I0091144

Dance Circles

DANCE AND PERFORMANCE STUDIES

General Editors:

Helen Wulff, *Stockholm University* and **Jonathan Skinner**, *Queen's University, Belfast*

Advisory Board:

Alexandra Carter, Marion Kant, Tim Scholl

In all cultures, and across time, people have danced. Mesmerizing performers and spectators alike, dance creates spaces for meaningful expressions that are held back in daily life. Grounded in ethnography, this series explores dance and bodily movement in cultural contexts at the juncture of history, ritual and performance, including musical, in an interconnected world.

Volume 1

Dancing at the Crossroads: Memory and Mobility in Ireland
Helena Wulff

Volume 2

Embodied Communities: Dance Traditions and Change in Java
Felicia Hughes-Freeland

Volume 3

Turning the Tune: Traditional Music, Tourism and Change in an Irish Village
Adam Kaul

Volume 4

Dancing Cultures: Globalization, Tourism and Identity in the Anthropology of Dance
Edited by Hélène Neveu Kringelbach and Jonathan Skinner

Volume 5

Dance Circles: Movement, Morality and Self-Fashioning in Urban Senegal
Hélène Neveu Kringelbach

Volume 6

Learning Senegalese Sabar: Dancers and Embodiment in New York and Dakar
Eleni Bizas

Volume 7

In Search of Legitimacy: How Outsiders Become Part of an Afro-Brazilian Tradition
Lauren Miller Griffith

Volume 8

Choreographies of Landscape: Signs of Performance in Yosemite National Park
Sally Ann Ness

Dance Circles

Movement, Morality and Self-Fashioning in Urban Senegal

Hélène Neveu Kringelbach

berghahn
NEW YORK • OXFORD
www.berghahnbooks.com

First published in 2013 by
Berghahn Books
www.berghahnbooks.com

©2013 Hélène Neveu Kringelbach
First paperback edition published in 2015

All rights reserved. Except for the quotation of short passages
for the purposes of criticism and review, no part of this book
may be reproduced in any form or by any means, electronic or
mechanical, including photocopying, recording, or any information
storage and retrieval system now known or to be invented,
without written permission of the publisher.

Library of Congress Cataloging-in-Publication Data
Neveu Kringelbach, Hélène, 1969-
    Dance circles: movement, morality and self-fashioning in urban Senegal / Hélène
Neveu Kringelbach. -- First edition.
    pages cm. -- (Dance and performance studies; volume 5)
    Includes bibliographical references.
    ISBN 978-1-78238-147-1 (hbk) -- ISBN 978-1-78533-038-4 (pbk) --
ISBN 978-1-78238-148-8 (ebook)
    1. Dance--Senegal. 2. Dance companies--Senegal. 3. Performing arts--Senegal.
4. Senegal--Social policy. 5. Senegal--Social life and customs. I. Title.
    GV1710.S46N49 2013
    793.319663--dc23

                                                                      2013020236

British Library Cataloguing in Publication Data
A catalogue record for this book is available from the British Library

ISBN: 978-1-78238-147-1 (hardback)
ISBN: 978-1-78533-038-4 (paperback)
ISBN: 978-1-78238-148-8 (ebook)

To my mother, Léone Neveu, and to the memory of Gina Burrows,
who loved a good dance

Contents

Figures

Abbreviations

AFAA	Association Française d'Action Artistique
AIF	Agence Internationale de la Francophonie
ANSD	Agence Nationale de la Statistique et de la Démographie
AOF	Afrique Occidentale Française
ARTE	Association des Ressortissants de Thionck Essyl
ASC	Association Sportive et Culturelle
CCBS	Centre Culturel Blaise Senghor
CCN	Centre Chorégraphique National
DRC	The Democratic Republic of Congo
ECOWAS	Economic Community of West African States
EDF	European Development Fund (FED in French)
Enda	Environnement et Développement du Tiers-Monde
EU	European Union
FCFA	Francs Communauté Financière Africaine
FESMAN	Second World Festival of Black Arts in Senegal (December 2010)
FESNAC	Festival National des Arts et de la Culture
IMF	International Monetary Fund
MCDS	Maison de la Culture Douta Seck
MFDC	Mouvement des Forces Démocratiques de Casamance
NGO	Non-governmental organization
OAU	Organization of African Unity
OECD	Organization for Economic Cooperation and Development
OHLM	Office des Habitations à Loyer Modéré
OIF	Organization Internationale de la Francophonie
PDS	Parti Démocratique Sénégalais
PS	Parti Socialiste Sénégalais
PSIC	Programme de Soutien aux Initiatives Culturelles
PSAC	Programme de Soutien aux Actions Culturelles
RTS	Radiodiffusion Télévision Sénégalaise
SICAP	Société Immobilière du Cap Vert
SOTIBA	Société de Teinture, Blanchiment, Aprêts et d'Impressions Africaines
UCAD	Université Cheikh Anta Diop de Dakar

UNESCO	United Nations Educational, Scientific and Cultural Organization
UK	United Kingdom
US	United States of America

Acknowledgements

The making of this book has been a long and bumpy road, and I would not have had the inspiration or the stamina to complete it without the encouragement and support of many colleagues, dancers, friends and family in several countries.

My deepest gratitude goes to David Parkin for his guidance and unfailing support since I embarked on this project in 2000. Since I joined the African Studies Centre in 2006, David Pratten has enabled me to grow as an anthropologist, and has exposed me to a world of ideas much beyond the confines of the discipline. From Stockholm, Helena Wulff has been an invaluable inspiration, mentor and friend, without whom I might not have started the daunting task of writing about dance in the first place. At the Anthropology Department in Oxford, I also wish to thank Nick Allen, my MSc supervisor, who introduced me to the discipline with great enthusiasm. Vicky Dean and Mike Morris have been very helpful at various stages in the process. Very special thoughts go to Gina Burrows, who sadly passed away before the completion of this book. She provided the kind of nurturing support one needs far beyond the academic side of things, helped with various funding applications, and even helped me to secure accommodation when I returned from fieldwork with a young child in tow. I am forever indebted to my thesis examiners, Wendy James and Roy Dilley, for their incredibly insightful comments on the first leg of this long journey. Wendy James advised me to let the dance take its rightful place in my work, and I have kept her wise words in mind when doing additional research for this book. My friend and colleague Ramón Sarró was always generous with ideas, encouragement, practical advice and contacts. I learned a great deal from him on the practice of ethnography, on West Africa, and on the value of thinking outside the box. I also wish to thank Katharina Lobeck Kane, who gave me useful contacts in Dakar before my first period of fieldwork, and has been a precious friend and colleague since.

In Senegal, the list of people who have made fieldwork an intensely rewarding experience over the years would be too long to acknowledge here. In particular, I wish to thank Ousseynou Faye, at the University Cheikh Anta Diop, for his constant support, patience and precious friendship. Ibrahima Thioub, Charles Becker and Cheikh Guèye were very helpful with ideas at the beginning of my fieldwork.

In the Dakarois dance world, I am particularly indebted to Jean Tamba, who welcomed me in his company and in the Kaay Fecc festival team, and offered his unconditional friendship over the years. Without him, this book would have turned to very different interests. My gratitude extends to the other members of his company,

La 5ᵉ Dimension, over the years: Oumar Diaw, Simone Gomis, Moustapha Guèye, Alioune Mané, Marianne Mbengue, Oumar Mbow, Vieux Tamba, Oumar Sène and Papa Sy. I am also indebted to the Kaay Fecc team, especially Gacirah Diagne, Nganti Towo, Honoré Mendy, Malal Ndiaye, Simon-Pierre Diatta, Pape Laye, Manga Sadibou, Mohamed Touré and Ibrahima Wane, now a colleague at the UCAD (Université Cheikh Anta Diop de Dakar). Massamba Guèye, always attentive, shared his passion for Senegambian oral histories, and his sharp insights challenged me to think in new directions more than once. At the National School of Arts, Mamadou Diop and Martin Lopy made me feel at home. Many other performers, choreographers, stage technicians and dance organizers have taken the time to introduce me to their art, and have been patient with my bizarre questions; in particular I wish to thank Germaine Acogny, Patrick Acogny, Ousmane Bâ, Coumba Bâ, Khady Badji, Fatou Cissé, Ousmane Noël Cissé, Marie Diédhiou, Djibril Diagne, Doudou Diagne, Djibril Diallo, Moussa Diallo, Longa Fo, Anta Guèye, Gnagna Guèye, Hardo Kâ, Thiaba Lô, Lamine Mané, Landing Mané, Ousmane Mané, Salif Mbengue, Marianne Niox, Andreya Ouamba, Onye Ozuzu, Kiné Sagna, Papis Sagna, Aziz Samb, Fatou Samb, Bouly Sonko and Aïssatou Bangoura Sow. Whenever we crossed paths, I have greatly enjoyed Esther Baker's friendship and insights on the Senegalese dance world. Didier Delgado allowed me to drive to Tubaab Jallaw with him on several occasions, and I always enjoyed our conversations during those trips. Antoine Tempé and Elise Fitte-Duval were always more than talented photographers, and in addition to their friendship, I have benefited greatly from their insights into the complexities of the dance world.

Outside the dance world, I was fortunate to have an excellent Wolof teacher, Aliou Ngoné Seck, with whom learning Wolof (a project far from completed) was as enjoyable as dancing. I also wish to thank Alassane Faye, from Enda (Environnement et Développement du Tiers-Monde) for introducing me to his protégés in Pikine. I enjoyed the long conversations with Djibril Kane, Alioune Ndione, Abdoulaye Ndiaye and others more than I was ever able to tell them. In Fass, Mame Cogna Ndoye, her family and Emilie Tamba, welcomed me in their homes and provided precious support in times of crisis.

In Dakar I also developed lasting friendships which have turned this journey into as much of a life project as an academic endeavour. In particular, I wish to thank Sulaiman Adebowale, David Bouchet, Tristan Cordier, Karim Dahou, Tarik Dahou, Jérôme Gérard, Nafy Guèye, Jules Kane, Mame Issa Ly, Yann Nachtman, Aminatou Sar, Yandé Sène, Aby Sène, Hélène Sow, Virginie Vanhaeverbeke and Saly Wade. They helped me settle into life in Dakar, or simply offered their hospitality and their unfailing support when it mattered most. It is no exaggeration to say that I would not have made it through fieldwork without them. I extend my warm thanks to Maïmouna Ndione, who looked after my young daughter daily, and in her own discreet way, looked after me, too. I am extremely grateful to fellow researchers Annie Bourdié, Tarik Dahou, Vincent Foucher and Jessica Libove, for sharing their insights and fieldwork experiences with me. Fellow dance scholars Funmi Adewole, Nadine Sieveking and Sarah Andrieu encouraged me to finish this book by promising to be the first readers. My friend Nafy Guèye acted as a research assistant for a short period of time, and introduced me to *Ndey ji Réew* Alioune Diagne Mbor, a living treasure of the Lebu community.

My long-time friends Marie-Laetitia Dumont, Christine Hehl and Hanne Søndergaard took the time to visit me in Senegal, and their interest in the project added an extra dimension to already intense friendships. In Paris, Roger Botte gave generous advice in the early stages. I have benefited greatly from the knowledge and challenging reflections of Ayoko Mensah, then a dance writer at *Africultures*.

In Oxford, I should not forget to thank the Institute of Social and Cultural Anthropology and Wolfson College for their financial support in 2000–2002 through the Godfrey Lienhardt Studentship in African anthropology. I would not have been able to finish this research without the generous support of St Anne's College, Oxford, through the Ioma Evans-Pritchard Junior Research Fellowship, which I was awarded in 2002–2004. My colleagues at St Anne's have provided intellectual stimulation and a warm environment ever since. In 2005–2006, a Postdoctoral fellowship from the British ESRC (the Economic and Social Research Council) offered me the opportunity to present my work at several seminars, to carry out additional field research and to begin working on the manuscript. Still in Oxford, I have been inspired by ongoing conversations with friends and colleagues, in particular my colleagues at the African Studies Centre and at the Institute of Social and Cultural Anthropology, especially Joe Arun, Mette Louise Berg, Amanda Berlan, Nomi Dave, Elizabeth Ewart, Sondra Hausner, Barbara Jettinger, Kristine Krause, Noel Lobley, Kathryn Nwajiaku, Caroline Potter, Nafisa Shah, Katie Swancutt, Richard Vokes, Suzanne Wessendorf and Zachary Whyte. Special mention should be given to Loredana Soceneantu and George Stroup for their unfailing support and friendship ever since we met each other in 2000.

Elsewhere, I have benefited greatly from the kind encouragement of Bob White, and have made good use of his historical database on the political use of culture by African states (www.atalaku.net). Jonathan Skinner has supported my interest in dance ever since we convened a panel together at the EASA (European Association of Social Anthropologists) conference in Vienna in 2004, and working with him on our edited volume on the anthropology of dance has enabled me to expand my ideas on dance. I also wish to thank my friend, dancer-choreographer and dance scholar James McBride, whose deep knowledge of the principles of human movement has informed my way of looking at dance over the years.

Finally, words fail to express my deepest gratitude and warmest love to my husband, Morten Kringelbach, without whose constant support and faith in my abilities I would not have lasted long as an anthropologist. I also wish to thank my mother, Léone Neveu, for her unfailing encouragement and help through many stages of the project, and my daughters Maya and Laura, for their patience with the nomadic life of an anthropologist's children. Apologies, girlies, for those times I have left you in the care of your father or your grandparents rather than taking you with me to Senegal.

The Shifting Faces of Dance

On a sunny winter afternoon of early 2012, I sat in a house in East London and chatted with a Senegalese dancer-choreographer-musician as he showed me some of the moves he had created in the various dance troupes he used to belong to when living in Dakar. A laptop sat on a table at one end of the room, showing Senegalese pop music videos on YouTube. We sat on the floor and talked, him occasionally getting up to demonstrates steps with careful precision, his arms sweeping the air in broad, wavelike movements which reminded me of my own jazz dance years in Paris in the late 1980s. In earlier conversations we had established that we were close in age, and had listened to the same kind of American pop music in those days. This made it all the easier for me to imagine his trajectory. Now established in the UK as a successful performer and teacher of West African dances and drumming, he reminisced about his dancing days in Senegal with visible pleasure. As a boy in Dakar, he had shown an early gift in bodily musicality, and had joined the Casamançais theatre and dance troupe in which both his parents performed. But he also enjoyed the breakdancing competitions that were popular with the boys in his neighbourhood, and the evening dances organized by his parents' hometown association, where he loved moving to the sound of Cuban music. Later, *mbalax* replaced breakdancing as the favourite dance style among the youths of his neighbourhood, to the extent that he choreographed sequences for the TV dance competitions that became the talk of the town in the mid-1990s. Concerned with his reputation in the Casamançais migrant community, however, he remained loyal to his parents' troupe, where he fine-tuned his drumming skills. Nevertheless, the urge to try something new was strong, and he also tried his hand at contemporary choreography, taking part in contemporary dance workshops and working with an up-and-coming company. His wide repertoire of skills caught the attention of a visiting choreographer from the UK. By the late 1990s he was teaching drumming workshops and working with a dance company in London, travelling back and forth between Senegal and various European destinations to teach and work with performers. This individual's trajectory draws out the main themes developed in this book: the making of mobile selves in urban Africa and beyond, the place of individual creativity in social transformation, the continuous importance of respectability and morality in the face of economic uncertainty, and the global circulation of performing practices.

More specifically, this book examines four interrelated dance practices in Dakar, Senegal: *sabar*, urban popular dances, neo-traditional performance and contemporary choreography. It is suggested here that exploring the range of interrelated, embodied practices people engage with, either simultaneously or at different moments in their lives, sheds light on the creative ways in which people use their bodily skills to negotiate their status in different social contexts, and to construct their sense of self. Performing and making dance are also about fashioning one's life and identity in the city, the nation and the world beyond. Drawing inspiration from Mbembe and Nutall's (2004) call to pay more attention to the complex aesthetics of African cities, this study is thus an impressionistic portrait of creativity and agency in a postcolonial city. It is also a conscious attempt to convey glimpses of the constructive, fun, and skilful dimension of social life in a modern African context, a much needed complement to the wealth of studies on violence and conflict dominating contemporary scholarship on the continent. Mbembe and Nutall (2004: 348) thus point to 'the failure of contemporary scholarship to describe the novelty and originality' of the African continent. In dominant historical and political scholarship, they say, Africa tends to be examined as 'a matter of order and contract rather than as the locus of experiment and artifice' (Mbembe and Nuttall 2004: 349). The study situates itself within the growing body of work that takes seriously the performative and the aesthetic domains of social life, particularly as they are embodied in music (Waterman 1990; James 1999; Askew 2002; Turino 2002; White 2008), dance (Argenti 2007; Edmonson 2007; Gilman 2009) and theatre (Barber 2000; Edmonson 2007). It is also intended as a contribution to the growing literature on the agency of African citizens in appropriating and creatively refashioning globalized practices, in this case individualized approaches to choreography.

This study also situates itself at the crossroads between social anthropology and dance studies. It draws the study of dance, both on stage and in social life, into an exploration of the key anthropological themes of self-making, gender, morality and social as well as spatial mobility. Its originality lies in the fact that it looks at the different ways in which people use their bodies in various domains of life, rather than focusing on a single genre. Here it is the movement *within* and *across* genres and techniques that is a central point of focus. This will be illustrated through a second vignette on a dance festival involving a multiplicity of genres.

Opening: Kaay Fecc, the 'festival of all dances'

Dakar, June 2003. By the entrance to the Maison de la Culture Douta Seck (MCDS), the state-owned cultural centre on the Avenue Blaise Diagne, three Austrians are struggling to stuff their filming equipment into a yellow-and-black Dakarois taxi. One of them, a woman, is a performer/choreographer. The two others are her manager and her filmmaker. The choreographer has just attended a 'traditional' dance workshop as part of the Kaay Fecc dance festival, and is now heading off to the National Theatre to rehearse for her company's contemporary dance performance the same evening. The filmmaker has been shooting at the nearby Tilleen market for a documentary on the company's work in Senegal. I have accompanied them to serve as a translator, asking reluctant market vendors for permission to film. Most refused, and the filmmaker quickly realised that 'bagging' images of people in Dakar was less straightforward than he had imagined, even against payment.

Like thirty-two other groups, they are here for the second edition of the Kaay Fecc international dance festival, a biennial event initiated in 2001 by an independent group of performers, choreographers and arts organizers, with the blessing of the government. Of the thirty-three groups invited, twenty-one are Senegalese and represent the full range of styles performed on the local stages: neo-traditional performance (*ballets traditionnels*), contemporary dance, hip-hop and popular dances. Inside the MCDS, the festival 'village' is buzzing with activity. There are food stalls where women from the adjacent neighbourhoods sell liver sandwiches and *fatayas*, fish-filled fried pastries. Next to them, a group of young men is sitting making *attaya*, the sweet mint tea that has come to epitomize urban young men 'hanging out' whole afternoons on end amidst a lack of formal employment. A tall, thin man wearing his hair in long locks is strolling about and selling cups of *café Touba*, a spicy and fragrant Senegalese version of the powdery Turkish coffee. The craft stalls feature batik dresses, miniature buses and toys or decorative objects made of recycled cans, and Senegalese glass paintings (*suweer*). The Communication stall has rotating shifts of well-dressed young men and women in charge of receiving journalists and distributing programmes and information to festival-goers. A few steps from there, technicians are balancing on poles high up above the outdoor stage, setting up the sound and lighting for the evening's performances. The site is full of young people chatting, strolling about and rehearsing. It is in the evenings that dance performances attract huge crowds, especially since entrance is free. Though there is an overwhelming majority of Senegalese on the site, the performers come from several African countries as well as Germany, Austria, France, Canada and the US.

In the main building, an open workshop in Sereer dances, attended by some forty participants, has now given way to a contemporary dance session with Paris-based Cameroonese choreographer, Pier Ndoumbé. He will later do a training session for the disabled dancers of Takku Liggeey, a Mbour-based development association which also features a dance troupe. In the evening there will be a contemporary piece by Austrian, Editta Braun, and a neo-traditional piece by the troupe, Bakalama. The equally packed programme of the next day will feature more workshops, performances and a sabar event in Dalifort, a smaller suburb between Dakar and Pikine. There Papa Sy, one of the performers in the festival organization, has set up a contemporary dance company with teenage girls and boys who rehearse regularly in the schoolyard. Dalifort also has a neo-traditional troupe, the Ballet-Théâtre de Dalifort. For the sabar, a large circle of plastic chairs will be made in the main sandy alley, and sabar drummers will be brought in from an adjacent neighbourhood, for a fee. The festivity will begin in the late afternoon, when the heat becomes bearable. Young residents and professional dancers involved with the festival will take turns to perform athletic sabar moves on the plastic sheet facing the seven drummers, who have set up their instruments on chairs at one end of the circle. Young people from both sexes will run forward, dance solo or in a pair and run back to the edge of the circle, charged with energy. At one point an adolescent girl dressed in a tight black top and fashionably slit white trousers will 'cut' her performance with a forward thrust of the pelvis, laughing before exiting the central space at full speed. The lead drummer will take a few steps towards where she stood, face her, and with his drumming stick in one hand, thrust his pelvis forward, too. The crowd will be laughing at the exchange. Later, in the fading daylight, the drummers will gradually decrease the tempo so that the older participants may come forward for their turn to dance. In the last twenty minutes or so, more mature women will come forward in pairs or several at a time, and execute perfectly-timed, but less aerial steps than the youths and professional performers who had dominated the first part of the event. Soon darkness will prevail, and this will be the end of the event. The lead 'speaker' will thank the drummers and the residents, for whom this event is unusual since half of the participants are not residents of the neighbourhood. The sabar and a couple of performances in the following days are part of Kaay Fecc's effort to 'decentralize' the festival to the city's poorer suburbs.

The MCDS, by contrast, is located at the heart of the Medina, one of the oldest neighbourhoods in Dakar. It is adjacent to the administrative and business centre, Le Plateau. Not far from the MCDS is a mosque marking the territorial and spiritual centre of the Lebu community, the original inhabitants of the Cape Verde Peninsula. There are several other mosques nearby, as well as St Joseph de Medina, one of Dakar's main Catholic churches. Almost every block in the Medina features a tailor's workshop. The neighbourhood is a tight-knit mesh of older urban compounds, single-storey houses with a square courtyard surrounded by a succession of rooms. Each room houses a household or a part of it, and most compounds are shared among several families. Dakarois housing has become unaffordable for many, particularly for young people and for families without migrants sending remittances from abroad. But for the nine days of the Kaay Fecc festival, the MCDS becomes an island of cosmopolitan activity, and Medina inhabitants occasionally drop in to see the free performances or the festival 'village'. This is what the Dakarois dance scene is about: a young, cosmopolitan, at times prosperous but also ephemeral, elusive milieu alternatively derided on moral grounds and valued as a route towards individual success. The Kaay Fecc festival reflects this milieu in all its vitality and diversity. But what is the connection between such aesthetically different forms of performance? How do the different genres relate to the ways in which young performers fashion their lives and their sense of selves?

My attempt to address these questions is informed by a number of interconnected anthropological themes, which include the relationship between moving bodies and self-making, gender and morality, and the interplay between performance and politics.

Moving bodies, self-making and agency

Following the fascination with subjective experience which grew out of a disenchantment with 'objective' social forms in anthropology in the 1960s, anthropological studies of the body have flourished. The reasons for the relative neglect of the body in the social sciences have been laid out very well in Brenda Farnell's (1999) review article. While phenomenological approaches have conceptualized the body as the locus of human experience,[1] a wealth of studies drawing on various anthropological traditions have looked at such themes as the body as a metaphor of society (Douglas 1969) or the locus of resistance (Comaroff 1985). Theories of performance and practice have been particularly helpful in moving on from earlier views of static bodies. Drawing on his earlier work on ritual and social drama, Turner (1982: 94) saw performance as the locus of human learning when he suggested that 'one learns through performing, then performs the understandings so gained'. Rather than separating staged performance from social performance, as was often the case until the 1970s, Turner saw the two as belonging to a continuum of presence and consciousness. A complementary approach is that of Bourdieu (1972), who built on Mauss's (1973 [1935]) earlier essay on the socially constructed nature of all bodily techniques to develop a theory of culture as transmitted through internalized bodily dispositions, or *habitus*. The work of these authors has been important because they have sought to address the perennial question of how human action produces diverse cultural practices. This is an issue that has yet to be fully resolved, perhaps because the contribution of disciplines outside the social sciences and the humanities is needed to improve our understanding of action. Meanwhile, theorists of performance and practice have established the notion that all culture is *embodied*. As Hastrup (1995: 90) puts it, 'there is no manifestation of the self outside the body, even if our senses and words help us project ourselves outward.'

Yet a dynamic perspective on embodied sociality remains elusive in anthropology. The body has often been regarded as a still object, as the recipient of illness for example, or as moving according to barely conscious dispositions, as captured in Bourdieu's (1972) notion of habitus. Much of what we do is neither entirely conscious nor entirely intentional, but in dancing we are intensely present (if not always entirely conscious), expressive, and often creative. Hastrup's (1995, 2004) reflections on performativity are useful to move on from the notion of habitus because she argues convincingly that the difference between staged performance and social performance is not one of kind, but rather one of awareness of the body's performative skills. In theatre, she says, performers are made aware of this difference through the 'projective space' that is the audience, whether actually present or imagined. For her, theatrical and other cultural performances are but 'variations of those "theatres of self", in which the motivated bodies act' (Hastrup 1995: 91). I found her analysis useful to capture the interplay between the dances of everyday life and choreographic production for the stage in Dakar. There is constant feedback between life and the stage, and people do not always make a clear distinction between the two. Indeed the bodily awareness Hastrup describes is often as intense in the dances of everyday sociality, such as sabar events, as will be evident in Chapter 3. This recognition came to me as fieldwork progressed. Inspired by studies of multiple genres or performative practices in a single context (Stokes 1992; Ness 1992; Wulff 2007), I followed the trajectories of informants and tried to gain a sense of all the activities they engaged with. This provided me with insights into the relationship between life and stage that would probably have eluded me, had I focused on a single genre.

Also important is the recognition that the study of dance opens a window onto aspects of social life not easily accessible through discursive forms alone. As Wendy James (2003: 93) points out, 'what can be said in language does not fully match all that is going on in life'. It is not that dance contradicts the verbal; it is rather that they supplement each other, thus enabling us to 'see' different things about society. In his work on Kuranko initiation in Sierra Leone, Michael Jackson (1983: 338) remarks that 'bodily movements can do more than words can say', and adds that 'techniques of the body may be compared with musical techniques since both transport us from the quotidian world of verbal distinctions and categorical separations into a world where boundaries are blurred and experience transformed'. It is precisely the transformation of experience that is at the centre of this study. How, then, do we understand the relationship between the repeated act of performing and individual agency, or the capacity to act upon one's life and that of others? And what role does performance play in self-making?

Looking at questions of agency and self-making would yield little understanding of people's actions and motivations if one did not recognize that the notion of individual agency itself is culturally determined. As James (2003) explains, the idea that individuals ought to be free to act of their own free will is a modern construct, and is influenced by the human rights discourse. In many contexts however, this discourse coexists with ideas of limited human agency. Throughout the Senegambian region, the notion that individuals are rarely in complete control of their actions is widely shared (Sylla 1994). This is evident, for example, in sabar dancing and in therapeutic practices, such as the *ndëp*, where movement is understood to be motivated both by the dancer and by external forces invoked by appropriate drumming rhythms. Likewise, destiny is understood to be in the hands of the divine, but also influenced by the morality of people's actions. This means that in order to grasp how performing actions relate to self-making, one needs to understand how people perceive their own agency as performers. What, then, becomes the significance of globalized contemporary choreography, in which individual performers are expected to be in complete control of their movements and to draw on their personal experience?

Drawing on the work of Hastrup and others, I want to suggest that in a social context in which music and dance feature prominently in social life, as they do in Senegal, self-making happens to a large extent through innovation in choreographic performance. Not all innovations in bodily techniques lead to enduring change, however, and thus the way in which innovation fits with 'sedimented' cultural practices (Hastrup 1995: 88–89) is important. Innovation is more than superficial change if it leads to discernible transformations in the capacities of individuals to act upon the world. These capacities are not just verbal, they involve the whole person, and exploring these may enable us to go further beyond the much contested Eurocentric mind-body duality. This study thus attempts to contribute to our understanding of the materiality of innovation in culture.

At this point, I should warn the reader that there will be a slippage, at times, between the notion of 'self-making' and that of 'social mobility'. There is a tension between the two that is left purposefully unresolved in the book. This is because I contend that social mobility is not, as the term is often understood, simply a matter of class. People do their best to put on new personas as they move across social fields, and therefore social mobility is often as much about constructing a new sense of self as it is about being accepted as a member of a new social category. But self-making is also closely linked to questions of morality, for the recognition of worthy membership in any social group involves a constant re-evaluation of a person's qualities within culturally defined moralities. Self-making, therefore, involves the actualization of morality, a process in which performance plays a central role.

Dance and morality

Since social acting is inseparable from an implicit morality (Hastrup 1995: 97), an important task in an ethnography of dance is to understand how different ways of performing may be associated with particular moral qualities, or with their absence. As Signe Howell (1997b: 4) reminds us, the challenge for anthropologists concerned with moralities lies in 'discerning the link between values which are derived from a larger metaphysical whole and actual behaviour and practices'. But how does one disentangle moral discourse from actual practice? Taken together, the papers in Howell's volume (1997a) suggest that one needs to look at specific activities that are meaningful to large groups of people within a single context. In Argentina, for example, Archetti (1997) found football to be an illuminating window into the moral codes of masculinity.

In Dakar, I suggest, dance constitutes a privileged window into the construction of gendered moralities and into the morality of social hierarchies. One way of getting to the heart of the matter is to look carefully at how different categories of people and institutions respond to different ways of dancing. Attempts at controlling dance are particularly illuminating because they are recurrent in modern human history. This is likely because dance carries an ecstatic dimension which often makes it unpredictable, and therefore potentially disruptive. Dance reminds us that as human beings, we enjoy the thrill of being together in ways that cannot be completely controlled. This may well be the main reason why world religions, in their attempt to impose a universal morality, have been consistently concerned with controlling dance. Establishing normative ways of dancing is not only an attempt to control people's bodies, it is also an attempt to define what acceptable behaviour is in relation to others, and to reflect on how moralities ought to be embodied. Looking at attempts to control dance over time and in a given context therefore illuminates changing ideas of morality. But people tend to challenge control attempts and normative practices, and therefore looking at the link between moral discourses and practice also involves focusing on 'active dissent' and what this tells us about 'reigning orthodoxies' (Howell 1997b: 4). Ultimately, the social control of dance speaks to the enduring difficulty, for human beings, of making sense of the relationship between morality and embodied practice.

Helena Wulff's (2007) historically informed study of Irish dancing provides an illuminating instance of a top-down attempt to instil new ideas about morality through normative ways of dancing. Wulff suggests that stiffness in the upper body, a characteristic feature that is strictly adhered to in competitive dancing, may have come about in the late nineteenth century, at a time when Ireland was under English domination and 'Irishness' had to be defined against 'Englishness'. The cornerstones of this cultural project were Irish Catholicism, the revival of the Irish language, the collection of folktales and new ways of dancing. English had to be trumped, and it is likely that a stiff upper body was regarded as the expression of a high moral virtue. In other words, competitive Irish dancing became a way of embodying new ideas about morality at this transitional period in Irish history. Wulff shows how there was active dissent, too, in the ways in which people hid to dance following the Public Dance Hall Act, a ban on dancing outside licensed halls requested by the Catholic Church in 1935. This spoke volumes about the 'reigning orthodoxy' of the Catholic Church in twentieth-century Ireland, and how people related to it in everyday life.

The disruptive potential of dancing also comes to the fore in Jane Cowan's (1990) ethnography of celebratory practices in the town of Sohos, northern Greece. Looking at weddings and the formal evening dances of civic associations, Cowan analyses dancing in terms of gender relations, but questions of morality are implicit throughout the book. Dance, she suggests, is problematic for men and women in different ways. Male youths and men are expected to put aside their antagonisms, and unite in the shared pleasures of dancing and drinking until they reach the altered state of *kefi*. For men, this is legitimate because they are expected to assert themselves as individuals. The quarrels that occasionally break out, Cowan says, are therefore valued as evidence of men's 'liveliness' and as an expression of their attempts to assert or challenge their social status in the Sohohian order. Women, by contrast, are much more restricted in the kind of performance that is appropriate for them, and their dancing is usually interpreted in terms of their sexuality. Women are therefore forced to affirm their individuality in much quieter ways than men; for example, through their clothing, hair style and restrained dance movements. But men and women from different generations and social classes hold conflicting views on appropriate behaviour at dancing events, and tensions are always just beneath the surface even as people share the pleasure of dancing. Here morality is embodied in different ways for men and for women, and dance serves simultaneously to elaborate gender identities and to provide a space in which different views on embodied morality can be confronted with each other.

In Dakar, it is morality that is the stuff of everyday conversation whenever people discuss dance. Indeed as we will see throughout the book, concern with young women's increasing autonomy and confidence in the public space is very often expressed in the form of judgments on how their dancing affects their respectability.

When people lament young women's inappropriate suggestiveness in dancing, it is morality in society that is being discussed, often passionately. Gender and age hierarchies are clearly at stake here, even more so as Senegalese Islam has become a powerful source of moral authority in all areas of public life. The importance of tensions over dance styles in the Senegalese context becomes clearer if we keep sight of local understandings of embodied morality. Indeed, in Wolof-speaking Senegal, morality is expected to be embodied differently depending on the social category, or 'caste' status individuals are identified with. I will return to the Wolof caste-like stratification in Chapter 2, but for now, suffice to say that the higher the status, the more restrained body movement is expected to be. Restraint and measure are highly valued, and a person of good moral standing is expected to make little display of emotions in public (Neveu Kringelbach 2007a), and to show self-control by avoiding loud speech, expansive movement and unnecessary gesticulation (Sylla 1994). Though this is generally valued behaviour throughout the region, the expectation to confirm to this is higher for the 'freeborn' *géér* than for those who belong to a hereditary category of artisans or performers, the *ñeeño* (see Chapter 2). In other words, ñeeño are understood to share the same moral values as their géér patrons, but ideals of behaviour are different for the two categories. In this context, dancers who perform expansive, energetic movement styles put their moral standing at risk, particular if they belong to high-status géér families. Given that an increasing number of youngsters from such backgrounds are attracted to the performing profession, a key question running through this book will be the extent to which the success of the performing profession at home and abroad is transforming local notions of embodied morality. I now turn to the bodies of literature on popular culture and dance that have helped to make sense of the genres discussed in this book.

The open-endedness of 'popular culture'

The growing literature on 'popular arts' and 'popular culture' in Africa has informed this study in many different ways. I have been particularly inspired by Karin Barber's (1997) pioneering work across a vast array of genres. Stressing the difficulty of defining 'popular culture', which in Europe implies a clear-cut distinction between 'high' and 'low' culture, she argues that it is more productive to conceive of it as the 'vast domain of cultural production which cannot be classified as either "traditional" or "elite", as "oral" or "literate", as "indigenous" or "Western" in inspiration, because it straddles and dissolves these distinctions' (Barber 1997: 2). Barber's characterization of the popular arts in Africa is particularly useful in highlighting the novelty and combination of styles and genres that is often central to the practices of city dwellers across Africa. In Dakar, youth dances like the ever-changing mbalax genre fit well within Barber's notion: they are neither traditional nor elite but borrow consciously from the older sabar genre. Moreover, the youths who perform these dances in nightclubs, at neighbourhood events or in front of TV sets revel in their novelty. They draw on a mix of Wolof drumming rhythms, themselves refreshed through constant innovation above stable musical principles, and rhythms from Cuban, European, Brazilian, North American and Arabic origins.

Without taking the elite-traditional-popular distinction too far, Barber's conceptualization is also useful in enabling us to draw out the uses of various dance forms as modes of distinction. According to her, 'retaining the distinction between elite, popular and traditional allows us to investigate the important question of how present-day African artists and participants in art themselves conceive of their activity and its status' (Barber 1987: 20). The ways in which people conceive of their activity, she suggests, comes across in the conscious relationship artists maintain to ideas of 'tradition'. In Senegal, I suggest, dancers' reference to tradition serves to construct a respectable status for the profession in a context in which the reputation of the public performer is always fragile.

A further aspect is that the distinction between 'popular', 'traditional' and 'elite' performers is not as clear as one might think from looking at the various dance forms performed in the city. Like in Wulff's (2007) study of dance in Ireland, it is often the same people who move back and forth between different genres in the course of their lives, or simultaneously but with different degrees of intensity. For example, the same dancer may join in sabar events in her neighbourhood or perform mbalax dances in nightclubs for fun, while working professionally with a neo-traditional troupe. At some stage she may take part in a workshop in contemporary choreography, and move on to a contemporary dance company while still performing with the neo-traditional troupe.

Finally, I found that the social organization of popular dances in Dakar fitted well with Barber's (1997) observation that popular culture fostered new identities, new publics and new collectivities. In this study, I suggest that dance and musical performance in Dakar do conjure new forms of association, particularly a sense of simultaneously belonging to a neighbourhood, a locality of origin and a transnational world of artists.

The performance of nationalism and regionalism

In his introduction to an edited volume in honour of Abner Cohen, Parkin (1996: xxxiii) points to the 'metaphorical capacity for cultural performance to say things sideways' as that which wins people's adherence more powerfully than propositional arguments do. This metaphorical quality means that performance is capable of encapsulating a multiplicity of messages. It is therefore a seductive way of embodying national or regional identities since it is flexible enough to accommodate changes in their contents. For example, the fact that hometown associations from the Casamance region in Dakar express their distinctiveness through performance is not because the Casamançais dance and play music better than others, but because this enables them to celebrate their distinctiveness while discreetly including elements of the dominant Wolof setting.

Studies of musical performance, nationalism and ethnicity politics in Africa have informed this book (Waterman 1990; Askew 2002; Turino 2002; Edmonson 2007; White 2008). In her work on musical performance in Tanzania, for example, Askew (2002) eloquently shows how nation-building is a process of mutual engagement between the state and its citizens. Ever since the United Republic of Tanzania was founded in 1964, one of its major challenges has been to bring together the islands (Zanzibar and Pemba) and the continental part of the nation into a unified whole. Music and dance were made to play an important role in this project, particularly through the patronage of a Swahili genre, *ngoma*, and the organization of performing competitions at a national level. Another popular music style, *taarab*, was side lined initially because it was considered foreign, and did not fit within the ideal of *ujamaa* socialism. But taarab was still performed during weddings and popular events, and was eventually co-opted by the state during the transition to multiparty-ism in the mid-1990s. Through historical sources, song texts and a rich ethnography, Askew shows not only how certain musical genres contributed to the emergence of a national identity, but also how the thriving presence of others showed the dissensions in state-led nation-building. Music expressed these tensions and provided musicians with a medium to reflect on them. It was in the songs and in the unpredictability of competitive events that the contradictions of nation-building were revealed, and Askew's ethnography of the musical scene helps to understand people's growing distrust toward the ruling party in the 1980s and early 1990s.

Away from Africa, Wulff's (2007) monograph on Irish dance demonstrates how several genres taken together (the traditional *sean-nós*, Irish Ballet, contemporary Irish dance, competitive dancing and commercial shows like *Riverdance*) enable people to explore the contents of 'Irishness'. Contemporary Irishness, Wulff suggests, involves both cosmopolitan mobility and a strong attachment to the materiality of the Irish land.

In Senegal, as in Tanzania and Ireland, the creation of a national identity remains an unfinished project. Despite a state rhetoric in which ethnicity is silenced ('ethnic' parties are forbidden by the Constitution), the southernmost region of Senegal, the Casamance, has suffered an armed separatist conflict since 1990. Though framed in a regionalist discourse, the separatist movement is led by Jola speakers (Foucher 2002), in a region otherwise linguistically, culturally and religiously diverse. Ironically, the neo-traditional performing genre that was championed by the state in the 1960s and 1970s has been most successfully appropriated by Casamançais groups. Thus, the genre that was created in order to help citizens imagine a unified nation (as well as establish President Senghor's moral leadership in West Africa) was appropriated as a vehicle of cultural distinctiveness, a goal not entirely opposed to nation-building but having the potential to undermine it. In the post-independence period, cultural diversity was valued as long as its representation remained controlled by the state. Today, however, it is in the hands of precisely those segments of the population that had been marginalized: Casamançais minorities, and to a certain extent ñeeño and people from other 'skilled' hereditary categories. The politics of artistic practices, then, shed light on the transformation of nation-building projects over time.

'Dance' and 'performance'

So far I have used the terms 'dance' and 'performance' almost interchangeably. This is meant to highlight the semantic challenge every study of dance is confronted with:

not only is the term 'dance' ambiguous, it also fails to capture the interplay between the different elements (oratory, poetry, song, music, movement) that is characteristic of many performing genres across Africa (Drewal 1991). Most dance scholars have come to acknowledge that it is impossible to come up with a universal definition of dance, even though, as Wulff (2001: 3209) says, 'dance anthropologists seem to converge on a consideration of bounded rhythmical movements that are performed during some kind of altered state of consciousness'. Dance anthropologists Kaeppler (1978) and Williams (1982) have refuted the idea of a universal definition, arguing that lumping widely different practices together obscured more than it revealed. Drawing on Saussurian linguistics (De Saussure et al. 1916), Rudolf Laban's (1970) movement theories, and in Williams' case on Ardener reflections on the anthropology of language (Chapman 1989), they have looked at 'structured movement systems' instead, and have analysed the semantic similarities in different practices within a single context.

Definition, however, is only part of the problem. An important challenge is to name very diverse practices so as to capture the way in which people experience them. The fact that many West African languages do not have a specific word for dance (Gore 2001) underlines the Eurocentric character of the category. Lassibille (2004) found that the WoDaaBe of Niger used three different terms to speak of dance: *fijjo* (play), *gamol* (dance) and *bamol* (dance or braid). In Wolof, dance is best translated as *fecc*, but this is not the most commonly used term. Rather, terms that designate a type of event or a genre are favoured. The term *sabar* for example, is used for a type of festive event, a range of drums, and a repertoire of rhythms and dances, with a recognizable structure and style. Style is indeed important to define a genre; one cannot, for example, dance sabar in a ponderous way. Gore (2001: 33) suggests that we should abandon the idea of isolating dance in culture, not only because this is 'conditioned by the deeply-ingrained Eurocentric habit of conceiving of art as compartmentalised and specialised practice', but also because this produces a discourse which devalues performance in 'socially and ritually significant contexts'. In practice, however, dance forms have often been ignored in studies of ritual, music or carnival, precisely because they were not seen to be interesting enough in themselves. I see no reason why dance should remain a substrate of another cultural form when participants obviously know how to distinguish it from other activities. As a compromise, I have therefore chosen to make generous use of the term *performance*, which refers to various genres, all involving codified movement, music, verbal arts, dress styles, and particular ways of using the space. My use of the term also draws on Schieffelin's (1998: 195) definition of performance as symbolic or aesthetic activities, and as 'intentionally produced enactments which are (usually) marked and set off from ordinary activities, and which call attention to themselves [. . .] with special purposes or qualities for the people who observe or perform them'. His definition has the advantage of drawing attention to the fact that performance is a conscious mode of action, for an audience (real or imaginary), and that it usually requires skills beyond those required for everyday activities. On the other hand, I have been conscious of only using the term 'dance' in contexts in which my informants do ('danse' in French or 'fecc' in Wolof).

Dance performances in Dakar, then, do not simply consist of movement and music. Barber's (2000; 2007) work on theatre and texts has been important in drawing my attention to the verbal and the textual, and from an initial focus on movement, I became gradually aware of the recurring references my informants made to language and to the world of theatre. Dance people often used terms like 'play' (*pièce*), 'text' (*texte*), 'theatre' (*théâtre*) and 'show' (*spectacle*). It was only when I started looking at the Senegalese dance scene in historical perspective that I discovered the strong connections with theatre. This, in turn, enabled me to see choreographic production as made of movement and sound as well as verbal, textual, spatial and material elements. This has been productive to uncovering the significance of texts to performers and audiences, of course, but also to shedding light on the exclusion of those without the literary skills to produce a 'text' explaining their artistic approach. In other words, focusing on different skills helps to uncover mechanisms of exclusion.

Finally, a crucial aspect of dance is that it is often intensely pleasurable to participants. The dry nature of academic writing makes it easy to forget that this is one of the main reasons why dance and musical performance are so powerful. I have written elsewhere about emotionality in Senegalese women's dances (Neveu Kringelbach 2007a), and to say that emotion is central to how dance 'works' does not imply that it is irrational. Indeed, recent research in the field of neuroscience suggests that emotions are an essential component of 'rational' thought processes (Kringelbach 2007). This actually supports what anthropologists have known for a long time. Parkin (1985), for example, attributed the universal power of performance to the 'moving together' of reason, emotion and body. A possible avenue to explore this further would be to look at the neuroscience of dance, but there has been little such research so far due to the difficulty of recording brain activity while people are dancing.[2] Throughout this book I attempt to draw out the sensual and enjoyable dimension of dance to show that such activities may well 'work' because they integrate human experience as a whole.

Attention to the ways in which people experience dance is also important to avoid seeing dance as nothing *but* the expression of something else. In his brilliant study of religious change, Sarró (2009: 4) has warned that 'the obsession with the liberating element of religion in colonial times risked [. . .] displacing attention away from the religious'. There is a similar tendency to focus on dance and music as simply reflecting social and political change. I suggest, rather, than it is more productive to think of these expressive forms as constitutive of society (Stokes 1997). I now turn to the existing literature on dance in Africa, to which this study contributes. I include scholarly texts as well as mainstream writings since both genres have shaped current perceptions on African choreographic practices.

Anthropology and dance in Africa

Although scholarship on African forms of performance has boomed in the last two decades, there remains a relative scarcity of studies on dance in relation to the ubiquity and social significance of choreographic practices. But the field is no longer as bare as when Margaret Drewal (1991) described dance as the least studied of all genres of performance in Africa, a state of affairs she attributed to the elusive character of what is often an improvisational practice. As she rightly foresaw, video recording, and images more generally, have made the field more accessible. Another important development has been the engagement of anthropologists who were themselves performers, and were therefore able to learn new bodily techniques fairly easily. But this development was long in coming.

In early twentieth-century ethnographies of Africa, dance was often mentioned only in passing, as a component in ritual. An early exception was Evans-Pritchard (1928), who dedicated his first published article to the *gbere buda*, the Zande funeral beer dance. A few years earlier, Radcliffe-Brown (1922) had dedicated a chapter of his *Andaman Islanders* to the 'function' of music and dance, which he interpreted as maintaining social cohesion through the ecstatic feeling of belonging these activities generated. Evans-Pritchard (1928: 460) challenged this view in *The Dance*, arguing that ceremonial dances involved other aspects, too, that were not easily visible in any other social form: the socialization of children, the shared sociality of young men and women, local notions of leadership, and the conflicts resulting from the tension between 'individual vanity and passions' and the 'constraining forces of the community'.

Much later, Clyde Mitchell (1956) wrote a landmark study of the Kalela, a competitive marching dance performed weekly by miners in the growing towns of the Zambian Copperbelt. But the focus of the study was urban ethnicity, and Mitchell did not linger on choreographic description. Instead he focused on the dress styles, the songs and the region of origin of the dancers. Nevertheless, the study provided inspiration for later studies of performance in the region. Ranger's (1975) historical work on the *beni ngoma*, for example, was the first important account of social transformation over more than a century, as traced through the trajectory of a genre of dance. In colonial East Africa, the beni ngoma developed as a march dance and a caricature of European military parades. Ranger showed how the beni associations helped people maintain a sense of continuity with the older Swahili stratification, all while acting as an ironical commentary on colonial society. Further South, ethnomusicologist John Blacking (1967) drew on his fieldwork with the Venda of Southern Africa to suggest that music and dance were central aspects in the socialization of children, and that they expressed the group's creative potential.

It all also worth mentioning Robert Farris Thompson's (1974) *African Art in Motion*, one of the first serious attempts to grasp the social significance of dance in West Africa. Unusually for its time, the book features a wealth of photographs and still shots from video recordings. Thompson's concern is with the aesthetics of dance, particularly the shared principles between dance and sculpture, rather than with dance in interplay with other dimensions of social life. As a result this rich, fieldwork-based work appears as a compilation of the artistic canons underlying 'African performance', and does not always avoid the pitfalls of generalization. Nevertheless, Thompson's historically informed reflections on aesthetics and art criticism in West and Central Africa remain highly innovative.

It was not until the early 1990s that a significant body of work emerged on various practices in which dance and musical performance played a central role. Deborah

Heath's (1990, 1994) work on dance, verbal performance and politics in Kaolack, for example, was important in showing how gender relations, social status and political influence in post-colonial Senegal were constantly re-negotiated through women's dances and verbal performance. She described women's dances as a scarce resource which people put to various uses depending on the context, for example as a contrast to high-ranking men's reserve, and thereby status: 'the identification of women, as well as lower-caste male performers and their drums, with sexual expressiveness allows certain men to maintain their reputation for reserve' (Heath 1994: 95).

There is also a growing body of work on masquerade in West and Central Africa. Argenti's (2006, 2007) work, for example, places masquerade at the centre of generational politics in the Kingdom of Oku, in the Cameroon Grassfields. Tracing back centuries of violent history in the region, he argues that both local and national polities have marginalized the youth and women, and that these groups have appropriated older genres of masquerade performance to contest their marginalization. In the Grassfields, masquerades embody the memory of the slave trade and the subsequent violent history of the region. At a more general level, Argenti argues for the capacity of performance to maintain and challenge social hierarchies simultaneously. In the practices I examine in Dakar, I am less concerned with the embodiment of memory, but here too, innovation in performance is driven by the desire of marginalized groups (youth, women) to re-negotiate their social status through strategies of extraversion (cf. Bayart 1999).

Writing 'dance' in Africa

As I have hinted already, this study distances itself from popular perceptions of dance in Africa as the expression of timeless traditions. The objectification of dance in Africa since the nineteenth century has been dealt with by other authors, and there is no need to dwell on it at length here. In her book on the *jali* (praise singers) of the Gambia, for example, Paulla Ebron (2002) includes an excellent discussion of Euro-American representations of African music in the light of Mudimbe's (1988) work on the 'invention' of Africa. Also inspired by Mudimbe, Francesca Castaldi (2006) writes about the manner in which colonial representations of African dances were used as evidence of the 'primitive' nature of the continent's people. She traces the tautological argument through which nineteenth-century European philosophy classified dance as an irrational and 'primitive' activity, then held the omnipresence of dance in African sociality as proof that Africans were indeed 'primitive'. She also suggests that Senegal's President Senghor himself had internalized this view when he created the National Ballet of Senegal. The genre the troupe performed, Castaldi says, was underpinned by an evolutionary view of African arts, and an idealization of the modernization narrative of the 1930s to the 1970s. Senghor held dance to be the quintessential African art, but by framing it in this way, Castaldi concludes, he helped to reinforce existing ideas on the 'primitiveness' of African cultures.

These ideas should be understood in the context of a longer history of objectification of black moving bodies. Not only European philosophy, but also anthropology, travel writing, colonial texts and the colonial press contributed to orientalist representations of African dances. These representations have created the illusion of a common spiritual and physiological basis in a diverse range of practices. By the time of the world fairs, the 'Hottentot Venus'[3] and other human exhibitions of the nineteenth century,[4] dances performed by Africans became conceived as the 'other'. As a result, writing on dance in Africa in the nineteenth and twentieth centuries has often crystallized the worst stereotypes on the supposed primitiveness of Africans. There is a wealth of texts in which this is evident, but a few examples should illustrate the point. The French colonial military magazine, *Tropiques*, thus published an essay by a respected psychiatrist, Henri Aubin (1951: 38), describing African dances as involving the body rather than the mind:

> The multiplicity of circumstances in which under-evolved indigenous peoples dance can be attributed to the fact that dance is a rather elementary activity: motor response, usually rhythmic, responding to stimuli where sensory and emotional data play the main role. Instead of being expressed through complex intellectual representations and a rich vocabulary, their emotional states become actions [. . .] of which dance is, after all, a privileged form.

Christian missionary writings also contributed to European representations of dance in Africa. In an illuminating review of missionary sources, Georgiana Gore (1999, 2001) notes that these texts often depicted dance as disgraceful, useless and indecent. In the French territories, missionaries encouraged the colonial authorities to ban dancing from public space for fear of temptation, and government anthropologists were not to write about dance in official documents. In Senegambia, Creole Catholic priest, Abbé Boilat, exiled to France following a dispute within the Church, published his memoirs in 1853 in an attempt to rehabilitate his reputation (Boilat 1853). His portrayal of regional dances as placing good Christian souls at risk is therefore predictable in this context. What is striking, though, is the similarity between his moralizing tone and some of the public discourse on popular dances in Senegal today. The following excerpt is taken from the section on the 'Moors' of Northern Senegambia, in which Boilat (1853: 370–371) describes evening dances held on gum trading boats on the Senegal River:

> Men and women dance separately; all their movements simulate fighting; but it is quite different with women: they, too, dance separately, and the young men come to watch; in general the movements they execute are most indecent. They form a large circle and each in turn enters the middle to dance while the others clap and sing in rhythm.
>
> The Negro women of the Walo do not remain indifferent to these pleasures; they embark with their *Griots* and drums and dance like the others, but in the manner of the Wolof who live on the edges of the desert. One easily imagines [. . .] that several [European] traders come to watch these evening festivities, where they forget the sacred moral duties and those of

faithfulness in marriage. They soon choose concubines among these beautiful dancers who cost them many *ballots de Guinée* [colonial currency], quite apart from the numerous gifts they are obliged to provide them with.

In Boilat's account, although both men and women dance, it is the morality of women dancing that is called into question; they are the ones who tempt innocent European traders and cause them to be unfaithful to their wives. As we will see in Chapter 4, this is not very different from today's public discourse in Senegal, where young women dancing in suggestive ways are held responsible for the moral ills of modern society.

Travel writing has been equally prolific in the stereotyping of dance in Africa. In his West African travelogue, *Africa Dances*, Geoffrey Gorer (1935) refrains from adopting a moralizing tone, but often describes the dances he has witnessed as pure entertainment, and hardly the product of a creative effort. But Gorer's book was not as widely read as the European printed press in the colonial period, a medium which made the exoticization of African dancing bodies widely available to European publics. Writing on African performance was particularly prolific during world fairs and colonial exhibitions, and the reviews of the magnificent 1931 exhibition in Paris are a case in point. The exhibition itself was an oversized display of imperial splendour, and a tribute to the French 'civilizing mission', *la mission civilisatrice*. Ordinary citizens did not have many opportunities to travel to the French colonies, and to entertain the millions of paying visitors who came over the course of six months, real and locally recruited colonial 'subjects' were brought in to perform scenes of everyday life in their native regions. The purpose-built site at the Porte Dorée took the visitor through 'a décor of pagodas, Indochinese temples, African huts, Arabic minarets and great Sahelian walls' (Décoret-Ahiha 2004: 49, translated from French). During those months, the French printed press was full of lyrical reviews by journalists and intellectuals posing as enchanted travellers to unknown parts of the world. On 22 August 1931, French weekly magazine, *L'Illustration*, published 'L'heure du ballet', a special insert on the dance programme at the exhibition. The text was supplemented with eleven photographs and four drawings, and writer Paul-Emile Cadilhac (1931: 13) commented on the African elements of the spectacle:

> All the peoples gathered in Vincennes are dancing. For the past three months it has been nothing but festivities, circus games and music-hall. Framed by torches, magnificent and barbaric parades have wandered through the alleys of the Exhibition in the evenings, [. . .] and every nation, every protectorate, every colony wanted to have its festivities, every palace its ball, every French or foreign section its theatre, its stage, big or small, its seats reserved for the privileged few or given up to the crowds. [. . .]
>
> Africa appears as more direct, simpler, closer to the primitive instincts. Its drums, its sorcerers, its processions – from Behanzin to the king of the Mossi – have seduced the crowds and carried them away. Success was such

that once a week the dances from West Africa, performed by indigenous riflemen, are now presented at the Cité des Informations by Commandant Décugis.

But of all these events, the most beautiful, the most complete, was undoubtedly the series of five soirées offered by the Governor of French West Africa, Mr. Brévié, and Mrs. Brévié in their red palace at the Exhibition. [. . .] A white platform had been set up against a fountain in the central courtyard, bordered by chairs on three sides and dominated by the high tower decorated with the shapes and faces of gods. And the dancers from Ivory Coast appeared. Almost naked, wearing a loincloth around the hips and bracelets around the ankles, they were laughing, showing their white teeth. On their heads were feathers or some sort of savage headdress, and they were holding long lianas which they alternatively stretched and released. They danced, accompanied by tambourines and a kind of triangle. Then they gave way to the court of King Behanzin. [. . .] Drummers came in a procession: Bambara, Soussou, Mossi and the women dancers of Siguri, wearing red and blue pants. Everyone danced in their own fashion, the Dahomeans on a very marked binary rhythm and the Soussou in an epilepsy-like manner which set in motion the shoulders, the arms, the whole body. From time to time, on the side, isolated individuals performed pirouettes, somersaults and cartwheels.

Meanwhile, the time of the Habbés[5] from Bandiagara had come. Naked above the waist, they wore a black tunic covered with thin plaited cords that looked like raffia. Their faces were hidden behind wire mesh masks. Small horns sat atop their heads, and in two cases also a sort of double swastika symbolizing the horns of the big antelopes of the bush. They performed for a long time, evoking through their cries, their calls, their songs, their gestures and their dances the wild beasts of Africa.

The performances are evidently new to the author, who does not quite know what to make of them. There is fascination with the flamboyance of the whole display and with the obvious popularity with the Parisian crowds. Cadilhac is also doing his best to show off his own erudition by naming ethnic groups and locations most French would not have heard of at the time. But there is also a running thread that is present in many texts from the colonial period: Africans dancing are portrayed as almost fused with the landscapes and the 'wild beasts' writers and readers alike imagine them to be living with. There is no place for either linguistic sophistication or elaborate choreographic work, and certainly not for urban culture.

From the mid-nineteenth century onwards, Africans dancing were thus constructed as driven by their emotions, their natural environment, and by mysterious forces outside the body, rather than individual agency and creativity. Ironically, as we have seen, this notion of limited human agency fits well with the perception of dance in certain contexts in Senegambia. The strength of this idea on both sides of the colonial divide may thus explain why it has been so enduring. This legacy of colonial representations is still with us in popular perceptions, albeit phrased in a different language, as we will see in the course of the book.

There is also, now, a growing body of literature written by dancer-choreographers themselves (Acogny 1994 [1980]; Tiérou 2001; Sanou and Tempé 2008), as well as films on contemporary dance in Africa.[6] A productive way of dispelling the myth of 'African dance' is to look at the ways in which specific practices have been shaped over time. There are, of course, limitations to do with the lack of historical data, and the difficulty of writing about performance in a way that does justice to the way it is experienced by participants. We can only propose tentative avenues for thinking about the significance of performance.

Fieldwork embodied

The main part of the fieldwork for this study was carried out over twelve months between May 2002 and February 2004. Shorter trips totalling about four months followed between December 2005 and April 2011. I stayed mostly in Dakar but also took trips to the rail city of Thiès, Tubaab Jallaw on the coast south of Dakar, the Siin Saalum region and Saint-Louis. Much as I would have liked to spend time in the Casamance, the region was not easily accessible at the time of my main period of fieldwork,[7] and the fact that I had a small child in tow prevented me from embarking on long road trips. On the other hand, fieldwork came to extend beyond Senegal: I visited some of the performers I knew as they travelled to France and the UK, and attended the Ninth Edition of the African contemporary dance biennale (*Danse l'Afrique Danse*, formerly *Rencontres Chorégraphiques de l'Afrique et de l'Océan Indien*) in Johannesburg in September–October 2012.

One of the main difficulties in researching dance is that people who are not professional dancers have little to say about it beyond comments on individual skills or the morality of particular dancing styles. Anthropologists researching dance and other embodied practices have often remarked on this. On masquerade dances in the Cameroon Grassfields, Argenti (2007: 27) notes that 'the passionate, transcendent sensations of pleasure, pain, fear, and sorrow that are achieved by the dancers and their acolytes cannot be visited again in language afterwards'. Researching dance in Dakar, therefore, required some degree of practice.

Over the course of several months I took weekly classes in West African dances with Salif Mbengue, also known as Zale, one of the most experienced dancers in the Dakarois scene. I attended a four-week workshop in 'traditional dance' organized for over thirty professional dancers by the Kaay Fecc association in October 2002. This consisted of a three-hour dance training session every day, followed by an hour of 'theory' during which Massamba Guèye, an expert in Senegambian oral traditions, taught in Wolof on the local practices the dances used to be integrated with. The four weeks were divided into three parts during which different styles were taught by experienced dancers: Lebu dances (*ndawrabin* and *gumbe*), Jola initiation dances, and finally the Ivorian *zaouli*. There was live drumming by players from several dance troupes. The workshop, which turned out to be an excellent way of meeting dancers, ended with a final 'restitution' performance attended by friends and relatives, other young dancers, and by Minister of Culture, Amadou Tidiane Wone. I also attended family ceremonies and neighbourhood festive events, but I rarely danced there, for although I learned the basics of sabar in dance classes, I found the dance circle intimidating.

I gained much more than a network through participation. Helena Wulff (1998) has written on how her background as a dancer had affected her rapport with ballet dancers. She noted that they could tell she had been a dancer from the way she watched them move. In my case, dancing with informants helped to legitimize my presence, and more importantly this enabled me to gain an experiential understanding of the local dance styles. In addition, taking up *djembe* drumming since then has given me a better grasp of the physicality of the rhythms. Being positioned as an apprentice, I also experienced how regional modes of apprenticeship differed from ways of learning how to dance in Euro-American settings. In this respect, it did help that I had extensive experience in various dance practices from studios in France, Denmark and the UK.

There was a lot of quiet watching, too, followed by mundane conversations. I had initially intended to focus on popular dances and hip-hop, but the serendipity of encounters decided otherwise. Early on, an acquaintance introduced me to a dance company, *La 5ᵉ Dimension*. I was intrigued by the combination of styles the dancers used, and they welcomed me to watch their rehearsals every week. Watching them at work, taking part in their informal meetings and having conversations with them turned out to be a important thread running through my fieldwork. Moreover the choreographer, Jean Tamba, had a long experience of the dance scene in Dakar, and his memories helped me to imagine what being a dancer between the 1970s and the 1990s must have been like. He was also one of the founders of the Kaay Fecc association, and the artistic director of the festival. In addition to the time spent with his company, I watched dance troupes rehearse at the Centre Culturel Blaise Senghor (CCBS)[8] a couple of evenings per week. One of the hearts of the choreographic scene in Dakar, 'Blaise Senghor' as the performers call it, is an aged, flat building with indoor and outdoor rehearsal rooms, a stage, offices and a small library. Dancers, musicians and theatre people hang out in the entrance hall every afternoon, and in the evening the building vibrates with the sound of loud drumming by three to five troupes rehearsing at the same time. I occasionally served as a photographer, snapping still and moving images of dancers at their own request, which gave me an excellent reason to be there.

Membership in the Kaay Fecc association early on enabled me to get glimpses of what was going on at the level of management and politics. I was part of the organizing team of the Kaay Fecc festival in 2003 and again in 2007, though the second time only for the duration of the festival. Fellow organizers included performers and choreographers, troupe managers, journalists, individuals with experience in the organization of events, stage technicians, and a secondary school teacher. Having previous experience as a festival volunteer in Denmark, I was in charge of recruiting and managing a team of about fifty 'volunteers', together with a visiting festival organizer from Ivory Coast. This enabled me to step into the role of a festival organizer, a position more tangible to most than that of an ethnographer.

Figure I.1 Soumbédioune, the Lebu fish market, seen from Fann Hock, 2002. Photograph by the author.

This was not my first visit to Senegal. I had spent several holidays there as a child and as a teenager visiting my Senegalese father and family, but my memories of Dakar were sketchy. I did, however, remember that the urban landscape used to be in a much better state and that the middle classes were better off in the late 1970s and early 1980s. I remembered the smell of fish, the fish market at Soumbédioune (Figure I.1) and empty beaches further north on the peninsula. I was surprised to see that a beach culture had developed in the meantime, with young people flocking to the sea at the weekends during the hot months. Smaller dance troupes without access to a proper space even rehearsed on the beach.

Through friends I came to live in the small neighbourhood of Fann Hock (Figure I.2), a fairly central location not far from the University and from the old Medina. From there I could easily catch a local minibus, a *car rapide*, or taxi to visit friends and informants across the city and its suburbs. In Fann Hock, people kept sheep in the sandy streets outside their homes, which the children washed with great dedication on Sunday mornings. There were mainly single-storey urban compounds in the 1950s style of the state agency SICAP (Société Immobilière du Cap Vert), though over the years more and more multi-storey buildings popped up. Sabar events as well as family ceremonies were held in the alleys from time to time. There were also *dahira* Sufi meetings on Thursday nights, with drumming and chanting well into the night. Loudspeakers made sure that the neighbourhood was momentarily taken over by the sound of prayer. I lived upstairs from a corner shop where neighbourhood youths met every day to chat, listen to Senegalese rap, make phone calls, watch the

Figure I.2 View of Dakar from Fann Hock in 2002. Photograph by the author.

girls, and sing the praise of their Sufi Muslim leaders, or *marabouts*. Next door to the shop lived a respected Jola traditional healer, whose courtyard was always filled with patients waiting from the early hours of the morning.

Friendships with other families in the neighbourhood meant that I was involved in circles outside the dance scene. Several friends worked for the local NGO, Enda Tiers Monde, and one of them introduced me to a cultural association in the dense suburb of Pikine (Figure I.3). The association was funded by a Belgian NGO with connections to Senegalese migrants in Belgium, and belonged to a sprawling constellation of associations that had benefited from the Senegalese decentralization policy launched in 1996. Their declared mission was to promote 'culture and the arts' in their district. When I told the first two members I met about my research, hoping to follow their work and attend neighbourhood events, they organized four afternoon-long group meetings for me to ask about dance practices in Senegal. I had not intended to carry out formal interviews at that early stage, but people were used to the principles of 'research-action' through their interaction with NGOs, and they expected me to follow the same model. These sessions turned out to be quite interesting. Although I sometimes felt uncomfortable with such a formal set-up, these were precious opportunities to discuss a wide range of issues, and not just performance. I came back regularly afterwards, spending most visits sitting and chatting outside the Women's Centre (often occupied by men) in this district of Pikine. These visits gave me insights into the world of local associations, many of whom were offshoots of the

Figure I.3 Views of one of Pikine's districts in 2003. Photographs by the author.

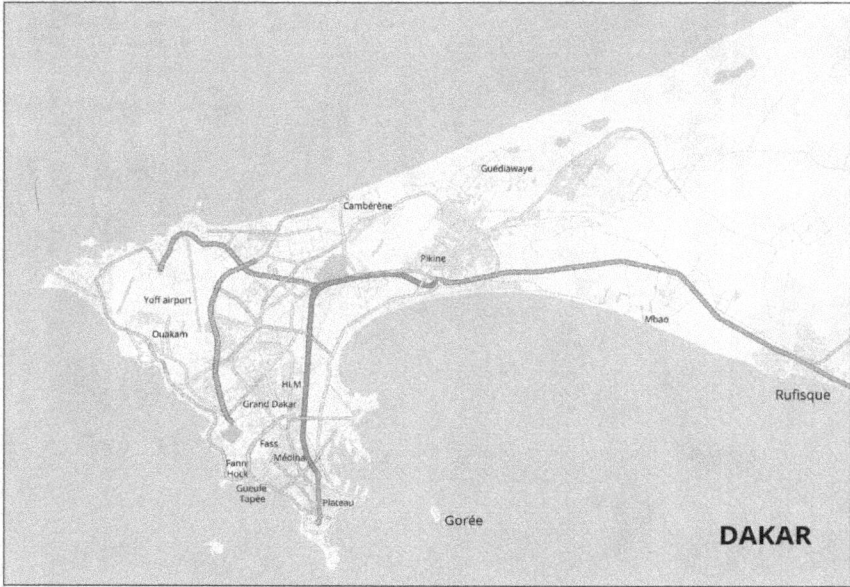

Figure I.4 Dakar and the Cap Vert Peninsula, with main fieldwork sites indicated. (Map created by ML Kringelbach using TileMill. © OpenStreetMap contributors).

ASC (Associations Sportives et Culturelles) movement, the youth sports and cultural clubs which I return to in Chapter 4. My fieldwork thus stretched over most of the peninsula (Figure I.4).

Though I started learning Wolof with a qualified teacher early into fieldwork, I was never fluent enough to conduct interviews exclusively in Wolof. Most of my conversations were in French, or in a mix of French and Wolof. On several occasions I relied on friends to conduct interviews with interlocutors who did not speak French, mainly women. But my linguistic limitations mean that my interactions were skewed towards people who had at least completed primary school. Nafy Guèye, a close friend with a keen interest in dance, introduced me to Lebu dignitary, Alioune Diagne Mbor, joined me at a few women dance events and helped to translate songs.

As a researcher, I worried constantly about 'giving something back' to the dance scene, and to key people with whom I spent time. This was all the more important as many informants were acutely awareness of exploitation issues. Thus the Senegalese NGO officer who introduced me to the association in Pikine did not hide the fact that he was deeply distrustful of the ethics of research in Africa by outsiders. As we waited for the two men to arrive from Pikine, he remarked in a sarcastic tone: 'I know how these things work, you know. You will do your research here, learn things from people and then you'll go back and be called an *expert*'. He then proceeded to tell me about an NGO-funded study trip he had made to Ivory Coast, during which a French 'expert' had lectured the African delegation on cocoa farming. 'Where had he learned this, if not from Africans?', he asked. To him, this captured the unfairness of research structures on the continent. When the Pikinois arrived, he introduced us and explained what I wished to do. He then stood up and said he would leave us to 'negotiate', but not without telling the visitors that I was going to offer them a workshop in film script writing. I extricated myself from the situation by offering to give English lessons instead, but the visitors had a hard time believing that I had never written a film script in my life. The officer's tactics were obvious: by making a surprise offer on my behalf, he made it clear that I would have to 'give something back', although not necessarily in the form of cash. Over time I found ways of making myself useful by becoming involved in practical tasks in the dance world, designing a poster and a website for a company, helping people with CVs, English translations, etc. I also became less conscious of people's expectations as relationships grew into friendships, with their usual tensions and expectations.

Although most of the data for this study was gathered through fieldwork, I have also spent time doing archival work. I have consulted the archives of the 1966 World Festival of Negro Arts at the National Archives of Senegal in Dakar, and consulted Senegalese newspapers from the 1930s onwards, both in Dakar (at the Centre d'Etudes Supérieures des Techniques de l'Information, or CESTI) and in Paris (Bibliothèque Nationale de France). I have also benefited greatly from Bob White's online database of newspaper articles on www.atalaku.net.

Finally, I have drawn inspiration from Jackson (1989)and Sarró (2009), both of whom highlight the importance of discussing ideas and writing with key informants. My three-week trip in April–May 2011 was thus dedicated to long hours of conversation with a dozen dance people about my book manuscript. I spent time explaining the contents verbally, since most of my informants were not fluent in English. In return, the feedback process yielded some of the most fruitful conversations I had had for years, and added a deeper layer to existing relationships.

Dance circles in an African city

Following this introduction, Chapter 1 places the study in historical context by tracing the history of public performance in Wolof-speaking urban Senegal, from the occupational trade of griots to a modern profession largely detached from traditional status hierarchies. It is suggested that the promotion of colonial school theatre, the cosmopolitan trajectories of the nationalist elites and President Senghor's patronage of the arts for political purposes were defining moments in the emergence of a profession with worldwide ambitions. These moments all fostered the emergence of new genres and new techniques of the body, which have paved the way for the current diversification in choreographic production.

Chapter 2 looks at the urban context in which this production takes place. Moving closer to the contemporary period, I focus here on the city of Dakar to show how the social transformations sketched in the previous chapter have provided young city dwellers with alternative routes towards social mobility. Since the Lebu from coastal fishing communities are regarded as the first inhabitants of the Cape Vert Peninsula on which Dakar sits, and since they have retained a strong discourse of autochthony despite a recent history of diminishing land tenure, I also look at Lebu performance in the context of official ceremonies. I suggest that successful performance in a particular space symbolizes moral authority and the capacity to command the allegiance of others. In other words, successful performance embodies the widespread West African notion of 'wealth in people'. Finally, in this chapter I suggest that the appeal of the performing profession for youths from non-Griot backgrounds is fraught with tension because of the shifts it indicates in the location of status and power in society.

In Chapter 3, I begin to address the issue of self-fashioning by examining sabar dance events as a social space in which persons are gendered. Looking at the differentiated performance of sabar over the course of city dwellers' lives suggests that the genre serves in particular to help girls, and later women, to experience in their own bodies what being a social person at different stages of life involves. Although the genre is dominated by the presence of women, I suggest that it has to do with male personhood, too, but through a gradual absence rather than sustained participation. In this chapter I also focus on the spatial and choreographic structure of sabar events to argue that the genre embodies the tension between social conventions and individual creativity.

Chapter 4 focuses on the mbalax genre and other popular dance offshoots of the sabar as embodied practices through which young men and women use their skills to create new forms of sociality, and make the best of a situation of uncertainty and growing economic inequalities. Through the lens of state-sponsored TV dance competitions, the chapter also shows how a crucial dimension of post-colonial politics is the state's repeated attempts to co-opt youth movements and cultural practices in order to avoid disorder.

Chapter 5 explores the politics of neo-traditional performance, with a focus on the appropriation of the genre for regionalist, transnational and individual career purposes. This links in to previous chapters as I suggest that the practice of neo-traditional performance alongside dances in youth clubs and neighbourhood events, either simultaneously or at different life stages, helps city dwellers to make sense of their engagement with different moral communities. Moreover, neo-traditional performance has become an industry as well as being a cultural and political project, and this chapter thus examines the commodification of 'tradition'.

Chapter 6 examines the individualized genre of contemporary dance. The history traced in Chapter 1 is supplemented here with a focus on the recent emergence of a pan-African contemporary choreographic scene promoted by French and other European funding. The existence of a biennial pan-African choreographic competition since 1995, in particular, illuminates the circulation of the genre, which is best described as a creative process. But rather than the passive adoption of new choreographic techniques, the chapter also sheds light on the local appropriation of the genre for purposes of social mobility and self-fashioning.

Chapter 7 begins with reflections on the uses of notions of tradition in contemporary Senegalese choreography. It then moves a step below the general to focus on La 5ᵉ Dimension, a contemporary dance company whose members have played an important role in shaping the Dakarois choreographic scene. This is a group portrait which gives a sense of the creative process involved in the local contemporary genre, and shows creativity to be shaped by individual aspirations as well as local and global discourses on the role of the artist in society. The growing phenomenon of cross-cultural choreographic collaborations is also presented as a factor which lies at the heart of contemporary choreography's attractiveness with African youths who are keen to participate in global culture on equal terms with their peers from elsewhere.

Chapter 8 concludes the book with remarks on the role of movement and imagination in the fashioning of urban livelihoods and identities in contemporary Senegal as well as among the growing Senegalese Diaspora. Throughout the book, all translations between English and French are my own unless otherwise indicated.

Notes

1. For comprehensive reviews of phenomenological approaches in anthropology, see for example Lock (1993) and Csordas (1999).
2. A pioneering experiment with the neuro-imaging of tango footwork suggests that dance is indeed a holistic activity, involving the 'integration of spatial pattern, rhythm, synchronization to external stimuli and whole-body coordination' (Brown, Martinez, and Parsons 2006). Also see the recent work on dance and neuroscience in Jola et al. (2011).
3. The 'Hottentot Venus' was a Khoisan woman named Saartjie Baartman, who was tragically paraded around European theatres and circuses between 1810 and 1816. Her life has been documented in several biographies (Holmes 2007; Crais and Scully 2008).
4. On world fairs and colonial exhibitions, see for example Greenhalgh (1988), Corbey (1993), Lindfors (1999), Bancel et al. (2004).
5. *Habbés* was the colonial name given to the Dogons of Mali.
6. See, for example, *Drums, Sand and Shostakovich* by Ken Glazebrook and Alla Kovgan, USA, 2002, 70 minutes; *Movement (R)evolution Africa (a story of an art form in four acts)* by Joan Frosch and Alla Kovgan, USA, 2007, 65 minutes; *Danse l'Afrique, Danse!* by Marion Stalens, France, 2012, 52 minutes.
7. On 26 September 2002, the *Joola* ferryboat linking Dakar to Ziguinchor capsized tragically, causing the death of nearly 2,000 people on board. For several years following this tragedy, the only way to travel between Dakar and Ziguinchor was by road or plane.
8. The Centre Culturel Blaise Senghor (CCBS) is one of the biggest sites in the network of state-owned cultural centres modelled on the former *centres culturels* built during colonial times to promote French language and culture. Most centres were built between the 1950s and the 1970s. The CCBS was built in 1977 with the support of UNESCO.

Chapter 1

Cosmopolitan Performing Arts in Twentieth-Century Senegal

In the second decade of the second millennium it may be difficult, at first glance, to see the agency of the state as significant in shaping artistic life in Senegal. Dance and music festivals are mostly funded by international sources, and the state is no longer a major patron of the arts. The controversial FESMAN (World Festival of Black Arts) held in Dakar in December 2010 at great cost and subsequent debt should not hide the fact that the flagship arts institutions of the post-independence period have either closed down or are threatened with closure. The biennial state-funded FESNAC, the National Festival of Arts and Culture held across Senegal since 1997, features dance, music and theatre competitions but it is notoriously underfunded. Participants in the 2005 FESNAC in Tambacounda spoke of performers having to sleep rough in schools and being left for long hours without food or water. Long gone, too, are the days when Léopold Sédar Senghor invited artists to the presidential palace and called them his 'dear children' (Harney 1996). Senegalese performers must now spend part of their lives abroad in order for their work to circulate. Yet most of them maintain connections to Senegal, and Dakar has a buoyant performing scene in which the state continues to play an important, albeit more complex role.

This chapter opens with historical sketches on the antecedents of the sabar genre I discuss further in Chapter 3. There are few written sources on the topic, and therefore this aspect of the historical context is necessarily limited. I then move on to the emergence of the modern performing profession in the colonial period, which introduced important transformations to the existing practices of specialized categories of performers (praise-singers, or *griots* in French) by promoting new audiences, new patrons and connections with arts worlds outside the region. This chapter examines the political agendas that have moulded the Senegalese choreographic arts into the social worlds they are today: at once locally grounded and outward looking. It is also suggested that the centralization of the modern performing arts in the Dakar region is a consequence of this history.

Women and griots: echoes of past dance circles

There are echoes of sabar performance in northern Senegal going back to at least the seventeenth century, when European travellers first mentioned dances performed to the sound of drums beaten with a hand and a stick (Tang 2007). Oral histories and the sparse written sources available do not paint a clear picture of what sabar performance may have looked like in the past, but it is likely that there was a suggestive dimension to the style early on. Thus in 1789, Lamiral (1789, cited and translated in Charry 1992: 33), gives a slightly more detailed account of an event very similar to a contemporary sabar, but with a more balanced presence of youths from both sexes:

> The boys and girls gather together in the middle of the village, they sit in a circle and in the middle are the musicians who entertain the party with dances and lascivious gestures. They pantomime all the caresses and raptures of love, the griottes approach the onlookers and seem to provoke them into an amorous combat, the young girls accompany them with their voices and say things appropriate to the matter at hand: they all clap their hands in time and encourage the dancers by their clapping. At first the music appears slow, the dancers approach one another and back off, the rhythm doubles, the gestures become quicker; the musicians thunder and the movements of the dancers get faster and faster, their bodies take all sorts of shapes; they hold each other and push each other away: finally out of breath they fall into the arms of each other and the onlookers cover them with their pagnes [skirt cloths]; during this time the drums make such a racket that it is impossible to understand anything that is said.

Several decades later, in Wolof-speaking regions, Abbé Boilat (1853: 323–324, translated from French) also witnessed what was probably the antecedent of contemporary sabar events:

> On moonlit evenings, the local drum announces the dance towards the end of the meal; the women seem electrified by this music, they rise all of a sudden and come running at great speed; soon the men follow. The first sequences are performed by the young men, the women sing and clap; suddenly they rush and perform dances that decency prevents me from describing here, and which are nothing but the representation of the most brutal passions. The Clerics and their families never take part in those festivities.

Christian attitudes to West African dances at the time, as well as Boilat's desire to convince his readers of his own moral purity, mean that the suggestiveness hinted at is not to be taken literally. Yet the observation that Muslim 'clerics and their families' did not take part suggests that mixed-gendered entertainment dances were already contested on moral grounds. There is also a suggestion that women were often the most enthusiastic dancers, even though Dakarois informants in their eighties remember that in their youth, men danced a great deal more during sabar events than they do today.

It is indeed likely that the current association between female societies and sabar dancing, which I return to in Chapter 3, has historical antecedents. Among Wolof speakers for example, age-sets (*mbotaay*) and female groups of friends (*ndey dikké*) have long formed the basis of networks of solidarity, even organizing collective work, such as washing, millet grinding or wood and water collecting (Sarr 2002). Most importantly, they helped each other to gather the resources needed to fulfil social duties in the context of family ceremonies, circumcision rituals and funerals. For the Pulaar speakers of the Fuuta Toro, Wane (1969: 27–28) highlights the importance of the female age-sets (*fedde rewre*) for similar purposes. According to oral historian and storyteller, Massamba Guèye, sabar dances used to be performed by married women when they gathered for domestic work. In the intimate space thus created, they were able to exchange secrets, playfully compare their bodily 'assets' and solve family conflicts, much as adult women do today. Historian, Ousseynou Faye, suggests that mbotaay were the closest antecedents to the modern *tours*, or closed festive events organized by women's groups (see Chapter 3), and did not have a direct equivalent among adult men because men already held power through more formal institutions. For him the mbotaay, therefore, always involved a subtle contestation of male power (Faye, personal communication, Dakar, October 2002). During the colonial period, the urbanization of the region gave rise to urban societies modelled on rural female societies. Women's sections of political parties, for example, were created at the initiative of women themselves, and played an important role in Senegalese politics from the 1940s onwards (Ndiaye Sylla 2001). Other organizational forms have appeared under the impulse of the state, such as the 'Groupements de Promotion Féminine' created in rural areas in the 1970s in order to integrate women to development projects. Women's associations have multiplied further since the 1980s (Dahou 2004), and many organize their sociality around dance events.

Another enduring aspect of dance in northern Senegal, which comes across in missionaries' and travellers' writings, is that performing in public, and with skill, has long been perceived as the prerogative of the griots. The emergence of a modern performing profession in colonial times has transformed this, but for many families there remains an underlying sense of 'griot-ness' in the act of dancing and singing for others. This is an important aspect in the context of this study, and a grasp of the transformations at hand requires, first, an explanation of traditional status hierarchies in the Senegambian region.

The first Arabic and European travellers had already reported the existence of endogamous groups with specialized trades in the wider region (Tamari 1997), which became known as 'castes' during the colonial period, in reference to the Indian case. Though the term fails to reflect the West African specificity (Wane 1969; Dilley 2004), for reasons of convenience I follow Roy Dilley (2004) in using the term 'caste' or 'caste-like' as shorthand. Sociologist, Abdoulaye-Bara Diop (1981), has given the fullest description of the Wolof model, albeit from the point of view of the higher-status groups. He identified two overlapping but distinct components in Wolof hierarchies, the first determining status ('castes'), and the second determining political power ('orders'). The orders consist of the royal and aristocratic lineages (*garmi* and *jàmbur*), the common freemen (*baadoolo*) and the slaves and their descendants (*jaam*). Diop describes the 'castes' as based on a complementary opposition between two main ranks, the *géér* and the *ñeeño*. The géér represent the majority of the population (eighty to ninety per cent), with the ñeeño making up the rest. In the past they included the *sab-lekk*, or performers, and the *jëf-lekk*, or artisans (blacksmiths and jewellers, leatherworkers, woodworkers and weavers). Among the sab-lekk were the *géwël* (musicians, praise-orators[1] and genealogists-oral historians) and the *ñoole* (buffoons). In Wolof, *géwël* literally means 'the one for whom a circle is made' (Panzacchi 1994). The sab-lekk included sub-groups distinguished by the style and function of their songs and by the instruments they played. Over time, Diop says, they were all subsumed within the géwël category, whose role was to validate the status of their patrons through a skilful combination of praise-oratory, drumming and dancing. Whereas drumming was the domain of géwël men, dancing was mostly associated with women, and singing as well as praise-oratory could be performed by either sex. In theory, the ñeeño were endogamous. The Haalpulaar'en of the Fuuta Toro, in the Senegal River valley, had an even more complex stratification system. Highest was the category of the *tooroBe* (singular: *toorodo*), the descendants of Muslim Clerics who took power in the Fuuta Toro in the late eighteenth century, and who initially included people of all backgrounds (Wane 1969). The Mande/Mandinka areas were similar to the Wolof model, and there the *nyamakala* were comparable to the Wolof ñeeño. By contrast the Jola, the Bassari and the Manjaco, in the Casamance, are said to have more egalitarian modes of organization.

Though on the whole, occupations are no longer determined by these hereditary categories, to a certain extent public performance rewarded by money remains associated with ñeeño or nyamakala status. This is occasionally expressed in the Senegalese printed media (Nouvel Horizon 2003: 39):

> Dance is not well perceived in our society, this is a well-known fact. [. . .] The phrase 'A *non casté* [géér] does not speak, sing or dance' would be repeated over and over again to those who wished to transgress this tradition. Dancing is strictly reserved to Griots, who are by vocation and by definition 'public entertainers'.

This association has long extended into perceptions of everyday movement and speech. As I have argued elsewhere (Neveu Kringelbach 2005, 2007a), dance, non-dance movement and speech form part of the same continuum of performance, which corroborates Wendy James' (2003: 78–79) point that 'the performative and experiential aspects of the various formal genres of patterned movement, ritual, marching, and dancing are not just a spill-over from the 'ordinary' *habitus*, but derive their power partly by speaking against, resonating ironically with, this very base'. In

Dakar, ways of dancing, moving and speaking may either reiterate status by birth or contest it. Thus restraint (*kersa*) is generally perceived as indicative of géér status, as is coolness. In Wolof this is reflected in the distinction between the speech style of the géér, *waxu géér*, and that of the géwël, *waxu géwël*. Waxu géwël is often described as 'loud, high-pitched, rapid, verbose, florid, and emphatic, with assorted phono-logical, morphological, and syntactic devices linked to those characteristics' (Irvine 1989:261). Géér who speak in such expansive ways are therefore at risk of being assimilated to géwël, as expressed in the condescending phrase 'ya ngiy géwëlee', literally 'you are becoming griot-like'. People often say they can tell from the way a person walks, dresses, speaks and dances whether this person is a géwël. By contrast, the speech style which indexes high status, waxu géér, is slower, spoken with a lower tone of voice, less emphatic and generally considered more thoughtful.

Beyond the seemingly rigid nature of the regional status hierarchies, there has always been a degree of flexibility to this, as I discuss in the next chapter. But over the course of the twentieth century, the single most important factor in the emergence of a modern performing profession, less tied to griot backgrounds, was colonial school theatre.

Musical theatre between colonial schools and European stages

The history of modern musical theatre in West Africa is intimately linked to the Ecole Normale William-Ponty, set up by the French authorities in Gorée in 1915 to train indigenous schoolteachers and administrators. Moved to Sébikotane, east of Dakar, in 1938, it attracted students from all over French West Africa. In 1935, Charles Béart, a Frenchman who had taught in Bingerville in Côte d'Ivoire, introduced the-atre to the Ponty curriculum, and was soon appointed director.[2] The students were asked to spend their holidays writing plays to illustrate their 'native' traditions, with the aim of encouraging them to preserve a connection with rural life. Indeed while these students epitomised the successful *évolués*,[3] there was also a fear that they might lose touch with the populations they would have to teach or administer on behalf of the French. This concern was evident in Béart's (1937: 14, translated from French) writings:

> Some pupils have asked the Director of the William-Ponty School to lend them the costumes made for the [end-of-year] party so that they may 'play' during the holidays. Tomorrow, as civil servants, they will meet their vil-lage brothers with sympathy, they will study the art forms neglected for so long and they will return them to their rightful place. It will be precious for those of us who care about Africa, because we will know it better; it will be precious for those who will find comfort from the minor worries of the profession in this unselfish and generous activity – the schoolteacher who will have discovered a new and enchanting legend or who will have transcribed an old epic song will soon forget that he has quarrelled with the major's interpreter.

The Ponty training probably exceeded French expectations in producing an elite of schoolteachers who were close to the populations they worked with. Vincent Foucher (2002: 148) says of the growing engagement of schoolteachers in politics in post-1945 Senegal that this was helped by their coverage of the territory and their good relations with the local populations, since they were 'not engaged in the direct exercise of colonial authority'. If it is difficult to assess the role theatre played in this political awakening, it certainly provided the Ponty students with opportunities to express anti-colonial sentiments in subtle ways, by imagining and staging the lives of resistance heroes. *Bigolo*, for example, was written by Casamançais student Bouli Dramé in the late 1930s and staged and choreographed by another Casamançais, Assane Seck (Ly 2009: 416), who was to become an academic geographer, a politician and a Minister of Foreign Affairs after Independence. *Bigolo* is a drama set in the Casamance during the French colonial conquest in the late nineteenth century. Bigolo is a courageous soldier who has defeated the French in battle. While the Casamançais soldiers dance and sing to celebrate their victory, word comes that the French retreat was just a ploy, and that they are heading back for a new attack. In a fit of rage, Bigolo destroys his fetish, which he believes to have betrayed him. He returns to war and is eventually defeated and killed as a punishment for his destructive action (Bingo 1953). Although we know nothing of Bigolo's dances and songs, the plot leaves sufficient room for various interpretations: the villain may be the French army or it may be Bigolo himself, who is not sufficiently cool-headed to control his anger, and eventually betrays the spirits who have protected him thus far. Before attending the lycée in Saint-Louis, Seck grew up near Sédhiou, in the Casamance (Seck 2005), and was undoubtedly familiar with the region's choreographic and musical practices. It is highly likely, therefore, that the songs contained an even more ambiguous message than the text in French.

In the same vein, in 1936, in the presence of the Governor of French West Africa, Jules Brévié, whose dance programme had been such a success at the 1931 exhibition in Paris (see Chapter 1), the Guinean students performed *L'Entrevue du Capitaine Peroz et de Samory*. This was a play which celebrated the courage of nineteenth-century Wasulu leader, Samory Touré, a well-known anti-colonial figure (Mouralis 1986). Whilst being works of historical imagination, many of the plays dealt with the moral dilemmas caused by the radical transformation of local societies under colonial domination. This was the case, for example, of the 1936 play *Le Retour aux Fétiches*, a drama on the misfortunes of a Porto-Novo family, in what was then the Dahomey (later to become Benin), who had abandoned their traditional divinities (Mouralis 1986).

The Ponty plays were interspersed with musical interludes and short choreographic pieces which the colonial administration perceived as innocuous folklore. Mbaye (2004) notes that the French staff controlled and sometimes censured the plays, but this rarely affected the musical interludes. French actor, Henri Vidal, who had witnessed the play *Téli Soma Oulé* by Lompolo Koné from Burkina Faso, echoed this tame view in a commentary written for *Traits d'Union*, the magazine created to promote the work of the network of 'cultural centres' set up across French West Africa from 1953 onwards:

This is an exclusively folkloric play, which allows the incorporation of men and women dancers who, as direct descendants of the legend characters, will dance what their grandparents danced in front of the famous chiefs of the time. (Vidal 1955: 66, cited in Mbaye 2004, translated from French)

The students were divided in their attitudes towards the colonial enterprise however, and musical performance provided a creative space where they could momentarily set aside their cultural and political differences. This came together beautifully in evening performances outside the school, when the students were asked to put together comedies, singing and dancing for official celebrations organized by the local chapters of French political parties. Of course, the printed press reported on these *soirées* in glorifying terms for the colonial authorities (Paris-Dakar 1947), but for the student-performers this must have been a fine balancing act between anti-colonial activism and the desire to be closer to the centres of power. After all, Dakar was then the capital of French West Africa (see Chapter 2), and this was where the future of the Empire was being conceived.

One of the reasons why modern theatre involving acting, music and choreography took root so quickly was the existence of regional performing traditions of a similar kind.[4] Before the arrival of Charles Béart at Ponty, the students were already staging plays with dances and songs, but for entertainment rather than as a formal part of the curriculum. In Bingerville, it was after being impressed by pupils putting together a short play about villagers announcing the arrival of a colonial officer that Béart had the idea of promoting theatre in schools (Mouralis 1986). Thus the emergence of a theatrical genre combining regional performing traditions with European ones was the outcome of mutual inspiration rather than a top-down French imposition. This is well documented in the literature on twentieth-century West African Francophone drama, but because of the near-exclusive concern with language in literary studies, very few authors have remarked on the importance of the musical and choreographic dimensions in these works.[5] A case in point is Bernard Mouralis' (1986: 136) well-informed text on Ponty drama, which emphasizes text and casts aside 'bodily expression' as 'not absent' but which 'only appears alternately with the spoken parts, to represent for example a festival, with songs and dances'. In separating text from the other elements of performance, Mouralis did not do justice to the integrated nature of the practices these plays were drawing on. Yet the success of the new genre far beyond colonial circles cannot be properly understood without reference to the musical and choreographic dimensions, and their resonance with older performing practices across West Africa. This is attested to by the gradual decrease of textual elements and the expansion of choreography, as modern theatre spread over time and space and was reconfigured in every location. I call 'neo-traditional performance' the choreographic genre which emerged in West Africa as a result of the circulation and codification of colonial school theatre. In several Francophone nations, neo-traditional performance would soon become the favourite medium through which educated elites attempted to turn entire populations into modern citizens.

One student, Guinean poet, Fodéba Keita, born in 1921 in the Maninka district of Siguiri, was to help transform this emerging theatre into an ambitious project of nation-building and cultural transformation. At Ponty between 1940 and 1943, Keita already displayed unusual performing skills: he composed poetry, sang, and played banjo in a student orchestra (Cohen 2012). In subsequent years he taught in the colonial capital of Saint-Louis, where he set up his first music band and dance troupe before returning to Guinea, where he worked as a schoolteacher and youth leader (Goerg 1989; Straker 2009). He soon made his way to Paris to study law. There he socialized with a cohort of Black students, among whom were Sédar Senghor and other founders of the international Negritude movement. Senegalese students who had moved into theatre, such as Assane Seck and Annette Mbaye d'Erneville, as well as Senegalese performer Féral (François) Benga, were also part of the festivities. Benga had arrived in Paris around 1923 to accompany his father on a trip. He had quickly risen to fame as one of Josephine Baker's lead dancers at the Folies Bergères, where he made his debut in 1926 in the music-hall show *La Folie du Jour* (Coutelet 2012). A successful dancer in a Parisian scene in search of exoticism, he used the fascination with black dancers to promote his own choreographic experiments, and appeared in shows at prestigious venues like the Casino de Paris and the Théâtre des Champs Elysées. By the time Keita arrived in Paris, Benga was staging shows at the cabaret-restaurant he had opened in 1938, La Rose Rouge (Sonar Senghor 2004; Coutelet 2012). His *Tam Tam*, staged at the Olympia in 1943, featured eight women dancers from West Africa (Décoret-Ahiha 2004). Another successful artist on the Parisian stages, actor Habib Benglia, from Mali (then the Western Sudan), took up roles in classical plays.[6] Future Senegalese President, Léopold Sédar Senghor had arrived in Paris in 1928, at a time of excitement and experimentation in the theatre world. Diaghilev had brought his Ballets Russes to Paris following the Russian revolution, where they had become the talk of the town with avant-garde choreographies. At this juncture, theatre and staged choreography reflected the struggle around the radical political changes that were taking place throughout Europe, including the contested rise of communism. We do not know whether Sédar Senghor saw these performances by West African artists, but he might have since Benga was a relative of his (Coutelet 2012). Moreover, when his nephew Maurice Sonar Senghor (hereafter 'Sonar Senghor'), who had been sent to Paris to study, decided to become an actor instead, he received theatrical training from Benglia (Sonar Senghor 2004). Parisian musical theatre, then, formed part of the intellectual milieu in which both Sédar Senghor and his nephew, Sonar Senghor, forged their ideas on the intimate link between arts, politics and the making of new citizens. These ideas would later lead them to support musical and choreographic performance as essential cornerstones in nation-building.

It was in this highly politicized, cosmopolitan environment that Fodéba Keita set up his Théâtre Africain, in 1949 (Straker 2009). The first performances took place at the Cité Universitaire, the home of some of the students from Guinée, Senegal, Mali, Côte d'Ivoire and Cameroon who made up the initial troupe (Bingo 1953). Keita had joined forces with musician, Facelli Kanté, whom he had probably met in

Saint-Louis (Cohen 2012), and six former students from West Africa. He had the support of Sonar Senghor, and Benga helped with venues and contacts. Keita's subtly anti-colonial scripts and his skills as a stage director and choreographer, combined with Kanté's modern music, produced almost immediate success. Keita wrote both poems and plays with varying degrees of anti-colonialism. His most famous drama, *Minuit* (Keita 1952), was banned in French West Africa because of its explicit anti-colonial stance, but others were less openly political. At the height of its successful trajectory in Paris, Keita's troupe, now renamed Les Ballets Africains de Fodéba Keita, re-staged Assane Seck's *Bigolo* at the prestigious Théâtre de l'Etoile in April 1953 (Bingo 1953). In 1954 followed a performance at the Théâtre des Champs Elysées, and by then Keita was sufficiently recognized as a brilliant artist that French President René Coty attended the performance with his wife (Bingo 1954). In the early 1950s, as the troupe began to tour around Europe and North America, the choreographic and musical dimension gradually displaced spoken dialogue (Straker 2009) because this was more appealing to international audiences. The repertoire featured choreographed versions of ceremonial practices and everyday movement styles from West Africa, with 'special emphasis on the Mandinka folklore of Guinea and Casamance' (Kaba 1976: 102), tinged with a Parisian touch. Then steeped in the Negritude movement,[7] Keita conceptualized his artistic production as a project of cultural revival, modernization and moral salvation all at the same time (Keita 1955).

The success of these first years led to a tour throughout West Africa in 1956–57, at the invitation of the Governor of French West Africa. This was a turning point during which Les Ballets recruited a new generation of young performers who were to replace the first Paris-based students. At Guinea's independence in 1958, the group was renamed Ballets Africains de la République de Guinée and toured the world as the nation's 'cultural ambassadors' under Kanté's leadership. Keita was appointed Interior Minister in Sékou Touré's first government, and although Touré later turned against him and had him executed in 1969, he played a large part in designing Guinea's cultural policy up to the 'cultural revolution' of 1968. The early 1960s were also a time of growing rivalry between Touré and Sédar Senghor over political and moral leadership in the region. The artists and their entourage, however, knew each other well from the Parisian years and the Ballets Africains returned to Senegal in 1961, after successful tours through Europe and North America (Paris-Dakar 1961a). During US tours the Ballets Africains had thus taken Broadway and other prestigious venues by storm, as evident in the reviews and adverts published in the major newspapers at the time (Figure 1.1). In the advert shown here, the presenters obviously draw on the stereotypes of Black bodies and African dances discussed in the Introduction. In some American cities, the troupe had even been the talk of the town as the women dancers were deemed too scantily clad, and were required to cover their upper bodies (Martin 1959a, 1959b, 1959c, 1959d; New York Times 1959). But this only served to reinforce the sensational character of the show, which became known in West Africa as a success on the worldwide stages. The creation of the National Ballet of Senegal in 1961, therefore, is best understood in the light of a complicated relationship of proximity and tension with neighbouring Guinea.

MAIL ORDERS NOW! 2 WEEKS ONLY– Beg. FEB. 16 thru FEB. 28

FROM THE HEART OF AFRICA, TO THRILL, BEWITCH AND ENCHANT YOU, COMES EUROPE'S MOST TRIUMPHANT THEATRICAL ATTRACTION!

LUBEN VICHEY *presents*

LES BALLETS AFRICAINS

DE KEÏTA FODEBA

"DESPITE ITS TITLE THIS SHOW HAS LITTLE CONNECTION WITH BALLET AS WE KNOW IT. IT IS FAR MORE EXCITING."

"EUROPE'S NEWEST DANCE SENSATION. LES BALLETS AFRICAINS HAS WON RAVES IN PARIS, LONDON, EDIN-BURGH."

PARIS
"Black magic, breathtaking, bewitching and mysterious, spontaneous and exuberant."

"INTOXICATES THE MOST BLASÉ SPEC-TATOR."

LONDON
"Sensuously impelling. Most uninhibited evening seen."

"AN IMPRESSIVE ACHIEVEMENT. A CON-COURSE OF ALL THE ARTS."

"Nothing so new, so fresh, so bursting with life."

"WOW! IT'S A JUNGLE FLAME. THE AUDIENCE GASPED."

"Sends an authentic thrill up one's spine."

"WHAT A SHOW!"

EDINBURGH
"A most spectacular event. They came, they sang, danced, leapt in the air and they conquered."

"SPECTACULAR, EXOTIC. A SOCK PER-FORMANCE."

MARTIN BECK THEATRE, 302 W. 45 ST., Circle 6-6363
PRIOR TO BROADWAY: Feb. 2-7, Shubert Theatre, Phila.—Feb. 9-14, Colonial Theatre, Boston

Figure 1.1 *An advert for the Ballets Africains published in the* New York Times *on 1 February 1959, p.X3. Image from ProQuest's Historical Newspapers, displayed with permission of ProQuest LLC.*

Choreographing the nation

At Senegal's independence from France in 1960, nation-building required that lin-guistically and culturally diverse populations be brought together around the idea of a single political unit. To establish a stable working state, governing elites needed people to 'imagine' the new entity to which they now belonged (Anderson 1983). Senegal's cultural policy at the time was dedicated to this project, and also to the strengthening of Senghor's moral authority. Alongside the visual arts, the performing arts became the flagship of this policy. Drawing on her ethnography of music in post-colonial Tanzania, Askew (2002) has argued convincingly that musical performance played a much bigger role in post-colonial nation-building than Eurocentric theories of nationalism had done justice to. The political uses of performance, however, have varied depending on the strength of regional performing histories and the personal preferences of post-colonial leaders. In Senegal, the involvement of musical and cho-reographic performance in nation-building was heavily shaped by the rivalry between Léopold Sédar Senghor and Sékou Touré. Behind the scenes, it was also shaped by the trajectories of individuals like Maurice Sonar Senghor, who had been steeped in the cosmopolitan milieu of Parisian theatre.

One of the major projects of the period was the creation of the National Theatre, which consisted of the National Ballet, the National Drama Troupe and the Traditional Instrumental Ensemble. The Daniel Sorano Theatre, a modern theatre built in 1965 with French funding, would later house the three troupes. This reflected the post-colonial state of affairs at the time: France's role as a patron was essential, but it remained mostly invisible so as not to threaten Senegal's status as a sovereign state. Sonar Senghor, who had returned to Senegal in the late 1950s, was appointed director of the new theatre. In 1959, future President Sédar Senghor had seen Keita's Ballets Africains perform in Dakar, and had been sufficiently impressed to write a long commentary in the Socialist Party magazine, *L'Unité Africaine*. This had been an opportunity for Sédar Senghor (Sonar Senghor 2004: 66, translated from French) to articulate his ideas on 'Black African dance', which he saw as embodying the 'emotional' nature of African cultures:

> Black African dances stay very close to the sources. They express dramas. For the Black African, dance is the most natural way of expressing an idea, an emotion. When taken by an emotion – joy or sadness, gratitude or indignation – the Black African dances. Dance so different from European ballet. Nothing intellectual. Neither pointe shoes nor straight lines nor elaborate arabesques or entrechats. These are earth-bound dances, bare feet flat on the ground, pounding the ground without either tiredness or rest.

In the same text however, he was also fiercely critical of a certain style of acting and of short sketches inspired by European and American humour. Intriguingly, he also criticized what he saw as an excess of eroticism in some of the dances, in a moralizing tone which prefigures contemporary moral panics about popular dances (see Chapter 4):

> The Ballet Master should avoid letting the show be taken over by the European spirit, and especially American. [. . .] There is a black humour, which is to approach life through laughter in the face of an inhuman situation. He should make generous use of this. Above all, he should not give in to eroticism, which is the intellectualization of sensuality and which becomes pornography. One might respond that 'Yonnou Gambie' is a Wolof dance. Admittedly, but this is one with an Arab-Berber flavour adapted to the American taste. This is not the best thing the Maghreb has given us. Fodéba Keita ought to return to a sensuality which embodies Black African spirituality. (Sonar Senghor 2004: 67, translated from French)

In addition to positioning himself as an expert in the performing arts, in this text Senghor displays a thinly veiled criticism of what he saw as Sékou Touré's lack of intellectual sophistication, through a critique of Keita's production. For Senghor, Touré was but a poorly educated trade unionist who had risen above his skills, and a strong animosity grew between them throughout the 1960s. Two years after writing this review, Léopold Sédar Senghor signed a decree to create a Senegalese National Ballet, clearly designed to outshine the Guinean troupe. He certainly believed he could win the upper hand over Touré on his own turf, 'culture and the arts'. Indeed Sédar Senghor had already gained a strong legitimacy as an intellectual in the Francophone world through his engagement in the Negritude movement, his poetry and his higher degree in French grammar.[8] Moreover, though he was not much of a dancer himself (Vaillant 2006: 124), it is evident in Senghor's poetry that he regarded dance as a quintessential African art. His *Prières aux Masques Africains* (Senghor 1956) ends with an allusion to Africans as 'people of the dance': 'Nous sommes les hommes de la danse, dont les pieds reprennent vigueur en frappant le sol dur'.[9]

Furthermore the notion that 'culture and the arts' could be powerful political instruments as well as vehicles of social change was a legacy of French colonial policy. In the first decades of the twentieth century there had been a debate in France on the pros and cons of 'assimilation' versus 'association' in the African colonies, which culminated with the international congress on the cultural evolution of colonial populations held in 1937 in Paris. Marcel Mauss, Marcel Griaule and Henri Labouret were among the anthropologists present at the congress, whose objective was to discuss the implications of social change in the colonies (Vaillant 2006: 196). Senghor spoke in favour of a colonial education model that would be adapted to African contexts without compromising on quality, particularly in the rural areas, and would enable the best students to access high-level positions on a par with their French peers. The congress did not result in a unified position on future colonial policy, or on the relative place that should be given to 'African' and 'French' culture. But the recommendations pointed towards a separation between African arts, which should be encouraged, and the social practices that could not be reconciled with French cultural values, which should be discouraged (Vaillant 2006: 202–3). In subsequent years, Francophone African political expression became confined to the arts. This was a domain that was left relatively free, as in the case of the Ponty plays. Senghor's insistence on the importance of the arts after independence was shaped by this history. In a more pragmatic way his cultural policy was also, to a large extent, funded by France.

In official discourse, the work of the National Ballet aimed at recovering regional histories while reframing them as 'national', celebrating the nation's diversity, and showcasing Senegalese 'culture' abroad. In practice, the first goal was elusive since there was never a simple transposition of performing practices to the stage. The Ballet staged tableaux that combined acting and choreography in an attempt to collapse images of contemporary rural life with those of the past. Urban life was seldom represented since it did not evoke the past. Choreography was the integrated product of Sonar Senghor's Parisian-inflected theatrical ideas, the dances his young performers had grown up with, and the troupe's creative work. Dancer, Ousmane Noël Cissé (Figure 1.2), who was one of the Ballet's lead dancers in the late 1960s and through much of the 1970s, remembered a typical working day:

> The day would start with a class taught by Sonar Senghor. Then every dancer, from Dakar or from elsewhere, would take turns to teach the others some of the steps they knew from home. Sonar Senghor would then select and rearrange the moves into a choreographic sequence. Later in the day, we'd rehearse for the shows.[10]

Figure 1.2 Ousmane Noël Cissé in front of the National Theatre in Dakar, April 2011. Photograph by the author.

This creative approach was confirmed by several other dancers who worked with the Ballet at the time. The dancers were usually young, and not as educated as the first generation of Ballets Africains performers in Paris. By the late 1950s, Dakar had a very active neo-traditional performing scene by virtue of the troupes set up by former members of the Guinean Ballets Africains and the success of the genre with hometown associations. The newly created National Ballet was therefore able to recruit young performers with stage experience, including some who had already performed abroad (Paris-Dakar 1961b). There were also many recruits among migrants from the Casamance region, from the Sereer-speaking Siin-Saalum south of Dakar and from towns like Louga and Coki in northern Senegal, all these being areas where school theatre had been particularly successful (for Coki, see Niang 1961). Finally, there were students from the School of Arts and youths from the long-established Cape Verdean community in Dakar, who often shone on the dance floors of Dakarois nightclubs pulsating with Cuban music. Young as these recruits were, they would have had limited knowledge of regional histories. Behind the discourse of historical recovery, therefore, the work of the National Ballet consisted mainly in the further codification of the genre which had blossomed across the region in the period post-Second World War.

The second goal was more realistic since the diversity of the nation was de facto celebrated by the Ballet's inclusiveness. There was, however, an implicit hierarchy among the different ethnicities. In continuity with the Ballets Africains as well as a colonial tendency to regard the forest areas as the repositories of 'authentic' African cultures,[11] a substantial proportion of the dances were inspired by ceremonial practices from the Casamance region and from the wider Mande areas. But this emphasis also indicated that Casamance was considered to be at the margins of the modern state. As such, Casamançais populations were those in most need of co-option into the nationalist project. Yet there is no evidence that this worked with the local public. In Dakar, audiences were mainly the Senegalese elite and European expatriates. Paying to sit in cushioned seats in the imposing air-conditioned room of the Daniel Sorano Theatre was evidently not aimed at the masses. This was a space in which the elite could congregate, elegantly dressed in suits, evening gowns and Senegalese *grands boubous*, and in one gesture show off their taste for the high arts as well as their commitment to the Senghor regime. The resonance of the National Theatre with ordinary citizens is more difficult to assess. Sonar Senghor (2004) writes at length about the Theatre's efforts to popularize its work by putting on performances in government-owned workplaces and in Senegalese towns outside the capital, but these very efforts betray the elitist character of the institution. It did, however, foster the performing arts as an attractive profession for youths with the right skills. One did not need to be articulate in French to become a dancer or a musician, and therefore recruitment was not restricted to educated youths. Musicians and singers tended to come from griot families, but dancers and actors came from more diverse backgrounds. In addition to the pleasure of dancing, the troupe represented an exceptional opportunity to acquire the highly desirable status of a *fonctionnaire*, a civil servant. There was also travelling for up to half of the year, and daily allowances on top of a very decent salary.[12]

But national audiences only represented one side of the project. The third goal behind the creation of the Ballet was to project Léopold Sédar Senghor's leadership onto the worldwide stage. The troupe was thus sent to perform around the world, and in particular to Europe and the US, where the President had kept contacts from his Parisian years and the Negritude movement. In the 1930s he had thus struck up a friendship with Mercer Cook, an African American academic who studied in Paris, and later taught Francophone literature at Howard University. Cook played an important role in making Senghor's work known in the Anglophone world since he was the first to translate Senghor's poems into English (Vaillant 2006). Also, as the son of a singer mother and a musician father, Cook was probably encouraging of Senghor's ambitions for the Ballet when appointed as a US Ambassador to Senegal and the Gambia in 1964. Showcasing the cultural wealth of the Senegal-Guinea-Mali region was Senghor's way of establishing himself as a key African leader, a role for which he competed with Sékou Touré, Kwame Nkrumah in Ghana, and Julius Nyerere in Tanzania. But by contrast with their more openly political agendas, he sought to impose his leadership in his favourite idiom, 'culture and the arts'. In so doing he was acting in continuity with the ideas debated at the colonial congress in 1937. This was unsurprising for a man who had, after all, mastered French education so brilliantly.

Outside Senegal, the troupe's success lived up to Senghor's high expectations from the beginning. The first European tour in 1961, for example, gained rave reviews in the printed press in the UK, Germany and France, and the tour was extended by several weeks (Dakar-Matin 1961a). But the Ballet also left its mark in more subtle ways as many of its performers stayed behind over the years. Many of them subsequently set up dance and drumming schools where they happened to settle. In addition to this, a significant number of European and American artists were inspired by the Senegalese performances they saw in their home countries. In fact, the 1950s and 1960s were a period of intensifying circulation of national troupes from various parts of the world, and this generated unprecedented artistic effervescence across performing genres (Shay 2002). The Senegalese Ballet's US tours in the wake of the Ballets Africains' first tours in the 1950s thus attracted the attention of many American artists, for whom Senegal represented an easily accessible yet 'authentic' door into Africa. The fact that it was Francophone did not seem to keep people away. Thus when the US State Department sent dancer-actor Gene Kelly on a tour of seven African countries in 1964, Dakar was the first stop of the tour. Kelly presented extracts of his films, met students and 'Dakar's cultural leaders', and attended a rehearsal of the National Ballet (Brinkley 1964: X15). More significantly, in 1966 Katherine Dunham was invited by Léopold Sédar Senghor to train the National Ballet, probably ahead of the 1966 World Festival of Negro Arts. Dunham was an African American dancer and choreographer from Illinois who had also studied Anthropology at the University of Chicago in the 1930s. After training in Laban-inspired modern dance and ballet in the 1920s, Dunham had set up one of the first Black dance companies in America, Ballet Nègre, in 1930. In the subsequent decades she developed her own modern dance technique and achieved tremendous success as a performer, choreographer and stage director. She appeared in several Hollywood musicals, staged numerous shows and collaborated with classical ballet choreographer, George Balanchine for the 1940 Broadway show, *Cabin in the Sky*. Her New York school had people like José Limón, a disciple of modern dance pioneers Doris Humphrey and Charles Weidman, teaching modern dance. By the time Dunham came to Senegal, she was a star of the American dance world. But it is very likely that this was a two-way process and that she learned a great deal from Senegalese performers since she was said to do dance ethnology everywhere she went. In 1968 she invited drummer, Mor Thiam, whom she had met in Dakar, to teach and perform in Saint-Louis, Missouri. Thiam subsequently settled there with his wife, Kiné Guèye Thiam. Although settled in the US, where their son later came to fame as singer Akon, the Thiam family continued to spend time in Dakar and were among many individuals in the expanding group of performers whose lives were stretched between Senegal and remote destinations.

By the mid-1960s, therefore, Dakar already pulsated with an effervescent choreographic scene of dozens of dance troupes, all galvanized by Senegal's generous cultural policy, in which the performing arts were celebrated as cornerstones of nation-building. In this favourable context, being a performer in a dance troupe was not the exclusive prerogative of individuals from griot backgrounds, even though griots made up a significant proportion of musicians and singers in the National Theatre and its offshoots. This transformed previous modes of transmission, when one learned to dance in the everyday context of family compounds, sabar events, weddings or name-giving ceremonies, and more recently in youth evening dances. There was now an additional route whereby younger dancers could teach each other, in ways that mirrored older modes of apprenticeship but without following age-based hierarchies. This was a highly cosmopolitan environment, in which young men and women without much formal education could travel around the world and earn a decent income. This new artistic community only partially overlapped with the hereditary griot trade that was still essential to the proper completion of family ceremonies. But most importantly, the 1950s and 1960s introduced the idea that bodily techniques, such as dance and drama, could help transform the youth into new, modern citizens, rather than remain the domain of specialists. These youths were outward-looking without losing sight of where they came from. Despite the fact that they were engaged in entertainment, therefore, they could be seen as morally virtuous so long as they embraced the interests of the new nation. But the following years would demonstrate that complete control of cultural production would remain forever elusive. This became evident during the most ambitious event of the Senghor presidency: the 1966 World Festival of Negro Arts. The festival embodied Senghorian ideas on the relationship between modern African identities and the arts.

The 1966 World Festival of Negro Arts

The idea of an international festival celebrating the contribution of Black people to world cultures was discussed at the second congress of the Society for African Culture in Rome in 1959, under the leadership of Alioune Diop, founder of Présence Africaine. Initially scheduled to begin in December 1965, the festival eventually took place over twenty-six days in April 1966, gathering delegations from more than thirty nations. Although long in the making, it is certainly no coincidence that the event took place at a time when Senghor's political power was being challenged amidst growing opposition. In 1964, he had claimed to thwart a coup by his former Prime Minister, Mamadou Dia, whom Senghor had forced to resign in 1962. Dia remained imprisoned until 1974. In 1967 a notable from Saint-Louis, Moustapha Lô, was executed for a bungled assassination attempt on the President at the Great Mosque in Dakar. Economically, things were taking a turn for the worse following the withdrawal of the French from most local businesses. In these troubled times, Sédar Senghor chose to assert his power in his favourite idiom: 'culture and the arts'. There were also hopes that the festival would establish Senegal as a destination for cultural tourism. The presence of prestigious figures like Ethiopian Emperor Haile Selassie and French Minister of Culture André Malraux was to help legitimize the project. But the festival faced a string of organizational problems and was fraught with political tension in Senegal, where it was heavily criticized by opposition leaders.

France footed a large share of the bill to build the Sorano Theatre and the Musée Dynamique, a Roman-style, imposing marble construction built on the sea front to house the festival's sculpture and painting exhibitions. But the most imposing delegation was that of the US where, at the height of the Civil Rights movement, there was intense interest in African diaspora connections. However, the American committee suffered from a lack of funds. There was also hostility from a number of prominent African-American artists, appalled to see the presidency in the hands a White woman, Virginia Inness-Brown. The head of the American delegation to the World Festival of Negro Arts carried great symbolic value, and the presence of a White person in this post was perceived as implying that no Black individual was good enough for the job. Although officially chosen by Senegal, in reality it is likely that Inness-Brown had been appointed at the suggestion of the State Department in an attempt to raise the $600,000 budgeted for the American participation. But the fundraising campaign was a failure, and the State Department was forced to give out a substantial sum to avoid a complete debacle. The failure unleashed a flood of criticism towards Inness-Brown's presidency, and the much reduced American delegation was marred by tension. The archive held at the National Archives in Dakar reveal that this was a major concern to the organizers, both Senegalese and American.

On the Senegalese side, not everyone agreed with Senghor's explicit choice to restrict the colloquium to Black participants, in effect excluding North Africans on racial grounds. In response to this, an alternative Pan-African Festival was organized in Algiers in 1969, with strong backing from Sékou Touré. In the middle of such a flamboyant display of Black creativity and power, 'race' still mattered in the most uncomfortable way, and the festival escalated existing tensions over political and moral leadership in Francophone Africa. Senghor's generous patronage of the arts did not translate smoothly into political gain, and 'culture' was not showing itself to be the 'engine of development' he had imagined.

Nevertheless, international and Dakarois audiences were delighted by the dance and music on display at the festival. Highlights included the concerts given by Duke Ellington and his orchestra, in what was already a well-established jazz milieu (Benga 2002). The Leonard DePaur chorus sang, and gospel singer, Marion Williams, took the predominantly European audience at the Cathedral by storm (Fuller 1966). The only American dance act was the Alvin Ailey Company at the Sorano Theatre, who had been flown in from Rome during a European tour. The performance was put together in haste after the initial plan to have a major show involving six choreographers, led by New York City Ballet dancer, Arthur Mitchell, was cancelled. But there were plenty of dance performances from other delegations. The National Ballet of Senegal performed, of course, as well as the national troupe of Mali, who received rave reviews, and troupes from Chad, Côte d'Ivoire, Niger, Sierra Leone, Zambia and Burundi. Of the WoDaaBe dancers from Niger, *Ebony* magazine (Fuller 1966: 102) wrote that they 'enchanted the sophisticated audiences with their astonishing charm and innocence and their strange, bird-like songs and movements' and that they 'wore feathers, painted their faces, and chirped like birds'. Unsurprisingly given the strained relations between Senghor and Sékou Touré, Guinea boycotted the event, and the Ballets Africains were conspicuously absent.

Concentrated in Dakar and with many paying performances, the festival remained largely an elitist event. But in the interstices of the official programme, people took to abandoned buildings and nightclubs and threw themselves into the cosmopolitan dance crazes of the moment:

> At the flag-bedecked Place de l'Indépendance, and at less imposing spots throughout the city, local groups in gay – and sometimes outrageous – costumes enlivened the streets and the Medinas with spontaneous explosions of song and dance. Long after the theaters had dimmed their lights, merry-makers crowded the floors of the nightclubs of the city and along the sea-cooled corniche, doing the frug and the Watusi until near-dawn. At Camp Mangin, a mid-city outpost recently abandoned by the French army, a Nigerian band played riotous Pied Piper to devotees of the High Life, that free-wheeling ancestor of the dance crazes currently sweeping the Western world. (Fuller 1966: 100)

Was it not telling that people chose a disaffected French army camp to dance to High Life played by a Nigerian band outside the official programme? Was this a sign that Senghor was not dancing to the same tune as the Senegalese youth? After all with his French classicist training, he never showed much sympathy for popular culture. There was much criticism of the festival, reflecting the fact that Senghor's version of Negritude had become highly contested, not only at home but also across Anglophone Africa. His critics pointed out that he had simply inverted the Eurocentric dichotomy according to which Western culture was based on reason and the African world on emotion. Many did not warm up to Senghor's idea of a common artistic impulse running through all Black cultures. Senghor was also criticized for legitimizing the power of a Europe-educated elite far removed from the concerns of ordinary citizens. Nigerian playwright, Wole Soyinka, who received the best play award for *The Road* at the festival, is famously remembered for his sidelong attack on Negritude. Even Senghor's guest, Katherine Dunham, was critical of what she saw as an overly intellectual elaboration of what Black people did (Garrison 1966). Ultimately, however, the presence of thousands of participants from more than thirty countries was to generate tremendous artistic effervescence in Dakar. It also focused international attention on Senegal, and encouraged performers from the US and elsewhere to engage in artistic exchanges with Senegal.

In the choreographic scene, cracks also appeared that revealed gaps of a different kind. The international press was not particularly impressed with the Ballet, which suffered from the juxtaposition with the Malian troupe. For the reasons mentioned earlier, there was as yet little institutional knowledge of the social context of the dances that had inspired the repertoire. This may explain why festival president, Alioune Diop, sent a late telegram, dated 18 March 1966, to Gray Cowan of the African Studies Association at Columbia University, asking him to recommend a speaker on 'traditional' African dances:

> Connaîtriez-vous experts signification danse traditionnelle – Si oui donner adresses – Amitiés. Président Alioune Diop.[13]

Gray Cowan must have suggested anthropologist Judith L. Hanna at the University of Wisconsin, for the festival archive includes another telegram addressed to her by Diop a few days later, on 23 March:

> Could you write a paper on the significance of the dance on a given tribe or ensemble of tribes for colloque – Could you also participate in eventual jury for dance prize. Président Alioune Diop.[14]

The archive includes a copy of a paper on dance in Africa, based on Hanna's fieldwork in Nigeria, but there is no evidence that she attended the festival. For the organizers, it must have been painful to face up to the fact that several years after the creation of the National Ballet, there remained little formalized knowledge of the region's performing practices in their social context. The recourse to an American expert on the dances of a 'given tribe' manifested the elite's disregard for urban popular culture, and its idealization of rural 'traditions'. But it also indicated the enduring 'bifurcation' of the urban and the rural, in continuity with colonial legacies throughout much of Africa (Mamdani 1996). New approaches would be needed to expand the state's control of cultural production. Building on local troupes fostered by the genre of school theatre discussed earlier, the state would therefore promote 'popular theatre'. This would swell the ranks of neo-traditional performance as a youth practice, and simultaneously pave the way for new forms of choreographic experimentation in Senegal.

Neo-traditional performance and popular theatre

Following the appointment of schoolteachers trained at William Ponty through the region, popular theatre flourished from the 1940s onwards in Senegalese cities, small towns, and in the rural areas of Casamance (Foucher 2002). This contributed in important ways to the genesis of the neo-traditional genre because many of the plays staged by youth troupes, often in schools or local youth clubs, included a choreographic and musical dimension. I return to the role of youth clubs in Dakar in Chapter 4, but for now, suffice to say that the state soon sought to co-opt this theatre in an attempt to control as much of the nation's cultural production as possible.

As had been the case in other domains, this was achieved by building on the legacies of the late colonial period, and in 1965 the Ministry of Youth created a supervisory body, the Fédération du Théâtre Populaire. Following a model initiated under French rule in the mid-1950s (Mouralis 1986), the Federation organized theatrical competitions between the various regions of Senegal. As eloquently demonstrated by anthropological studies of cultural policy elsewhere in Africa, performing competitions and festivals have often been an effective instrument of control in the construction of ethnicities and moralities in young African states (Askew 2002; Apter 2005; Edmonson 2007). By setting up rules and by bringing people together to perform formatted productions, dance, music and drama competitions have enabled states to shape moral ideas of what it means to be a good, modern citizen. Competitions have also helped to build a sense of common culture across ethnic boundaries, thereby contributing to the emergence of national identities. They were initially held in the context of 'youth weeks' *(semaines de la jeunesse)* because they had the Youth Ministry as a patron. The role assigned to popular theatre in nation-building was framed as educational, and this was made explicit in official speeches and government publications (Sénégal d'Aujourd'hui n.d.):

> From a purpose of protest before 1960, after Independence the troupes have tried to adjust to the new reality. There was, and there still is, a need to educate the population so that it may participate in the development of the country. In fact research is oriented towards this goal. Thus the troupes perform scenes evoking the diversification of agriculture, denouncing waste etc . . .

It was in this competitive context that several troupes came to fame across Senegal, and served as templates for offshoots set up over the years by performers keen to become leaders of their own. This was the case, for example, of the youth club/theatre troupe, Cercle de la Jeunesse, in Louga on the northern edge of Senegal's 'peanut basin'. Set up by performing artist and songwriter, Mademba Diop, and his friends around 1958, the troupe won the main awards over a number of years. Diop was eventually appointed as a Youth Ministry officer, where he worked to include music in the activities supervised by the Ministry. Schoolteacher, Mor Sadio Niang, who had written enthusiastically on the importance of youth theatre in the state newspaper *Dakar-Matin*, citing the contribution made by young men and women migrants from his hometown of Coki (Niang 1961), followed a similar trajectory. Recruiting artists into the state apparatus was thus one of the ways in which popular theatre was co-opted to 'educate' the citizens. The other was to award top prizes to troupes like the Cercle, who presented the moral and economic issues addressed by Senegalese policy in a favourable light. These awards were attractive for the money and prestige that followed, and also because they resulted in invitations to festivals abroad: between 1962 and 1981 the Cercle represented Senegal at festivals and sports events in Finland, France, Mexico, the UK, Italy, Germany, Switzerland and Poland (Wade 2007). 'Education', at this juncture in Senegal's history, was an attempt to refashion the educated youth away from of the anti-establishment ethos that remained from the colonial period, towards national 'development'. A similar enterprise was taking place in neighbouring Guinea with Sékou Touré's promotion of militant youth theatre in the forest areas (Straker 2009), but with more openly revolutionary objectives than in Senegal.

Following the regional performing histories discussed earlier, popular theatre included all elements of performance (narrative, acting, singing, live instruments and dancing), and was able to modulate them depending on the context (Sénégal d'Aujourd'hui n.d.):

> These troupes' theatrical work is very diverse. They can be asked to entertain during folkloric evenings (without presenting a play). These pieces are drawn from our national folklore (Gumbe, circumcision, harvest festivals, etc.). These troupes also carry out research. They perform ballets on specific professions.

This ability to modulate the different elements remains one of the essential features of Senegalese (and West African) neo-traditional performance today. As we will see in Chapter 5, it was also this malleability which allowed local troupes to pursue their own agendas from the 1980s onwards, once the state had lost much of its capacity to act as a patron. By contrast, the repertoire of the National Theatre was more rigid because of its role as a flagship of national culture. Its productions struggled to shrug off their elitist flavour, as apparent in Sonar Senghor's later reflections on the use of French in the troupe's work in rural areas. During the first part of the show in a countrywide tour in the 1970s, a spectator complained loudly, in Wolof, that what was going on was a 'grotesque squeaking' incomprehensible to anyone, and that the real show, surely, ought to start very soon. The 'squeaking' was in fact a comedy in French, which had been fairly successful when performed in Dakar (Sonar Senghor 2004: 167, translated from French).

Although more versatile, popular theatre troupes were eminently caught up in state projects in the first two decades of independence, to the extent that little about their production can be described as 'popular', in the sense of being entirely from the grassroots. Rather, the label 'popular' was appropriated by the state in an effort to convince local audiences that the plays addressed their concerns. This was not entirely misplaced since the artists who created the plays drew inspiration from their own lives. For example, the Cercle de la Jeunesse, which would initially have included youths with experience of working in the surrounding peanut fields, became known for its choreographic evocation of agricultural work. Indeed, collective work in the fields has a long history due to the communal nature of land tenure in the region. During harvest time this was a rhythmic activity, often with musical support from griots and with collective singing. Youth theatre was also 'popular', precisely because its actors had fun doing it, as Straker also points out in Guinea's case around the same period (2009). The practice offered opportunities for youths of both sexes to spend time together in ways that would not have been appropriate otherwise.

But the other side of the coin was that only those plays that fitted the official agenda received awards in major competitions. In 1961, for example, the award for the best theatre troupe in Dakar was given to the Ballets Sérères for a play in homage to fishermen and farmers in villages along the coastline south of Dakar (Dakar-Matin 1961b). One of the farmers, a good and hardworking man, is bitten by a snake while working in the fields, and after a dramatic brush with death due to the villagers' ignorance about modern vaccines, he is eventually saved by an old witch doctor, the only man with the traditional magical knowledge necessary to save the poor farmer. The competition judges must have been seduced by the combination of hard work, traditional knowledge in the hands of its rightful guardians, and a demonstration of the benefits of modernity (the vaccines).

Conversely, those plays that did not fit with Sédar Senghor's views or competed with his favourite productions failed. Over the years, however, free space appeared in the interstices of the state apparatus since there were never sufficient resources to support all theatrical initiatives. An independent theatre developed, either 'popular' or with the ambition to stage classical plays, and with a degree of freedom to engage in experimental work. But even independent theatre depended partly on governmental approval, at the very least to avoid censorship. And in any case, state funding made all the difference between success and struggle for survival. Thus in 1971, a group of young graduates from the National School of Arts, for whom the National Theatre had no vacancies, set up the Tréteaux Sénégalais.[15] This was, as former leader Mamadou Diop told me, a Dakar-based troupe aimed at 'creating new theatre aesthetics, radically more modern than what people were doing at Sorano'. Diop had trained as a ballet dancer in addition to his training as an actor, and was looking for new ways of incorporating choreography into theatre as a narrative element in its own right rather than, he said, as 'added decoration'. The troupe struck a chord with the Ministry of Culture when they decided to set up *Chaka*, a play written by Senghor on the legendary Zulu King. Sédar Senghor gave a generous donation[16] which enabled the creation of two further pieces. One of these, *Le Train de la Liberté* (Freedom Train) paid homage to Nelson Mandela and the fight against apartheid. The *Train* does not seem to have found further favour with the President, perhaps because of the ambiguity inherent in portraying a struggle against a government in place, in contrast with the anti-colonial epics in *Chaka*. Sédar Senghor subsequently found their work too radical, according to Diop. Whether or not this was the reason, state funding was no longer forthcoming, and within ten years the troupe's demise was complete.

Although formally under state control, the youth clubs to which I return in Chapter 4 enjoyed a degree of autonomy by virtue of their localized character. Finally, an important factor in the rise of independent popular theatre was the increasing movement from the rural areas of the Casamance and Sereer-speaking Siin and Saalum to Dakar from the 1950s onwards. Rural migrants soon began to organize themselves in hometown associations which often set up their own theatre troupes. Hometown associations from the Casamance region were particularly active in this respect because many of their members had known school theatre from home, a factor that will be illustrated in Chapter 5. The promotion of 'popular theatre' by the Senegalese state in the 1960s and 1970s turned the attention of young citizens towards the moral values needed to build the nation, and generated common experiences for thousands of youths across the country. But as I will suggest later, it also had the effect of providing alternative cultural agendas with an idiom through which they could express themselves. While this was underway, in the second decade of Senghor's presidency, priorities moved on from the creation of a national culture to strengthening the Senegalese leadership in the international arena by creating avant-garde Pan-African institutions, and by encouraging a deeper engagement with the wider world.

Making Pan-Africanism through dance training

Once Sédar Senghor's power had been consolidated and dissenting voices silenced, the state was free to carry out its modernization project. For those among the intellectual elite who were sympathetic to Senghor's notion of 'rootedness and openness' (*enracinement et ouverture*), fostering artistic professions independent of the caste-like trades required proper training in Western techniques. For Senghor and his educated, like-minded artist friends, Senegal would be a modern nation, and its arts would express 'African' contents while using Western technical mastery (Harney 2004). It was in this spirit that the National Arts Institute was created in 1972 following the reorganization of the previous National School of Arts, itself an offshoot of the Mali Arts Centre set up in the 1950s (Snipe 1998). In the 1970s the performing arts section was mostly devoted to drama, but dance became an increasingly important part of the curriculum. At the dance department, cosmopolitan cohorts of students were taught classical ballet, music and stage techniques on the model of European arts schools. Mamadou Diop discovered classical ballet there when haphazardly walking in on a class taught by a French woman, Mrs Boblin. He was initially puzzled by what he saw but quickly found himself drawn to ballet:

I was stunned. I had never seen anything like this. I thought 'What is this, gymnastics?' But she told me to try it. I did, and after that I kept coming back to the classes. I was hooked. (Personal communication, Dakar, April 2003)

Diop eventually graduated as the 'first classical ballet dancer trained in Senegal'. For him and for subsequent generations of dancers who trained there, the national institute was a cherished symbol of Senegal's capacity to train professional artists at a decent international level. Choreographer, Jean Tamba, who graduated from the School in the mid-1990s, expressed this when speaking to the dance students at the end of a week-long workshop in March 2003:

The *conservatoire* [performing arts section] is our pride. We were trained here, by Senegalese. We didn't have to go abroad to be trained.

Others remembered with pride that in the 1970s, the school attracted students from other African countries. The notion of a performing profession led by Senegalese people, yet with a Pan-African outlook, is a recurrent theme in the local dance scene. In artistic circles at least, post-independence cultural policy was successful in making people see themselves as citizens of a small nation with a disproportionately prominent role on the continent.

For all the talk of a locally-made profession, however, many artists still had to go abroad to get further training, find work or both. The increasing strain on state finances from the mid-1970s onwards, following years of drought in the Sahel and the oil crisis of 1973, meant that there was no longer enough arts funding to sustain a profession now much too dependent on state patronage (Diagne 2002). As a result, performers began to leave for longer and longer periods of time. In the early 1980s Mamadou Diop, for example, benefited from a bilateral agreement with the Soviet Union, which included a programme of cultural and artistic exchange. While selected Senegalese artists and intellectuals were invited to study in the Soviet Union,

Soviet counterparts travelled to Senegal in various capacities. As a graduate of the National Arts Institute, Diop was selected and spent five years studying choreography at the Russian Academy of Theatre Arts in Moscow. Coming from a country with no classical ballet tradition and having made a late start by the standards of the ballet world, he struggled to catch up with the Russian dancers. Yet he showed talent as a choreographer of 'variety theatre', and after winning the second prize at a chore-ography competition in Moscow, he was invited to create shows for several Soviet theatres. Upon return to Senegal he was keen to integrate the state-sponsored world of arts, but his application to the National Theatre was turned down. He went on to teach at the National Arts Institute, where he remained for many years as the head of the performing arts department. The head of the dance section at the time of my fieldwork, Martin Lopy, also spent time abroad after his initial training as a classical ballet dancer at the National School in the early 1970s. In 1976, he travelled to Paris to study ballet and modern dance with French dancer-choreographer, Aline Roux. He had intended to stay for a few years, but the experience was cut short when he was asked to return to take part in the Senegalese delegation at FESTAC, the second Black and African Festival of Arts and Culture held in Lagos in January 1977.[17]

The emergence of a new generation of performing artists with international connections provided Sédar Senghor with welcome assets in his political competi-tion with regional rivals. Following the 1966 Festival, it had been agreed that Nigeria would organize the second worldwide celebration of Black cultures, but Senegal's views were eventually marginalized in the run-up to FESTAC. This was especially painful as this came after the 1969 Pan-African Cultural Festival held in Algiers under the auspices of the OAU (Organization of African Unity), where the Negritude philosophy had been severely criticized by the North African nations (Apter 2005). Senegal had hoped that FESTAC might provide an opportunity to rehabilitate Negritude, and by the same token Senghor's leadership in regional politics. When the regional organization ECOWAS (Economic Community of West African States) was established in 1975, Senghor failed his diplomatic battle to have the headquarters located in Senegal rather than in Nigeria. The flamboyant FESTAC held in oil-rich Nigeria at a much bigger expense than the 1966 Festival, therefore, looked like a direct slap in Senghor's face (Apter 2005). Predictably, the President and some of his Caribbean and African American friends (Aimé Césaire, Langston Hughes) were conspicuously absent from the festival. The slap was quite literally captured in the banners carried by the disproportionately big Guinean delegation at the opening ceremony in Lagos, which read 'Let us bury Negritude forever' and 'No Whititude, no Negritude' (Gaye 1977a; Gaye 1977b). The state-owned Senegalese press took the opportunity to publish thinly veiled criticisms of FESTAC's organi-zation and of Sékou Touré's version of Pan-Africanism, which rejected Senghor's emphasis on Black Africa and sought to include Guinea's North African allies, Algeria in particular (Le Soleil 1977a, 1977b).

Once again, time had come for the President to showcase his intellectual sophis-tication in an attempt to outshine his rivals. While the National Ballet's original troupe, La Linguère, focused on *jembe* rhythms from the wider Mande area, Sédar

Senghor decided to create a second national troupe. This was Sirabadral, named after a fourteenth-century Sereer princess from Senghor's region of birth. The two troupes would be able to specialize in different styles, and Sirabadral thus introduced Sereer and Wolof rhythms as well as 'modern dance' under the leadership of Ousmane Noël Cissé. This was a division of labour, with the first troupe acting as an outward-looking 'cultural ambassador', and the second focusing on domestic audiences now expecting a higher degree of innovation. Indeed the political significance of being innovative was not lost on Senghor. While Nigeria celebrated its traditional dances at FESTAC, Senghor chose a strongly modernist approach to the arts. The most ambitious artistic project of the decade was thus the creation of a prestigious Pan-African dance school, Mudra Afrique, housed in the sumptuous building of the Musée Dynamique. The school opened in 1977 with funding from the Senegalese state, UNESCO and the Gulbenkian Foundation, the latter two making a joint donation of $100,000. At the opening ceremony, Senghor framed the project as an attempt to create a new Black African dance aesthetic:

> Beyond the establishment of an inventory of Black African dance steps and movements, Mudra Afrique must absorb the steps and the values of other dance forms in order to generate a new kind of Black African Dance that can be understood and appreciated by people of all cultures. (Acogny 1994 [1980]: 4)

Under Senghor's protection, two individuals drove the project. The first was French choreographer Maurice Béjart, whose Mudra school in Brussels was well established as a leading training institution for professional dancers. Béjart's father, philosopher Gaston Berger, had been a Creole from Saint-Louis, and Béjart himself had travelled to Senegal before. He had even auditioned dancers in Dakar, including Ousmane Noël Cissé, who was invited to attend Mudra in Brussels for a couple of years, and Mamadou Diop.

The other leading figure was Germaine Acogny, a sports teacher and dancer originally from Benin. In the late 1960s Mrs Acogny had opened a dance school in Dakar, and following performances by her students, in 1972 she had been appointed leader of the dance section at the National Arts Institute. The students there had included Martin Lopy as a promising young dancer. In the section's annual report for 1972, Mrs Acogny made explicit reference to the need to codify Senegal's 'traditional dances' into a vocabulary and a set of techniques so as to preserve them. She illustrated the richness of the region's performing repertoire with dances from the Sereer-speaking regions and from the Casamance, where she had been posted briefly as a sports teacher in Ziguinchor. This discourse, clearly influenced by the Euro-American ballet tradition as well as by Senghor's interest in African linguistics, would play a crucial role in fashioning the world of 'African contemporary dance' later on.

The first cohort at Mudra Afrique in 1977 included twenty-five students from all over Francophone Africa, as well as a Haitian and a Swiss student. Over a three-year course, they attended classes in classical ballet, in Mrs Acogny's 'African

dance' technique, in American modern dance (Martha Graham technique), in singing and drumming. Master Drummer, Doudou Ndiaye Rose, taught sabar drumming. Dancers from Béjart's Ballet du Vingtième Siècle were brought in to teach
classes with the support of a Russian pianist. There were also performances choreographed collectively by the teaching team and the students. A modern *Cinderella*
was performed in a village in the Casamance (Waksman 1980) and in Paris. By any
standards, Mudra Afrique was an extraordinary artistic enterprise in Africa, by virtue
of its global ambitions and its contrast with the surrounding urban life. A former
student I knew smiled broadly as she remembered the puzzled faces of city dwellers when they saw the dancers sitting on the seafront in their tight leotards. Three
cohorts completed their training before Mudra Afrique was forced to close down
in 1983 due to lack of funds. By then, Senghor had passed on the presidency to his
former Prime Minister, Abdou Diouf, who was left to implement the severe cuts in
state expenses required by the first structural adjustment programmes (SAPs). The
Musée Dynamique was turned into the Supreme Court, and there was no place in
the new neoliberal economic policies for such artistic luxuries. Although several other
African countries had initially agreed to contribute financially (mainly by paying
for their students to be trained at the school), in this economic climate Pan-African
funding never materialized.

Aside, therefore, from the promotion of popular theatre to expand the reach of
national culture beyond the capital, the 1970s were marked by an internationalization
of the Senegalese choreographic scene. Avant-garde institutions like Mudra Afrique
encouraged choreographic experimentation of a new kind, one which valued more
egalitarian modes of creation, in contrast with the more traditional master-apprentice
model adopted by the National Ballet. This was an important, often underestimated
rupture that was hastened by a conjunction of factors. The most important factor was
probably the desire by dancers who had come of age during the effervescence of the
early post-colonial days and witnessed the 1966 World Festival, to try out something
new. There was also a growing interest from artists from other parts of the world
thanks to Senghor's image as a man of culture. But the state spectacle staged by his
'dear children' increasingly struggled to hide the cracks in a strained economy and a
declining presidential popularity at home. It was as if, to follow Apter's (2005) analysis of Nigeria at the same period, increasingly elaborate cultural productions served to
mask a lack of substantial economic development. But soon the cracks would become
a void, and the vacuum left by the Senegalese state would leave the stage to other
actors, both domestic and international.

Informalization and appropriation

As we will see in Chapter 2, by the mid-1980s the Senegalese economy was ailing.
The flagship institutions of the Senghor period, therefore, had to be closed or scaled
down. The performing arts department at the National Arts Institute closed shortly
after Mudra Afrique, only to re-open in a smaller version in 1990, once again under
the name of National School of Arts. A new performing arts degree offered a dance,
music or drama option over a six-year curriculum, later reduced to five. By the time

I began fieldwork in 2002, the National School of Arts had been moved to a temporary location, and its derelict state reflected the more general situation in which state-funded cultural institutions found themselves. The shabby-looking building on the Avenue Faidherbe was difficult to notice at first, trapped as it was between the Gare Pedersen bus terminal, Chinese trinket shops and a web of car repair shops smelling of oil and rust. The dance section was in a small extension at the back of a courtyard adjacent to the main building. In the courtyard, women from the nearby houses cooked and did laundry for neighbourhood clients. The only 'luxury' item in the dance room was a large mirror. There were metallic bars across the grey walls for ballet work, but the concrete floor, covered with small tiles and broken in places, subjected the dancers' bodies to a painful regime. There was a single shower, and no toilets. The walls in the small office of section leader, Martin Lopy, were covered with older photos of ballet dancers from across the world. Despite the poor conditions, people at the school were intensely preoccupied with what was happening in the choreographic scenes elsewhere. On one occasion I walked in to find Lopy, Jean Tamba and a handful of students absorbed in watching a video recording of the pan-African choreographic competition, Rencontres Chorégraphiques de l'Afrique et de l'Océan Indien, held in Madagascar two years earlier. This was Lopy's own video player, which he had brought from home. There was, as usual, lively commentary about the quality and creativity of the performances as people huddled around the small screen. But there was also a sense of being isolated in a corner of the global artistic scene. A couple of years later the School was relocated into a new building on the VDN (Voie de Dégagement Nord), in one of the newly built areas on the outskirts of the city. In this brand new building the dance room was, if anything, smaller than before. The floor was made of marble-like tiles utterly inappropriate for dance training, and Lopy used the balcony as his office since it enjoyed better ventilation. When I visited the new premises in early 2006 there were no dance students, apparently due to lack of state bursaries.

The National Theatre also suffered from cuts in state funding in the 1980s. The National Ballet kept its main troupe, La Linguère, but shut down its second troupe. The civil servant status was dropped in favour of contractual arrangements on a seasonal basis. By the time I visited the Sorano Theatre in the early 2000s, everything from technicians' overtime hours to bulbs for the stage lights seemed to be a scarce resource to be fought for. Backstage, the only signs left of the old splendour were faded black-and-white photographs of the Theatre's productions hanging on the walls, as if nothing remarkable had happened since the 1970s. There were rumours that the rate of defection during tours abroad had become so high that the troupe was, at times, barely able to honour its engagements for lack of performers. Ballet director, Bouly Sonko, told me how he had taken to collecting the passports of performers on the way to the Dakar airport in an effort to minimize the problem.

Indeed one of the important effects of the drying up of state funding in the 1980s was to accelerate the emigration of artists. What had been the coming-and-going of people whose activity was by definition transnational was now an option of choice. This was compounded by the emergence of the World Music phenomenon, which raised hopes that African artists could achieve global success. A marketing initiative launched in 1987 by UK-based 'independent record company executives and enthusiasts' looking for 'ways to market to British-based consumers already-circulating commercial recordings of popular musics from many parts of the world' (Stokes 2004: 52), the World Music circuit expanded the audience base of well-established Senegalese musicians like Youssou Ndour, Ismaël Lô, Baaba Maal, or bands like Tourékounda and Xalam. This in turn attracted further interest from young people who would not have considered musical careers earlier because they did not belong to griot families, thereby extending the dissociation between public performance and hereditary status already initiated during the colonial period. This success of Senegalese music abroad benefited dancers via engagements to perform alongside musicians, and via a surge of interest in 'African dance' classes throughout Europe and North America. The main source of income for West African dancers abroad soon became teaching rather than choreography or performance.

Bruised by the closure of Mudra Afrique, Germaine Acogny left Senegal in the mid-1980s and settled in Toulouse with her husband Helmut Vogt. Together, they opened a new dance school there, the Studio-Ecole-Ballet-Théâtre du 3è Monde. But Mrs Acogny retained a connection to Senegal through dance workshops for European students which she organized every year in Fanghoumé, a village in the Lower Casamance region (Barry 1987). In 1995 she returned to Senegal, and in 1998 she officially opened her training and choreographic centre in the Lebu village of Tubaab Jallaw, some 50 km along the coast south of Dakar. The centre was nicknamed Ecole des Sables as an evocation of its location on a windblown patch of savannah. For the first time since the closure of Mudra, a large and well-equipped space was entirely dedicated to choreographic production. This was going to become one of the main centres for the creation of a new choreographic genre which emerged across European and African studios: 'African contemporary dance'. Mrs Acogny herself described the school in the same terms as she described Mudra Afrique twenty years earlier: the 'sacred grove of modern times'. The Senghorian idealization of tradition and the Pan-African ambitions of the now-deceased former President lived on in this made-up space where dancers from all over the continent and further afield could come to work, meet other artists, be inspired.

The Senegalese dance scene, however, was never confined to big institutions. In spite of the demise of state funding in the 1980s, popular theatre and independent dance troupes continued to exist alongside what was left of the National Theatre. Among Senegalese artists who had known the golden post-independence years, the 1980s are often described as a time when little happened except popular TV dramas in Wolof. Yet this was a time during which youth neighbourhood troupes flourished, as we will see in Chapter 4. The vacuum left by the state soon filled up with independent initiatives, though in a much reduced scale. For example, in the 1980s, textile manufacturer, SOTIBA,[18] sponsored a male youth dance group, the Sotiba Boys, who advertised the company's textiles by performing during fashions shows, TV adverts and various promotional events. Most of these boys also attended Ousmane Noël Cissé's Manhattan Dance School, where they learned American-style jazz dance and worked on their own creations. Despite the scarcity of funds, small-scale initiatives flourished in Dakar throughout the 1980s and 1990s.

Since the mid-1990s, the local choreographic scene has been transformed by external funding sources, channelled either through NGOs or via the local offices of multilateral institutions such as the European Union, the AIF (Agence Internationale de la Francophonie) or UNESCO. There has also been limited funding from associations and individuals in the Senegalese diaspora, and some corporate funding in the form of advertising or donations in kind during festivals. In an increasing number of cases, Senegalese migrants have helped to direct NGOs towards funding cultural and artistic projects in Senegal. Thus the association I followed in Pikine organized a biennial arts festival as well as occasional workshops in such activities as poetry in Wolof or painting. It was funded by a Belgian NGO who had taken an interest in Pikine as a result of personal connections with Senegalese migrants in Antwerp. The most substantial funding, however, came from the EU, which overtook the role as main patron of the arts via its local agencies, the European Development Fund (EDF)-funded PSIC (Programme de Soutien aux Initiatives Culturelles, 1995–2000), later followed by the PSAC (Programme de Soutien aux Actions Culturelles, 2000–2007). Crucially, France has continued to fund the performing arts through creation bursaries, training and performing space via its Africa-wide network of cultural centres. The French centres in Dakar and Saint-Louis have consistently supported choreographic creation, even though in practice priorities are set by the director in place at a given moment. Some funding has also been attributed directly to music bands and dance troupes for national tours.

These sources have facilitated the emergence of a wealth of workshops and independent festivals of music and dance. The Kaay Fecc dance festival, for example, benefited from PSIC funding for its first edition in 2001, and there have also been local festivals focusing on neo-traditional performance, hip-hop, theatre, film, and a whole range of musical genres. Since 1996, under the impulse of Senegal's decentralization programme some of these events have been held in regional centres rather than in Dakar. Ultimately, the rise of independent funding sources has generated a renewed interest in the arts as a field in which decent careers can be made, not only as artists but also as managers, organizers and promoters.

During the twelve years of Wade's presidency (2000–2012), it became gradually evident that the new regime attempted to regain a degree of control over this wealth of activity. This was unsurprising given the history of entanglement between the performing arts and politics in Senegal. After all, Abdoulaye Wade had been coached into politics by Senghor before setting up his own Parti Démocratique Sénégalais (PDS) party in 1974. The FESNAC and its competitions were still being held in different Senegalese towns every other year, and in addition there were signs of a broader re-appropriation of artistic production. Indeed in the 2000s, the Ministry of Culture often appeared either side-lined or simply put in charge of running cultural projects initiated by the President and his family.

It would be beyond the scope of this book to paint a full picture of the links between culture and politics, but a few examples will illustrate the point. For the

2003 and 2005 editions of the Kaay Fecc festival, most of the funding came from international sources, but it is significant that two members of the presidential family became involved. The President's wife, Viviane Wade, attended the opening gala dinner-performance, and in 2005 she was the festival's honorary patron, even though funding and logistical support from state institutions actually decreased that year (Kaay Fecc 2005). Meanwhile the presidential couple's daughter, Sindiély Wade, put her Public Relations agency at the service of the festival in 2003. She attended the closing show, where she gave a short speech and declared her enthusiasm for cultural initiatives of this kind. She later became a special adviser to her father, and was appointed coordinator of the 2010 FESMAN. Following two decades of withdrawal of state patronage, the Wade regime seemed determined to revert back to Senghor's old tactics, albeit with fewer resources. Without a novel ideology to legitimize control, Pan-Africanism was being conveniently recycled (De Jong and Foucher 2010).

Conclusion

Historically in Wolof-speaking Senegal, skilled performance in public, and in exchange for compensation of some kind, was associated with hereditary griot status. In addition, dancing during important moments of social life was regarded as mainly being the domain of women, despite the fact that young men also danced in well-defined contexts. This began to change during the colonial period, with the emergence of school theatre with a musical and choreographic dimension.

Encouraged by French authorities keen to reinforce schoolteachers' and colonial administrators' connection with their 'cultural origins', theatre became an important form of expression among young, French-educated literati. Contrary to French expectations, this theatre carried the seeds of political activism from its early days. This became confirmed later, as the same cosmopolitan elite who had staged plays under the approving gaze of the colonial authorities mobilized around anti-colonial movements after the Second World War. In Senegal, where Dakar was the capital of French West Africa and attracted students from all over the region, this theatre galvanized the emergence of a theatrical profession throughout the 1950s. Over time, the first students and schoolteachers were replaced with new generations of performers from diverse social backgrounds and with more diverse levels of schooling. These new generations gave pride of place to choreography and music, and the new genre of 'neo-traditional performance' that emerged as a result seduced audiences both at home and abroad.

After Senegalese Independence, President Senghor emulated Sékou Touré from neighbouring Guinea, and promoted the genre for nation-building purposes. The international success of Senegalese dance troupes extended the division between griot trade and professional performance by attracting youths from high-status, non-griot families towards state institutions like the National Ballet and the National School of Arts. In terms of bodily techniques, however, the most significant transformations happened in the 1970s, when regional rivalries encouraged Senghor to promote modernist approaches to choreographic production. The establishment of the Mudra Afrique school was a defining moment in the introduction of modern choreographic techniques to the Dakarois performing world, and seemed to reinstate Senghor's intellectual and moral leadership in Francophone Africa. The effervescence of high modernism was to be short-lived, however, and the economic decline of the 1980s meant that the state's all-encompassing patronage could not be sustained. Reflecting on several decades of Senegalese cultural policy, Souleymane Bachir Diagne (2002) perceptively asked whether those who bemoaned the drastic reduction of state funding for the arts were not looking at things from the wrong end: was the state ever supposed to be in complete control of artistic production in the first place? In any case, the withdrawal of state funding forced the Senegalese performing world to develop new strategies of 'extraversion' (Bayart 1999), on the same model as the state itself. Most significantly for this study, the post-SAP (Structural Adjustment Programme) years created the conditions for new modes of transmission of performing techniques, and new ways of fashioning the body and the self. How this happened in practice will become clearer from Chapter 4 onwards. But having located the study in time, I will now situate it in space. Indeed it is significant that the transformations sketched in this chapter were centred on the capital city of Dakar, from where they radiated to the rest of Senegal and beyond.

Notes

1. I follow Irvine (1989) in her choice of 'praise-oratory' rather than 'praise-singing' because oral performance is not as much a song as it is a succession of emphatic, well-articulated speeches.
2. For an excellent study on the role of the Ponty school theatre in the formation of an elite urban culture in Francophone West Africa, see Jezequel (1999).
3. The term designated African individuals who were literate, educated in the French system, wore European clothes and displayed modern lifestyles.
4. See for example Labouret and Travélé (1928) on Koteba comedy theatre in Mali, and Diop (1990) on traditional theatre in Senegal.
5. A notable exception is Jay Straker's (2009) study of youth theatre and the Guinean Revolution, which gives a place of pride to Fodéba Keita's *Ballets Africains*.
6. Benglia famously appeared in Jacques Richepin's *Le Minaret* in 1913 and in a wealth of plays and films in the subsequent decades, including Gaston Baty's *L'Empereur Jones* at the Théâtre de l'Odéon in 1923 (Coutelet 2008).
7. Negritude was originally a literary and artistic movement founded in Paris by Léopold Sédar Senghor, Aimé Césaire and Léon Damas. It was an attempt by Black artists and intellectuals educated in France to come to terms with the cultural devaluation imposed by colonialism. Without denying their attachment to French culture, they aimed to bring about a reassessment of Black people's contribution to world history, and were influenced by their exposure to the highly politicized African American literary milieu in Paris in the 1930s. Senghor's version of Negritude was defined as a modern form of cultural development that would strike a balance between the revival of useful African traditions and engagement with worldwide cultures. On Negritude, see for example, Irele (1965), Jules-Rosette (1998), Wilder (2005).
8. Léopold Sédar Senghor was the first African student to pass the most prestigious competitive exam in France at the time, the *Agrégation*. Having chosen French grammar over literature due to an interest in the formal study of Senegal's local languages, Senghor thus

became an *agrégé de grammaire* in 1935, aged 28. For an excellent biography of Senghor's life, including his Parisian years, see Vaillant (2006).

9. 'We are the people of the dance, whose feet regain strength by pounding on the hard ground'.

10. Interview with Ousmane Noël Cissé, Dakar, April 2011.

11. Sonar Senghor's first scouting trip in Casamance had been commissioned by French Director of Information Services Pierre Fromentin a couple of years before Independence (Sonar Senghor 2004: 57).

12. Informants' memories of their earnings vary, but the salaries of ordinary National Ballet dancers in the 1970s seem to have ranged between 25,000 and 40,000 FCFA. This places performers on similar levels as school teachers and mid-level public administration officers.

13. 'Do you know any experts in the meaning of traditional dance – if so, please send addresses – yours truly'. ANS st928/FMAN/Pl.

14. ANS st1033/FMAN/Pl.

15. Ndao (2008) puts the beginning of the Tréteaux in 1969. 1971 is the date given to me by Mamadou Diop during an interview. Diop himself did not mention the lack of employment opportunities with the National Theatre as a motivation for the creation of the troupe.

16. Mamadou Diop gave me the figure of 1 million FCFA in an interview, but Ndao (2008) puts the figure at 3.5 million FCFA. In either case this would have been a considerable amount at the time.

17. For an illuminating analysis of the politics of FESTAC, see Apter (2005).

18. For a history of Sotiba and the Senegalese textile industry between 1960 and 1975, see Boone (1992).

Chapter 2

A City across Waters

It is no wonder that the French chose Dakar as their stronghold in West Africa. Beautifully located at the Western tip of the region, the Cape Vert Peninsula was ideally placed to become a transatlantic crossroads. The most populated of Senegal's fourteen regions, Dakar is a booming metropolis of concrete buildings rising from a tight grid of sandy alleys and traffic-jammed arteries. A fifth (20.7 per cent) of the country's population is concentrated in Dakar, an estimated 2.59 million inhabitants out of a total of 12.5 million in 2010. In 2002, according to the latest census, Dakar represented a little over half of the urban population (ANSD 2011). It is also politically strategic: Dakar gathers migrants from every corner of Senegal, and political control of the capital is vital to any regime in place.

Speculation about the origin of the word 'Senegal' has given rise to the endlessly repeated metaphor of the nation as a fishing boat. Wolof speakers like to say that the word comes from *suñu gal*, 'our boat'. Although historians generally attribute the country's name to the Zenaga Berbers from what is now Mauritania, the boat metaphor is fitting for a society with a long history of engagement with the Atlantic world. In the early 2000s the metaphor took a new dimension as the international media became filled with images of West African migrants trying to reach Europe on fishing boats. People in Dakar often remark that the desire to travel is the country's greatest wealth as well as its potential downfall. Indeed, the most constant feature of coastal Senegal's history is mobility.

Between the fourth and the thirteenth centuries A.D., the Empire of Ghana, which made the kingdom of Tekrur in the Senegal River valley a vassal, played a dominant role in the trans-Saharan trade. Through trade, Tekrur became the point of entry of Islam in the region, and the kingdom's Pulaar-speaking aristocracy was probably converted as early as the fourteenth century (Tamari 1997; Dilley 2004). During the heyday of the Mali Empire in the fourteenth century, parts of today's Senegal belonged to the Empire's political centre, the Mande. The first Europeans in the region were Portuguese navigators who explored the Senegal River in 1444. Although trans-Saharan and regional slave trades already existed then, the reorientation towards the transatlantic slave trade that followed drastically modified the political make-up of the region (Barry 1988). By the sixteenth century, Senegambia had become an important source of slaves for the transatlantic trade, and not only the Portuguese, but also the Dutch, French and British were competing for the control of trade routes and for the most profitable alliances with the local monarchies. France eventually outlawed slavery in 1848, but did not give up its interests in Senegambia. Peanuts for export were introduced as an alternative to slave trading, encouraging the government of Napoleon III to strengthen its control over Senegal after 1850. The Wolof and Sereer states were conquered by Louis Faidherbe during the 1850s-1860s, and became the first French colonies in Africa. Expansion continued until 1886, when the kingdom of the Kajoor was re-conquered from Lat Dior Diop, who had mounted a rebellion forcing the French to withdraw in 1871. In the Fuuta Toro, Muslim cleric El Hadj Oumar Tall attracted a large number of followers to his anti-colonial revolts between 1854 and 1857. He eventually agreed to tolerate a French presence in the region, and from the late nineteenth century onwards, colonial expansion had the simultaneous effect of weakening the old aristocracies – the four Wolof kingdoms of the Jolof, Bawol, Kajoor and Waalo were destroyed by the mid-nineteenth century – and of making space for the expansion of the Muslim Sufi brotherhoods, the *tariqas*. Indeed mass conversion to Islam was facilitated by the tariqas' antagonistic relationship to the old monarchies, whose authority had been undermined by their involvement with the transatlantic slave trade (Diop 1981; Barry 1988). Further south, by contrast, the Casamance resisted both French colonization and conversion to Islam until the 1920s.

As they gained a stronger foothold in the region in the mid-nineteenth century, the French expropriated the Lebu[1] villages located along the shores of the Cape Vert Peninsula. They had an ideally positioned base from which to achieve this: their old trading post on the island of Gorée, where they had settled in the eighteenth century. From 1862 onwards the French settled on the Peninsula for good, beginning with the establishment of a military port in what was to become Dakar. Following major building works in 1904–10, and again in 1926–35, the port was turned into the biggest commercial hub on the coast of West Africa, capable of handling the lucrative exportation of peanuts as well as the maritime traffic between Casablanca and Cape Town (Tall 2009). Between 1882 and 1885, a railway line was built between Dakar and Saint-Louis, then the main French trading post. Colonial Dakar initially developed around these two labour-consuming infrastructures, the port and the railway, and their adjoining facilities and services. The Lebu fishing villages were forcibly displaced several times over the years in order to make way for colonial expansion. In one of the most dramatic episodes of French colonization, in 1914 the colonial authorities used a devastating bubonic plague as an opportunity to displace the settlements that still occupied land near the port area, and relocated them in the purpose-built Medina. There remains a persistent rumour that the epidemic was caused by the colonial authorities. At the very least, it is likely that they let it develop to such a degree that forcible relocation became justified (Faye 2000).

Early on, the French developed a policy of cultural assimilation which became particularly advanced in the colony of Senegal. The most significant indication of this was the regime of the Four Communes, a distinctive feature in the history of the region that still shapes urban identities today. In 1890, male residents in the four oldest trading posts – Saint-Louis, Dakar, Gorée and Rufisque – were granted citizenship rights. In practice, this meant that they had access to French education and could elect their own representatives to the French Parliament. Although the 'communes' represented no more than five per cent of Senegal's population, their elites became highly influential throughout French West Africa, the AOF (Afrique Occidentale Française). By 1939 Senegal had gained a leadership role in the French colonial system that was disproportionate to its modest size. The 'special relationship' between Senegal and France has remained an important feature in both countries' trajectories ever since.

Urban expansion and the formation of middle classes

In 1902 Dakar became the capital of the AOF in place of Saint-Louis, and the base from which the French extended their domination over the region. The making of Dakar as a capital was a gradual process that entailed the marginalization of former centres, Saint-Louis and Rufisque. This was achieved by systematically stripping them of their administrative and economic functions, such as the storage of peanuts for Rufisque (Tall 2009). Saint-Louis remained the capital of the colony of Senegal until 1957, when the status was transferred to Dakar. From the 1950s, Dakar's population began increasing exponentially, both from organic growth and as a result of immigration. There was some emigration too, mostly to France and to other Francophone African countries (Mauritania, Mali, Côte d'Ivoire, Gabon), but this was minimal compared to the numbers who came to the new capital in search of employment and education.

This influx produced a competition for property that remains a defining feature of the capital today. Between 1950 and 1973, Senegal embarked on massive building programmes through its agencies SICAP (Real Estate Company of Cap Vert) and OHLM (Organization for Housing at Moderated Rents). This was achieved in part through French funding, through the CCCE (Central Economic Cooperation Bank). My neighbourhood of Fann Hock, on the site of an old Lebu village, was one of the first 'SICAP', as the planned neighbourhoods were called. The main beneficiaries of the early property development programmes were civil servants and private sector employees with stable jobs, who were offered affordable mortgage schemes to buy accommodation. Those who were not employed in the formal sector during the expansion period were excluded, and most never formally gained access to property. Tall (2009) suggests that this resulted in the constitution of a property-owning middle class acting as a buffer between the wealthy elite and a massive disenfranchised population. Urban residents without access to property schemes began building slum housing extensively from 1970 onwards, meaning that large tracts of urban land were developed outside the control of the state. Many Lebu owners benefited from this period of informal development by selling properties that were still under customary land ownership. They had understood that the state would make it difficult for them to acquire individual property documents and therefore sold out wholesale, at fairly low prices. Though the Lebu were the Peninsula's original inhabitants, little wealth was therefore accumulated to pass on to future generations. This has undoubtedly been a determining factor in excluding the post-independence generations from accessing property, and thereby making emigration a necessity.

In sum, social classes in Dakar were largely solidified between the 1950s and the 1970s, on the basis of access to, or exclusion from, property schemes. This is important to this study since the Dakarois performing world is split between those who grew up in families housed in SICAP neighbourhoods and those who grew up in informal settlements in more remote *quartiers* (poorer, often overcrowded neighbourhoods and suburbs).

Lebu symbolic power

Though the Lebu did not maintain ownership of the land, their status as the Peninsula's first inhabitants remains politically significant, and they have retained a political power which bears no relation to their numbers in the capital.[2] This is only possible because their symbolic power still matters, as I found out as I got to know the *ndey ji rew*,[3] Alioune Diagne Mbor. My friend, Nafy Guèye, knew him in her capacity as a member of a local environmental NGO, Association Sénégalaise des Amis de la Nature, which he headed. Together we visited him several times at the Thierigne Mosque in the Medina, where he sat almost daily with other Lebu notables, helping to settle disputes. It was in the context of official ceremonies with the environmental association that the Lebu symbolic power became most visible to me. Indeed the choice of environmental issues as a theme for civic engagement was probably no accident, given the Lebu claim to a special connection, both historical and spiritual, with the land on which Dakar was built.

One such occasion was the inauguration in February 2004 of the new facilities built for the association with German funding. The site had been leased by the municipality of Mbao, in the Greater Dakar area. From early in the morning, the day was packed with dances, drumming, praise-singing by griots and visits of the facilities. There were also speeches by Alioune Diagne Mbor himself and by government officials, including then President Wade and Mbao Mayor, Mamadou Seck. Outdoor seating covered with canopies had been set up for the officials while hundreds of women in matching outfits cheered, sang, danced and blew their whistles. Galvanized, and undoubtedly paid by the local women's section of the PDS (Parti Démocratique Sénégalais) in power at the time, they held signs carrying the photograph of the Mayor while singing 'Avec Mamadou Seck jusqu'à la mort!'[4] at the top of their voices. Though this looked like any official ceremony in Francophone West Africa, what was remarkable was the Lebu presence, despite the fact that this was in no way a Lebu ceremony. Lebu notables and representatives of the community in Santhiaba, where the Thierigne Mosque is located, sat in a separate area under a white canopy. They were clearly more numerous than any other group of notables in attendance, and a sign hanging from the canopy indicated that they were Lebu from Santhiaba.

In the morning, the ceremony began with a series of dance and drumming performances. The most striking dance was performed by a group of Lebu women dressed in dark blue and yellow outfits, their hair styled in traditional Lebu fashion underneath headscarves, their lips and gums dyed black as a marker of Lebu identity. Whereas the other women who cheered and danced were stuck in the crowded areas behind low fences, the Lebu women were clearly occupying the centre stage. They performed a Lebu dance, the *ndawrabin*, in a perfect line facing the government officials. Performed to the sound of Wolof sabar drums, the ndawrabin is visually striking, and has many variations. At the beginning of the dance, the women come forward, taking small steps and alternatively lifting each leg, the knee bent high up before being thrust to the side. The arms are also held high above the head and follow the movement of the knees on each side. The ndawrabin is designed to be performed by a group rather than an individual, and as a result displays harmonious lines not easy to achieve with the more athletic sabar dances. Having learned the ndawrabin during a Kaay Fecc workshop in 2002, I felt the way in which the leg movements were designed to create a fluid movement in the long wrap-around skirts worn by the dancers underneath their *mbubb*,[5] similar to lifting the lower part of a curtain. It is also significant that the ndawrabin used to be performed during important Lebu festivals. Diagne Mbor told me that this dance used to be performed during the May-June festivities, at the very beginning of the rainy season, when stock was taken of the year past and people sang about memorable events. Everyone took part in the ndawrabin, which he described as having a 'regulatory function' in society. Diagne Mbor added that it was also performed during the *baonaan*, a Lebu rain-making ceremony during which people dressed in rags so as to 'appease the spirits'.[6]

That day, however, no one in the audience gave any sign of appreciation, even though the women performed with perfect coordination, dignity and graceful confidence. But then, neither did they react during the other performances. The higher the status, the more dignified audiences are during performing events gathering people of both sexes and of diverse class backgrounds and age groups. Yet the ndey ji rew, who had brought the dancers, seemed satisfied. He had made a statement by showing the PDS officials seated in the shade that Lebu power still mattered: the women PDS militants had been outperformed. That it was possible for Lebu notables to make such a show of status in a non-Lebu event confirms the importance of their symbolic power. Even though the Lebu were marginalized by the Wade regime in comparison with the political purchase they enjoyed during the PS (Parti Socialiste) years between 1960 and 2000, Wade's PDS seemed intent on maintaining the status quo, since both sides needed each other's goodwill. The Lebu, for their part, knew full well the importance of 'performing' their old rights to the land if they were not to lose whatever power they had left in the governance of the capital. As Tall (2009: 64, translated from French) says, the marking off of Lebu social and spiritual space in the form of twelve *pinthie*, or Lebu spatial and political units across the Dakar region, serves as a kind of 'psychological marker for a power whose territorial manifestation is gradually disappearing'.

This vignette was meant to illustrate the power of performance in both marking and making power in Dakar. The ability to stage the best dance during public events is essential in demonstrating the underlying power to mobilize and discipline people. It shows the possession of moral authority (*kilifteef*), and the capacity to command the allegiance of others. Yet, the Lebu skill in playing the performing game has not prevented a growing gap between those urban residents who have access to property ownership, often international migrants, and those who do not. Increasingly, power lies in the performance of absence.

A growing divide

Few ordinary citizens can now afford to buy property in the city or its suburbs. As Tall (2009) and Melly (2010) have shown, most houses built in the recent construction boom have been paid for by migrants and returnees. Both authors explain that for many migrants, the most tangible sign of success is investment in property, whether for their families or future families to live in, for speculative purposes or for renting. Disciples of the Mouride Brotherhood often give priority to building in the holy city of Touba, but this does not exclude building in Dakar. This has contributed to high levels of inflation in the past two decades, pushing tenants and owners who did not benefit from migrants' remittances further into the peripheries. Among my own informants, only those who lived with relatives were able to reside within reasonable distance from the city centre, and avoid wasting exhausting hours sitting in minibuses in gridlocked traffic. A few families managed to rent in neighbourhoods like Fass, Medina, HLM (Habitations à Loyer Modéré) or Grand Dakar, not too far from the city centre, but this usually implied several people sharing a small room. Otherwise people lived further away in Ouakam, Pikine, Dalifort, Cambérène, Guédiawaye, Yeumbeul and even Keur Massar and Mbao, on the Peninsula's throat.

Inflation and housing shortages are only some of the manifestations of the difficult economic situation into which Senegal has found itself since the late 1970s. When Léopold Sédar Senghor was elected to the Presidency at independence in 1960, Senegal received economic and military support from France in exchange for its loyal support of French foreign policy in the region. The Senghor regime welcomed the privileged access to the French market that followed for its peanuts, phosphates, fish and produce. But as elsewhere on the continent, the oil crisis of 1970–73 had the tragic effect of cutting short the development of major infrastructures and productive industries. In Senegal this combined with soil erosion, periodic drought throughout the 1970s and falling peanut prices, which hastened the demise of the agricultural sector. It probably did not help that the centrally planned economy favoured city dwellers at the expense of the rural areas (Sharp 1994). In cities, the manufacturing sector was in crisis following the liberalization initiated in the 1970s (Thioub et al 1998). In a country that was still relying heavily on borrowed funds, and with few natural resources, the effects of this downturn were devastating. In 1980 the Senegalese government called the IMF and the World Bank to the rescue, and the Structural Adjustment Programmes (SAPs) implemented from 1981 onwards imposed massive spending cuts on health, education and administration. Since those were the sectors that offered stable employment, this had the effect of pushing the emerging middle classes back into poverty.[7]

It is in large part the economic downturn of the past three decades which accounts for the growing popularity of performing careers. Many young performers in Dakar today are the children of the emerging middle classes whose hopes for the future were cut short, as they were elsewhere in Africa (Ferguson 1999). The 1980s, therefore, are often remembered in sharp contrast to the hope that characterized the first years after independence, particularly in artistic circles. The prevailing feeling by 2010 was the sense of a growing divide between the wealthy and the poor, with the middle classes being pushed further down. Apart from those households who have recently gained access to migrant remittances, most of the Dakarois I have known since 2002 have found it increasingly difficult to make ends meet. This has been particularly marked since 2006, which coincides with a higher cost of energy, the crisis in the global finance sector and the concomitant repercussions on inflation. In 2002, many of the middle-class urbanites I knew were still fairly optimistic about their future. This had been a mixed year, marked first by nationwide euphoria when the Senegalese football team made it all the way to the quarter finals in the World Cup, but later by tragedy, when the Joola ferryboat capsized along the Ziguinchor-Dakar route. Despite a poor handling of the disaster, President Wade was re-elected for a second term in February 2007 with fifty-six per cent of the votes. Legislative elections were held a few months later, in June, and a coordinated boycott by several opposition parties allowed Wade's Sopi coalition to maintain a comfortable majority in Parliament.

By early 2009, however, disillusion with the regime had grown, not only among the middle-class urbanites and youths who had wholeheartedly supported the regime change in 2000, but also within the Dakarois population at large. Many spoke about the social fabric in pessimistic terms, and more people than before seemed to be making active plans to leave the country. The failure of the Senegalese economy to generate stable employment does not explain everything. After all, the lack of stable employment has been a defining feature of the Senegalese economy for at least two decades. If anything, in Dakar the first half of the 2000s saw an improvement at some level, if an indicator like the incidence of poverty is anything to go by, which, according to official figures, decreased from 33.4 per cent to 25 per cent of house-holds[8] between 2001 and 2005 (ANSD 2008). Yet by the late 2000s, the dominant sentiment was the perception of growing inequalities. In this context it came as little surprise that Abdoulaye Wade's PDS was forcefully defeated in Dakar and in several strategic cities at the local elections of March 2009. This was an early sign of the resounding defeat inflicted on the PDS when President Wade ran for a highly contested third mandate in 2012, and lost to his former Prime Minister, Macky Sall.

Shadows of the Casamance

I have already alluded to the intense involvement of migrants from the Casamance in the Dakarois performing world. I will return to this involvement in more detail in

Figure 2.1 Senegal. (Map created by ML Kringelbach using TileMill. © OpenStreetMap contributors).

Chapter 5, but for this to make sense, a few words must be said about the historical relationship between the Casamance and the rest of Senegal. Indeed the integration of the region into the nation has been one of the most pressing challenges faced by successive Senegalese governments. Separated from the northern regions by the Gambia, the Casamance is a linguistically, culturally and religiously diverse area roughly covering Senegal's wet tropical zone (Figure 2.1). Jola speakers are dominant in the Lower Casamance, in the Ziguinchor region.[9] But the Middle and Upper parts of the region, around Sedhiou, Kolda and Velingara, are more diverse, with an important Mandinka and Pulaar-speaking (Fulani) presence. In addition, there are smaller groups, like the Manjaco, the Mankañ and the Balanta, who live across the Gambia, Guinea Bissau and Guinea.

The region has seen a low-intensity separatist conflict since 1982, when the newly formed MFDC (Mouvement des Forces Démocratiques de Casamance) organized a march in Ziguinchor, in protest against ongoing repression by the Senegalese army. But armed forces were not mobilized until 1990, sparking a conflict that has yet to be resolved. A peace agreement was signed in December 2004 between the Senegalese government and the MFDC, only to be broken in 2007. The MFDC is now split into two main factions, and the guerrilla conflict is deeply entangled in the politics of the three neighbouring countries. Though the violence is fairly recent, there is a longer history of Casamançais separatism. Indeed a political movement named MFDC already existed during the colonial period, formed in 1949 in Sédhiou by two Casamançais schoolteachers, Emile Badiane and Ibou Diallo. But scholars of the region disagree on whether the current MFDC is a direct successor of the former. At any rate, the idea of independence or at least autonomy for Casamance is not new, and there are a number of competing explanations as to its root causes.[10] One of the most common explanations, and one that is espoused by the movement itself, is the gradual emergence of a regional consciousness over the course of the twentieth century. In the first instance this was caused by the marginalization of the region in the French colony, and later by what people from the region regarded as the government's sabotage of their economic development. In short, this approach views the growing sense of being 'left out' of the nation's development, combined with the cultural and geographic distinctiveness of the region, as the main factors behind the conflict.

Though these analyses are undoubtedly valid, they do not account for the absence of an armed rebellion in other parts of Senegal with similar histories of difference and marginalization. With this in mind, Vincent Foucher (2002) looked at schooling in the Casamance and migration to Dakar and found that the geographic spread of the Casamançais movement fitted neatly with a high rate of primary schooling. Drawing on Anderson's (1983) notion of 'imagined communities', he argued that education was one of the two main factors that prompted a Casamançais, and particularly Jola consciousness to emerge in the Lower Casamance. The other factor was migration to Dakar, which took off extensively in the 1950s and 1960s, and which raised hopes, among educated Jola youths, that they would be integrated into the state apparatus on a par with northern Senegalese citizens. It is significant, Foucher (2002) argues, that the rebellion started at a time of economic decline, when Casamançais aspirations were cut short by the drying out of state employment.

In Thionck Essyl, a town that is significant to my study, Alice Hamer (1981) found that by 1978 migration had indeed become an integral part of village life, with fifteen per cent of the population engaged in seasonal migration and eighteen per cent in permanent migration. Half of the 'permanent' migrants lived in Dakar. She also found that most of the women who held a waged job in Dakar worked as house employees (eighty-four per cent). This fits with the claim by several of my informants that many women performers in the 1950s to 1970s were working as house employees during the day, and rehearsing in the evenings. The dance troupes provided them with a space of fun, relief and sociality away from the hardship of the *mbindaan* work.[11] Coming from a part of the region where dancing is less associated with a compromised morality than it is in Wolof-speaking Senegal, they were also relatively free from the expectations of restraint that made it difficult for Wolof women from high-status families to perform in public.

Despite a long history of regional mobility (Linares 2003; Lambert 2002), the region remains perceived in Senegal as a bastion of timeless, rural traditions (De Jong 2007). I will suggest in Chapter 5 that this perception stems in large part from the success of Casamançais troupes in Dakar. The neo-traditional genre, in particular, is dominated by Casamançais migrants and their descendants, who account for at least a third of performers according to my own estimates. But not all dancers and musicians in Dakar have links with the Casamance. In spite of the historical transformations sketched in the previous chapter, for many others the association between ñeeño lineage and public performance remains a discreet yet salient feature shaping social status.

Griots, géwël, artists

Although the introduction of colonial school theatre had initiated a degree of detachment between public performance and ñeeño status, as we have seen in Chapter 1, there remains underlying continuities in the social perception of dance/musical performance. For the purposes of this study, the most important enduring aspect is that the power one may derive from performing skills is highly ambiguous.

Mastery of speech and music-making on behalf of others is known to be a source of power throughout the region, and skilled praise-orators are essential in validating, even establishing the status of their patrons (Wright 1989; Irvine 1989; Rasmussen 1992; Hale 1999; Ebron 2002). They receive money or gifts in exchange for their artful delivery of praise in a public setting, and conversely, prestige is conferred by having a skilled griot amplify one's speech in public. The nature of this power is contested, however, and the literature on status in Sahelian societies is thus divided into two broad perspectives. According to the first, 'caste' stratification in the region contains an inherent form of inequality (Silla 1966; Wane 1969; Irvine 1974; Diop 1981; Tamari 1997; Mbow 2000; Ngaïde 2003). By contrast, the second perspective argues that different groups own different forms of power (Richter 1980; Wright 1989; Rasmussen 1992). Following Dilley (2004), I situate myself between the two approaches: I suggest that it is important to recognize the existence of different 'versions of difference', while also acknowledging that for people who are categorized as ñeeño, the experience of difference is often one of marginalization. This is also confirmed by my recurrent observation that people of géér descent who choose dance or music as a professional activity are rarely keen to become associated with ñeeño status, yet this remains mostly unspoken. As the following story illustrates, social tensions around 'caste' are most evident in marriage disputes where the preference for endogamy is threatened.

Ousmane identifies himself as a Wolof géwël, even though both his parents belonged to other ñeeño groups. As we sat over a dish of rice and discussed the 'caste' issue, he once told me that nowadays, géér/ñeeño marriages were tolerated in most families. He added that whenever disagreements arose, they were usually resolved. For example, when a match was refused by an individual's father, the intervention of the mother's brother could be solicited. Nevertheless, he said, the problem did not occur very often because the ñeeño themselves favoured endogamy, and were reluctant to 'take spouses from the géér'. He added that this also applied internally within ñeeño families since the géwël were often reluctant to take spouses from other ñeeño categories:

You see, our women [géwël] are raised to be extremely generous and hospitable, because these are our values. So, if a woman who hasn't had this kind of education comes into the family, she won't be able to keep up. Her husband's sisters and the other women in the family will keep making gifts to her, and she won't keep up. We'd rather not take their women, to save them the humiliation.

Although not from a géwël family but from a different ñeeño background, his talent as a story-teller or *communicateur traditionnel* in the modern jargon, made him identify with the géwël, who epitomize the broader ñeeño category (Panzacchi 1994).

Further into the same conversation, however, he told me a personal story which completely contradicted his argument. As a high school student, Ousmane had fallen in love with a géér girl whom he had hoped to marry. She was also in love with him, but upon discovering that he was a ñeeño, her mother had ordered the girl to leave him. Nothing was said to him directly, but a friend of Ousmane's, who was also the girl's cousin, soon published a tale in the school magazine. It was the story of a ñeeño who had made the mistake of thinking himself worthy enough to ask for the hand of a géér. Ousmane understood that this was directed at him, and found this all the more painful as it was coming from a friend. Feeling humiliated, he broke off the relationship himself. Intermediaries acting on his family's behalf then went to visit the girl's family, he said, and told them about the exploits of his illustrious ancestors. Upon hearing about his lineage, Ousmane said, the mother confessed that she had made a mistake. But Ousmane's pride had been irremediably hurt. He told the girl that although he loved her, he could never marry someone whose relatives had insulted the 'life [his] parents had given [him]'. A few years later, he married a ñeeño woman.

Regardless of the accuracy of the story, this reflected Ousmane's contradictory feelings about the social classification that shaped his life. His first remark about the alternative solution in cases of dispute provided an ideal vision of Wolof society as harmonious, with shared values and safeguards to guarantee a fair degree of freedom for individuals. His second remark inverted the dominant géér discourse according to which generosity is a mark of their superior status: in his tale, no one could compete with the generosity of the géwël. Finally, his personal story contradicted the discourse he had so beautifully crafted by showing that endogamy could still be enforced in subtle ways, at great emotional cost for the individuals involved. Ousmane's testimony also raises the possibility that people perceive the different status groups as associated with different moralities ('our values'), a point that is recurrent in anthropological studies of morality (Howell 1997a). How, then, do performers navigate these different moral domains while preserving their reputations across all the social fields they engage with? I will address this question throughout the book, but rather than providing a single answer, I will illustrate the way in which people attempt to resolve tensions about morality within different genres of performance.

Historians seem to agree that the power of griots was most prominent during the mighty days of the Senegambian kingdoms, between the fourteenth and the eighteenth centuries (Leymarie 1999), when they were at the service of royal lineages in constant need of the reaffirmation of their authority through the manipulation of genealogies. Until recently, some géwël families were attached to high-status lineages by birth (*géwël juddu*), and a relationship of the géér/géwël juddu type remains more valued than a temporary exchange of praise for cash because it involves a deeper historical knowledge. It is particularly valued when the performer is skilled in amplifying – or inventing – glorious events and concealing anything that may tarnish the family's reputation. Consequently, the monetary reward depends on oratory skills and the knowledge of individual and family histories. Thus a guest at a wedding I attended in early 2004 reprimanded me for having given too much to a griotte who had been dancing and reciting praise in front of me. 'You should take your money back', the guest said, 'this is too much for her; she doesn't know you, she can't say anything about you, so she has no right to take that much'. I had only given her a modest sum (1,000 FCFA), but this is symptomatic of the resentment that comes with ephemeral patron-client relationships today. This is, in reality, a discussion of changing morality in society. When patrons (who may or may not be géér) complain about the griots' pursuit of 'quick money' and when griots complain that patrons have grown increasingly stingy and individualistic, each party is in effect lamenting what is perceived as a deplorable effect of modernity: a rising tendency to take shortcuts towards the achievement of a respectable moral standing. This is particularly significant in relation to the widespread notion, throughout the region, that a person's moral qualities should be developed over a long time, through lengthy apprenticeship and a degree of self-sacrifice (Sylla 1994).

Most telling about the ambiguity of ñeeño power is the widespread notion that the bodies of ñeeño are the repositories of forces that remain inaccessible to others. As Dilley (2004) has analysed in the Haalpulaar case, whether this power is understood as a positive or a negative force depends on the context and individual perspective. Whereas skilled griot performance is regarded by patrons as vitalizing for the lineage as a whole, poor performance – especially deliberate – is an insult and may have negative effects on the person's prestige and well-being (Wright 1989). I have often heard people say that when a griot is talented, his or her praise will 'make your blood run faster' and will physically compel you to pull out cash to reward the performance. The power exercised by a skilled griot is described in physical terms, as a force which affects a person's conscious control.

On the other hand, for many géér, sexual intercourse with ñeeño, sitting in their seats or eating from the same bowl carries a risk to one's well-being. There is also historical evidence that the Wolof and the Sereer used to bury griots in hollow baobab trees, thereafter called *guy géwël*. [12] It was feared that the soil would become sterile if they were buried in it (Boilat 1853; Mauny 1955), and violent incidents over the burial of géwël in cemeteries in the early 1960s (Paris-Dakar 1961c) testify to the fact that this is recent history indeed. But ñeeño often turn the discourse around and attribute such beliefs to the fear inspired by their exceptional powers. Ousmane, for example, explained that 'in some villages, the older griots had so much power that they could not be buried in the soil' for fear that they might spoil the harvest.

Similarly, the géér notion that their children are better educated because parents and older relatives spend more time with them (whereas the géwël are said to be too busy tending to others' ceremonies) is often reversed. I have thus shared meals with géwël who assured me that they taught their children a wider range of life skills than the géér, including the love of nutritious food or the art of elegance. While eating the entrails of fish in a dish of *ceebu jën*,[13] for example, they explained that most géér had never been taught that this was the tastiest and most nutritious part of the dish. To what extent, then, are young performers from géér families perceived to assume the physical (and thereby also moral) attributes of ñeeño? I will suggest in later chapters that this depends on the kind of dance people perform, and the social fields they engage with. But for now I turn to the tensions arising from a gradual dissociation of occupation and 'caste' status.

As I have alluded to in earlier chapters, in a context of uncertainty affecting all social categories, occupations traditionally associated with ñeeño have become attractive to others. Being a dancer, a choreographer or a musician is increasingly regarded as an alternative avenue towards success, which challenges the widespread perception that these are degrading activities. Many youths believe (often wrongly) that dancing requires intense physical training but no formal education, in return for endless travelling opportunities. As a result, many young géér who are keen to become performers are school leavers with a passion for dance and music as well as a desire to travel. Needless to say, this creates tensions with performers from ñeeño families, many of whom are not keen to see competition from those who scorn them. As a result the term 'artist' has become increasingly used within the performing world as a way of obscuring people's genealogical background. By presenting themselves as 'artists', people are able to work together without having to address the issue openly.

The competitive nature of contemporary géér-ñeeño relations is further complicated by the fact that not all ñeeño families value the performing professions, a trend Cornelia Panzacchi (1994) already noted in the early 1990s. Indeed, many invoke the low morality of the modern performing profession, perceived as fostering substance abuse and sexual promiscuity and being morally inferior to the traditional griot trade. These families often place a high value on formal education, as if to beat the géér at their own game. Already in the colonial period, ñeeño had begun to gain access to high-ranking administrative positions through formal education. Kiné Lam, a Senegalese diva and self-identified géwël, thus dedicated her song, *Tabasky Thiam*,[14] to the ñeeño who had earned degrees without denying their origin. This is a short extract from the song:

| Tëgg dawul mbar | The smith has not escaped the workshop |
| Diplom yi la ko tontu | He has replied with degrees |

The emphasis on formal education in ñeeño families is particularly visible when parents who practise a hereditary trade insist on their children getting degrees first rather than simply learning their own trade. A lead drummer I knew, who identified as a ñeeño, thus had a fifteen-year old daughter who was consistently noticed as a skilled dancer during sabar events. She wanted to become a professional dancer, but her father would not let her practise with the troupe he had recently set up. Once on my own with her, I asked what she thought the reason for this reluctance was. She replied that her father wanted her to get an education first, and that rehearsing several times per week would jeopardize her schooling. When I asked the father about it on a different occasion, however, he replied that she was a gifted dancer, and that he did not want her to be exposed to other people's envy too early. He explained that there were 'evil tongues' out there, and that people might want to harm her if they realized how gifted she was. If she waited for a few years, he continued, she would be better protected against them. Though this was evidently an idiom to talk about the danger posed by envy in the family or neighbourhood, this also pointed to the idea that the power to neutralize (or otherwise manipulate) malevolent forces came with age and experience. Ultimately, however, it is likely that the father's reluctance had to do with both a concern for her schooling and a desire to protect her from harm.

Yet many ñeeño complain that those who rise 'above their status' are never completely free from the scorn of the géér. Silla (1966) remarked on this in post-independence days, when the few ministries headed by ñeeño were nicknamed *mbar mi*, the smithy, or artisan workshop more generally. I witnessed similar scorn on several occasions. In a youth club I visited occasionally, one of the committee members was a man in his mid-thirties who held a Bachelor's degree in Law. Having failed the Bar exam several times, he was getting by with various ill-paid jobs. Unlike the other committee members, who dressed in T-shirts, jeans and caps despite their advancing years, he was always impeccably turned out in a suit and tie. As I remarked on his sartorial taste to another committee member on one occasion, the man replied in a contemptuous tone:

> He thinks he can be a man of culture by wearing a suit. But he is a Griot, his family are Griots. He wants people to forget this, that's why he's wearing a suit.

Thus the increasing popularity of dance and music as professional avenues is fraught with tension because this hints at potential shifts in the location of power in society. I once asked an experienced informant, who identified as a ñeeño himself, to estimate the proportion of ñeeño in the dance troupes that he knew. His guess was that ninety per cent of drummers were ñeeño, but that the proportion was lower for dancers, probably around seventy per cent. My own observations have led me to conclude that the proportion of ñeeño in general is probably less than half for the dancers since one must adjust for the fact that Jola and Manjaco performers, who are quite numerous, do not recognize this type of stratification. It is undoubtedly much higher for dance troupe musicians, mostly drummers. Ñeeño are therefore overrepresented in the performing world, but this is far from the complete dominance one would expect. Yet making a performing career acceptable to families remains problematic for many youths from high-status families. Whereas in some cases attitudes change when the individual starts bringing money home, travelling and helping others find work, in other cases would-be dancers or musicians must choose between giving up their passion and being cut off from parts of their families.

One dancer-choreographer I knew, for example, was a Haalpulaar who had grown up in Dakar in a *tooroBe* family. When I asked him what his family thought of his choice, he replied that his parents were open-minded people who had always supported him. Visibly reluctant to discuss the subject, he added that he neither knew nor cared what the rest of the family thought since he had very little contact with his parents' siblings. As it happened, someone I knew had met some of them in a different context. Apparently, some of the family members strongly disapproved of his choice, and according to my interlocutor this was the main reason why they had so little to do with him. This did not seem to be a problem in his neighbourhood, however, where he enjoyed respect as the leader of a dance group that kept youths away from mischief.

The situation was equally ambiguous for a drummer who lived in the Medina, and also belonged to a high-status Haalpulaar family. His father had been against his career choice from the outset: 'You will not bring sabar [drums] inside this house as long as I live!' he had shouted upon discovering that his son was learning to play with a dance troupe. But the young man had a passion for music-making. He continued to play in spite of his father's wrath, he said, because he 'couldn't help it'. Following a couple of years of discreet practice, he began to play onstage with the troupe and to earn a decent living for his young age. A fast-learning and talented drummer, he was also paid to play at neighbourhood parties and family ceremonies. The flow of cash apparently prompted his father to change his mind:

> When my father saw me come home with 50,000 [FCFA], he asked: 'How did you earn this?' I said it was the drumming. In the beginning he didn't believe me, but after a while he told me to go out and drum some more [laughing].

When I visited him at home, a wide range of drums were displayed in his small room. His musician friends often came by to chat, listen to Senegalese rap, repair the drums and drink *attaya*. He said his family had come to terms with his drum-beating (*tëgg*), but that they still hoped he would eventually grow out of it and turn to a more respectable trade. A few years later, however, he settled in France, where he has been teaching drumming and performing since. By contrast, a close friend of mine had not been able to pursue her passion for dance. She had always loved dancing, but her family had told her that this was not an appropriate occupation for a Wolof géér. She insisted that if she had been a teenager now that the profession had become more respectable, she would have become a dancer.

What these individual cases point to is an enduring moral ambiguity around public performance, despite the increasing attractiveness of the profession for young Dakarois. I suggest that this stems partly from the association with ñeeño status and morality discussed above, and partly from the very transformations sketched out in Chapter 1. Indeed when people find they are no longer able to ascribe 'caste' and moral attributes on the basis of the trade people exercise, when young géér become performers, while géwël and other ñeeño distance themselves from performing altogether, the uncertainty about 'who really is who' generates a great deal of moral anxiety. As we will see in Chapter 4, this anxiety is often expressed in the idiom of religion, at a time when Senegalese Islam is becoming more prominent in public life.

Conclusion

In this chapter I have sketched the urban context in which musical and choreographic performance have become increasingly attractive activities for youths across social categories. The previous chapter had already suggested that the introduction of colonial school theatre, and later the use of the performing arts in nation-building, had fostered the emergence of a profession of educated performers, and had begun to dissociate public performance from the hereditary trade of Griot families. In this chapter, I have moved closer to the contemporary period and focused on the city of Dakar to show how these transformations have provided young city dwellers from impoverished middle-class backgrounds and from underprivileged neighbourhoods with alternative routes towards social mobility. But the social significance of performance also goes much beyond the socioeconomic aspect. In this chapter I have thus drawn on the Lebu history of diminishing land tenure to suggest that successful performance in a particular space symbolizes the possession of moral authority and the capacity to command the allegiance of others.

Finally, I have suggested that the appeal of public performance for youths from non-Griot backgrounds is fraught with tension because it makes space for potential shifts in the locations of power in society. Indeed, family conflicts often arise when 'respectable' géér families see their children embrace the trade of their former 'clients'. In addition, this suggests that young people may have a form of power of their own if they know how to use their vitality and bodily skills. Indeed, one should not underestimate the shifts in authority that may come from a young performer being able to support older members of his family. But issues of social classification in relation to public performance are only one side of the coin. There is another domain which cuts across all categories because it has to do with the making of persons in an urban context: it is the women-dominated sabar genre, to which I turn in the next chapter.

Notes

1. The Lebu are the original inhabitants of the Cap Vert Peninsula. They do not constitute a separate ethnicity but speak a distinctive version of Wolof. Their presence along the coast is attributed to their flight away from the centralized Kajoor monarchies in the sixteenth century.
2. According to Tall (2009), the Lebu represent approximately 3 per cent of Dakar's inhabitants.
3. *Ndey ji rew* translates as the 'mother of the republic'. In practice, this is the head of the Lebu assembly.
4. 'With Mamadou Seck until death!'

5. A *mbubb* (*boubou* in French) is a loose robe often made of damask cotton cloth, worn with a wrapper underneath (*pagne* in French; *sér* in Wolof) and a headscarf (*musoor*). There are mbubb of varying lengths and sleeve shapes. For funerals and the Friday prayer, an embroidered see-through shawl is thrown over the head, also covering the shoulders. The mbubb is the women's ceremonial outfit par excellence, the equivalent for men being a long caftan with loose trousers. Mbubb are now described as 'traditional' Senegalese dress, and indeed photographs taken in Saint-Louis and Dakar in the 1930s and 1940s show many women wearing them, but they were not as widespread as they are now. Heath (1992) traces the popularization of the mbubb to the post-independence nationalist period, when urban elites invoked 'tradition' to legitimize their power.

6. Sylla (1994) similarly described the rags worn during the *baonaan* as designed to show people's humility in the face of the divine.

7. Mbembe (2001: 74–75) nicely sums up the criticism leveled at the liberal ideology of the 1980s that justified the SAPs and the broader 'tutelage of international creditors': 'throughout the 1980s, the dominant explanation for the "African crisis" consisted in placing responsibility on the state and its supposed excessive demands on the economy. [. . .] But, by doing everything possible to dismantle state intervention in the economy [. . .], without making the state more efficient and giving it new, positive functions, the result has been that the state's (already very fragile) material base has been undermined, the logics underlying the building of coalitions and clienteles have been upset (without being positively restructured), its capacities for reproduction have been reduced, and the way has been opened for it to wither away'.

8. 'Poor' households are defined as those which do not have the capacity to buy a standard basket of goods (including both food and non-food items) valued at 638 FCFA per person, per day in 2001–02 and 681 FCFA in 2005–06 (ANSD 2008b).

9. There are various spellings of Senegal's ethnic groups; in this case Diola (mostly in the literature in French), Jola and Joola are the most widely used.

10. For a comprehensive review of the different approaches and an analysis of the original MFDC, see Foucher (2002).

11. *Mbindaan* is the Wolof term used to designate a female house employee. There are tens of thousands of poorly paid house employees in Dakar, some of whom are younger relatives from the rural areas. Most come from the Casamance, the Siin Saalum and from neighbouring countries (the Gambia and Guinea Bissau).

12. *Guy* is the Wolof name of the baobab tree.

13. *Ceebu jën* ('rice with fish') is a very common dish of spicy fish, rice and vegetables cooked in oily tomato sauce.

14. Kiné Lam *Balla Aïssa Boury*, 1991, cassette. Translated from Wolof with the kind help of Nafy Guèye.

Chapter 3

Drums, Sand and Persons[1]

The scene is a women's *tour*[2] in a house in Fass, near the Medina, in the late afternoon. I have come with a woman friend and the six drummers who are due to perform. My friend and I have been invited to attend by one of the drummers, whom I got to know through the dance troupe he plays with. As we make our way to the tiled rooftop, the hostess, a married woman in her thirties, has already greeted the first guests. She snaps at the musicians for being late, and gives me a cool greeting when the drummer I know introduces me as his 'student'. The ensemble sits at one end of the rooftop and begins to play sabar rhythms while the space fills up. Before long, some fifty women, several teenage girls and a few children, girls and boys, are seated on the plastic chairs set up in a circle. They all wear colourful *mbubb* and *taille basse*[3] outfits in the fashionable light green, yellow, pink and two-colour combinations. My senses are overwhelmed by the strong smell of *cuuraay*,[4] the shiny fabrics, the thick layers of make-up and glittering jewellery. As the women greet each other and take their seats, there is a graceful brushing of damask cloth and matching party bags. Pointed satin mules make clicking sounds on the tiles. Headscarves are folded into the latest *jalgáti* ('bend the rules') or *uppukaay* ('fan') shapes, elaborately held together with sewing pins. The women are all friends and neighbours, but the sharp glances at each other's outfits leave little doubt as to the highly competitive nature of the event.

When the drummers begin to play dance rhythms, a woman gets up, takes off her shoes and holds the lower rim of her thigh-length mbubb while stepping forward in rhythm. The other arm is waving back and forth in a rounded movement that seems to be carrying the upper body forward. One step opening the knee to one side, then to the other; the initial steps are meant to get into the rhythm and attract the attention of the participants (Castaldi 2006). The woman steps forward until she is a few steps away from the musicians, facing them; she jumps to find support on the left foot while her right leg is thrown upwards, stretched, and then the right leg beats the air downwards at amazing speed. This is the basic beginning of many sabar dances: the jump is initiated just before the first beat, and both feet land on the ground on the beat. The woman leaps upwards again three times on alternate legs, both knees bent, then pivots on the left leg, arms folded away from the body and pointing upwards. Finally she jumps on both feet to re-establish her balance, and starts again.[5] The rhythm steps up. She dances solo for about thirty seconds and runs back to her chair, laughing heartily. Her friends congratulate her in high-pitched voices, and the energy of the group builds up. Gradually, more women get up and step into the central space, taking turns to dance solo or in pairs, challenging each other playfully. The rooftop fills up with the sounds of loud drumming, laughter and chatter.

One woman is attracting attention of a different kind. Sitting in a quiet corner, she collects 1,500 FCFA[6] from every participant and records the names and amounts in her notebook. This is the *yaayu mbotaay*, literally the 'mother of the age-set'. The climax of the evening will be the lottery: the names of the participants entitled to take their turn that week will be written down on bits of paper, and a single paper will be picked randomly from a basket, under the surveillance of the yaayu mbotaay and three other women appointed as witnesses. It is of the utmost importance that the 'ritual' of the lottery be followed carefully so as to prevent cheating. As the name of the winner is announced the woman lets out a loud cry, twirls and performs a few dance steps while her friends congratulate her.

Later in the evening, the energy level rises along with the sexual suggestiveness of the dances. Loud cheering resonates when the drummers initiate the *Lawbe*[7] rhythms, such as the *lëmbël*. The women encourage each other to be daring, to roll the buttocks generously and to perform creative steps drawn from the sabar repertoire and from the popular mbalax[8] genre. The high level of energy is palpable and there is frantic to-and-fro movement. Chairs are taken and quickly left again to perform in the central space for a few seconds to half a minute. The few women who refuse to dance at least once, lacking confidence in their skills, are made to pay a symbolic fine. Some of the dancers walk across the space and playfully lift their friends' skirts. Others stand up, turn to their friends and quickly lift their wrapper to reveal their *beeco*, or underneath wrapper, and their tiny thongs decorated with motifs, such as a sunflower or a cat's head. Revealing one's latest underwear design is part of the fun, and outbursts of laughter resound with every skirt being lifted. One of the women, standing with her back to the musicians at the very edge of the circle, beats her friends in boldness and reveals the full extent of her female anatomy. 'You know what we, women, say', my friend tells me, 'the bigger, the better!' Others remove their wrapper and go on dancing in their beeco, bare legs beating the air. Some of the beeco are made of white cotton painted with bawdy inscriptions. Meanwhile the two *tama* players have started moving around the rooftop, acting as if they were aroused by the sight. They comment on the underwear ('it is Sotiba[9] that is teasing us!'). Suddenly, there is a commotion. One of the drummers has grabbed a woman wearing a painted beeco from behind, and is thrusting his hips at her, mimicking sexual intercourse. She laughs and plays along while the other women gather to take a closer look. My friend laughs: 'Have you seen the drawings on her beeco? It was too much for him, he couldn't resist!' A few seconds later the game is over, and so is the *tour*. Darkness fell a while ago, and the rooftop is only illuminated by a few street lights. Once the drummers have stopped playing, the women disappear down the stairs as quickly as they arrived, as if in a rush to get home. On the way out, I ask the musicians whether they had been genuinely aroused by the women, or just pretending. One of them smiles and eludes the question, replying that this is their job and that they are used to it.

A scene like this takes place hundreds of times most days in Dakar, though not during Ramadan and Muslim holy days. Here I want to suggest that dance events in their various forms play a central role in the construction of personhood in urban Senegal. Personhood has to do with the shaping of individuals as socially recognized members of the group. Ever since van Gennep's (1960 [1909]) seminal essay on the three-fold structure of rites of passage, personhood has often been studied through the lens of rituals marking the transition of one life stage to the next. But anthropologists have also come to recognize that the making of persons is a continuous process, a social and bodily training that needs to be maintained in everyday practice. There is thus an infinite range of activities that may be said to contribute to the making of persons (Battaglia 1995). Among the Mende of Sierra Leone, Mariane Ferme (2001) thus demonstrates that gendering takes place throughout childhood through a wide range of practices leading up to the actual initiation stage into either Sande (female) or Poro (male) societies. In practice, she says, the social construction of gendered selves is a gradual process 'wherein gender is defined, and contested in principle, by distinct bodily practices, rhythms, and symbolic postures well before this stage' (2001: 219).

In Dakar, dance events are an essential component of the socialization process from the moment children are able to walk confidently. These events are dominated by girls and women, which suggests that they are connected with womanhood in important ways. This is particularly salient in a society in which polygamy remains the norm, and where social relations amongst women are often fiercely competitive. As we have seen in Chapter 1, men used to participate in similarly structured dance events to a greater extent however, which raises questions regarding the recent dominance of women (Castaldi 2006). Males remain important participants during many events, however, as drummers, young boys, professional dancers or distant observers. But their presence is consistently explained away, as if they are not really men in those contexts. Most women, for their part, only perform the dances in their full amplitude until their late twenties to their mid-thirties, depending on their skills and energy. Later in life, those who still dance perform the movements in the more restrained manner that is appropriate for their status as mature women, although they may perform very differently depending on the degree of intimacy of the event.

Beyond the shaping of personhood, urban dances are all the more important to this study as they constitute the movement and sound environment in which Dakarois performers develop their skill. Many dancers say they acquired a passion for dancing during such events, and they continue to participate in them in their respective neighbourhoods. Even more importantly, the sabar genre embodies one of the enduring aspects of personhood as it is widely understood in the region: it is the notion of limited human agency to which I alluded in the introduction. Indeed in sabar, dancing is produced by both the skill and experience of the individual dancer and by external forces seen to be mediated by skilful drumming. As we shall see in later chapters, the individualized techniques of choreographic production that constitute the contemporary dance world represent a radical shift from this notion of distributed agency.

Style and skill in the dance circle

Sabar events take on different names depending on the time of the day and the nature of the occasion. A *tànnibéer*, for example, takes place in the evening (see Figure 3.1), and the dancing is expected to be more sexually suggestive than during an afternoon sabar (Castaldi 2006). I have broadly identified three categories of events during which the genre is commonly performed: weddings (*séetal*) and naming ceremonies (*ngénte*); neighbourhood events and the regular gatherings of women's associations, or female societies; and the rallies organized by political parties or civic associations. The overwhelming majority of women in Dakar belong to at least one, and often several societies of kin, friends, neighbours, or fellow members of a Sufi brotherhood. All the women I knew had been members in a society at some point in their lives, but some had withdrawn when they had moved to a new neighbourhood, fallen on hard times or when they could no longer take the pressure of keeping up with the latest fashions.

The female chapters of Muslim associations (*daa'ira*) do not normally organize dances, but some of their members dance in other contexts. Many societies and *tours* simultaneously serve as rotating credit associations or 'tontines' (*nat*). 'Tontines' are groups constituted on the basis of friendship, age group, residence, kinship or a mix of several of these factors. The groups meet weekly, fortnightly or monthly, and between 2002 and 2010, contributions could be anything from 500 to 50,000 FCFA per participant. Most groups, however, only required modest amounts, usually between 500 and 2,000 FCFA. The upper end of the scale gathered the wealthiest women, often businesswomen in their own right.

Before discussing the making of persons through sabar, a few words must be said about the musical aspect of the genre. Sabar drums are beaten with a hand and a stick, and a complete ensemble includes at least six different drums (Tang 2007). Each ensemble makes up its own combination depending on its favourite drums and the availability of players, who often specialize in a particular drum. A common combination includes the *nder* (usually the leading drum), the *mbëng-mbëng*, the *tungune*, the *lamb* (also known as *cól* and *ndënd*), the *talmbat* (or *gorong talmbat*) and the *gorong yeguel* (or *gorong mbabas*), a recent addition named after the *mbabas* dance (Tang 2007: 35–38). Those drums are divided into two broad categories that produce different kinds of sounds: the closed-bottom drums and the open-bottom ones. The very popular *tama*, the small 'talking drum' strapped over the player's shoulder, is also used intermittently, but according to Patricia Tang (2007), it is a recent addition to the Wolof sabar tradition. Until the fairly recent past, sabar drums served a wide range of purposes, from inter-village communication to warfare, agricultural

Figure 3.1 Three photographs of a tànnibéer in Fann Hock, April 2003. Photographs by the author.

work, Senegalese wrestling and festive events. Importantly, drumming remains a domain of practice tightly controlled by men from géwël families. Tang's (2007) vivid ethnography of sabar in Dakar focuses on the Mbaye family, and the two other main families are the Sing Sing Faye, and the family of internationally renowned Master Drummer, Doudou Ndiaye Rose. Exceptionally in a male-dominated activity, Ndiaye Rose taught his daughters and daughters-in-law to play the sabar. But this remained an exception and their ensemble, *Les Rosettes*, performed during concerts rather than sabar events (Marshall 2001).[10] In practice however, not all drummers are griots, as I alluded to earlier.

Sabar dances are open to infinite variations depending on individual creativity and skill. Nevertheless, many Dakarois distinguish the dances that belong to the older repertoire, such as *ceebu jën*,[11] *Baar Mbaye* or *kaolack*, from those which have been more recently revived or created in the ever-changing fashion of popular dances. In addition, every géwël family has its own distinctive rhythms, or *bàkk*, invented by the most gifted drummers and passed on to the next generations. Some dances and the rhythms they are associated with are known to be particularly suggestive, such as the lëmbël mentioned in the vignette. In the lëmbël, a woman turns her back to the lead drummer, bends the knees and rolls the hips in tune with the beat, increasing the speed when the beat accelerates and breaking the movement when the drumming stops. A good dancer shows her skill by moving in tune with the beat, and also by interrupting the movement with absolute precision in relation to the drumming (Castaldi 2006). By doing this she shows that she is attuned to the ending 'call', and in a perfectly timed conversation with the lead drummer. Other sabar dances are more aerial than the lëmbël, but the principle of interaction between dancing and drumming remains. At first it would seem as if the lead drummer calls the shots. In its best moments, however, the interaction between dancers and musicians follows a thrilling call-and-response pattern.[12] The best dancers challenge the lead drummer to play more complex, faster rhythms. If inspired, he will respond by initiating new challenges for the dancers. A lead drummer I knew compared the sabar to a conversation, adding that if a dancer was good, he simply needed to 'look at her leg to know what she [was] going to do next'. This interaction, which involves much playfulness, is also crystallized in the analogy that exists between speech and drumming: well-known drumming rhythms can be transcribed directly into sabar speech, and vice versa (Castaldi 2006; Tang 2007). An experienced dancer I knew used to express this by saying that 'sabar is like Wolof, and if you don't understand Wolof, you can't dance sabar properly'.

For the drummers, the conversational aspect of performance is crucial. This is what enables the best players to show off their skills, and the thrill of the conversation compels participants to give more money. Even though drumming ensembles are paid a fee before or after events, the money placed in the drummers' clothing during a good performance can add up to significant amounts. Lead drummers are often seen interrupting the session and walking around the circle during an event, shouting out bawdy jokes in Wolof and embarrassing people into giving money by refusing to play until a gift has been made. They will, for example, loudly lament the rise of selfishness and greed in Wolof society. People are more likely to give if the jokes are good, so that the verbal skills of a lead drummer (or alternatively, one of his more experienced apprentices) determine the ensemble's income for a particular event. I have heard lead drummers threaten people to make their private parts 'fly away' if they do not give generously, generating outbursts of laughter and making the cash flow faster. They may also sing people's praise, which requires rewarding, but this works best if they know some of the participants and their family histories.

Sabar and the making of persons

The motif of the circle (*géew*) is fundamental to the performance of sabar, and the preparation of an event is always announced by the presence of a circle of plastic chairs several hours before the event. The circle, sometimes supplemented by an open-sided marquee when people can afford the rental, physically delineates a space that is set apart from everyday social relations. A portion of the street will often be closed off for the occasion, and in some neighbourhoods people are required to pay a small fee to the local police for permission to do so. The drumming ensemble is expected to arrive before the participants, and to set up in a semi-circle at a designated edge of the space. The spatial arrangement and its careful preparation signal that something is being *made* in that space, not just performed in an elusive moment. What takes place, in the géew, is the continuous shaping of urban personhood, and I begin here with the gendering of persons.

Although this has not always been the case, the sabar circle has come to delineate a domain of female control. Men are almost always present as drummers, as spectators watching from windows and rooftops and as occasional participants, but they do not have much agency to shape the event, and their presence is at the whim of women. Young men and boys occasionally come forward to dance in a movement style which parodies the female style, much to the women's laughter. But once women stop laughing and cheering, men are no longer welcome. The men's relative marginality in such contexts is also marked by their dress style: unlike women, they do not dress up in their best attire. Rather, they appear to have dropped in almost by accident, wearing their usual (albeit suitably fashionable) T-shirts, jeans, caps and trainers. Women and girls, meanwhile, will have spent long hours and sometimes significant sums of money getting dressed, made up and their hair done, especially for weddings and naming ceremonies. The géew also excludes strangers, those who do not participate in the event. I have sometimes edged closer to sabar events I had not been invited to, and waited to see what would happen. During big tànnibéers, watched by several circles of spectators this went unnoticed, but in smaller events organized for a wedding or naming ceremony, someone would eventually come forward and ask whether I wished to join in. This was done in the same polite manner as when one inadvertently looks as people eating, and they offer one to share in the meal. One is no more meant to accept sharing a frugal meal than one is meant to stand aimlessly, watching people dance without being part of the circle.

The sexual suggestiveness of some of the dances also delineates a female domain. As I have argued elsewhere (Neveu Kringelbach 2007a), extremely suggestive dancing de facto excludes men from active participation, unless they are young boys under the age of puberty or professional dancers. Adult men who do not belong to a dance group but enjoy dancing in public are always at risk of being classified as effeminate (*goorjigéen,* literally 'man-woman'), which nowadays has become synonymous with 'homosexual'. As a result the dancing style of those who do take part, as professional or aspiring professional dancers, often has the aesthetics of a statement of masculinity. Whilst the basic structure of the steps remains the same, the movement style is more athletic, with wider arm movements, higher jumps and the legs thrown higher up in the air. In her thesis on sabar and Mandinka neo-traditional performance in a small town south of Dakar, Tholon (2009) takes note of this ambiguity between dance and masculinity, and argues that this is the reason why male dancers in sabar events take great pains to demonstrate their athleticism and technical skill. As I also observed in Dakar, she notes that the 'cutting' phase of the dance is often done in a style that suggests a powerful masculine sexuality, with a strong forward thrusting of the hips and grabbing of the crotch, hip-hop style.

Women's dance styles, on the other hand, signal confidence, emotionality, play and sexual innuendo. This is in sharp contrast to the expected modesty of women in most aspects of Senegalese public life, as also noted by Castaldi (2006). It is not that women are absent from politics, business or the arts; indeed a number of women of a certain wealth and status are very powerful in these domains,[13] but even they are expected to show modesty (*sutura*), reserve and deference (*kersa*) towards men as well as women of a higher status. In fact, powerful women and female celebrities often make a point of publicly declaring their modesty and submission to their husbands. This not only highlights the moral status that is gained from such outward compliance with male authority, it also betrays the moral risk powerful women run from being exposed in the public space as strong, independent figures.

This is momentarily reversed in the sabar circle, albeit at different degrees for different categories of individuals. There is little reserve and deference there, and there are echoes of the rituals of inversion studied by anthropologists elsewhere in Africa. In her study of spirit possession in Kel Ewey Tuareg society, Rasmussen (1995) highlights the dominance of women in possession-inducing curing rituals, and argues that the inversion from gendered behaviour in other domains of life serves to explore and shape ideas of Tuareg personhood. Sabar events also provide a space in which urban Wolof notions of personhood can be explored and commented on, in particular in relation to aspects of gender, generation, 'caste' and class. Sabar events thus provide a space in which girls become women, and therefore potential daughters-in-law, sisters-in-law and co-wives. This is also a space in which girls can 'act out' male attributes in a playful way, and boys take on female attitudes framed as parody. Although it is inappropriate for more mature men to take active part, their very absence, their presence as background observers, or even their invisible role as patrons (by subsidising events or being conveniently absent so that the festivities may go on undisturbed) plays into the definition of a respectable and generous masculinity (Heath 1994).

The characteristics of female personhood as it is shaped through sabar events come into sharper focus if one looks as the form participation takes across the different life stages. Ideas of morality, too, become visible through the tensions surrounding notions of appropriateness and inappropriateness in participation. Heath (1994) pointed out quite rightly that sabar dances were framed as a domain of female inappropriateness. However, they are not equally inappropriate for all female individuals in all contexts. It is thus more appropriate for young girls, unmarried women and ñeeño women to dance in public than it is for married, older and géér women.

From around the age of two, young children in Dakar's *quartiers*[14] learn to perform by watching adults, by taking part in the early stages of real events and by practising among themselves. In my corner of the city, most afternoons a group of five to eight children gathered under the shade of a tree and practised. A couple of them used sticks to drum on an empty tin can and a piece of cardboard. Meanwhile the others would draw a circle in the sand, take off their sandals and line them up neatly on the edge of the circular 'dance space' delimited by their bodies. The party was obviously led by the oldest child, always a girl. The children would take turns to step into the circle and dance for a few seconds at a time. It always struck me how well they mimicked the suggestive poses of adults, sometimes from the age of two. In addition to the 'drumming' they would encourage the dancer by clapping their hands in rhythm. The adults nearby did not seem to pay much attention, but the older girls and young women sitting nearby, chatting and braiding hair, would occasionally join in the hand-clapping. The group of men sitting on the other side of the street making *attaya* and playing checkers, on the other hand, did not even seem to register their presence. The leading girl would often decide whose turn it was to dance or who the best dancer was, and this seemed to be the cause of many arguments.

Such miniature versions of a dance circle play a highly formative role. The children obviously learn to accept the authority of those older than themselves, even in a matter in which they are not complete beginners. They learn to perform a repertoire of sabar dances fashionable at a given moment, while also acquiring the movement style characteristic of the genre, with its speed, its aerial flow of energy and its turns. Most importantly, they experiment with the challenging call-and-response interaction between the dancing and the drumming. When taking part in 'real' events, they also learn from the comments they receive from adults. A good sabar dancer attracts attention to herself right from the first steps, she is perfectly attune to the smallest rhythms variations, and she is able to show her individual creativity by innovating within the conventions of the genre: a particularly suggestive and sudden hip movement for the cutting phase, the *danël*, which may even become a person's 'signature' as a dancer; the parody of a fashionable move from a music video; or a well-timed interruption of the movement to let the participants admire a particular pose. Children who display these skills receive considerable praise from the adults, either verbally or through a hand gesture in which people place the thumb and index of the right hand on the dancer's head and turn clockwise once, mimicking the killing of lice on the person's head. In the early childhood years both boys and girls may learn to dance sabar. The drumming part is a bit different since it is children from géwël families who are most likely to learn proper sabar rhythms from family members. Géér children may learn, too, but it is rare that adults encourage them to master the art of drumming.

Afeeru jigéen: from girls to women

Gender differentiation becomes much more marked around puberty. From then on, it is mostly girls who are seen dancing, and what goes on during sabar events is often described as *afeeru jigéen*, 'women's business'. The participation of boys becomes gradually restricted to short episodes with a strong flavour of parody, and to boys from ñeeño families as well as professional or aspiring professional dancers. For adolescent girls, dance events become more obviously linked to the making of good marriage partners. Thus sexual suggestiveness in girls' dancing attracts increasing praise by adult women. Girls and young unmarried women, who belong to the same intermediate stage as social juniors, no longer dance on the edges of the circle but gradually move to the central space. Rather than practising under a tree, they take part in real events. For events organized entirely by girls or young women, anywhere from the age of puberty to the early twenties, preference may be given to hiring a DJ to play mbalax tunes since this is cheaper and provides more opportunities to display the latest moves from music videos. More mature women, by contrast, tend to favour live sabar ensembles if they can afford the expense. This is not only because they create a better space in which to display wealth and prestige, but also because the interaction with the male drummers makes suggestive dancing more exciting. As much as the dancing may be a playful competition amongst women, the presence of male drummers allows for much livelier acting than a DJ hidden behind a sound system.

One of the new skills acquired during those years is a manner of rolling the eyes upwards at the height of a solo performance in the sabar circle, facing the drummers. According to some interpretations this symbolizes sexual swooning (Castaldi 2006). The girls and women whom I have asked, however, have either appeared to do this unconsciously, as an effect of the thrill of the dance, or they have claimed to be rolling their eyes upwards in concentration, as if the dance was making them turn 'inwards'. In either case it is quite likely that the eye movement signals a change in the inner state of the dancer at the height of the sequence, when the interaction with the polyrhythmic drumming is most challenging, but also thrilling. In other words, this may be a socially mediated expression of a fleeting trance-like state. Indeed, the same aesthetic effect of showing the whiteness of the eye is also valued in the Lebu *ndëp*, a therapeutic ritual of possession still used in the treatment of mental illness in the coastal regions. Indeed in both types of events, many women participants insist that certain rhythms take control over their bodies against their will.

This is also the life stage when girls learn to draw confidence from their dancing skills. Drawing on his earlier ethnography of the dances of boys and young men/warriors among the Samburu of Kenya and on texts on the Bori cult among the Hausa in northern Nigeria, Spencer (1996) argued that in both places, skilful dancing served to enhance the confidence of the performers in the importance of their social role. Ultimately, Spencer argued, this generated confidence from the wider society in their physical and spiritual powers. In Dakar, too, skilful dancing during this stage of transition into adulthood helps to build up confidence in forms of female power linked to sexuality, but not easily visible in everyday sociality. Sabar events thus provide a space in which girls can experiment with emergent capacities in socially accepted ways. This may explain the inversion of behaviour from everyday life; instead of showing the restraint (*kersa*) that is expected of them, girls allow themselves to get carried away in intense displays of strength and pleasure. Their speech is louder than usual, the gestures wider, and the body seems 'charged' with unusual flows of energy. This was something I felt strongly whenever I brushed against the bodies of young women I knew during sabar events. Once, at the end of a tànnibéer in Fann Hock, the girls who had been dancing were beginning to disperse in the nearby streets, and some of them were still filled with energy. When two men who had been watching from a distance made provocative comments about their attractiveness, the girls made scary faces and started running after them. It was all done jokingly, but it was no coincidence that this was taking place at the end of a sabar event: the girls were full of confidence, and it was acceptable in this context not to show deference to men.

Among the important skills learned during those years are ways of preparing the body for dance events. As already suggested, this extends well beyond conforming to social expectations, and also has to do with becoming an attractive woman, a sociable friend, and with developing a person's social and physical potentialities more generally. In Wolof-speaking Senegal the idea of beautifying the body as a whole is expressed through the term *sañse*,[15] which encompasses several layers of beautification from the skin to the outer dress. Becoming a social person is very much about learning how to manipulate and dress the body in elaborate ways. The transformation of the body into a symbol of wealth, status and moral standing is especially important in the context of family ceremonies. In other words, the more elaborate the beautification, the more valued the event.

Ahead of important dance events, girls are taught by kinswomen or friends to perfect the beautifying techniques they have been watching since childhood. The body must be washed and scrubbed properly, and moisturized with cream. In Dakar's quartiers, many women then use skin-lightening creams or home-made skin-bleaching mixtures. Skin-lightening is called *xeesal*,[16] and although the popularity of xeesal varies depending on women's social position, the fashion of the moment and the impact of public health campaigns, in Dakar it is said to have been a widespread practice since the 1960s. For many women in Dakar's quartiers, a fair complexion represents a competitive advantage in the seduction game, and a statement of self-mastery: the treatment involves daily discipline in applying cream, as well as resistance to suffering in the many cases when the skin gets badly damaged. Working on the skin is all the more important as sabar events are privileged opportunities to appraise the body. In this predominantly polygamous society,[17] social relations amongst women are marked by solidarity as well as competition: among co-wives, sisters-in-law, and half siblings from the same father, the *doomu baay*. Through ways of fashioning the body, young women learn to compete with their peers, not quite as much for the attention of men as for status in the female world. In the afternoon preceding an important event, those girls and women who can afford it flock to beauty parlours with friends to have their hair re-styled and thick layers of make-up applied, while also exchanging the latest gossips and building up the excitement necessary for a successful event.

The next stage is the inner dress, the mastery of which is perceived to be essential for married women to 'tie'[18] their husbands. Although there is less pressure on girls to appear with perfect inner dress, many of them enjoy the playfulness involved. The most important piece of underwear is the *beeco*, a wrapper of variable length made of light cotton, either plain or with a netting of fashionable patterns. Market vendors give them playful names, referring to female concerns or commemorating a significant event, which helps to ensure a fast turnover of designs. *Mbaal* ('fishing net'), *Coupe du Monde* (in tribute to the national football team during the 2002 World Cup), *Ma yër li nga yore* ('let's see what you're wearing', a song by Coumba Gawlo Seck), *Fatou Laobé* (a Senegalese diva whose songs praise Senegalese women's sexual attractiveness) or *Kayitu yi kër gi* ('the deeds of the house') were some of the designs in fashion in 2002–06.

The beeco is supplemented by several ranges of waist beads (*fer*), and sometimes a thong in a fashionable design. There are changing fashions of waist beads, which are usually worn in rows of five. In the privacy of the house, both underwear and waist beads are carefully suspended over clay pots (*and*) filled with ash and burning cuuraay. The sensuality of this powerful combination of elements resides in the suggestion of something that is present yet always elusive, just a little out of reach, even to those for whom it is intended. Thanks to the 'bathing' of accessories in fragrant incense, the slightest movements of the body gives off fragrant wafts, and during dancing the presence of the waist beads is suggested by discreet click-click sounds. To produce maximum effect, the inner dress must be revealed gradually as a dance event progresses towards its climax, in a sequence which mirrors the sexual act. Thus girls become initiated to the manipulation of the senses that is important in sexuality, even though this may not be articulated so blatantly. Mastery in the art of underwear in Dakar is said to give the wearer a great deal of power over men. However, it is in essence very difficult to know how this becomes actualized in practice, and as far as I could make out, the art of underwear is really about competing with peers while also showing compliance with socially valued norms of femininity which emphasize women's dedication to their husbands.

Finally, the outer outfit, which may be a mbubb, a taille basse or a camisole with a wrap-around skirt (*sér*), must be carefully designed to make a striking impression. Whereas in the 1950s and 1960s, any young woman who could afford it would wear a European-style dress to go to a dance, the 1970s and 1980s saw a revival of the Senegalese styles.[19] Status has now become symbolized by heavily embroidered damask cloths and in the matching headscarves, jewellery, bags and locally made shoes. Dress in the sabar genre thus seems to embody a dialectic relationship between a young woman's individuality (as expressed through innovation and competitiveness) and her identity as a social being. It is not surprising, therefore, that the keenest participants at sabar events are girls and young women in this phase of transition into womanhood. But this phase is also perceived as vulnerable for particularly skilled dancers, as we have seen in the previous chapter.

On the other hand, this is a life stage during which young people of both sexes are free to act out the attitudes of the other sex during sabar events. Girls do act out male attitudes in ways completely inappropriate in other contexts, and boys are allowed into the circle to a much wider extent than later in life. This, I suggest, points to sabar events as a space in which persons become gendered, not only through differentiation but also through experimenting with the potentialities of the other sex.

Perfecting the art of suggestion: married women dancing

Many married women I have known in Dakar felt caught in a dilemma: on the one hand, they were expected to show more restraint than they did before marriage, and on the other hand, they felt compelled to show that they had achieved a confident femininity. Looked at it this way, sabar events held in fairly closed-off quarters delineate a social space with sufficient freedom to attempt to resolve this tension in a playful manner.

There is no major difference between the dancing style of married women and that of unmarried ones or girls. However, since it becomes more important to show mastery than youthful energy, the same risqué moves tend to diminish in amplitude. Dances like the lëmbël are ideal because when performed to a slow beat and with skill, they are far more suggestive than the more athletic styles in the sabar repertoire. Adult women who have retained a taste for dancing – this is not always the case – continue to experiment with innovative gestures that will mark their individuality and make their friends laugh. At a wedding sabar I attended, one of the women performed a slow-moving lëmbël during which her legs, knees bent, performed a rotating movement which opened her wrap-around skirt to reveal, not only her beeco, but also her waist beads. She was facing seated friends, and her slow hip movement revealed a bracelet dangling from her waist beads, just below the navel. As she danced, the bracelet made circular movements in tune with her hips. As if to make the trick even more explicit, she placed her hand in front of the bracelet and followed its rotating movement with an index finger stretched forward, causing an outburst of laughter among her friends. It is no coincidence that this was performed at the edge of the circle since it is often there that the most daring moves are performed. Thus on different occasions, I have seen mature women stand at the edge and lift their skirts and boast to their friends about the size of their inner 'assets'.

The climax of a married women's tour often involves revealing elaborately decorated beecos. Rather than the standard designs hanging from market stalls, the married women I knew preferred more individualized designs that carried stronger statements about the wearer. Those who could afford it bought tailor-made, crocheted beecos, decorated with beads for up to five times the price of the standard items. When one of my friends bought one for me, I realized that these crocheted nets were as visually striking as they were uncomfortable when seated. This revealed the fleeting use of underwear items designed to be worn for dance events rather than for everyday wear. Beecos featuring painted or embroidered erotic drawings can be made to order or purchased 'behind the counter' from market vendors, who try to outdo each other in the bawdiness of the inscriptions. These range from fairly mild ones such as *saf na* ('it's spicy'), 'love' (in English) or 'chéri je t'aime – je t'adore – je ne veux que toi' ('darling I love you, I adore you, you are the only one) to much more explicit sexual interjections in Wolof.[20]

In addition to the display of a confident femininity, dance in urban events embodies a relationship between organizers and participants. It is a form of exchange in which the organizers spend time and money bringing people together, and participants dance to acknowledge this. The more people dance at someone's event, the higher the organizer's status is likely to be in the neighbourhood. As a result, young women who are not very popular with their peers may hesitate to organize events for fear of the embarrassment that will follow if people fail to turn up, or remain defiantly seated. Not being 'danced for' both reflects and brings about social exclusion. This is especially important in the case of family ceremonies because they are very much *about* relations of exchange also expressed in the circulation of cloth, money and words via the oratory skills of griottes.[21]

The tension between the lack of restraint displayed by participants in sabar events and the importance of preserving a good reputation is one that is never completely resolved. This comes across in the reluctance with which most Dakarois speak of their experience of dancing. When I asked women I knew whether they danced during such events, the responses varied depending on their status, their age and on who was listening, but as I will illustrate, this was rarely a straightforward issue. In the presence of men, well-off married women often denied taking part altogether. Some married women over the age of thirty-five to forty confessed to have had fun dancing when they were younger, but insisted that they had become too old to dance in public, and that they would feel ashamed (*rus*) if they did. To illustrate this particular point, historian, Ibrahima Thioub (personal communication, Dakar, 2002), told me about his aunt, who 'loved to dance but couldn't allow herself to do so, because of her rank'. Thus during family gatherings 'you could always tell that she was there, from the tapping of her feet underneath the table', he explained.

There are festive moments when it is appropriate for mature and older women to perform certain styles, such as the *ndawrabin* mentioned in Chapter 2. On the whole, however, open dance events are problematic for women from their early forties onwards. Yet it does happen that mature women abandon themselves to the pleasure of dancing, which is probably in continuity with such therapeutic practices as the ndëp ritual. Though doing a few steps jokingly is usually taken as a sign of appreciation of the event, going on for too long, or too vigorously, becomes inappropriate with age. Thus an older woman in my neighbourhood used to get carried away in the dance during sabar events. She always wore the same outfit of pink damask cloth, which was taken as a sign that she could not afford new outfits or did not have close friends from whom she could have borrowed outfits for the dances. People used to comment on her participation by saying that she was mad, and she was always elbowed out towards the edge of the circle after a couple of stints at the centre.

Participation in sabar events could put the reputations of younger women at risk, too, and many were reluctant to talk about it in front of men. During a group interview I conducted in Pikine with five men and two (unmarried) young women, one of them, soon to be married to one of the young men present, insisted that she did not know how to dance. As she said this she shifted uncomfortably on her chair, smiled a little and did not elaborate further. Yet when I later asked what a particular dance looked like, she spontaneously got up and demonstrated the moves perfectly.

In middle-class neighbourhoods, sabar events are much less frequent than in Dakar's more crowded quartiers because family heads there do not wish to host them. There is, therefore, an unspoken class dimension to sabar which partly overlaps with 'caste' hierarchies, even though private sabar parties with a hefty entrance fee are sometimes held in some of the new, affluent neighbourhoods like Les Almadies. Several of my women friends from middle-class backgrounds insisted that they were very poor dancers because there had been few sabar events in their part of the city as they were growing up. One of them recalled that girls from her neighbourhood would go over to some of the poorer quarters to dance so as not to be seen by senior family members. Her own lack of dancing skills was a matter of pride since this confirmed her social standing, and on the few occasions when I saw her dance at events, she cultivated this by inventing ridiculous steps and exaggerating her own clumsiness. On a different occasion, she laughed heartily at the memory of a sabar event organized in her affluent neighbourhood by Ndèye Khady Niang, a well-known former dancer who passed away in August 2010. She remembered how the dancer had lifted her skirt to reveal her elaborately decorated intimacy. 'The kids in my neighbourhood threw stones at her, she couldn't believe it! She was crying afterwards, she had to flee in a taxi', my friend recalled. Whether or not this actually happened, the memory was revealing for the pride my friend took in juxtaposing her own lack of dancing skills with the cold reception Ndèye Khady received in her neighbourhood. Sabar dancing of this kind had no place there; even children knew this.

So far I have mainly discussed female participation in the sabar genre, and yet I also alluded to the fact that there are often men present. How may one explain the contradiction between the Dakarois qualification of sabar events as 'women's business' and the ubiquitous presence of men?

Invisible men and intermediary categories

I want to suggest here that in Dakar, male agency plays a mediating role in the construction of female personhood through dance. Indeed men, or male attributes, are an integral component of sabar events even when absent. Thus men may serve as sponsors for female relatives, but they also participate directly as drummers, and occasionally as dancers or discreet observers.

Sponsoring female relatives can be achieved in many different ways. In the cases I have seen, this was done by contributing financially to family *tours*, but without taking part in the gatherings. Thus one *tour* I knew of had three men out of a membership of forty-one, and the men paid their contributions but did not attend the meetings. Women members explained to me that the men would be ashamed to take part in the dancing or to be seen to watch. Drummers and professional dancers, by contrast, are often present in the géew, but their presence is brushed off as accidental or insignificant. Men who had caught glimpses of *tours* in their own households said that they just happened to be there and were not supposed to know what was going on: 'even when we [men] are around, we have to pretend we don't see anything,' one of them said. On the presence of male musicians, comments such as 'they are just musicians' were commonplace, as if this disqualified them from being real men. The fact that these men may play an active role in acting out responses to women's suggestive dancing was rarely acknowledged verbally.

Anthropological studies of personhood in the region may help to understand this apparent paradox. Mariane Ferme's (2001: 79) work in Sierra Leone, for example, highlights the importance of intermediary categories in Mende understandings of the person. One of these, the *mabole*, is a category of women who undergo some aspects of both female and male initiation rituals, and are allowed to take part in both women's and men's activities. Whilst 'visibly woman but in many ways male', the mabole is barred from the most important and dangerous moments in other women's lives, such as childbirth. The capacity of the mabole to play a role in both the female and the male world stems from the very incompleteness of her gendering, yet this also associates her with powers to be feared by virtue of their ambiguity. Ferme argues convincingly that what she calls 'figures of mediation' are essential in the preservation of social order amidst change. For her, their presence embodies domains of ambiguity in communal life which are purposefully left unresolved because they help to work out conflicts and tensions. The 'figuration of mediated space', Ferme (2001: 221) suggests, 'allows social actors to perceive conflicts as ways to establish new forms of sociality'. In an analogous manner, male participants in sabar events all belong to intermediary social categories: drummers and professional dancers are classified as ñeeño in this context, and children are not yet fully formed persons. If this works as what Ferme describes, the new sociality produced by the 'mediated space' of the dance event remains to be explored further. Given what we have seen thus far, it would not be too far-fetched to suggest that this points to the reconfiguration of female personhood in Dakar. This may go a long way to explain why men who are not professional performers, and thus are not classified into one of the 'mediating' categories, have become nearly invisible in sabar events.

It is also significant that women's dances have come under increasing scrutiny as the repository of urban morality precisely at a time of intense uncertainty about the future. This may well have something do with the socioeconomic power that women construct through the dance events and societies from which men are largely excluded. Women are thus able to retain control of such important aspects of life as marriage negotiations and the use of their own money (Neveu Kringelbach 2007a).[22] Thus the novelty may not reside so much in women's economic autonomy as in men's reaction to it. I want to suggest that perhaps an increasing number of Senegalese men experience this autonomy as a threat to their masculinity. In my view, this explains why women's suggestive dances are readily accused of being responsible for the 'moral decline' of society, as I return to in the next chapter. The 'crisis of masculinity', as it has been called in Africanist scholarship, is vividly expressed in popular cultural forms such as songs. In Senegal, the géwël genre allows for metaphors to be interpreted as praise or as lament depending on the context, and is characterized by a malleability that is akin to the Yoruba oríkì genre brilliantly analysed by Karin Barber (1991). Women singers, therefore, are able to critique the current tensions in gender relations without openly holding anyone to account for them. There are many instances of this in Senegalese pop music, and I have chosen the 1991 song *Boroom Kër*[23] by Kiné Lam, a diva with the National Lyrical Ensemble in the 1970s and 1980s who also enjoyed a solo career:

Boroom kër[24]

Boroom kër ya kaaru mbar mi	*Boroom kër* you are the hut's saviour
Bul gawa sa ngëm	Do not lose faith
Yàlla boo gawa sa ngëm boroom kër	May God prevent you from losing faith, *boroom kër*
Bul gawa sa ngëm	Do not lose faith
Gungel ma njaboot gi, boroom kër	Guide the family for me, *boroom kër*
Boroom kër xool naa la xool yërëm la	*Boroom kër* I have looked at you and I feel sorry for you
Ma dellu ko xool yërëm ko	Again I looked and felt sorry for him
Boroom kër ya kaaru mbar mi	*Boroom kër* you are the hut's saviour
Soo joge si mbar, mbar mi rës	If you leave it, it will fall apart
Fajar fekk na nga jóg	Before dawn you are up
Lan lay yobbu jafe loolu	Transportation is difficult
Booy dem dangay lang ak axëlu	When you leave, you hang on to the back [of the mini-bus, to avoid paying] and you think
[. . .]	
Lu ca root dal nga yobbu sa njaboot	You bring the fruit of your labour back to your family
Takk sa biir bi xiif ak mar	You deprive yourself of food and water
Waw waw ngir sa njaboot	Yes, all this for your family
Waw waw ngir sa njaboot	Yes, all this for your family
Soo waccee ba togg	As soon as you come home from work and sit down
Xale yi wër la dal	The children begin to surround you
Situut soxna sa nuyoo	Your wife immediately comes to greet you
Waw waw yori kayit	Yes, she is holding papers
Nga xamnee lep ga ak ndox ma	You guess that these are the debts and the water [bill]
Moo ko tax di wax	That is what she came to talk about

Situut Diallo nuyoo taxaw feyyu	Diallo[25] immediately drops by to ask for his money
Ñun jigéen ñi nañu bàyyi feyyu bor guddi	We women must stop talking about debts at night
Ñu bàyyi xuloo guddi	We must stop quarrelling at night
Baaxul ci boroom kër	It is no good for the *boroom kër*
Yalna yàlla waccee xéewal yu bare	May God bring prosperity [on the family]
Bul gawa sa ngëm	Do not lose faith
Yàlla boo gawa sa ngëm boroom kër	May God prevent you from losing faith, *boroom kër*
Yalna doom yi baax ba fey la	May God protect your children so that they can repay you
Bul gawa sa ngëm boroom kër	Do not lose faith, *boroom kër*
Yalna yàlla waccee sa boroom kër	May God free you from everything, *boroom kër*

(Kiné Lam 1991, translated from Wolof with the kind help of Nafy Guèye)

On the face of it, the song is a tribute to the modern household head as a man who soldiers on to support his family, even in dire economic circumstances, with little stable employment available. The tone is one of compassion, which has a positive connotation in the Wolof context since it suggests that the pain is shared among social equals. But the praise is also ambiguous because it contains hints that the household head has lost some of his authority alongside his capacity to act as a breadwinner. The word *mbar* used to designate the home refers to a light and unstable construction, perhaps an artisan's workshop. The dominant image is not that of an uncontested figure of authority, but rather that of the *goor goorlu*,[26] the city-dweller who struggles daily to bring cash home, at the constant risk of being shunned by his family if he does not succeed.

Conclusion

In Dakar, sabar dance events play a crucial role in the gendering of persons, which is facilitated by the skilful drumming of gëwël. Drumming, here, possesses the same transforming force as the skills of craftsmen, and it is no coincidence that both drummers and craftsmen are associated with the ñeeño category. It may seem, at first sight, as if sabar is exclusively linked to the gendering of female persons. However, I want to suggest that it is linked to male personhood as well, but through gradual invisibility rather than sustained participation. Indeed many young boys learn to dance and take part in sabar events, when they are not yet fully gendered. After puberty, emergent male personhood is signalled in part by a gradual avoidance of dance events. Things change, however, and in the 2000s it has become fashionable for young male professional dancers to display their skills as well as their popularity in their neighbourhood by organizing sabar events of their own. These are mainly 'open' tànnibéer, rather than the more private *tours* that remain dominated by women. The recent popularity of events organized by well-known male dancers, often trained through the circuit of

TV dance competitions, probably accounts for some of this masculinization of sabar. But there may be further, mutually compatible interpretations. Given that most of these dancers are school-leavers with few prospects of formal employment, carving a renewed space for young men within the modern sabar genre may well be an attempt to appropriate some of the ambiguous power associated with skilled performance that was introduced in Chapter 2. In a more practical sense, this may also signal a desire to prolong the in-between stage of youth, as we will see in the next chapter.

The circular motif of sabar events also points to the social significance of the genre. Circles of dancers with musicians in the middle are a widespread structure throughout Africa (James 2000), and although its significance differs from one region to the next, the structured circle always marks the social importance of what takes place within. In sabar, I suggest that the circle symbolizes the interplay between individual agency and the extrasocial domain, between the male and the female, and between the inside and the outside of the body. The interplay between the individual and the extrasocial, or forces beyond human control, is epitomized in the perception (reflected in the introductory vignette) that the small 'talking drum', the *tama*, has the power to override women's concern with their social position and forget all decency in dancing. In a common Senegalese trope, some Muslim leaders even talk about the tama as a manifestation of the devil (*seytaan*). The play with the boundaries between the inside and the outside of the body is captured in the playful use of inner and outer outfits in the dance, and in the excitement about the intimacy that is being displayed at the edges of the géew. By codifying the tension between individual autonomy and social norms, the sabar genre thus fuses older notions of morality widespread in the region, characterized by a constant negotiation between what is given and what is being made (Jackson 1989), with an urban, modern aesthetic. I suggest, therefore, that sabar embodies the constant tension between social norms and individuality that is an enduring aspect of human life.

Finally, the pleasure participants take in the sabar genre points to the fact that social conventions would not make much sense if people did not find elements of playful sociality in them. Beyond the anthropological concern with patterns, norms and categories, it would be missing the point to forget that one of the main reasons why the genre is successful is because it provides a space in which people have fun together across generations and social categories. It is easy to see how this might be especially valued in times of uncertainty.

Notes

1. This is inspired by the film on contemporary dance in Africa *Drums, Sand and Shostakovitch* by Ken Glazebrook and Alla Kovgan (2002).
2. *Tours* are gatherings, usually involving dancing, organized on a regular basis by female societies of various kinds. The French word 'tour' refers to the fact that this is a fixed-membership group in which members take turns to organize the festivities.
3. A 'taille basse' (*taay bas*) is an outfit including a long skirt (fitted or wrap-around), a tight-fitted top with sleeves and a head scarf (*musoor*). The style was inspired by European dress and made its appearance in the 1930s (Rabine 2002), so more recently than the *mbubb*.

4. *Cuuraay* is a form of fragrant incense made of crushed seeds or woods, blended with perfume extracts.
5. For vivid images of sabar dancing in Dakar, see the short documentary made by Dutch anthropology graduate Sophie Schouwenaar (2007), *Sabar Dancing in Senegal.*
6. In 2004 this was approximately £1.50. As a yardstick, the price of a minibus ticket then was 50 FCFA, a kilo of ordinary imported rice cost 150 – 200 FCFA and a single room in Fass could be rented for 20 – 30,000 FCFA per month. This sort of contribution meant that this was a fairly middle-class association, hence the live drumming.
7. The *Lawbe* are an endogamous category of woodworkers, mainly Pulaar-speaking. Lawbe women are widely stereotyped as the best market vendors of waist beads, Senegalese underwear, incense and potency enhancers. Though there is no evidence that the more suggestive sabar dances, such as the *lëmbël*, were invented by the Lawbe, their reputation for sexual expertise reinforces this perception. Some of the market vendors encourage this as a marketing tool for their artefacts.
8. Mbalax can be described as a popular music offshoot of the more traditional sabar.
9. Sotiba, located in the outskirts of Dakar, is the biggest textile manufacturer in Senegal.
10. See the documentary film, *Djabote: Senegalese Drumming and Song from Master Drummer Doudou N'Diaye Rose* by Béatrice Soulé and Eric Millot (1993).
11. Some of my informants, in their mid-forties in 2003, reported that the *ceebu jën* had not changed since their childhood. Acogny (1994 [1980]) mentions that it was already known in 1928. The ceebu jën rhythm, which is fast and physically demanding for the dancers, is sometimes executed with sticks beaten on a metallic dish turned upside-down.
12. See Penna-Diaw (2005) and Tholon (2009) for descriptions of the different phases in sabar dancing.
13. These women are called *diriyànke* in Wolof. They are stereotyped as voluptuous women who live affluent lives, are independent entrepreneurs in their own right and take great care of their appearance. Historian, Ousseynou Faye (2000: 420–421), who traces the word back to the arrival of American soldiers in Dakar during the Second World War (*diri yankee* might have meant 'to bring a G.I. home to tame him'), describes the figure of the diriyànke as a social 'mirror of fantasies' with whom moral norms can be perverted so that they can be better defended afterwards. At any rate their moral standing is perceived as highly ambiguous. This may explain why they often make a point of being married women, even though they often lead autonomous lives and enjoy travelling for business purposes.
14. The French word 'quartier', or neighbourhood, is not as widely used in Dakar as the plural form, 'quartiers', which designates the densely populated, generally poorer neighbourhoods than the Plateau (the central administrative and business district) or the more affluent residential areas like Fann Résidence, Mermoz, Point E or the recently built villas of Almadies.
15. See Heath (1992) and Mustafa (2002) for illuminating discussions on the Wolof notion of *sañse*, etymologically from the French 'se changer'.
16. The term derives from *xees* in Wolof, 'to have a fair skin'.
17. Around the year 2000, forty per cent of Dakarois women were found to have lived in a polygamous union by the age of forty (Adjamagbo, Antoine, and Dial 2004). The 2002 census puts the proportion of polygamous marriages in Dakar at 26.3 per cent of all marriages, lower than the national average of 38.1 per cent. The ANSD interprets this as a consequence of a higher cost of living in Dakar rather than resistance to polygamy (ANSD 2006).

18. The Wolof term *takk* means both 'to marry' and 'to tie', as well as referring to the secret practices some women resort to in order to ensure exclusivity in their husband's attachment.
19. The dress styles of young Dakarois women in the 1950s and 1960s are vividly described in Nafissatou Diallo's (1975) memoirs. Rabine (2002) argues that the re-emergence of Senegalese dress styles in the 1970s and 1980s is linked to the decline of jobs in the formal sector and the concomitant emergence of a skilled profession of tailors for whom embroidered Senegalese outfits provide better opportunities for individual creativity than European-style clothes.
20. Fall's (1998) richly illustrated book on the art of seduction in Senegal includes images of this underwear fashion.
21. For detailed descriptions of these exchanges, see Diop (1985) and Buggenhagen (2004). On women's songs, see McNee (2000).
22. In Senegambia, it has long been customary for married women to keep their own income or the money given by their relatives for ceremonial expenses and clothing. Household heads (ideally men, but this not always the case in practice) are expected to provide for the family's daily expenses of food, health and children's education.
23. *Boroom kër* literally means 'master of the household'. The term has a strong male connotation.
24. I am grateful to Ousseynou Faye for useful comments on the interpretation of this song.
25. Diallo is the generic name given to small shop owners, who are (often wrongly) assumed to be Pulaar-speakers from Guinea.
26. The figure of the *goor goorlu* is captured very colourfully in a cartoon by Alphonse Mendy, alias T.T. Fons. The cartoon was adapted into a very popular TV series in 2002 by director Moussa Sène Absa.

Chapter 4

Images of a Mobile Youth

In this chapter I focus on Senegalese popular dances in the age of mass media and digital technologies as a lens through which social tensions around morality can be illuminated. The dances I examine here are mainly the popular music offshoots of sabar, the *mbalax* repertoire. As the sabar tradition becomes transformed into new modes of youth sociality and commodified for public consumption, so the moral stakes of the popular dances that emerge in the process rise to a new level. When images of dancing circulate throughout Senegal and the diaspora via TV channels, the internet and mobile phones, it is no longer possible for women and youths to attribute dancing that 'spills over' to an agency beyond their control. The daring moves and outfits of young popular dance aficionados are increasingly fingered as being both a mirror and the cause of urban society's moral decline. Yet at the same time, the most successful dancers enjoy all the addictive benefits of stardom: huge followings of loving fans, money, status, and travelling opportunities. As a result, they constantly walk a thin line between social marginalization and success: whereas they may be shunned on moral grounds, they also project the image of rapid success that captures the imagination of many young Dakarois. But men and women performers' reputations are fragile in different ways, and to illustrate this, I touch briefly on two male genres of performance: wrestling dances and the dances involved in the 'lion game' (*simb*).

The choreographic forms in this chapter also contribute to the formation of an urban sense of belonging connected to the neighbourhood, among those both present and absent (i.e., former neighbourhood residents living abroad). Neighbourhood-based identities have been in the making in Dakar for many decades, of course, and were probably strengthened in the wake of the economic decline of the 1980s. Mamadou Diouf (1992, 2002) has written eloquently on the youth movements of the 1980s in Dakar, such as the *Set Setal*,[1] as an expression of an alternative to the nationalist memory of Sédar Senghor and Abdou Diouf's post-independence regimes. For him, student strikes, the Set Setal and the rise of mbalax were all ways in which young city dwellers used their bodies to create their own version of history, and new forms of belonging in the process. This echoes Barber's (1997) point that popular culture has the capacity to call into being new identities and new collectivities. Here I suggest that popular dances are part of a social world in which the youth explore the possibilities afforded by the city and its media, against the background of economic hardship discussed earlier.

In sketching the recent history of popular music in the first part of this chapter, I suggest that the appropriation of dance crazes by the political elite demonstrates the power of these cultural forms to inflect the moral domain. I also show that the rise of the music video has brought the visual and choreographic aspects of musical experience to the fore. Next, TV dance competitions are introduced as projecting images of youth success and crystallizing wider social anxieties about changing moralities. Wrestling games and simb ('lion game') performance are given specific attention as the locus of masculine self-fashioning in the city. Taken together, competitive dancing, wrestling and simb, I suggest, could be described as a dance which locks the aspiring youth and the elites together: the latter attempts to harness youthful energies to serve its own agendas and maintain social order, while the urban youth attempts to appropriate the spectacle of its talent to achieve social recognition and mobility faster than ever. Finally, I suggest that dancing, as a livelihood, is problematic from a moral and religious perspective.

From cosmopolitan dance crazes to Wolof mbalax

To understand where the current popular dances are coming from, we must begin by looking back to the history of popular music and dance in Senegal. Just like the theatrical forms in Chapter 1, twentieth-century popular music in Senegal has been produced by engagement with musical styles from other parts of the world. A determining moment was the Second World War, during which tens of thousands of young men from across West Africa were recruited and sent to North Africa, East Africa, Europe and Asia to fight alongside the allied forces. The recruitment of the 'Senegalese riflemen' (*tirailleurs sénégalais*), as they were called, was administered from Senegal, and this is where many of them were sent back. Their return, alongside the presence of American soldiers in 1945, turned Senegal into one of the most cosmopolitan music scenes in West Africa. Between 1945 and the late 1970s people listened to jazz (Benga 2002) and danced to jive, Cuban rhythms in their Cuban and Senegalese versions (Shain 2002, 2009). Ballroom dances and swing were very popular in Dakar and Saint-Louis in the 1950s (Diallo 1975). Informants who were born in the 1960s spoke of how their parents would sometimes dance the twist during neighbourhood dance events very similar to contemporary sabar festivities. There were also students and other *évolués*[2] returning from Europe for the holidays with record players, spreading dance crazes as far as rural Casamance. In the 1950s and 1960s in Casamance, Foucher (2002: 112) evokes the school holiday atmosphere in which young migrants returning from Dakar would demonstrate their modernity by partying to the sound of modern music:

Ballroom-dancing was the other activity which saw a particularly rapid development in rural Lower Casamance. In all villages, the youth would provide for a cemented floor and a record-player with the latest songs. Ballroom-dancing had the educated young men in suits meet with the young maids in European dresses, demonstrating their new urbanity in a way quite different from traditional dances, which set genders apart.

As we will see in later chapters, this moment was significant in the re-shuffling of age hierarchies throughout the region. Interestingly, this echoes Sarró's (2009) analysis of youth dances on the Upper Guinea Coast in the 1950s, when young people of both sexes defied the authority of the elders by imposing mixed-gendered dance parties.

Then a shift took place in the urban music scene in Senegal in the early 1980s: it became more consciously nationalistic, and at the same time the music produced became more of a global commodity. This probably related to the political and economic shift sketched in Chapter 2, and it was during that period that mbalax really took off. During this transition period from a pan-African outlook to a re-centring on national interests, those cultural forms that promoted Wolof culture were favoured. Abdou Diouf's regime was indeed keen to accelerate the 'Wolofization'[3] process underway since the 1960s, and as the iconic form of popular culture in Senegal, music was the perfect medium to lead the movement. Castaldi (2006) rightly points out that the overwhelming success of sabar and mbalax not only reflects, but also contributes to this on-going process. Indeed mbalax has come to dominate the pop music industry in Senegal, and the fact that it is sung almost exclusively in Wolof both reflects and shapes the pervasive image of Wolof culture as the core of the nation. Simultaneously, in the 1980s mbalax was one of the first genres to circulate globally as part of the newly created World Music market.

Mbalax is one of the rhythms in the sabar repertoire, and singer Youssou Ndour appropriated the name for the genre he helped to develop in the 1970s and 1980s. He and his band, Super Etoile, mixed sabar rhythms played on sabar drums with Western instruments (electric guitars, wind instruments and keyboards) and rhythms drawn from Funk, Cuban and Reggae styles. The styles Ndour has drawn on have changed over time, reflecting his own interests as well as the trends of the moment: Cuban rhythms and funk in the 1970s, Egyptian music in the early 2000s. But in the 1980s Ndour and Super Etoile focused consciously on the sabar tradition. As quoted in Duran (1989: 277), Ndour said: 'I took the word mbalax because it's a beautiful and original word, it's a purely Wolof word and I wanted to show that I had the courage to play purely Senegalese music.'

Like sabar, mbalax is based on polyrhythms that interact with each other in codified ways, with an increase in tempo over the course of a piece. This makes it difficult for untrained ears to dance to it, and reinforces the genre's nationalistic flavour. Youssou Ndour, therefore, produces different versions of his albums for home and for the global market. From the outset, then, the success of mbalax was based on the musicians' capacity to adapt the genre to seduce the Senegalese youth as well as African music-lovers abroad.

Mbalax is performed during tours, weddings, naming ceremonies and youth neighbourhood parties (*furël* or *xumbël*), when a DJ is paid to come with his equipment and blast out the latest tunes. The music reaches far into the neighbourhood, much in the same way as religious chanting and drumming that is played over loudspeakers during the Thursday evening meetings of the local Sufi chapters, the dahiras. For the organizers of festive events, this is one of the ways in which statements of belonging and social prestige are made: one momentarily 'takes over' the neighbourhood's sounds. Mbalax also dominated the night-club scene during my main period of fieldwork in 2002–04, along with Cape Verdean zouk (also called *cabo love*), hip-hop and Anglo-American R&B. But the most important vehicle through which mbalax circulates is the hundreds of music videos produced every year, mostly with very small budgets. Virtually all mbalax videos feature four to ten dancers performing the latest fashionable styles. They are mostly young, in their teens or early twenties, with increasingly lean body shapes.[4] Boys and girls perform different moves, and whereas boys are always clad in European outfits (T-shirt, jeans or loose cotton trousers, sneakers and a cap, or European-style suits), the girls' dress styles mirror the urban tension between 'modern' and 'traditional' girls: they are either dressed in cool urban clothes (tight-fitting tops and trousers, all sewn locally) or in short mbubb with a wrapper and beeco showing underneath as they dance.

From a choreographic perspective, mbalax resembles sabar, but with a faster turnover of simple innovations produced by the singers or their dancers. The emergence of the music video in the 1990s has indeed given dancers a more prominent role than they had when mbalax was either performed in live concerts or listened to on the radio and on cassette players. In the 1970s and 1980s musicians like Youssou Ndour and Thione Seck had dancers on stage with them, but they were few and often remained loyal to their band leader for years. It was the development of videomaking and later digital technology that made it possible to make music videos with a small budget, thus creating professional opportunities for the thousands of young dancers who practised in their neighbourhoods every year. The videos also enabled musicians to market their cassettes, and later CDs, more aggressively: a new hit came with a new dance, and therefore the tune itself did not have to sound much different from previous ones. As long as there was a cool dance to go with it, it would sell. In the 1990s and early 2000s therefore, much innovation in mbalax has been primarily of a choreographic kind.[5] New dances are usually simple enough that people can master them in a matter of weeks before a new dance comes along. It is now the carousel of dance fashions that is the mbalax industry's most effective marketing tool. Innovation, meanwhile, happens in other musical styles, such as hip-hop.

The language of mbalax forms an important part of its appeal, and musicians compete to come up with dance names expressing ironical commentaries on people's everyday concerns. In 2002–03, city dwellers vibrated to the sound of Coumba Gawlo Seck's *joggati* ('go on stamping'), the *jalgáti* ('to bend the rules', 'to cheat'), Papa Ndiaye Géwel's *raas* ('to pick' or 'to hunt'), Pape Thiopet's *bu ko racati* ('don't spill it') and Ndongo Lô's *tarkhiss* ('stumbling over'). Aware of the power of music and dance to shape consciousness (Barber 1987), politicians often attempt to appropriate these styles to establish their legitimacy. Askew (2002) and Edmonson (2007) have both shown, for example, how the Tanzanian ruling party, CCM (*Chama cha Mapinduzi*, or Party of the Revolution in Swahili) had successfully appropriated Tanzania's most popular music styles through the patronage of devoted performing troupes. Similarly, Abdoulaye Wade and his PDS did their best to appropriate the jalgáti to boost their image as the party of the people. In 2002, the state-owned TV channel, RTS, conspicuously promoted it as the national dance in support of the 'Lions' during the unprecedented performance of the national football team at the World Cup. The team made it as far as the quarter finals, and football, dance and music blurred into a flamboyant national celebration, matched only by the festivities that had followed the change of regime two years earlier. There was football and dancing everywhere: in front of the TV in Dakarois homes, among groups of children in the streets, on the pitch as the players performed the jalgáti after every goal. Even the city's marketplaces seemed to vibrate to the sound of the jalgáti: makeshift stages were set up to advertise soap, milk powder or stock cubes by way of jalgáti dance competitions for children. The association between football, dance and victory was not lost on the PDS, which promoted both the jalgáti and the national team as embodying 'Senegal that wins' (*Le Sénégal qui gagne*). Speaking to the celebrating crowd in front of the presidential palace, Abdoulaye Wade showed his skills as a populist leader when he reminded the Senegalese that the football victories were the result of hard work, a virtue he had always preached.[6] Although the enthusiasm was short-lived, in that moment many believed him, and danced away while imagining a new world order with Senegal among the dominant nations. Youths shouting mantras like 'Europe is finished, now it's Africa's turn!' could be heard in all corners of the city. Never had the sense of national unity seemed as strong as during those weeks, when the colours of the Senegalese flag were painted on every surface from walls to live sheep, and the inside of every *car rapide* was covered with portraits of the players.

That the Wolof word, *jalgáti*, referred to cheating, by-passing the established rules, seemed only to reinforce the frisson of the moment. It also paid tribute to trickster figures, among whom football players featured prominently: rather than the straightforward outcome of hard work and skill, their victory was seen as also involving the occult power of their marabouts, who had undoubtedly 'worked' on the team beforehand. When the Senegalese team lost out to Turkey in the quarter finals, many disappointed fans concluded that the Turkish team must have benefited from better protection from *their* marabouts. It was only later that questions about the physical condition of the players were raised. President Wade was playing on the same register when repeating his work mantra 'Il faut travailler, toujours travailler, et encore travailler!'[7] Wade is known for his impeccable command of the Wolof language, and it could not have been lost on him that the Wolof term for 'work', *liggey*, also refers to the 'work' of occult forces. His political rivals had long nicknamed him *njomboor*, the hare. In the Wolof oral tradition, the hare is the trickster figure par excellence. Wade's appeal to work in this context, therefore, was playing on a local perception that success is best achieved through a combination of hard work and clever trickery.

Thus the success of the jalgáti dance pointed to the power of popular performance to evoke shared ideas of morality and success at a particular historical moment.

The jalgáti also had the advantage of being simple, and therefore easy to learn even for people with few dancing skills: the basic structure involved two steps to the right with a coordinated swaying of the hips, arms bent in front of the body and the hands thrown sideways with the beat, then the same steps repeated to the left. But it was also meaningful that the jalgáti looked good on TV and videos given the visual turn taken by Senegalese music during the 1990s.

Music videos and TV competitions

Between the 1980s and the late 1990s, mbalax videos were mostly broadcast during designated programmes on the RTS. Since then, the liberalization of the media has resulted in the multiplication of private channels, and it is now possible to watch music videos around the clock, MTV-style. These videos form the background décor in many Senegalese households and small restaurants, and are as popular as football and Latin American soap operas. This is magnified by the high TV receiver rate.[8] Cable TV channels also feature music videos and, despite their cost, many households have access to them thanks to the ingenuity of the local *bricoleurs*. In the second half of the 2000s, music videos have been increasingly accessed via smart phones and the internet as both technologies have spread into urban life. Watching music videos or soaps together has become a convivial activity, a way of 'killing time' together. [9] More importantly, people often learn new dance moves in front of the TV before displaying them at neighbourhood or family events.

Indeed mbalax dances can be performed with a live sabar ensemble, where participants adjust their performance to the call-and-response principle. Whether one is going to a night-club, a furël, a tour or a tànnibéer, there is always a context in which to display newly acquired moves. As well as having fun, this is an opportunity to demonstrate the richness of one's social life and one's capacity to keep up with the fast pace of urban life. Furël, in particular, provide a space in which girls and boys can socialize and have fun together without this being frowned upon. Dance events thus help to form urban identities in which neighbourhood competes with, and often overrides, ethnicity. Many Dakarois youths identify with their neighbourhood alongside, or even before any ethnic background, although in some cases the two are linked. For example, the small neighbourhood of Dalifort near Pikine was set up by Haalpulaar migrants to the city and has a majority of Pulaar speakers; former Lebu villages like Ngor, Yoff, Ouakam and Thiaroye still have important Lebu populations. A few neighbourhoods are associated with a particular Sufi brotherhood, such as Cambérène with the Lebu Laayen. But all neighbourhoods are ethnically and religiously diverse, and the bigger suburbs located on the outskirts of Dakar, Pikine and Guédiawaye, are said to represent the nation on a smaller scale. Dance events there bring people together, in the dance circle as well as in the organization. They provide opportunities for individuals and families to show off their social leadership and commitment to neighbourhood life. One furël I attended was thus organized by a friend in her early thirties who had moved out of Pikine a few years earlier after getting married. Her mother and several of her siblings still lived in the family compound but her friendships had grown more distant despite her frequent visits. My incessant questioning gave her the idea of organizing an evening furël just outside her family compound. She knew that I was keen to attend and record the event on video, and also felt that this would be a good way of showing her sisters and friends there that she still cared for their status in the neighbourhood. She was pleased when the event was well-attended, and when several young women who had their eyes on her younger brother as a potential husband made a point of showing their best dance skills.

Riding on the back of this phenomenon, TV dance competitions contribute to the formation of localized urban identities, and inflect the moral contents of these identities. This is not simply a grassroots phenomenon, but rather another facet of the state's attempt to control youthful energies and to shape the moral domain. The competitions I focus on form the core of a hugely popular TV show known as the *Oscars des Vacances*. Running every year over July-September since 1993, originally on the RTS channel and since 2007 on the privately-owned channel 2S TV, the show was created by former football player Aziz Samb. Officially, this was meant as an innocuous way of occupying the youth over the school holidays. Samb had lived in Côte d'Ivoire through the 1980s and had been involved in variety TV there, at a time when Abidjan was a centre of musical production in West Africa. Upon his return to Senegal in the early 1990s, Samb (personal communication, Dakar, April 2011) started *Carlton* and *Grand-Place*, musical shows aired on the state-owned radio station. Success was immediate, and Samb and his producers were offered to start a TV show in 1993, *Loisirs des Vacances*. From a modest beginning in one of Dakar's smaller theatres, the show eventually moved to a basketball stadium, and 'Loisirs' was changed to 'Oscars' to evoke a cosmopolitan atmosphere, even though the focus on mbalax dances styles makes it a distinctively Senegalese, urban event. Given the timing and the support from the Abdou Diouf regime, this was an obvious attempt to court the youth and to control potentially dangerous energies. Indeed the weakening power of the PS had been laid bare during the civil unrest of the late 1980s, a period marked by student strikes, a short-lived but bloody conflict between Senegal-Mauritania conflict and the Set Setal movement.[10] In this context, leaving the urban youth idle during the school holidays was risky.

Rather than mobilizing talent from scratch, the Oscars co-opted already existing youth clubs, the ASC (Associations Sportives et Culturelles) promoted by the state in the 1970s and structured within the ONCAV (Organization Nationale de Coordination des Activités de Vacances). There was, early on, a political dimension to the ASC movement: although officially promoted by the state, in the late 1970s some of the ASCs served as a relay for political activism at a time when Senghor had forced opposition parties underground (Faye, personal communication, Dakar, July 2002). Sports and the performing arts were imposed as mandatory activities, but these quickly became popular with the urban youth, probably because they fitted well with the modern identities the Dakarois youth strived for and provided an alternative to forms of association based on a locality of origin.[11] Inter-neighbourhood football competitions, the *navétanes*, were organized between July and September every year and became a central part of urban youth culture. The performing groups included theatre, dance and music. The plays staged by theatre groups mostly fell within the 'theatre for development' genre, and as Barber (1987) has observed in other parts of Africa, this did not generate an enduring practice. Dance and music groups blossomed, on the other hand, and it was those groups the TV Oscars co-opted from 1993 onwards. Neighbourhood-based youth dances have since gained momentum, and Samb himself has become a media celebrity.

There has been increasing corporate involvement in the competitions through sponsorship, advertising (especially with the private 2S TV), a cash prize of 3 million FCFA for the winners in the group category, and job opportunities for some of the performers. Aziz Samb thus gave me examples of performers and beauty pageant candidates who had been given jobs with sponsor companies, often in communication or marketing for the young women, and marketing or private security for the young men. This 'professionalization' of the competition has made it particularly attractive at a time when state resources for the youth clubs have long dried up. NGOs like Enda Tiers-Monde had filled in only a little of the gap left, mainly through organizational and logistics support (Faye 1996).

Though different styles and categories appeared over the years (junior, senior, solo and groups), most notably with the introduction of rap, a set piece in a different style every year,[12] a short play and a beauty pageant, mbalax in all its variants has remained the show's centrepiece. Performers are also quizzed, in a school-like manner, on their knowledge of *culture générale* (general knowledge); but the questions, in fact, usually revolve around the state's achievements in various development-related fields. While Samb himself presents the show and galvanizes the groups offstage, the jury is made up of well-known figures in the Senegalese musical and artistic world (such as visual artist and playwright Joe Ouakam), state officials and representatives from the corporate sponsors.

For our purposes, what matters is that the competition provides opportunities for the wider audiences and for the increasing numbers of migrants who watch the show via satellite TV abroad to debate issues of morality. Discussions often revolve around the appropriateness of the outfits and the dance movements, the treatment of social issues in the short plays, and the moral standing of previous winners. Whereas some regard the show as entertaining and as a good way of turning idle youths into good citizens by teaching them the value of hard work, competitiveness and humility, others argue that the Oscars, just like football, prevent young people from giving sufficient attention to schoolwork. Yet others are worried about the reputations of girls rehearsing alongside boys for whole days, sometimes until late into the night over several weeks. The trajectories of previous winners have come to the fore as what was previously a holiday activity became a breeding ground for professional performers[13] as well as an alternative route towards celebrity, money, status in one's neighbourhood, attractiveness to the opposite sex, and in some cases jobs and travelling opportunities. As I return to later in the chapter, for the dancers, their immediate social environment and for TV audiences, the question then becomes: how may one achieve rapid success through such a morally risky activity as performing popular dances in public, while at the same time preserving one's reputation?

The Oscars competition could thus be described as a 'social space' into which young performers, established artists, audiences, media producers, state and corporate officials all project their own ideas of how material success may be achieved without compromising moral standing. This is particularly salient for female performers given the association between dance and female sexuality evoked in the previous chapter. Young men, meanwhile, find their own mix of risk, fun and opportunities for rapid success in the competitive fashioning of hyper-masculine bodies.

Choreographed masculinities: wrestling and 'lion game'

Whereas competitive dancing is practised by boys and girls alike, there is a popular practice in which dance unambiguously expresses a powerful masculinity: wrestling. Wrestling without punching (*mbapat*) was traditionally practised by young men during harvest celebrations across the region. It is said that mbapat was the highlight in the ritual celebration of fertility during the grain harvest, as well as an opportunity for young men to display their strength, courage and endurance. In other words, in wrestling games young men showed that they were ready to enter adulthood.

While wrestling is still performed during harvest season in many parts of rural Senegal, it has also become a lucrative sport in cities. It was in Dakar in the 1950s that entrepreneurs combined the mbapat with boxing to create wrestling with punching, or *làmb* (Faye 2002). They recruited strongly built, competitive youths with the promise of cash earnings for fights, and turned wrestling from a ritual to a pugilistic sport held seasonally in big stadiums. In Dakar and in many other Senegalese cities, làmb has become the most popular sport alongside football.[14] It is now a thriving business and a flamboyant spectacle, complete with dancing, sabar drumming and oratory performance. At home in front of TV sets, people gather to watch the fights, cheering, arguing and shouting as their favourite wrestler clasps his adversary's body. People often cheer for a champion who represents their neighbourhood or region of origin, or simply a wrestler whose style they like. 'Style', in wrestling, is as much about performance as it is about fighting skills, as we will see shortly. For the big events, an afternoon of fights between lesser known wrestlers will climax with an encounter between two champions at sunset, often lasting no more than two minutes. The winner is the one who successfully pushes his opponent's shoulders to the ground.

There has been a growing literature on Senegalese wrestling in the 2000s. Faye (2002) has described wrestling as a manifestation of the shadowy connections between sports, business and politics in twentieth-century Senegal. The most relevant to this study is Havard's (2001) work, which has looked at wrestlers as icons of new understandings of masculine success built on youth, moral strength, body building, and the appearance of autonomy. Indeed, in recent years the most popular wrestlers have appeared to challenge traditional forms of authority from marabouts, political leaders and older relatives (Havard 2001; Baller 2007). Around 1995, Mouhamed Ndao 'Tyson', a young wrestler born in Kaolack and raised in Pikine, became a role model for many young men, and an icon of the *bul faale* generation.[15] In urban Wolof, 'bul faale' means 'don't worry about it' or 'who cares?' The term was popularized by rap group, Positive Black Soul with their 1994 cassette *Boul Fale*, with lyrics speaking of the obstacles faced by young men in their struggle to become social adults. They sung about being self-reliant and getting on with life despite the lack of decent jobs and the difficulties of love relationships for young men with limited options. With his rags-to-riches story, his hard work ethic and his defiant attitude towards the prejudice he encountered as a young wrestler who had refused to wait for his turn in one of the established 'stables', Tyson embodied the bul faale ethos. His was a masculine strength against all odds, and the bul faale dance he invented became a fleeting craze in the mbalax repertoire. His popularity was damaged by his association with the Socialist Party during the 2000 presidential election, however, and the bul faale dance went out of fashion. But the 'Tyson moment' marked a renewed interest in wrestlers and wrestling dances.

According to *ndey ji rew* Alioune Diagne Mbor, himself a keen wrestler as a young man, dance and oratory skills were always integral components of the wrestling ritual. He told me that in his youth, an accomplished wrestler was someone who was also a skilled dancer and composer of sung poems. These poems would evoke the wrestler's moral virtues, and by extension reflect on his family. Wrestling was a display of moral as well as physical strength, and both had to be demonstrated in the dancing and oratory performance leading up to a fight. With wrestling now taking place in big stadiums, the oratory dimension has receded to the background even though the rituals surrounding the fights still involve the singing of praise poems (*taasu*) for the champions. More spectacular from a distance and on TV, the dancing that precedes a fight has come to the fore. It is performed to the sound of sabar drumming by the wrestlers, their 'stables' (*écuries*) of large groups of male assistants, coaches and apprentices, some of them young boys. Nowadays they wear matching sports outfits printed with their corporate sponsor's logo. During the fights, however, wrestlers strip themselves of all clothing except the traditional loin cloth and amulets tied around the arms.

The wrestling dances are simpler than many other styles, with which they nevertheless resonate. Rather than innovative steps, they emphasize strength and a defiant posture. The image of strength is reinforced by the colossal, worked-out (and nowadays medically boosted) bodies of the wrestlers. In continuity with traditional wrestling, the basic position involves the knees bent low in a sitting-like position. While one foot faces the front, the other is turned outwards to the side so that the legs are opened at a 45-degree angle, upper body straight and strong on the bent legs. The progression from there involves variation in the steps and rhythms. In the bul faale dance for example, the dancers moved forward in this position, shuffling the feet forwards in small steps to the beat of the sabar drums. The arms moved up and down in scissor-like movements, each arm movement ending with control rather than release. The style seemed designed to exude strength, confidence, rhythm and control. Wrestling dances are indeed the main component in the ritualized performance designed to impress the adversary before a fight. This is attested to by the value placed on the *bàkk* (person-specific call-out rhythms) of individual wrestlers.

Star wrestlers have their own drummers who play with them regularly and compose bàkk for them. When played with skill, these rhythms are said to give the wrestler mental strength, and therefore only the best lead drummers get to play for wrestlers. The bàkk and the dances also help to turn what is, after all, a fairly short affair into a flamboyant spectacle. At the centre of the spectacle is the masculine figure of the wrestler, an individual who is at that moment stripped of anything but the strength of his mind and body, and the protective power of the amulets.

There is another spectacle which projects a similarly powerful image of masculinity, and in which dance also occupies a prominent place. It is the simb, a ritualized game called *jeu du faux-lion* in French. In the simb, performers dressed in lion-like outfits, their faces painted in red and black or in yellow in the manner of animal masks, try to catch some of the participants. If caught, participants are forced to dance or complete a task set by the 'lion'. Adults today describe it as an event they used to fear as well as be excited about as children. The simb has structural similarities with sabar in that it also involves a circle of participants, sabar drumming and dancing, and praise poetry sung by géwël. The origins of the simb are unclear; whereas a commonly told myth traces the ritual back to a time when men who had survived a lion's attack became invested with the animal's powers, informants in the Senegalese performing scene described it as a ritual of rebellion and a vehicle for secret communication during the colonial period. Though it is beyond the scope of this study to dwell on this practice, there are obvious aesthetic continuities with the youth masquerade performances of the Casamance and the Upper Guinea region.[16] A significant difference with wrestling is that the simb spectacle expresses a powerful masculinity by juxtaposing it with an extreme performance of femininity: the figure of the *goorjigéen*, the effeminate man. The presence of goorjigéen dancing and taunting the audience is nothing new, for Diallo (1975) had fond memories of it as a teenager in Dakar in the 1950s. The goorjigéen performers I saw wore heavy layers of make-up, brightly coloured Senegalese outfits, and performed sabar dances in a feminine style. In this sense, the simb seems closer to the sabar genre, which draws on the presence of intermediary categories to hint at the ambiguity of gender categories.

In Dakar today, therefore, it is not only a female sense of self that is being shaped through dance; it is also male selves, through the projection of a powerful masculinity in public spectacles like wrestling and simb. Using recognizable elements of regional 'traditions' and transforming them through sports and the modern media, these practices celebrate the physical power and moral strength young men acquire by cultivating their body. In reality, money and politics are very present behind the scenes, as Faye (2002) eloquently demonstrates with wrestling. As in boxing, there is little doubt that power is in the hands of the promoters and not, with a few exceptions, in that of the would-be champions or the 'lions'.[17] This was confirmed in the run-up to the presidential election of 2012, when it was rumoured that the PDS was paying wrestlers to form youth militias in Dakar's *quartiers*. Yet the image of the endurance of youth against all odds that is being projected into the city and further beyond Senegal's boundaries from stadiums and

TV screens is highly seductive. It provides respite from the uncertainty of everyday life, and reflects the aspirations of young men with little prospect of reaching social adulthood any time soon. Young men identify with these figures of fast success because they, too, can move like them.

Popular dances and Islam

The seductive power of dance and its capacity to embody moral tensions have not been lost on religious leaders, who increasingly compete to occupy the public space. This may be one of the main reasons why the appropriateness of popular dances has been increasingly called into question in recent decades.[18] This is perhaps unsurprising since the literature on Muslim societies suggests a recurrent tension between musical performance and Islamic practice. Van Nieuwkerk (1995) thus showed the ambivalence with which women performers had been regarded in Egypt since the nineteenth century, despite the social value attached to their trade. For her, the moral status attributed to this occupation in Egypt depends on the context and the audiences. Women dancing for other women at wedding celebrations, for example, are seen as more respectable than women dancing in front of men in nightclubs. The differentiation Van Nieuwkerk describes is similar to what I observed in Senegal, where age and marital status are important in determining respectability. As suggested in Chapter 3 on sabar, it is thus less appropriate for a mature mother to dance in front of men than it is for a younger, unmarried woman.

This is an issue for professional performers, many of whom are devoted Muslims.[19] For musicians this is less of a problem because singing the praise of Sufi leaders makes their occupation morally acceptable. But for this to make sense, some background needs to be provided on the specific character of Senegalese Islam. Senegalese Sufi Islam is largely dominant in Dakar, and virtually all Muslim performers claim allegiance to one of the two main tariqas (the Tijaaniyya and the Muridiyya) or one of the smaller ones (the Qaddiriyya and the Laayenes). The tariqas are all organized around the hierarchical order of the Khalife-marabout-disciple (*taalibe*) trilogy: each brotherhood is headed by an all-powerful head, or Khalife, surrounded by a council of senior clerics, or marabouts. These senior clerics are represented locally by devoted marabouts, who animate the tariqas' local chapters, the *dahiras*, act as spiritual leaders, organize the work of the young disciples, receive gifts in exchange for their blessing, and more generally attend to the welfare of their followers.

Among the performers I knew there was an over-representation of Mourides and Niassènes, two highly popular movements among the urban youth. These included a significant proportion of converts from other tariqas, particularly among the Niassènes. The Niassènes represent one of the more recent branches of a much divided Tijaaniyya. Analysing the reasons for the relative dominance of these two movements is beyond the scope of this book, but preliminary points can be made. The Muridiyya was founded in Senegal in the late nineteenth century by Cheikh Amadou Bamba, himself the son of a famous Qadr marabout. Since the late 1980s, when it moved from its mainly rural base, the Muridiyya has been immensely successful in recruiting disciples among the urban youth. The fact that the performing scene is fairly young is therefore an explanatory factor. But additional reasons may be found in Mouride practice, in which performance, in the form of loud chanting and the recitation of Cheikh Amadou Bamba's poems (*xasaids*) is highly valued.

The Niassène branch of the Tijaaniyya also values devotional music. Historically, it has also been more inclusive of ñeeño categories than the other Tijaaniyya 'house', the Tivaouane-based branch founded by El Hadj Malick Sy in 1902. The Niassène branch was founded by El Hadj Abdoulaye Niass in Kaolack in 1924 following an internal conflict within the brotherhood. Niass was the grandson of a Blacksmith (*tëgg*) from the Jolof kingdom, who married a géér woman against strong opposition from his fellow Tijaans. Indeed, although Muslim theology postulates that believers can only be distinguished according to their degree of piety, Senegalese Islam has not worked very hard at doing away with the 'caste' stratification (Behrman 1970). In the Fuuta Toro, Dilley (2004) argues that the framing of *nyeenyBe* knowledge (the Haalpulaar equivalent of the ñeeño) as anti-Islamic has even served to exclude the 'men-of-skill' categories from high-ranking positions in the tariqas. In the newly formed Muslim communities of the late eighteenth and early nineteenth centuries, the role of griots as public performers was problematic, and some of the converts were encouraged to abandon their trade and work for their marabouts (Diop 1981). There was never a complete rejection of the griots' oratory skills, however, since brotherhood life requires muezzins, song and ritual specialists, and praise-orators for the marabouts, *géwëlu Yonent* (Diop 1981). But they have rarely made it up the ranks of the tariqas, and few ñeeño have been chosen to become *muqadam*, the high-ranking clerics who represent the Khalife.

In this context, Niass' acknowledgement of this ñeeño background must have been revolutionary and, though it is rarely mentioned, I have no doubt that it is a widely known fact across the Senegalese Tijaaniyya. Several older géér I knew, who were Tijaan disciples, were mortified when I asked whether their allegiance was to the Tivaouane branch or to Kaolack, because the implication that they may be Niassènes suggested that they would have accepted the moral authority of a ñeeño. Given the high proportion of ñeeño in the performing world, the conversion of urban youths to the Niassène branch can be construed as an aspiration to egalitarianism.

It is also in continuity with the disciple-marabout (taalibe-marabout) relationship that is at the centre of Senegalese Sufi Islam (McLaughlin 1997). This may explain why Senegalese popular music has blended quite well with religious practice. The chanting by young disciples in praise of their marabouts during Thursday evening dahiras bears aesthetic similarities with singing in non-religious contexts. McLaughlin also reflected on the appearance of the *cànt*, a new type of Mouride ceremony, during the 1990s. She described cànt, which have grown increasingly popular and often draw thousands of youths from across the city, as '*animation musicale* for a living marabout' (McLaughlin 1997: 566). Music also forms part of religious practice in other tariqas, and in the performing world I have often heard people comment on the strong musical character of Niassène and Qadr ceremonies. This was echoed by McLaughlin (1997: 566):

Far from being sombre events, Sufi ceremonies are associated with an important element of entertainment. This is especially apparent in the ceremonies
of the Qadiriyya, which an amused Tijani described as "folkloristic-some-
where between a gammu and a sabar" [. . .]. He went on to say that those
ceremonies were not very sacred in character, and that he had even heard
people at them singing secular songs by pop stars such as Youssou Ndour.

Popular musicians have made increasing use of religious themes, often encouraged by
Sufi marabouts, who have become their most loyal patrons. There is hardly a recent
cassette or CD of Senegalese pop music that does not include songs in praise of high-
ranking marabouts or tariqa founders, particularly Cheikh Amadou Bamba. Some
musicians, like Youssou Ndour, promote the illusion of a unified Senegalese Islam by
dedicating songs to leaders of all the main tariqas.

Dance is a more problematic activity because it is not associated with Islamic
devotion in the same way, and because women's dancing is explicitly associated with
sexuality. It is particularly in public, on TV and on the internet that religious morality is at stake. This is complicated by the fact that the boundaries of public space are
fuzzy: a neighbourhood event may be considered private or public depending on the
organizers, the purpose and the participants. TV and the internet, on the other hand,
are unambiguously public since they are accessible to all. Women being seen to dance
on those media are therefore the most likely to see their morality being questioned.
On countless occasions when I have been visiting friends in Dakar, chatting in front
of music videos, people have made negative comments about the inappropriateness
of the women dancers' dress, which was immediately linked to the dubious morality of the dancers. Men often remarked that they would never let their wives or
daughters dance like this in public, and yet, they obviously enjoyed the spectacle.

The media often capture this uneasiness in interviews with women dancers.
Dancers and singers will give interviews for publicity purposes, and to manipulate
those moments to establish their moral credentials. This was evident in an interview
with Ndèye Guèye, a dancer then in her early twenties, published in a daily newspaper. Guèye had come to fame through the Oscars, with Oumou Sow's Amazones de
Dakar. Born in Pikine, she tells the journalists that her father is a football referee, and
her mother a trader. Like many dancers in Dakar, she discovered her dancing vocation
during family ceremonies and sabar events. Most dancers have been influenced early
on by a relative or a friend, and she is no exception: her older sister was a dancer with
one of Dakar's major troupes, the Ballet Mansour Guèye, and Ndèye Guèye says that
she wanted to be like her. From the moment she started earning money from dancing,
she says, some of her older relatives tried to prevent her from dancing in public by
hitting her. Invoking the sense of losing control discussed earlier, she says she went
on dancing because she could not help it. She goes on to explain that her exceptional
sensitivity to drumming stems from her naming ceremony, held at the customary age
of eight days, when drumming and dancing went on for a whole day.

In 2005, after four years with the Amazones, she and two fellow dancers left
to set up their own girl dance group, Les Gazelles de Dakar. Like the Amazones,

they appeared in music videos, in mbalax concerts, in nightclubs and as entertainers during sports events. During the interview, she is taunted by the journalists for being 'too sexy', and for wearing dancing outfits so provocative as to have embarrassed President Wade during a concert at the National Theatre, as well as the director of the RTS during an Oscars show. Obviously prepared for this, when the interviewers ask her about her hobbies she replies: 'Going to religious ceremonies'. When they ask whether this is in contradiction with her profession, she responds:

> I'll give you a phone number. Call this person and ask them about my hob-
> bies in life. They'll tell you the same thing. I even organize 'diangues' [prayer
> ceremonies in commemoration of a deceased] every year for my deceased
> elder sister. I go to nightclubs, it's true, but I spend most of my time in
> religious ceremonies. (Konté and Kossi 2006, translated from French)

This was only one of the many instances when scantily clad women dancers were presented in the Senegalese media as the most visible indication of society's moral decline. As a result, dance people go out of their way to express their concern with decency in dancers' dress, even though this is often in stark contrast to practice. Thus Aziz Samb is always keen to reassure viewers and the families of the young dancers that decency is a major concern at all stages of the Oscars competition:

> This year, my team and I went to see the groups in their neighbourhoods,
> with their parents and sometimes the local mayors present. [. . .] This was an
> opportunity to explain to the participants some of the rules of the competi-
> tion. For example, I told them that if a jury member catches a glimpse of
> a girl's breasts during the competition, points will be taken off the group's
> score. (Nankasse 2005, translated from French)

Consequently, dancers who appear on TV, particularly young women, are con-stantly walking a tenuous line between desirability and moral dejection. Whilst being expected to appear as icons of urban Senegalese beauty, they must also remain careful not to compromise their reputation to the point of becoming unmarriageable (Neveu Kringelbach 2007b).

The issue of marriage is indeed recurrent in media 'scandals' about women danc-ers. A revealing instance of the fragility of female dancers' moral standing was the 'Goudi Town'[20] affair in September 2007, which ended up with three performers being charged in court. At the centre of the furore was the circulation of images of young women dancing particularly suggestive variations of the lëmbël to the sound of live sabar drumming. The context was an evening of competitive dancing in a Dakarois nightclub in 2005. Ndèye Guèye and several other women took turns to dance in front of a jury of European businessmen. Some performed lying on the floor, face down and the hips raised in the air, moving in tune with the beat. They wore net-like beecos, and what looked like minimal underwear underneath. The winners were given cash on the spot to thunderous applause from the audience. This is not particularly unusual: sabar parties called *soirées Sénégalaises*[21] are routinely held in nightclubs. I attended such a soirée led by former Youssou Ndour band member, Mbaye Dièye Faye in 2003. In contrast to the restrained manner of most people on the dance floor, the young women who came on stage late into the night danced in a highly suggestive style. Such soirées are expected to have a bawdy character, and this is part of the fun. The winners are sometimes selected to perform during Senegalese pop concerts abroad, the ultimate prize for many years being a stage appearance at Youssou Ndour's annual show at the Paris Bercy venue. The fun, the money in cash and the lure of international touring are enough to encourage dancers to perform their most suggestive moves.

What gave the Goudi Town event a twist was that the competition was recorded surreptitiously from a hidden camera, and the images later posted on the internet. From then on they were copied onto mobile phones across Senegal, and spread to the diaspora via the internet. Indeed it was in the company of Senegalese dance people in London that I first discovered the footage. They knew the women personally, and alternated between authoritative comments on the obscene nature of the dancing and details on the dancers' lives. They also expressed outrage at the way in which the European 'jury' encouraged bawdier moves by waving cash in front of the dancers. The fact that this differed little from the common practice of 'spraying' money onto singers and dancers to reward good performance, a practice documented elsewhere in Africa, [22] was of little relevance here. The fact that the patrons were Europeans apparently gave the gesture a dubious character.

This would probably have remained the stuff of tabloids and Senegalese blogs, were it not for the fact that one of the dancers brought the matter to court upon discovering the images on the internet. She and the other dancers had been duped, she complained, since the organizers had assured them that there would be no filming. In the process of getting married, she was worried that the images may cause her marriage to fall through, and wanted the culprits charged. But things did not turn out this way. A prominent Muslim association and a consumer association sued everyone involved in the event. Charged with being complicit in public acts of indecency, Ndèye Guèye and two other dancers were jailed for two weeks. The moment when she walked out of jail was widely covered by the media, as if to set an example (Ndoye 2007; Ciss 2007; Sarr 2007). In the following weeks, a debate raged in the media and in blogs between those who found the court too lenient, and those who argued that the freedom of citizens was threatened by this type of action. Though not in Senegal then, I was able to follow the debate through the media and conversations with friends in Dakar. Within neo-traditional and contemporary dance troupes, people were quick to blame the three women for degrading the profession by doing 'pornography' and calling it 'dance'. This was a golden opportunity for stage dancers to assert their moral superiority over the world of concert and competitive dancing, even though this was blatantly ignoring the fact that the same individuals often participated in both worlds.

In everyday life, many Muslim dancers focus on a strict religious practice as a way of compensating for the choice of a 'tainted' profession. Christians often keep a low profile when it comes to religious matters and respond to salutations in the Muslim way, or open their hands upwards in the sign of Muslim prayer at the end of meetings. It is in the privacy of their homes that their faith is displayed openly through Christian iconography. Some confessed that they were annoyed by people constantly trying to convert them to Islam since they felt this expressed a condescending attitude towards Christianity, despite a dominant discourse of religious tolerance that is one of Senegal's points of pride in international relations.

Muslim practice is thus highly conspicuous in the dance world. At the Centre Culturel Blaise Senghor (CCBS) in Dakar, prayer mats pop up everywhere at prayer time, and dance troupes often wait until the end of prayer to begin rehearsing properly. For workshops that take place before the most important prayer of the week, the early afternoon prayer on Fridays, young dancers come dressed in their best outfits so that they may be ready for prayer later. Young men who wear casual European clothes the rest of the week are seen wearing clean, starched caftans, and women dancers bring their white prayer shawls. Some of the men dancers go to the mosque together for the Friday prayer, while those who do not keep quiet about it. There is an understanding that a reputation as a good Muslim brings the respect of one's peers.

Whenever I asked dance people how they reconciled their profession with being 'good Muslims', answers were often uneasy and elusive. One of the more experienced dancers, who never missed a prayer, replied that his dancing skills were a God-given talent. God, he said, would understand that he used his talent to a good end, to feed his family. He added that he would redeem himself in due course, when he could no longer earn a living from dancing. There was thus an uneasy tension between the God-given character of talent, which helped to recast dance as a virtuous activity, and the notion that it would have to be redeemed later in life. The manager of a neo-traditional troupe, a Niassène, confessed that his livelihood was morally problematic for a committed Muslim like himself. But this was compensated by his devotion to the local chapter of his brotherhood, into which he had drawn some of the performers in his group, and with whom he organized Thursday evening dahiras at his house. They took part in a *zikr* every other Sunday, a religious ceremony involving praying and chanting well into the night, and he insisted that the group had integrated zikr rhythms into their performance.

I also interviewed several Muslim clerics, mainly Tijaani, on how they viewed dancing. They all replied that dancing was not recommended because it could so easily distract believers from their religious path. On the whole however, they were fairly accommodating. Several explained that among the many degrees of deviation from proper practice, dancing was acceptable as long as the performers were 'properly covered'. One of them added that committing adultery, for example, was a much more serious offence. When I asked what they would recommend people did with the money earned from dancing, several clerics suggested that although 'performance money' was tainted, it could be rendered clean if used according to the highest moral standards, such as supporting one's family. There was a surprising homogeneity of views among these clerics, who had received their religious training in Senegal, Morocco or Egypt. One contrasting view was that of a Sunni leader who lived in a village in northern Casamance, just below the border with the Gambia. Through family contacts, I had the opportunity to interview him while he was on a short visit to Dakar to undergo medical tests. Probably in his mid-forties, he said he had been trained in the Casamance by people who had 'studied in Saudi Arabia'. I had met his much younger wife a few days earlier at a family wedding, where she sat among the guests and was the only young woman who did not wear any makeup and did not dance at all. Sitting with her baby on her lap, she wore a brown *hijab* and barely spoke. When I interviewed her husband he said outright, in a forceful manner, that Senegalese Islam as it was practised today was wrong, corrupted by the older marabouts. He said he had a growing number of followers in his village, ordinary family men who visited him in secret:

> I tell them exactly what is in the Qur'an, not what the marabouts say, because they don't know. Ask me anything, and I will tell you *exactly* what is in the Qur'an.

So I asked him what the Qur'an said about dance. He became agitated and explained that there were only two moments in life during which dancing was permitted: 'when your child gets married, and your heart is cool'[23] and 'when your child has borne a child, and your heart is cool'. In other words, dancing is appropriate as an expression of joy and gratefulness to God at weddings and naming ceremonies. Aside from these two moments, he was adamant that dancing was contrary to the recommendations of the Qur'an. Indeed, he said, dancing mirrored the movements of those who had ended up in Hell, and were trying to avoid the flames by jumping around. He added that there could even be aggravating circumstances, such as when a married woman dances in front of other men, or when 'people who normally respect you' watch you dancing. Though such prescriptive views are more likely to be found in Muslim reformist circles than in mainstream Senegalese Islam,[24] this expresses more widespread concerns about the morality of women performers. Many clerics take a more accommodating view, nevertheless dancing under the gaze of strangers or people of a lower status places moral and religious respectability in a fragile equilibrium.

For this reason, families often tolerate rather than welcome dancing as a livelihood. Some simply turn a blind eye as long as the performer shares his or her earnings with the household. Others make it clear that they will only accept such 'deviation' for a limited period of time. At times, relatives even exercise pressure to make the individual quit. This is done, for example, by withdrawing financial support, arranging a marriage or even through physical violence, as Ndèye Guèye narrated in her interview. I have also known women dancers who chose to quit of their own free will, either because they wished to avoid family conflicts or because the moral issue provided them with a good reason to quit a highly competitive profession that requires grinding daily hard work and is difficult to combine with family life. Arranging a marriage may be particularly effective since few husbands tolerate seeing their wife perform in front of strangers, unless they are in the performing world themselves. One of the most frequently repeated comments I heard in response to the Goudi

Town scandal was that one of the women was married, and that such exposure was deeply immoral in her situation. How could her husband walk head high after this?

Conclusion

The commodification of sabar performance into the mbalax genre, fostered both by musical experimentation at home and by global marketing as part of the World Music phenomenon, has served multiple agendas in Senegal since the 1980s. The tensions among these agendas, I suggest, are expressed in the framing of mbalax dances by the media and some of the political and religious elite as embodying the very morality of urban society.

The first of these agendas was the desire by the Abdou Diouf regime to prevent the urban youth from disrupting the political status quo established during the first decade after independence. With the threat contained in the youth movements of the 1980s, co-opting artistic activities and sports seemed all the more important as part of the simmering unrest was galvanized by the youth clubs, the ASCs. As other authors have documented elsewhere in Africa,[25] musical performance was regarded as a privileged medium through which a sense of self-worth could be instilled in young people. At the same time, co-opting the neighbourhood-based youth clubs had the advantage of undermining ethnic identities, at least on the surface. Youth clubs have been successful in promoting a local sense of belonging by virtue of the amount of time people spend on collective practices, and through competition against other neighbourhoods. This is expressed in dance group names like Les Pirates de Dieupeul, Les Diamants Noirs de Pikine, Xale yi Parcelles ('the children of Parcelles' from the neighbourhood 'Parcelles Assainies'), Alliance Dakar Plateau Farbis, Rufisque Diaspora Dance, etc. Multi-neighbourhood groups like Les Amazones de Dakar thus signal their ambition to make a name for themselves beyond the confines of the neighbourhood. Encouraging competition in mbalax dancing, wrestling and other sports, then, has been very much about controlling the youth and furthering the construction of a national identity. The fact that images of local groups circulate widely on TV and the internet is not in contradiction with the strengthening of neighbourhood identities; rather, it is emblematic of the way in which people's lives increasingly take place between that which is close and that which is far away, at least in imagination.

The second agenda could be described as the appropriation of the first by young people themselves. Though it would be an over-interpretation to frame this as a coherent strategy by a homogenous group, there is little doubt that many of those who distinguished themselves through these competitive activities consciously used their skills and their status as youth icons to gain access to the professional world, either as musicians, dancers and choreographers or in the corporate world. This will come through in some of the individual trajectories sketched in the chapters that follow.

A third agenda could be characterized as a more diffuse struggle for the moral high ground in public life. Testimonies from performers as well as the intensity of the negative coverage of popular dances in the Senegalese media indicate that this competition has increased since the mid-1990s. Given the timing, this may well be linked to intensified competition in both the political and the religious fields. Indeed, with the election of Abdoulaye Wade in 2000 and the regime change from the PS to the Sopi coalition, the perspective of a single party staying in power for a longer period of time has vanished. In a context of widespread disillusion towards the old political elites, the capacity for parties and individuals to present themselves as morally superior to their predecessors is crucial. Political competition is mirrored by a competition among the different strands of Senegalese Islam. For both political parties and religious movements, public expressions of outrage about the appropriateness of youth and women's dances serve as statements of their own moral standing, however illusory this may be.

Since these agendas are not always compatible with each other, the tension among them comes to the surface particularly strongly in times of crises, and it is expressed in moral terms. It is thus no coincidence that the Goudi Town affair was turned into a court case with heavy media coverage during Abdoulaye Wade's second mandate. Early in his first mandate, in 2000–02, he had revelled in the unconditional support of a young electorate of both sexes, and it had made sense to show his approval of popular dances (the jalgáti), football and wrestling. By 2007, however, much of the urban youth was much less enthusiastic about the regime, and on the other hand the most youth-friendly sections of the Senegalese brotherhoods, such as the Tijaan Niassènes and the new Mouride movements led by Seriñ Modou Kara or Cheikh Bethio Thioune, were gaining ground. It was expedient, therefore, for the Wade regime to court the youth through these movements, and to shift the public discourse from an ethics of hard work – there were few jobs to work hard for anyway – to the field of morality. This was confirmed subsequently when Abdoulaye Wade spoke out on several occasions, against what he phrased as the 'obscenity' of some of the dances shown on TV:

> It was during the annual meeting with press editors and distributors, for the presentation of the press world's new year wishes, this Wednesday at the presidential palace, that President Abdoulaye Wade expressed his displeasure with the tendency of Senegalese TV channels to show obscene dances. For him, TV must go beyond entertainment and educate the citizen. [. . .] 'I am in favour of televisions refraining from showing certain dances that verge on the obscene. We are not gaining anything from pretending to be in Las Vegas.' (Nettali.net 2011)

With this public moralization of popular culture, the President was gesturing towards the religious leaders while also trying to outdo them in maintaining high moral standards for Senegalese society. As for young performers, they are fully aware of walking a thin line between success and moral rejection, and this has only increased with the intensified circulation of images in the past decade or so. It is in this light that their constantly renewed attempts to appear as good Muslims must be understood. For this purpose, it remains useful at times to invoke an urge to dance coming from forces beyond one's control (as in Ndèye Guèye's interviews), even though the mbalax genre as it is now performed for TV competitions and music videos is very much choreographed.

This chapter also sheds light on one of the main features of popular culture: the constant tension between experimentation and subversion on the one hand, and appropriation by established institutions on the other. This fits well with Barber's (1987) characterization of the popular arts as those activities that take place outside the realm of the controlled, the privileged, the elite, and which innovate by mixing elements from established genres and loosening their conventions. The mbalax repertoire of popular dances thus draws on the older sabar genre as well as on American music videos, sports, fashion, and a range of popular music styles from across West Africa.

I focused on mbalax in this chapter because this has been the most popular music and dance style in Senegal since the early 1980s, but over time popular genres are inevitably replaced by others, and this is the case here. In parallel with a thriving Senegalese rap scene, hip-hop dancing has grown in popularity throughout the 2000s, mainly among secondary school children and school leavers. The phenomenon of hip-hop 'battles' is now well-established in Dakar, and Kaay Fecc-organized workshops by foreign hip-hop artists are always well attended. It is, however, significant that the hip-hop dance scene, which is mixed-gendered but noticeably dominated by boys and young men, is much less subjected to moral judgments than mbalax practice. But then it is probably a characteristic of most societies that morality is expected to be embodied differently for men and for women.

As mentioned in the introduction, competitive youth dances are often an important lead in the trajectories of professional performers. Many practitioners of popular dances move on to neo-traditional troupes later so as to learn the 'African' skills expected of them in global performing circuits. By contrast with common assumptions by audiences abroad, therefore, these urban practices often precede the styles qualified as 'traditional' in dancers' individual trajectories. In the next chapter, I turn to the equally commodified world of 'neo-traditional' performance.

Notes

1. The *Set Setal* movement of the late 1980s – early 1990s was a neighbourhood-based youth movement aimed at 'cleaning up' the urban environment, both in a literal sense (*set* means 'to clean' and *setal* 'clean up!' in Wolof) and in a moral sense via attempts to eradicate corruption, prostitution and delinquency. The movement found a graphic expression in the covering of urban surfaces with inscriptions and paintings (Bugnicourt and Diallo 1991).
2. In French colonial language, the *évolués* were African individuals who were literate, educated in the Francophone system, wore European clothes and displayed modern lifestyles.
3. The term 'Wolofization' refers to the multiple ways in which Wolof cultural elements impose themselves on, and become appropriated by, people who do not classify themselves as ethnically Wolof. This refers mainly to the use of the Wolof language in everyday social life, but also to the practice of Islam within one of the two major Sufi brotherhoods, the Tijaaniyya and the Muridiyya. However ethnic boundaries in Senegal are fuzzy, and

Wolof self-identification could best be described as 'a process, which relates to a range of subjects: urbanization, migration, religion, statehood' (Cruise O'Brien 1998: 27).

4. See Neveu Kringelbach (2007b) on the re-fashioning of body shapes in the Dakarois dance scene.

5. There have been exceptions to this, such as Youssou Ndour's album, *Sant* (*Egypt* for the international market) and Thione Seck's, *Orientissimo*, both released in 2004.

6. See Ralph (2006) for a more detailed description of Wade's political use of the team's victories.

7. 'One must work, always work, and work even more!'

8. By 1996 there were 320,000 known receivers in Senegal, out of a population of 10 million (Fair 2003). But the real number of viewers was probably far greater, and has grown since then.

9. See Schulz (2001) for a fascinating analysis of music videos and women's sociality in Mali. Also see Ralph (2008) for a vivid ethnography of young unemployed men 'killing time' around the brewing of tea in Dakar.

10. For an analysis of the political transition of the 1980s in Senegal, see Diop and Diouf (1990).

11. This was not restricted to Dakar, and De Jong (2007: 99–103) describes a similar phenomenon in Ziguinchor.

12. For the set pieces, the tune is imposed but every group is free to create its own choreography. In recent years the novelty styles have included Ivorian zouglou and Bollywood dancing, all performed with a visible movement influence from mbalax.

13. Despite Samb's insistence that this is purely a holiday activity, the Oscars have become a talent show. Some of the most popular bands and groups of concert dancers have emerged through the Oscars, from the Pirates de Dieupeul (winners in 1994), later renamed Wapyrat, to Oumou Sow and her girl group, the Amazones de Dakar.

14. Football even surpassed wrestling in popularity in 2002–03, but this was undoubtedly linked to the exploits of the national team. According to Baller (2007), in previous years Senegalese audiences had become rather indifferent to the fate of a national team that seldom distinguished itself in major tournaments.

15. For an illuminating article on the bul faale generation, see Diouf (2002).

16. See, for example, De Jong (2007) on Jola and Mandinka masquerades in the Casamance.

17. Wacquant (1998) makes a similar point in the context of boxing in Chicago.

18. This is also one of the central points in Heath's (1994) pioneering study of women's dances in Kaolack.

19. Muslims are in a majority in the performing world because Senegal is predominantly Muslim, but Roman Catholics are over-represented in the dance world: according to my own estimates, they account for up to twenty per cent of dance troupe members, against fewer than five per cent in the overall population. This is most probably because a significant proportion of dancers originate from the Casamance region and the Sereer-speaking areas of Siin and Saalum, where the Christian minority is concentrated.

20. *Guddi* means 'night' in Wolof. The printed media tend to use French rather than Wolof orthography.

21. See Castaldi (2006) for a vivid ethnography of a *soirée sénégalaise*.

22. I have observed the 'spraying' with cash of musicians, and occasionally mbalax dancers, in Senegal and in Côte d'Ivoire. Askew (2002) writes about the significance of 'tipping' taraab singers in interpersonal relations among women in Tanzania. In the DRC,

White (2008) describes this practice as important in establishing the status of individual audience members.

23. To have a cool heart, in Wolof, means to be happy.

24. Reformist Islam has been present in Senegal since the 1970s, but it was through the 1980s and 1990s that Sunni movements really took off. On contemporary Islam in Senegal, see Augis (2002) on the Sunni *Jama'aatu Ibadu Rahmane*, as well as Guèye (2002), and Diouf and Leichtman (2008).

25. See, for example, White (2008) for the relationship between popular music and politics in Mobutu's Zaïre, or Nyamnjoh and Fokwang (2005) on music and politics in Cameroon.

Chapter 5

The Politics of Neo-Traditional Performance

Dakar, November 2002

The scene is the Centre Culturel Blaise Senghor (CCBS) in zone B, between Fass and Grand Dakar. Most evenings, four or five neo-traditional troupes rehearse there. Space is scarce, and there is a hierarchy in the way in which it is occupied. Established troupes like Sinoméew, Bakalama and Forêt Sacrée work in the theatre room, which features a stage at the back; the workshop room or the inner courtyard. Meanwhile, smaller and more recently formed troupes rehearse in the interstices of the building. That evening, the troupe rehearsing in the theatre room is Bakalama, a Jola troupe based in Dakar but tracing its origin to Thionck Essyl, in the Lower Casamance. Dancers and musicians arrive from Fass, the Medina or Ouakam, having walked or taken a bumpy ride with a car rapide. Rehearsals begin when everybody is there, or when the prayer is over. Upon arrival, those who are early chat with friends from other troupes and with those who populate the Centre on a daily basis: stage technicians, troupe managers, 'animateurs culturels', and youths with time to kill. Drummers from the various troupes start playing as the dancers warm up. There is gossiping about the latest love affairs or performers who have vanished during a tour abroad. Managers and choreographers, often a bit older than the dancers, discuss Senegalese politics and reminisce about the old days, when there was money for the arts and when spaces like this were not derelict. Those days did not last very long, but in retrospect it seems as if they did.

When the rehearsal finally begins, the warming up consists of single movements taken from the Bakalama repertoire, repeated over and over again. It is led by one of the most experienced dancers in the group. When a public performance is planned over the following weeks the rehearsal then focuses on the programme, usually drawn from an existing piece. This week it is *Kañaaleen*, one of Bakalama's favourite pieces. Men and women rehearse separately for some of the time, then together. Time must be spent making minor improvements to the choreography, rearranging the lines to fit the space that will be available, 'cleaning up' the movements, working on the synchrony between dancing and drumming, improving the acting where it is needed, and training the less experienced 'apprentices'.

Some of the other troupes working in the space finish the evening with a sabar-like moment during which people stand in a semi-circle or in two lines with the drummers at one end, and take turns to improvise short sequences. There are sabar dances, Mandinko steps, and anything people enjoy doing. Creative steps and difficult acrobatics draw the loudest cheers. This is the moment when bodies are exhausted, but also free to indulge in favourite moves and be admired by fellow performers. For Bakalama, however, many evenings end up in a different way: this is the time when the group sits together in a circle, outside the dance space, to discuss the work accomplished. Bakalama is a Jola troupe, and its members take great pride in their egalitarian approach to work.

London, September 2010
I am at the house of Landing, a former Bakalama member now settled in the UK with his wife and two children. He teaches drumming in schools across the UK, occasionally performs with a small group of drummers and dancers, and holds 'drumming and team-building' workshops for businesses. He is known in the small world of African performance in Britain as a talented, professional and reliable artist. His parents are visiting from Thionck Essyl. His father, Lamine, is one of Bakalama's founders. He says, jokingly, that he does not really speak Wolof even though he has spent thirty-five years of his life in Dakar. Yet he speaks to his grandchildren in perfect Wolof. His French is perfect, too. But I suspect the point is that he feels Jola, and that half a lifetime in Dakar has not changed that. His wife speaks Jola and Wolof, but little French. Lamine does not like being in England because he does not speak much English, and feels isolated. He is tired, too, because this is Ramadan and he is fasting. A family friend arrives shortly after me. He too is a Jola, raised in Dakar by parents who were migrants from Thionck Essyl. His father was also a founding member of Bakalama, and he had joined the troupe as a teenager himself but had not stayed long because, he says, he was a poor dancer.

Later in the afternoon, Landing sits in front of the computer in the living room. He logs on to Skype and makes a call. 'This is a surprise, you'll see', he tells me. The person takes the call and they chat in Jola. Before long it is my turn and I am speaking to a Bakalama dancer I have known since the 2002 Kaay Fecc 'traditional dance' workshop in Dakar. She is teaching dance in Madrid, and provided she can get a visa, she will soon make her way to Sweden, where another Bakalama member is organizing a dance workshop. In Madrid she is staying with former Bakalama members, and has learned just enough Spanish to get by. She is also in touch with other Bakalama members across Europe through Facebook. There is a Bakalama diaspora within the Jola diaspora, and its northernmost boundary is now northern Sweden. Life, they know, is made of movement.

These vignettes illustrate the range of social worlds a Senegalese dance troupe may stretch across. It is no coincidence that this one is a Jola troupe, given the prominent role of migrants from Casamance in the Dakarois performing scene. There are dozens of neo-traditional troupes in Dakar which explicitly claim a Casamançais identity. As migrants or their children, they provide an interesting lens through which the complexities of nation-building can be examined since they identify with regions held to be at the 'margins' of the nation. Kelly Askew (2002: 12) has argued that there was a gap in the literature on nationalism, which is the ways in which nationalist projects become re-appropriated 'from below'. She suggested that nation-building was a mutual process of engagement between the state and its citizens, and that 'this very element of mutuality, of sharedness, of common participation, admits the possibility of dissension from those excluded from state activities'. Drawing on this notion of politics 'from below', this chapter moves on from state-led efforts to appropriate popular culture, to the appropriation of neo-traditional performance for regionalist, transnational and individual career purposes. This links in to previous chapters as I suggest that the practice of neo-traditional performance alongside popular dances in youth clubs and neighbourhood events, either simultaneously or at different life stages, helps city dwellers to make sense of their engagement with different moral communities. In making this argument, I draw on Lambert's (2002) and De Jong's (2007) work on the translocal character of many Jola communities, and on Foucher's (2002) analysis of migration to Senegalese urban centres as one of the root causes of the Casamançais separatist movement. In the first part of the chapter, I focus on the case of one particular troupe derived from a hometown association of migrants from Lower Casamance as an exemplar since Casamançais troupes in Dakar have played a prominent role in the development of the genre (see Chapter 2).

Bakalama from Thionck Essyl

In 2002, veteran theatre leader Mademba Diop, of the Cercle de la Jeunesse in Louga, estimated that there were at least three hundred dance troupes in Senegal at any given moment (Dumas 2002). They are concentrated in the Dakar region, in Casamance and in the coastal resorts south of Dakar. Since dance troupes have an average size of fifteen to twenty members, it is fair to say that thousands of Senegalese have been involved with dance troupes at some point in their lives. The troupe I focus on here is an exemplar of the genre's development in the capital, with ramifications elsewhere in Senegal and beyond.

Bakalama presents itself as a 'ballet' from the 'village' of Thionck Essyl. Now a *commune* in its own right, Thionck Essyl was classified as a rural settlement until the 1990s, despite having a population of more than 8,000 inhabitants. Most are wet-rice cultivators, Jola speakers, and almost exclusively Muslim (De Jong 2002). Located in the region of Ziguinchor in the Lower Casamance region, Thionck Essyl is also in the heartland of the separatist movement. This is significant because the culturalist discourse chosen by the movement (Foucher 2002) means that all cultural performance produced by people from the region has a direct bearing on the movement, whether or not this is intentional.

The official meaning of the troupe's name is that it means 'calabash' in Jola, in reference to the calabash tree with its strong, far-reaching roots. The troupe's name, therefore, symbolises a strong attachment to the place of origin in spite of migration. Indeed Bakalama was an offshoot of the hometown association of Thionck Essyl, the ARTE (Association des Ressortissants de Thionck Essyl) that had existed in Dakar since 1952. One of the initiators of Bakalama was Lamine Mané, thirty-five years old in 1972. He had first lived in Dakar in 1953–54 for a year before returning in 1959, initially with plans to travel to Côte d'Ivoire, where he had heard from a relative that there was plenty of work. While trying to earn enough money to embark on a boat for Abidjan, he joined the French army on a whim. There he received training in radio transmission. At independence, he was recruited into the newly formed Senegalese army and transferred to the Intelligence Services. He would have preferred to stay in the French army, but with less than two years of service he was not eligible to do so. Fellow association member, Lamine Diédhiou, worked as an engineer in a soap factory in the outskirts of Dakar. Others worked as civil servants, often in the police or the army, or as employees in the private sector.

Throughout the 1960s, Mané and others in the association performed Jola dances during name-giving ceremonies and other festivities. This is when his performing skills became known, although he says he acquired them in childhood. Mané said he was a 'returning child' who had died and returned several times, causing a great deal of grief to his mother. He had a scar beneath the shoulder that was evidence of this, the same scar which had been noticed on the babies who had died before he was born. Having lost several children, his mother had been taken into the *kañaalen,* a Jola sorority of women who have not been able to carry healthy children. Lamine was born after his mother had undergone the fertility rituals required to stop the cycle of return. He had subsequently grown up taking part in Jola women's ceremonies, where he had learned to dance and sing. The Thionck Essyl association, along with others from Casamance, also organized evening dance events in neighbourhood cultural centres. Interestingly, the most popular style at these parties was Cuban music: not only was it very popular with the Dakarois youth, but also, according to early members, those who had attended secondary school in Ziguinchor in the 1960s had already developed a passion for Cuban rhythms there.

By 1972 popular theatre was booming across Senegal, and the association decided to create a repertoire of performances blending drama, music and dance. The different wards of Thionck Essyl and the families considered to be indigenous to each ward – Niaganan, Batine, Kamanar and Daga – were represented, thus concealing from outside view the existence of profound dissensions among the wards.[1] Lamine Mané, from the Niaganan ward, says he was chosen as Bakalama's first director because of his experience as a performer. Members of the association who were students in Dakar wrote plays which followed the conventions of Senegalese popular theatre. This was no coincidence since most of these students had already tried their hand at theatre in primary school in Thionck Essyl. By contrast with the National Theatre's emphasis on Wolof-speaking heroes and the moral values appropriate for good Senegalese citizens, Bakalama's plays portrayed Jola heroes like Aline Sitoe Diatta, a prophetess whose cult was violently repressed by the French in 1942. They also portrayed the dilemmas of young Jola men and women caught between the old and the new. The initiation play *Gambacc*, for example, told the dilemma of a schoolboy who was forced to choose between two worlds when time came to go into the sacred grove for initiation. The boy wished to remain loyal to Jola tradition, but school had taught that such practices were morally wrong and should be abandoned. One of the performers I interviewed said he was chosen for this role in 1980 because he was then a schoolboy himself. There was a piece on changing gender relations in rural Casamance (*Manding Mousso*, 'the rebellion of the Manding woman'), and *Djurumpa*, a piece on the kañaalen.

One of the 1970s students, Saliou Sambou, who wrote *Kañaalen*, later became an important figure in national politics, rising to the post of Governor of Fatick and later Governor of Dakar. Other amateur playwrights included Lamine Diédhiou, Victor Diatta, Laye Badji, Martin Mané, and Toumani Camara (who wrote *Manding Mousso* and *La Reine de Kabrousse*, the play on Aline Sitoe Diatta). Mané continued his work in Intelligence Services by day while being a troupe organizer and choreographer by night. He says he had to conceal this because membership of civic associations was forbidden in the army. His hobby was not discovered until five years into the troupe's existence. Around the same time the troupe was chosen to represent Senegal during festivals abroad, so this does not seem to have been an immediate problem. After retirement from the army in 1980 he held a post at the Interior Ministry, and continued to work with the troupe while also helping to stage Casamance-related shows for the National Theatre.

Though fairly conventional within the established genre of school theatre, the Bakalama plays differed from theatre made by Wolof speakers in that they emphasized Casamançais cultural elements, especially those that were visibly distinctive from northern Senegalese ones. Whereas the songs were in Jola and the texts in French or Jola, Wolof language and history were carefully excluded. Thus work in the rice fields, an important marker of regional culture (De Jong 2007), featured prominently but not peanut cultivation, despite the fact that peanut farming had been widespread in the region since the 1930s (Mark 1977; Lambert 2002). Some of the founders of the troupe had indeed worked seasonally in peanut farms. But peanut farming did not appear in the performances because of its association with the Wolof-dominated Senegalese state rather than with Casamançais identity. Islam did not appear explicitly in the performances, either, despite the fact that most of the troupe members were practising Muslims, and that Islam became dominant in the region during the colonial period (Lambert 2002). Rather, practices framed as 'traditional', such as Jola initiation,[2] were portrayed as if they had remained untainted by the presence of Islam and Christianity. Yet anthropologist Louis-Vincent Thomas (1965) reported the presence of Muslim clerics as an integral part of a *bukut* ceremony in the village of Niomoun, and De Jong (2007: 60–62) has shown that the male initiation process in Thionck Essyl had been modified as a consequence of widespread conversion to Islam in the first half of the twentieth century. Circumcision is thus performed during the early years of a boy's life rather than as part of male Jola initiation, and the 1940 cohort was the last one to be circumcised in the sacred forest.

Although the plays involved drama, dancing and singing from the early days of the troupe, over time drama gradually receded until dancing and musical performance came to fill most of the time on stage. Troupe members say that theatre was used to explain stories to people, whereas dancing was used to 'express' things. But they also acknowledge that dance enables more flexibility in the composition of a show, and that it makes it easier for audiences anywhere to follow without feeling excluded by language. An additional reason mentioned to me by members from the 'second' generation, now in their forties, is that few of the younger performers (the 'third' generation) have a strong enough command of French to be comfortable performing the original texts.

Despite the troupe's emphasis on Jola rhythms, instruments and songs, performers present what they do as representative of Thionck Essyl, of the Casamance as a whole or even of Senegal, depending on the context. Those pieces the troupe identifies as Jola, however, are subject to less aesthetic manipulation than those referring to neighbouring groups, especially the Mandinka. Until recently, the performers strongly identified with Thionck Essyl, where most of the men had undergone initiation. This is also where the troupe performs every year, and those trips to the hometown are emotionally meaningful for the troupe members; it is important to them that the local audiences recognize the dances, songs and rhythms and identify them as 'authentic'. Several members thus told me how moved they were whenever they performed *Kañaalen* in Thionck Essyl, and women from the sorority spontaneously joined in the songs. There is, therefore, somewhat less room for innovation than with dances from other parts of the Casamance. One of the troupe's long-term performers expressed this in gender terms:

> In Bakalama's creations, you're free to mix and match, but when you play for the women in Thionck Essyl, you must respect tradition. (Mané, personal communication, London, March 2012)

In a context in which the preservation of Jola identity has long relied on women (Linares 1992), I suggest that this points to the importance of maintaining Jola-ness at the core of the troupe's work.

There is undoubtedly a political aspect to this, since the constant slippage between Jola culture and the broader Casamance is in striking continuity with the separatist discourse. Several authors have suggested that the framing of the Mouvement des Forces Démocratiques de Casamance (MFDC) as a regional rather than an ethnic movement served to legitimize the separatist discourse in a state where the ethnicity argument alone carries little political weight (Faye 1994; Lambert 1998). In his introduction to the MFDC's manifesto, Darbon (1985) notes that although the authors make a point of framing economic and political marginalization as a problem for the Casamance as a whole, the references that permeate the text are Jola: Jola heroes, Jola movements of rebellion, the destruction of forests, rice fields and fishing environments. He notes that the Mandinko and Pulaar speakers are not mentioned once, even though they are in a majority to the east of Ziguinchor. Equally, when troupe members spoke to me about their work, they always used 'Jola' and 'Casamançais' interchangeably, and yet the themes they bring to the stage are first and foremost Jola. The cultural production of Jola troupes in Dakar thus draws on the regionalist discourse and provides substance to it at the same time.

In addition to the performance of a Jola identity, in its early days Bakalama also carried a dimension of gerontocratic authority. Those who had joined the troupe as children in the 1970s and 1980s said that the idea then was to 'keep the youths from Thionk Essyl busy', to give them a space in which to have fun among themselves and to 'prevent them from turning to drugs and banditry' when faced with unemployment and the difficulties of urban life. But this argument fits within the construction of cultural distinctiveness: what was implied was that the Jola youth had to be protected from the 'corrupting' influence of the Wolof, whom many Jola regard as having lower moral standards. Involving the Jola youth in the troupe was an effective way of keeping a degree of separation since this involved spending a great deal of time together outside school, and going back to Thionck Essyl for cultural events and holidays. In the mid-1990s, some of these youths took over the troupe following an inter-ward conflict among the first generation, by now 'elders' in their own right. Though I have only been given a superficial explanation for the conflict, it is likely to have been related to the inter-ward conflict over initiation and politics in the first half of the 1990s, and which De Jong (2007) described in detail in his monograph. Indeed, the troupe manager, an outsider himself, alluded to the long-standing tensions between the Niaganan and Daga wards that were carried into the troupe's internal politics. This was implicitly confirmed to me when Saliou Sambou, originally from Daga, told me how he had distanced himself from the troupe at a time when 'politicians had tried to use Bakalama for their own benefit.'

I will return later to the consequences of this generational shift, but I now turn to the contents in one of the troupe's favourite pieces, *Kañaalen*, to show how the troupe's work was initially designed to help construct a moral community of Thionck Essyl *ressortissants* away from the town.

Kañaalen in life and on stage

Kañaalen is a full-length choreographic piece ('ballet'), and a Bakalama favourite by virtue of its distinctively Jola features. I have not had the opportunity to attend kañaalen rituals in real life, but I have drawn on the existing body of literature to gain a sense of the relationship between the theatrical version and the ritual in its social context, and over time.

Several authors have looked at fertility rituals in the Casamance (Journet 1981; Fassin 1987; Mark 1994), in the Gambia (Weil 1976; Hough 2008) and in Dakar (Fassin 1987). Although there are different versions of the ritual in different parts of the region, anthropologists seem to converge on the notion that the kañaalen (*kanya-leng* in Mandinka) involves powerful female societies and liminal practices aimed at neutralizing the forces that prevent some women from having many healthy children. In Jola and Mandinka societies, the authors suggest, a woman's status is linked to her productive capacity as a mother and a food producer. The core principle of the ritual is that the inability to achieve healthy motherhood, whether it is caused by infertility or by the death of children at a young age, must be repaired through the sacrifice of ordinary social life and dignity for a prolonged period of time. Women who join the sorority are thus called upon to leave their families and go through a period of liminality in a different location. This period could last three to five years in the past, but it is now often shorter, particularly in cities (Fassin 1987). During this time, initiates (*añaalena*) may have to endure daily humiliations, often being given ridiculous names or being encouraged to eat food leftovers by licking a bowl on the ground, like dogs. During festivals and family ceremonies, they must also dress like fools, act like buffoons, dance in a bawdy style, and generally act in ways that would be completely inappropriate in other contexts. On specific ceremonial occasions which include the feasts organized at the return of an initiate and when babies are born to her later, society members even adopt behaviour normally associated with men, such as fighting over food and wrestling (Weil 1976). There are thus echoes of the liminality of sabar and of the ritualized gender reversal present in both sabar and simb performances. If the cycle of infertility is indeed broken, further sessions are required to maintain the efficacy of the ritual protection; these were the rituals the young Lamine Mané attended as a child. In addition, sorority members are expected to re-enact their role during weddings and name-giving ceremonies later in life (Figure 5.1).

How, then, does Bakalama's *Kañaalen* relate to the fertility ritual? I first watched and recorded the piece in its forty-five-minute long version during the 2003 Kaay Fecc festival at the MCDS in Dakar. It featured a succession of tableaux with male and female dancers performing separate choreographies, and led by drummers and a lead singer/dancer who played the role of the añaalena. After a rhythmic opening played by three musicians on four Jola drums, the piece began with a synchronized dance by six men. They sang in Jola, each holding a fake *kajendo*, a tool with a long

Figure 5.1 Casamançais wedding in Dakar, January 2004. An initiate wearing her beaded calabash can be seen among the guests dancing behind a mask on stilts. Photograph by the author.

handle and a figure-of-eight-shaped spade used for rice cultivation. The dance suggested the rhythmic movement of this type of work, with ample forward-throwing gestures. The men wore dark green sleeveless, half-length tunics maintained on the sides with straps, and light green loose cotton trousers. At the end of the sequence, the voices of women rose loudly from the back of the stage. The men froze and looked at each other with a theatrical expression of surprise, and ran away from the stage just as a group of seven women entered. They wore half-length, colourful batik-printed *boubous* with matching, ankle-length wrap-around skirts. They sang in Jola and stepped in rhythm, with small, perfectly coordinated footwork while holding raffia baskets on the head with both hands. The baskets contained real rice plants. Once in three lines facing the audience, the women lowered the baskets to the ground and went on singing and stepping in rhythm while simulating the re-planting of rice, bodies bent over the ground.

The next scene, performed in the style of silent drama, introduced the main characters: a young man and woman. The man courted the woman, they fell in love, and their wedding stretched over a succession of tableaux featuring recognizable practices from Casamance, but not exclusively Jola. One of the women following the bride, for example, carried the suitcase she would bring to her husband's home. Indeed the 'suitcase' ritual has long been performed in many societies of the region (Diop 1985), and I have witnessed it at weddings in Dakar. The bride entered, surrounded by her kinswomen, her head completely covered by the customary embroidered white cloth. But her happiness did not last. In the following tableaux it became obvious that within a few months the bride, Akintou, had been rejected by her husband because she had failed to become pregnant. She was scorned by everyone in the village, and once alone she launched into a monologue in French. She prayed for fertility and lamented the harassment she suffered from other women. Apart from the songs in Jola, Akintou's monologue is the only textual element that is left from the original play, *Djurumpa*. I recorded the performance on video, and this is the monologue as it was performed in June 2003:

> Je suis fatiguée de marcher. Je suis fatiguée de me soumettre aux critiques des autres. Ô mon Dieu, faites que j'aie un enfant. Faites que je devienne comme les autres femmes. Je ne puis continuer de vivre ainsi. Ma co-épouse a toutes les faveurs de notre mari, qui ne daigne même pas me prêter son attention. Je suis triste et abandonnée. [Women singing in Jola] Qu'ai-je donc fait pour mériter ce châtiment? Bannie des femmes, méprisée des hommes, Akintou ne sait plus où aller. J'ai fait le tour du village. Les sorciers, les marabouts, les sages, tous ont reçu ma visite. [. . .] Les enfants fuient sur mon passage. Les mères se méfient de moi et me maudissent. [. . .] Dès l'aube, furtivement je regagne ma chambre de peur d'éveiller ma co-épouse et sa marmaille. [. . .][3]

The village women were then seen on stage, gossiping and harassing the husband. Two of them ostensibly courted him while Akintou went to see kañaalen priestesses in the forest. She agreed to submit herself to the ritual, here portrayed as a succession of joyful, energetic, therapeutic dances. At this point, loud cries of enthusiasm rose from a large audience made of ordinary Dakarois, performers from other troupes, families and friends of the troupe, festival organizers and media people. At long last Akintou was healed, and the piece ended up with the whole village marvelling at the sight of her new-born baby.

Songs, rhythms and material culture were the most distinctively Jola elements in *Kañaalen*. The calabash Akintou brought with her into the forest carried the hanging fringe of beads characteristic of the decorated calabash carried by real-life initiates, and with which they are meant to go around begging for food. During dance sequences, the women clapped small wooden sticks against each other in poly-rhythmic beats characteristic of the Lower Casamance region. The movement style was emblematic of Jola dances: both legs alternate in a rapid and powerful stomp, feet flat, with the knees bent and the body leaning forward at a forty-five-degree-angle. The arms are held away from the body and, by contrast with the Wolof sabar, they are never higher than the shoulders. The energy emanating from this movement appears directed towards the ground, as opposed to the aerial style of the sabar.

Jola-ness embodied

I would like to suggest that this type of choreographic work serves at once to construct particular images of Casamance with audiences outside the region, and to maintain a sense of moral community in a migration context. As I have argued elsewhere, performance is a particularly effective way of giving shape to modern identities within post-colonial states because it is sufficiently malleable to accommodate the rapidly changing contents of these identities (Neveu Kringelbach 2012). I will now turn to these two analytical points in turn. Firstly, the construction of particular images of Casamance was evident in the selective choice of elements in the staged *Kañaalen*. Anything to do with the pain and humiliation inherent in the real-life ritual as a form of humility in the face of divine forces was removed, even though this was a central aspect of the ritual. Part of this undoubtedly arose from the conventions of the genre, as well as from a desire to showcase Jola culture in a positive light. Indeed when I interviewed Saliou Sambou in Dakar, he was explicit about the need to use cultural performance to undermine the region's marginalization:

> The problems between Casamance and Senegal are fundamentally problems of cultural misunderstanding. If the Senegalese knew us, they would like us. We need to show who we are. We set up Bakalama at the time so that people would come to understand us. (Saliou Sambou, personal communication, Dakar, April 2011)

Since, as we have seen, discourses around performance are often indicative of contested moralities, it is likely that troupe members regarded the exclusion of the more painful elements of ritual as necessary to win the moral high ground over the northern Senegalese. Moreover the emphasis on wet-rice cultivation, at the exclusion of the region's dry-land crops (peanut, millet) was very significant in light of the importance of wet-rice in the history of the Lower Casamance. Indeed the tidal swamp rice varieties indigenous to the region require specific expertise to cultivate (Linares 1992; De Jong 2007; Lambert 2002) and therefore mastery of this crop is perceived as a marker of autochthony. This was reinforced by the theatrical representation of Jola culture as bounded and timeless, whereas in the 1970s and 1980s, several authors noted an increase in fertility rituals of the kañaaleen type (Weil 1976; Journet 1981). Among the Mandinka of nearby Gambia, Weil even argued that the recent emergence of kanyalang associations in this part of the region was linked to an increased pressure on women as producers of rice and children (an essential resource for labour-intensive dry-land cultivation), and the concomitant search for wives from the old rice-producing tidal swamp areas. For migrants from a region like the Lower Casamance, where autochthony is contested among the Jola, the Bainunk and the Mandinka, therefore, the act of 'performing' autochthony on stage is a significant political claim.

The second point I wish to make about this type of cultural production is that it helps to maintain a sense of local belonging among very diverse groups of migrants living away from Thionck Essyl, by sustaining the obligation to send children back to the Lower Casamance to build up proper 'Jola bodies'. In his monograph on the performance of secrecy in Thionck Essyl, De Jong (2007) demonstrated convincingly how male initiation was a key feature in the making of Jola ethnicity. But I would like to suggest that there are additional ways in which Jola ethnicity is embodied: through localized versions of the language of course, but also through rice cultivation techniques and wrestling. One of the performers from the second generation, who had grown up in Dakar, explained to me how he and his brothers had been sent back to Thionck Essyl for a year when he was about ten or eleven years old, around 1980. His parents, he said, had been worried that they may not grow up to be sufficiently Jola. It was especially important that they learned to speak the proper Thionck Essyl-version of Jola, to cultivate rice and millet, and to wrestle. Cultivation involved learning how to hold and use a *kajendo* tool in the manner used in a particular locality, something my informant insisted remained in the body throughout one's life. Those children in the family who learned the farming techniques well drew a great deal of pride from this, whereas those who were not keen on life in the rice fields were scolded. My informant was not specific about what happened to them, but it was obvious that a status distinction was made, from then on, between those who had developed the proper body practice and those who struggled, or consciously resisted. This is consistent with Lambert's (2002: 41) observation that in the Jola village of Mandégane, not far from Thionck, 'the willingness and ability of men to cultivate is a point of honor'. My informant remembered proudly how his father had called upon his own brother to come and watch him work in the rice fields, and had said: 'Look at him, he isn't that little Wolof boy you've known any more. Now he's a Jola!'

The embodiment of Jola-ness extended into performing techniques, of course, and my informant explained that one could always tell the difference in the way Jola rhythms were played and danced, between Jola who had grown up in Casamance, those (like himself) who had grown up in Dakar but had spent childhood time in Casamance, and finally those who had never lived in the region. This was because, he continued, learning to dance, sing and play music was much more than learning techniques; performing in the proper style required knowledge of the culture and the language. This is not specifically Jola however, and reflects widely shared regional ideas of performance as integrated to social life. My informant acknowledged that Bakalama's performing skills had changed character with the decrease in the proportion of performers with life experience in the Casamance, and that it was important for the troupe to keep recruiting youths who came straight from Thionck Essyl to preserve its Jola character. Now that a third generation was gradually taking over, the second had overtaken the role of the 'elder', watching over the preservation of a moral community by laying down rules for what counted as a proper 'Jola body'.

The other aspect of identity-making present in the troupe's work had to do with emphasizing 'difference'. Since Barth's (1969) ground-breaking work on the construction of ethnicity through the maintenance of boundaries, it has become well-established in anthropology that ethnicity is both contextual and relational, and that ethnic identities are constructed by emphasizing and cultivating otherness. Surprisingly however, there are comparatively few studies of the role of bodily techniques in this process.[4] In the case of Jola troupes in Dakar, difference has been cultivated contextually in relation to the Wolof, the Mandinka and smaller groups in the Casamance. Differentiation from Mandinka speakers is the most subtle, perhaps because the two societies are so closely entangled. In Bakalama's *Manding Mousso*, for instance, author Toumani Camara imagined the rebellion of a group of women exhausted by domestic work and farming in the rice fields. Determined to transform gender roles in Mandinka society, they eventually succeed in forcing men to share the work. This is now a choreographic piece derived from the original play written in the 1970s, and I have not had the opportunity to interview the playwright. Regardless of his original intention, it is significant that the second-generation performers I have spoken to, chose to interpret the piece as a reflection of the Jola's superior social organization. One of them thus explained that Mandinka men did not learn to cultivate rice, and left this important task to women. Mandinka men, he continued, concentrated on dry-land peanut fields, which required most attention at the beginning of the rainy season; this left them idle the rest of the year, while women did all the difficult rice work. Given the importance of rice cultivation in Jola society, there was an obvious value judgment in this interpretation.

This emphasis on egalitarianism extends into the social organization of groups, as a mark of distinction from both the Mandinka and the Wolof (Neveu Kringelbach 2012). This is because egalitarianism is widely regarded as a marker of Jola identity. In a nation dominated by the highly stratified Wolof, the absence of 'castes' in Jola history has been used by the separatist movement and the Senegalese state alike to explain Jola 'cultural difference'.[5] This also came across in interviews with performers:

First performer: This piece, I didn't do it on my own, it's all of us. When we're sitting in a meeting or in rehearsal, I can give a step and if everybody thinks it's nice . . . Or let's say, I give a step, and Y. B. [woman dancer] looks at it and says 'if you add to it like that, it's better.' Then I do my step and I add what she says. That's how we put things together. It's not someone who comes and does his choreography, no. We help each other out [*on s'entraide*].

Second performer: It's got to fit with the count [marks the metre of a rhythm by knocking on a chair].

Third performer: In Bakalama it's always consultation [*la concertation*] that comes first. You cannot say that you're the one who created this piece, period. (Bakalama 2007)

Egalitarianism is also cultivated through weekly meetings at the rehearsal space. This is the time when new projects are discussed, problems involving troupe members brought forward, mistakes from recent performances evoked, solutions discussed. Women's voices are equal to those of men, and seniority in the troupe matters more than gender.

I have also described elsewhere how the idiom of kinship is used to speak of social relations within neo-traditional troupes (Neveu Kringelbach 2012). This is particularly strong in the case of Jola troupes, and is reflected in the treatment of younger apprentices: whereas in many other neo-traditional troupes there is constant talk of exploitation, in Jola organizations a share of the income is often set aside for them while they are being trained. The group may even intervene in family conflicts on behalf of junior members. In other words, it is not only the people's attachment to Thionck Essyl and the Jola identity that holds the troupe together, nor is it simply a matter of money. What matters, at least equally, is the troupe's capacity to act as a surrogate family, in particular by creating an atmosphere of togetherness and by protecting those in need of care. Such practices are necessary to retain members and maintain continuity in the repertoire, but they also fit perfectly with the people's imagination of Jola culture. Discourse and practice reinforce each other in a constant feedback loop, even though Bakalama and other Jola troupes are actually stratified on the basis of experience.

Performative flexibility and generational change

A closer examination of the life of the troupe off stage indicates, however, that such projects as the construction of regional and local identities through migrant performance are always at risk of being undermined by generational changes. In Bakalama's case, this occurred when the children of the founders took over the leadership of the troupe.

For the first twenty-five years or so, profits from performance were mainly redirected towards the hometown association, but this changed in the 1990s. Whereas their parents had held fairly stable jobs and performed in their spare time, the second generation were now professional performers with families who depended on income from the troupe. Following a conflict with some of the early members, the second generation won the right to keep most of the profits for themselves and the upkeep of the troupe. This is likely to have been precipitated by the growing integration of young performers into Dakarois youth culture, characterized in part by strong aspirations of individual success. Members of Jola troupes in Dakar are often passionately engaged in the neighbourhood-based youth clubs and popular dance groups described in the previous chapter, and Bakalama's second generation was no exception. Two of Lamine Mané's sons, Landing and Ousmane, both worked with Ousmane Noël Cissé for his Sotiba Boys and Manhattan Dance School, and Landing Mané also choreographed for youth groups which took part in the first series of the Oscars des Vacances competitions. They also worked with a prominent contemporary dance company in Dakar, all while touring with Bakalama throughout the 1980s and 1990s.

Despite the professionalization of the troupe, members continue to make contributions towards various 'development' projects in Thionck Essyl (healthcare, the Great Mosque, schooling, etc.). The troupe also maintains a connection to the hometown through an independent dance festival held occasionally since 2003, when other troupes from Dakar are invited. It is a forum for the local troupes to show their work, and for Bakalama to hold training workshops for its junior troupe of aspiring migrants.

This multiple engagement is not as recent as it may appear. In the late 1970s already, the troupe had collaborated with the National Theatre to stage *La Reine de Kabrousse*, when Jola-speakers were needed for the songs. Lamine Mané says he had become involved in the promotion of Senegalese popular theatre as early as 1974, when he became president of the local federation of theatre troupes in Dakar, a post he says he held until 1993. It is in fact puzzling that he would have accepted an official post of this kind, albeit at a middle level, while trying to conceal his involvement in Bakalama and the Association des Ressortissants de Thionck Essyl (ARTE) from the army. Mané says he was also involved in organizing the state-sponsored *semaines de la jeunesse* in the Lower Casamance. Whether or not the army knew of his 'civic militancy', there is little doubt that he was involved in the state-controlled popular theatre circles in Dakar, and that this served Bakalama well: from the mid-1970s onwards the troupe took part in youth festivals across the country (Le Soleil 1987), performed at the arrival of the Paris-Dakar Rally, and represented Senegal abroad on a number of occasions, from a carnival in France in 1977 to a world fair in Japan in the early 1980s, and the 2009 Pan-African Festival in Algiers. In the early 2000s, Bakalama introduced a sabar programme. Though the core of the troupe's repertoire retains a strong Jola flavour (Figure 5.2), this enabled the group to widen its repertoire, and therefore the range of events at which it was invited to perform.

Everyday religious practice among performers shows that far from being reducible to a Christian minority or a bastion of traditional religion, many Jola migrants are fully integrated into 'mainstream' Muslim Senegalese practices. A certain strand of analyses of the Casamançais problem have portrayed the conflict as a clash of religions,[6] yet the Lower Casamance region is now predominantly Muslim, and therefore

Figure 5.2 Bakalama dancers in an 'animation' (short piece without a narrative), Dakar, April 2003. Photograph by the author.

separatism cannot be reduced to a religious issue (Foucher 2005). Nevertheless, the tension between male Jola initiation and Islam is problematic for some of the migrants, and indeed also for some of Thionck's residents (De Jong 2007). By no means a new problem, this was reflected in Bakalama's early plays. Since then, the performers have, on the whole, left such tensions unresolved. When the Kaay Fecc association held a 'traditional dance' workshop in Dakar in October 2002, one of the three styles in the intensive four-week programme was thus the Gambacc style performed by people of both sexes at the end of male initiation, and taught by dance master Fodé Badji. The training was followed by sessions in Wolof during which some thirty dancers from all parts of Senegal were taught about the 'traditions' associated with the dances. For the Gambacc dance, two Bakalama drummers, who had themselves undergone the initiation, gave their account of the different stages of the initiation process and circulated photos of themselves wearing the distinctive outfit of the initiates. Yet in different contexts, the same individuals questioned the appropriateness of Jola initiation for good practising Muslims.

Similarly, the leader of the Pikine-based Jola troupe told me that such was the importance of the male initiation for the diaspora that people felt compelled to come all the way from Dakar and even Europe when time came for them to be initiated.[7] Now an elder himself, he had been initiated in his father's village as a young man. Later in the conversation, however, he pointed out that he would not allow his sons to be initiated. He was a good Muslim, he said, and good Muslims 'should not be doing these things any more'. He added that many other fathers in Dakar's Jola community held the same view, but did not wish to elaborate further on why his youth troupe continued to stage the Jola initiation nevertheless. Ultimately, religious dilemmas of this kind are the daily bread for many citizens across all ethnicities, and performers may well be better off than most since they are able to dramatize these tensions.

I want to suggest here that it is the ability to modulate the mix of Jola, regional and national elements depending on the context which has ensured the success of troupes like Bakalama, both at home and abroad. But there is more to this mixing than a mere artistic strategy: it also speaks of the growing integration of Jola migrants into Dakarois life, and perhaps into the Senegalese nation as well. It also provides the younger generations of migrants with the social and symbolic capital they need to become successful and respected citizens in all the contexts across which their lives are stretched. Then this works as a feedback loop, and the enthusiasm with which many Jola performers in Dakar take part in sabar events, for example, is bound to have an impact on the construction of their multiple identities: as Senegalese city dwellers, as the children of Jola migrants and belonging to a Casamançais locality, as belonging to a Dakarois neighbourhood, and as transnational artists.

One should not, however, idealize this translocal engagement. Indeed 'engagement' may be a more appropriate term than 'integration', for as the gerontocratic aspect of the earliest troupes suggests, sociality with non-Jola people outside the Casamance is not completely free of all control. Marriages, for example, remain as controlled as they have been for much of the twentieth century,[8] and it may be easier for a Jola woman to marry a foreigner than a Wolof man. Within one of the troupes I knew, a Jola woman dancer had thus born a child to a Wolof man a few years earlier. She told me how her parents (both of whom were Jola) had refused to let her marry him because he was a Wolof. When I met her, she had recently married a Haalpulaar man who also belonged to the performing scene. Her parents had reluctantly accepted the love match, probably giving in because she already had a child, but not everybody in the family had been in favour. Years later her husband was still regarded as a stranger, even though he did his best to get to know Jola culture and had visited her hometown several times.

Nevertheless, looking at dance and drama as part of the 'work' of community-making in several locations brings an additional dimension to existing studies of Jola migration, which have shown for a while now that Jola mobility was no longer (or perhaps never was) purely a form of labour migration. Rather, a number of authors have shown how Jola communities are now genuinely translocal, and how the engagement of migrants from the rural areas with urban life was more profound that just making money and going back: as Lambert put it, 'in the city they [migrants from the Jola village of Mandégane] purchased homes, formed associations, joined unions and political organizations, and raised children' (Lambert 2002: xxii). Through theatre and dance, these associations have enabled their members to infuse their translocal lives with meaning, and to engage with urban contexts without losing their sense of belonging.

Though this is less well documented, the ability to move with ease across cultural contexts has also extended into Jola migrants' transnational lives. My exemplar here, Bakalama, has now grown into a transnational community with a strong sense of a shared identity and artistic vision. The transnational expansion of the troupe has to do with its history of mobility, as well as with the development of a transnational 'African dance' world in which Senegambian performers have played a central role.

Transnational connections

Whereas the first generation of founders performed in their spare time, for the newer generations travel is a necessary step towards securing a living. Indeed most of those who live in Senegal on a permanent basis are obliged to supplement their income with other work or to remain dependent on spouses and (often older) family members for a living. Over the years, therefore, a number of troupe members have settled abroad for longer periods of time, often marrying partners from the countries in which they ended up residing.[9] I know of Bakalama members living in Belgium, France, Spain, Sweden, the UK and Australia. Others teach in the US from time to time, drawing on long-established contacts through African Diaspora festivals held there in the 1970s, where the troupe had been invited to perform. New members have been recruited in Dakar to fill in the gaps (the 'third generation'), but the troupe also regroups abroad to perform during folklore festivals. Members settled in Europe often continue to support the troupe financially, and sometimes help with perform- ing opportunities. But visa restrictions and the vulnerable situation in which some of the migrants find themselves make this increasingly haphazard.

Women performers are now almost as mobile as men. Married or not, they increasingly travel on their own. In fact the mobility of women on their own seems to be more significant in Jola troupes than in others. This is in striking continuity with the way in which the circular migration of young women became generalized in Lower Casamance from the 1950s onwards, a phenomenon which has been described extensively in the literature (Hamer 1981; Linares 1992; Lambert 1999; Foucher 2002; Lambert 2002). In the various countries in which they reside, the more successful performers, Jola and non-Jola alike, teach 'African dance' or drum- ming to European aficionados in dance studios, community centres and increasingly, in schools and summer camps. Teaching and performing dances and rhythms from all over Senegal is another way in which Casamançais performers participate in the wider nation's 'cultural work'.

Apart from the obvious potential to earn cash, travelling is a symbol of success, and many performers would prefer to travel back and forth, were it not for the dif- ficulty of getting visas. As a result, people often choose to overstay rather than risk immobility should they return home. But overstaying is not always regarded as a positive move forward, particularly in a performing scene in which people know about the harsh living conditions faced by irregular migrants. What is valued as a scarce resource is the ability to move, to experience new adventures and to return, rather than being forced to stay away for years at a time. In Senegal, therefore, the traveller is a much more significant figure of success than the migrant. Stories of travelling thus constantly appear in conversation with performers, which is revealing of the place travel (*tukki* in Wolof) occupies in people's imagination. A drummer whose group had been invited to participate in a three-day festival in Sweden, for example, told me that they had declined the offer because the festival could not pay for their plane ticket to Sweden. Visibly trying to see things positively despite the missed opportunity, he added jokingly:

> What's the point of going for three days anyway? If people see me here this week and they see me here again next week, they won't believe that I've been travelling . . . So what's the point?[10]

The prestige of travelling is also obvious in people's pride in showing photographs of themselves in transit situations: at the airport, dressed smartly and carrying a suitcase, in a plane, or standing beside a travelling football team.

The transnational character of Jola performance thus forms part of a much broader phenomenon, from the 1980s onwards, of Senegambian artists travelling and migrating to destinations outside the continent, mainly to Europe and North America. There was mobility in both directions before, as exemplified by African American dancers like Katharine Dunham, Doris Green, Judith Jamison and Chuck Davis travelling to Senegambia to study 'performing traditions' in the 1960s and 1970s. But the decline in the state's capacity to act as a patron of the arts in the 1980s accelerated the process. In turn, the establishment of transnational connections between Senegal and the wider world fostered the transformation of the performing scene from a political (nationalist or regionalist) project into a web of smaller-scale, local or individualist projects. Indeed individual career pursuits were driven by the success of the neo-traditional genre abroad, which added a strong economic dimension to what was originally a political project.

Money matters and the social organization of dance troupes

As performers often lament, neither the local audiences nor hotel owners feel that neo-traditional performance deserves substantial monetary reward. The reason for this must be sought in the status of the performer in Senegambian societies, as described in Chapter 2, and in shared ideas about dancing not requiring particular skills. As a consequence, even well-established troupes like Bakalama must cope with irregular earnings. People do not generally get paid for rehearsals, although some troupes set aside fee money towards transportation expenses. But for most, no performance means 'no income'. I have encountered only one group that was able to pay its performers a monthly salary, and this was facilitated by the leader's ownership of a dance school, as well as the fact that her husband earned a good salary in a different field. Apart from the main choreographer, group members earned about 44,000 FCFA per month in 2003, significantly more than most performers with similar profiles. As a point of comparison, according to my own estimates a beginning primary schoolteacher would have earned about 50,000 FCFA per month, a taxi driver in the range of 40–70,000, a qualified electrician 80–130,000, and a house employee 5–30,000 FCFA. Official figures for 2003 put monthly average earnings in Dakar at 58,200 FCFA, but with huge disparities between the informal sector and state employers (Ministère de l'Economie et des Finances du Sénégal 2004: 169). In this context, a dance troupe that was able to provide a regular income was extremely attractive, and performers travelled from Dakar's suburbs for several hours to come and rehearse for half a day, five or six days of the week. The troupe leader told me that she would not be able to continue paying her performers unless she found engagements abroad, but when an invitation to a festival in southern Europe eventually materialized, the trip had to be cancelled at short notice because the performers were refused a visa. A few years later, the leader was still struggling to keep her now-downsized group alive. Yet these were considered to be decent conditions in a profession dominated by uncertainty, and several of her performers supported a whole family with their monthly allowance.

At the upper end of the spectrum, some of the biggest troupes in Dakar were able to charge 200,000 FCFA per evening for official ceremonies or upper-class weddings. Regardless of the status and competence of the troupe, however, the best opportunities were perceived to be 'African' or 'folklore' festivals abroad, followed by luxury hotels in Senegal and internationally-funded local festivals. In 2003, when the Kaay Fecc festival was at the height of its success, each troupe was thus granted a fee of 250,000 to 500,000 FCFA depending on the 'degree of professionalization', which was at the upper end of the scale in the regional performing world. Once the money had been distributed among twenty or more performers, in some cases, there was little left for each individual to take home. However the comparatively low average incomes were modulated by intra-group hierarchies. Mostly left unspoken, they often translated into significant differences in earnings. Jola troupes were well aware of this, and since they cultivated an egalitarian ethos, they made a conscious effort to minimize income differences. Nevertheless, there were always ranks linked to experience, age, gender and artistic contribution. My sense was that women performers in neo-traditional troupes were generally paid less than their male counterparts, but this was difficult to establish since people were generally reluctant to discuss earnings in detail. Experience usually mattered, however, and an experienced master drummer was generally in a better position to negotiate than his fellow musicians since he could not be replaced easily. In addition, master drummers often have active networks in the artistic community by virtue of their association with Griot families. This, in turn, gives them special status because they are capable of finding players to replace missing performers very quickly. Importantly, too, they control the production (or sourcing) and maintenance of the drums.

The neo-traditional scene does not exclusively consist of big troupes with well-trained performers. Whilst one end of the continuum is occupied by troupes like the National Ballet, Sinoméew[11] and Bakalama, at the other end are semi-professional troupes who perform for high-status weddings and political rallies. They often consist of members of the same wider family or neighbourhood peers, and are less demanding of their members' technical skills. Some of the dancers may be older and perform 'chorus dancing' rather than physically demanding moves, whereas the well-established troupes rarely have older dancers, especially women. In 2002–04 these groups could be paid as little as 20–30,000 FCFA for a several hour long performance, to be shared among ten to twenty individuals. On the other hand they had more opportunities to perform, particularly if they had built up a reputation as good entertainers within a linguistic minority.

The middle of the continuum could be defined as the large number of neo-traditional troupes who perform in hotels, schools or local associations. A skilled lead drummer in one of these troupes, who also played for a 'contemporary' company, said he usually earns 7,000–10,000 FCFA per hotel performance, but that most of his fellow group members only earned 3,000 FCFA regardless of the hotel's standing. His drumming lessons to foreign students earned him 5,000 FCFA per hour in 2003. In good seasons he would have one or two students at a time for a couple of hours per week, giving a maximum of 20,000 FCFA per week for private teaching. But he kept the hotel work because foreign students only came on a seasonal basis. On the other hand, foreign students represented potential opportunities for travel, and these teaching hours were thus as much an income as they were an investment in the future. He lived in a small room on the first floor of an unfinished house[12] in one of the poorer *quartiers*. The room was furnished with just a foam mattress, a chair and a small table, an open shelf, a nylon curtain and a radio-cassette player. The Mouride cleric who owned the house allowed him to live there for free. A couple of times per week he would visit his mother at the family house in one of Dakar's suburbs. He did not complain because he was waiting for an opportunity to emigrate. As a dedicated Muslim and hard-working musician, he had faith that his turn would come, and indeed a few years later he married a French woman and moved to France.

For the lucky few who manage to get contracts abroad, a few performances in Europe or North America may generate the equivalent of a year of hard work at home. To achieve this, a common trajectory is to begin as an apprentice in a neighbourhood troupe,[13] then move on to a bigger troupe with more touring opportunities.

One lead drummer in a bigger troupe required a fee of 300,000 FCFA per show when on tour abroad, but was not always given satisfaction. Having been on a tour a few weeks before his wife gave birth to their fifth child, he spent most of his earnings on a lavish name-giving ceremony. This was his gift to her, he told me. She had always dreamt of a ceremony with more guests than anyone in the neighbourhood, and expensive new outfits for herself. But previous births had not coincided with a tour abroad, and so he had not been able to afford this. Some months earlier however, the musician had spent some of his savings to set up a dance troupe in the neighbourhood. A ñeeño himself, he had recruited youths from both géér and ñeeño families, all impressed with his touring credentials and his superior drumming skills. Although the troupe had not yet been paid to perform in public, he had paid for the instruments, the costumes and the rental of the local cultural centre for rehearsals. Above all, he was keeping the youths occupied, and hopeful. Three times per week they trained, the drummers with him or one of his apprentices, and the dancers (a majority of girls and a few boys) with his male 'ballet master'. This position as the patron of a dance troupe gave him considerable status, and people I knew in the neighbourhood talked admiringly about him as a 'cultural actor' or a 'group leader' rather than as a géwël.

An experienced dancer in another troupe said he had received 200,000 FCFA for two performances in a luxury hotel in the French Caribbean. But on return he had to contribute 50,000 FCFA to the group's savings, which were spent on costumes and redistribution to troupe members who had not been selected for travel. He added that such redistribution was necessary to avoid discouragement from those still waiting for their turn to perform abroad. Indeed, although people probably understated their earnings to avoid envy, it is nevertheless the case that many troupes redistribute so as to minimize the turnover of members, though admittedly not as much as the Jola troupes.

In both examples mentioned here, the men involved were experienced performers in their thirties. They were also skilled negotiators, which gave them an advantage over younger troupe members. For many others, the promise of financial salvation through touring could be deceptive. Many women dancers, in particular, had little formal education, and not being able to read fluently in French, they only had the leaders' word for how much the group was being paid to perform. Many complained that they were given no information beforehand, and that they were expected to comply with the authority of the male leaders. Younger performers of both sexes often felt exploited, and many eagerly waited for opportunities to travel or to do independent choreographic work, as we will see in the next chapter. One dancer thus recalled his time with a troupe ten years earlier, in which the leader eventually married a European woman. Now able to share his time between Senegal and his wife's country, he occasionally brought his troupe from Dakar to European festivals. The dancer confessed that he had been bitter upon being repeatedly excluded from these trips, even though he was, in his own view, one of the best performers. He was convinced that the leader only ever selected the very young and inexperienced ones so that he could exploit them. They were all too grateful to be travelling, and whatever happened, they did not complain. Though there may have been entirely different reasons why he had not been chosen, it was significant that he explained his marginalization in the light of exploitative practices. In this environment, this was an entirely credible story. Fortunately, a few years later he had the opportunity to travel to France to teach youngsters, marry a French woman and settle there.

Other performers expressed their frustration that touring was not just a source of income but was costly, too, as this performer in his late twenties:

> You go to Europe for two or three months, you dance almost every day and then come back with 100,000 or may be 200,000 [FCFA]. It seems like a lot of money, but when you start thinking about it, it's not much for all this work. By the time you've lived and bought gifts to bring back home, there's nothing left. Most of the time you don't even know where the money goes.

As we will see in the next two chapters, the fear of exploitation is one of the reasons why many are attracted to contemporary dance; by doing individualized choreography, dancers hope to retain more control over their bodies, and their future. Another common strategy is to pursue activities alongside performing work, such as the trading of drums or the construction of 'tradition' as a commodity, as I turn to now.

The commodification of tradition

Remodelling existing narratives about 'tradition'[14] and turning them into commodities is by no means unique to the region, but the existence of a rich story-telling culture has facilitated the process. In addition, the nationalist period's emphasis on re-staging regional history has facilitated the objectification of historical narratives. Outside the continent, a renewed interest in African forms of performance, in the wake of the World Music phenomenon, has made people aware that their 'culture' could be valued beyond the borders of the region. But how does one turn 'culture' into a commodity?

The Dakarois world of neo-traditional performance as I have come to know it features an entrepreneurial sense that there is nothing wrong in giving people what they are prepared to pay for. There is also a sense in which this is morally justifiable because of Africa's past and present exploitation by European interests. There is an explicit discourse according to which 'Africans' should in turn be able to exploit the only valuable thing that they have left: their 'culture'. Thus I was often told that White people had traded their souls for wealth, and that they looked towards Africa in search of spirituality. In fact, this was the rationale on which Germaine Acogny's dance workshops in the Casamance in the late 1980s – early 1990s were based (Barry 1987). For many Senegalese performers, the sustained global interest in 'traditional' African dance and music forms part of this quest. Far from being oblivious of the moral value of what they do, people thus frame the business of selling bits of 'culture' in moral terms. A dancer-drummer with experience in several neo-traditional troupes, for example, told me casually about the dancing and drumming workshops he organized twice a year for European high school students on cultural trips to Senegal: 'If they only want the dance classes I ask for 30,000 FCFA per hour [for the whole group]', he said, 'but if they want the little stories about tradition as well, I ask for the double'.

Making a business of the 'little stories' was not the prerogative of men. During my first few months in Dakar, people had often suggested that I speak to Ndèye Khady Niang, a former dancer with the National Ballet whom I introduced in Chapter 3. In her late fifties when I met her, she still danced occasionally, including on TV shows. A friend of mine knew her nephew, and after a couple of phone calls she agreed to see me. She had made it clear that she expected to be paid, and seeing my reluctance to pay someone to speak to me, my friend tried to reassure me by pointing out that Ndèye Khady was a Griotte, and that women like her always expected to be paid. By the time we arrived at her house at 10.30 am as agreed, she had already left. Someone from the household let us in, and we decided to wait in her spacious living room. It had all the attributes of a middle-class Dakarois house:

expensive-looking, locally made armchairs and a sofa, all covered in synthetic velvet. There was a low glass table, shelves with glass-covered showcases filled with trinkets, and plastic flowers. A scent of curaay was floating in the air, and the walls were covered with framed portrait photographs of Ndèye Khady alone, with family and with well-known artists and politicians, including a centrally placed photograph in which she posed with Abdoulaye Wade. There was also a large portrait of her as a modestly dressed young girl, surrounded by both her parents, as well as a framed photograph of the Kasbah in Mecca. Informed by phone of her whereabouts, we finally tracked her down at her family home in a different neighbourhood, where two older ladies teased Ndèye Khady's nephew about his delay in getting married. Looking over to me, one of them joked that if he wanted to marry a *tubaab*,[15] he could choose someone with my skin colour, but no lighter. We were offered soft drinks. The door to the street was permanently open, and our chat was occasionally interrupted by a neighbour's greeting or a street peddler selling anything from vegetables to kitchen utensils and teddy bears. Ndèye Khady made a flamboyant entrance, apologizing for a delay which was, she said, caused by her being summoned to the presidential palace this very morning. While she insisted that she did not 'sell her art' because this was a 'gift from God', she requested to be paid, and we negotiated the price of the interview. She argued that the kind of information I was looking for was priceless and that having worked with American and Dutch scholars in the past, she knew the value of knowledge.

As my friend and I proceeded to interview her in a mix of French and Wolof, she consistently refused to talk about her career, except to mention the numerous official distinctions she had received, and her past invitation to teach at Maurice Béjart's dance school in Geneva. She did, however, enumerate the sabar rhythms she mastered, and proceeded to describe the 'traditional costumes' of sabar, even though I had not asked her to do so. When I asked her to tell me about the social context of a dance that had been one of her favourites, she replied that this was the sort of dance one performed during official visits, with TV crews on. When I insisted that there must have been other occasions when this dance was performed, she became visibly irritated. With a dismissive hand gesture, she replied that this dance used to be performed during weddings and name-giving ceremonies, and hastened to change the topic. After half an hour she said that my time was up, and demanded to be paid. Although Ndèye Khady may simply have been offended by my interviewing style, I had a strong sense that her irritation came from the fact that I had unsettled her expectation that she would make up whatever stories about 'tradition' she thought I deserved to hear.

Indeed she had done this before, which confirmed Leymarie's (1999) observation that one of the modern specializations of the Wolof Griots was to work with foreign researchers. In Dakar I came across this phenomenon often. Early on, I met a very articulate man who introduced himself as a story teller and 'expert in tradition'. He claimed to know a great deal about the region's dances, but warned me that he would not share his knowledge with me. Indeed I had to deserve his trust. As I met him regularly over the following months, he did share stories with me, but was consistently evasive on the question of his sources. He said his knowledge came from his upbringing in a rural area, and from years of personal interaction with elders. It gradually became clear that he did possess a great deal of knowledge, but that far from being from lived experience alone, this came from a mix of oral tradition, storytelling, novels and scholarly literature. There were references to Marcel Griaule's work on the Dogon and to Cheikh Anta Diop's work on the historical link between West Africa and Egypt. His self-conscious construction of tradition gave him a certain status – albeit contested at times – in the performing world. He often participated in TV or radio programmes on Senegambian traditions, and worked with foreign researchers as a matter of course. But he also confessed to feeling exploited by foreign scholars, and that he had therefore taken to asking hourly payment for sharing his knowledge. I did not react to the subtle hint, and he hastily added that my case was different because my project was also an 'existential quest'.

This individual belonged to a category of people who made a genuine effort to develop a body of knowledge about regional social histories, and to make it available to the performing world. He often told youths that they ought to know the history of the dances they were learning because they needed to have 'real values' to offer to the world. For him, traditional knowledge and morality were intimately connected. But there were also individuals with far less knowledge, who simply gravitated around foreigners in the hope of selling access to 'tradition'. This worked well with cultural tourists easily excited at the prospect of meeting 'authentic' Griots. One of them, a young man in his mid-twenties, said he was from a family of practising Griots, and offered to tell me everything I needed to know about traditional ceremonies. He also suggested, quite explicitly, that I give him some kind of compensation. He had just been 'working' with two French students for a week, mainly introducing them to some of his dancer friends, and was hoping to repeat the success with me. He became a little confused when I told him that I was more interested in his own background, but he answered my questions graciously. It turned out that he was not at all a practising Griot. He was a trained welder and enjoyed his trade, but was out of work for the time being. He had a relative who was a musician at a club in Paris, and who had encouraged him to learn to play the sabar. Hoping that this might give him opportunities to travel, the young man had been a drumming apprentice for a couple of years, but had eventually found that he did not possess much talent. He was now trying to recruit drummers for the Parisian club, and was hoping to get a visa to travel with them. When I asked how he had acquired the knowledge he was hoping to sell, he told me that his grandfather was a Wolof Griot with a deep knowledge of oral history. The young man himself had never been interested in his grandfather's stories until he realized that he could make money from them. He had therefore taped the stories and listened to them again and again, trying to extract their deeper meaning. It was obvious that he was not yet confident about his own knowledge. When I told him that I would try to attend family ceremonies in Dakar, he immediately offered to sell me video tapes of 'authentic' Griot ceremonies, on the grounds that géwël ceremonies were more traditional that the others. When I declined, he pulled out another set of services: he could introduce me to 'famous dancers' who performed in mbalax videos, and would negotiate the price of dance lessons on my behalf. I did not take up his offer, but when I met him again a few weeks later, he had been luckier with a young American woman with whom he was 'working'. Less than a year later, he had become an assistant manager in a newly formed dance troupe, and was still waiting for his visa to travel to France.

Conclusion

As Cohen (1993) and Parkin (1996) have argued, there is a dialectical relationship between cultural performance and politics: cultural performance lends itself to appropriation for political purposes, while political agendas must be performed to become meaningful in people's everyday lives. In post-colonial Senegal indeed, the genre of neo-traditional performance that was promoted by the state for nation-building purposes was soon appropriated by those who had been marginalized in this project. The colonial history of school theatre described in Chapter 1 meant that Casamançais hometown associations in Dakar, led by students and migrants with primary-level schooling, took the lead in appropriating the genre. Their staging of localized themes for both local and national audiences fostered the imagination and articulation of a Jola identity, which then fed into the separatist discourse in the southern region.

Dance and drama have been particularly seductive in this context because their flexibility has allowed for a multiplicity of messages to be perceived differently by different audiences: within the associations, the work of acquiring bodily techniques associated with the Casamançais landscape has helped to maintain a sense of belonging as well as distinction from ethnic 'others'. For audiences from outside the region, Casamançais 'culture' was imagined through the performance of Casamançais troupes, while tensions internal to the region were hidden from view. Tensions between Jola and Mandinka, between the different wards of a locality, or between individuals with different wealth and educational backgrounds, for example, were silenced in this cultural work. Performance thus helped to create an illusion of Casamançais unity and egalitarianism, which in turn is occasionally framed as a sign of the region's moral superiority over the rest of the nation. Flexibility is also reflected in the way in which the practice of popular dances in youth clubs and neighbourhood events helps youths from migrant backgrounds to make sense of their belonging to different moral communities.

In the introduction, I suggested that agency in performance was central to processes of self-fashioning, and this is a good point at which to return to the issue. By contrast with sabar dancing, in the neo-traditional genre the agency for movement is understood to be with the group, albeit distributed unequally depending on individual experience and creativity. But there is little sense left of a form of agency residing outside human control. Here skilled drumming helps to mobilize individual and group creativity, but it does not call upon extra-human forces. Indeed I have never heard dancers say, in connection with the neo-traditional genre, that they danced because they could not help it, as is often said about sabar.

The neo-traditional genre has also become an attractive livelihood for many youths without prospects of formal employment. In reality, however, the hierarchical organization of neo-traditional troupes often makes it difficult for youths with little

performing experience to achieve the autonomy and social mobility they had imagined. As we will see in the next two chapters, the difficulty in fulfilling these aspirations is at the centre of the enthusiasm for contemporary choreographic production
since the mid-1990s.

Notes

1. On inter-ward conflicts about local politics and the male initiation cycle, see De Jong's
(2007) detailed ethnography.
2. In Thionck Essyl, male initiation is called *garur*. It is called *bukut, futamp* or *kombutsu*
elsewhere in Lower Casamance (De Jong 2007).
3. *Kañaalen* performed by Bakalama, Dakar, 5 June 2003. Monologue: 'I am tired of walking. I am tired of being subjected to the criticism of others. Oh God, please give me a
child. Please make me become like the other women. I cannot continue to live like this.
My co-wife has all the favours of our husband, who does not even bother to show that
he cares about me. I am sad and abandoned. [The women sing in Jola] What have I done
to deserve this punishment? Banned by the women, despised by the men, Akintou no
longer knows where to go. I have been everywhere in the village. The witch doctors, the
marabouts, the elders, I have visited them all. [. . .] The children flee when they see me.
The mothers do not trust me and curse me. [. . .] At dawn I sneak back into my bedroom
so as not to awaken my co-wife and her flock of children'.
4. In the Africanist literature, Askew's (2002) and Edmonson's (2007) studies addressed
this gap in important ways. The performance of ethnicity is also treated beautifully in
Alexander's (1996) monograph on Black British youth identities.
5. Foucher (2002) shows how the culturalist argument, which emphasizes the distinctiveness
of Jola culture, has been appropriated by both sides of the conflict.
6. For a review of these studies, see Foucher 2005.
7. Foucher (2002) and De Jong (2007) also suggest that Jola male initiation has become
stronger as a marker of identity since the beginning of the conflict.
8. See Lambert (2002) for an analysis of the control of the migration and marriage of young
women in the Jola community of Mandégane, in the Lower Casamance.
9. I use the term 'ended up' purposefully because in most cases destinations were the outcome of encounters and circumstances rather than a choice from the outset.
10. Conversation with performer, Dakar, September 2002.
11. Sinoméew was set up in 1990 by Doudou Ndiaye Rose's eldest son Mamadou Thiouna
Ndiaye Rose with performers from the National Ballet's second troupe, Ballet Sirabadral,
after it had to shut down due to a lack of state funding.
12. See Melly (2010) for a perceptive analysis of the role of unfinished houses in Dakarois
residents' imagination of the future.
13. In 2002–05, neighbourhood troupes included, for example, Ballets et Rythmes and Jant
bi in Pikine, Kibaro Baleya in Dalifort, the Farafina Guy Gui Ballet in HLM, or the
G.I.E. Goorgoorlou in Yëmbël.
14. In everyday speech most people either use the French word or the Wolof term *cosaan*,
which roughly translates as the origin, or the past.
15. The term refers both to race and to socioeconomic category. It is mostly used to designate
a White person, but may also be used to denote a privileged social position. Thus a
wealthy, educated Senegalese person who speaks French at home may be called *tubaab* in
some contexts.

Chapter 6

Senegalese 'Contemporary Dance' and Global Arts Circuits

We should not close ourselves in a 'ghetto'. In the West they tap from other cultures; for example, when Picasso came to Africa, his paintings took another direction – so we too can do the same. We can borrow. We are free to take/appropriate. We have to be open and see what other people are doing and learn from them. But how can we do it without getting lost? That's a question I'm asking myself. (Kettly Noël in Douglas et al. 2006)

Every time there is a dance gathering somewhere, we discuss Africa. But really I don't care about Africa. As far as my dancing is concerned – when I'm creating – I care about myself. I care about my grandmother and the people who are around me. When I create I'll probably make some money and I can buy her a piece of cloth that she needs or I can buy her medicine and yeah, that's to quote the Argentinean writer Jorge Luis Borges, I would say that, while writing, I strictly write for myself, for a few people and what is the course of time . . . my time. I don't care about Africa because Africa – at least my portion of Africa – the one that I experience in my flesh, doesn't care about me. (Faustin Linyekula in Douglas et al. 2006)

This chapter starts with words of dancer-choreographers Kettly Noël and Faustin Linyekula, spoken at a panel discussion organized as part of the Jomba! Contemporary Dance Conference held in August 2004 in Durban, South Africa. The symposium was entitled 'African Contemporary Dance? Questioning Issues of a Performance Aesthetic for a Developing and Independent Continent', and its proceedings were published in an article edited by dance writer Adrienne Sichel (Douglas et al. 2006).[1] Both choreographers live in both France and Africa, Mali in Noël's case and the Democratic Republic of Congo (DRC) for Linyekula, and both have links to the Senegalese scene. National and regional politics, it turns out, are not the only dimensions at stake in choreographic dance worlds across Africa: they also form part of the global 'contemporary dance' phenomenon. In Senegal, contemporary dance is related to neo-traditional performance since it is often the same individuals who are involved in both genres, either simultaneously or at different life stages. But whereas the neo-traditional genre illuminates contested attempts to articulate nationalist and regionalist discourses, this more individualistic field of practice places people in global circuits, while also allowing for more autonomous selves to emerge.

The quotes above point to the existence of a pan-African artistic consciousness. Kettly Noël, who is originally from Haiti, is the leader of choreographic centre Donko Seko in Bamako, and performs across the world. In Mali and in Benin, where she lived for a few years before moving to Mali, she has facilitated the emergence of a new generation of choreographers. Faustin Linyekula studied Literature and Drama in Kisangani before leaving for Kenya in the mid-1990s, where he formed the Gàara Company with Kenyan dancer, Opiyo Okach. He now has his own Studios Kabako in Kisangani, and also performs across the world. Both Noël and Linyekula belong to the small but growing elite of African or Africa-based choreographers who travel widely to show their work, while also being able to speak about it in articulate ways. I brought in their reflections on the nature of what they do because they echo ongoing debates on the African-ness of contemporary arts throughout the continent, including in Senegal. Indeed, the local dance scene is very much shaped by interactions with performers elsewhere in Africa and across the world. Most Senegalese choreographers, however, find it essential to ground their work in their own lives. I treat the Senegalese contemporary scene, therefore, as an instance of how locality is 'constructed, enacted, and rhetorically defended with an eye (and ear) on others, both near and far' (Stokes 2004:50). The eye that is turned towards the local is concerned with contesting hierarchies of social status ('caste'), gender and generation, and this is done by shifting creative agency towards the individual artist. A new category of fairly young 'dancer-choreographers' has emerged in the process. The eye that is turned to the wider world, on the other hand, is concerned with individual success and participation in global cultural production on equal terms with artists from other parts of the world.

By the time I began fieldwork in May 2002, I knew of the National Ballet and the neo-traditional genre, and I knew of Mrs Acogny's current choreographic centre as well as of the Mudra Afrique adventure in the 1970s. But I had little awareness of the existence of a 'contemporary dance' scene. A chance encounter early on meant that I was able to go and see the company, La 5ᵉ Dimension, rehearse soon after arriving. As I walked into the small sports centre in the port area, the choreographer, Jean Tamba was sitting on the floor, next to a CD player. This was a proper dance room, with a concrete floor entirely covered with a thin rubber mat, and a large mirror along the wall. The dancers were facing the mirror, and Tamba was facing them. Behind the dancers, opposite the mirror, were large doors opened onto a courtyard paved with concrete, with a water fountain and a few plants in the middle. Between the open doors was a bench on which two drummers sat. A small group of four dancers, a woman and three men, was working on *Bujuman*, a piece due to have its premiere a few months later. One of the young men was experimenting with a short sequence he had choreographed, mixing high-energy double 'jazz pirouettes'[2] and slower moves with sweeping arms. The young woman was also working on her own, but with neo-traditional Mandinka-style moves, which she interrupted abruptly before beginning again. The remaining two men were working on a duet which seemed to include both mime and contact improvisation. The group was introduced to me as 'the first contemporary dance company' in Senegal.

Trying to make sense of the creative process I was witnessing led me to reflect on the relationship between this genre and others in the city. It emerged that none of the dancers had started with contemporary dance, and that all had been trained in neo-traditional performance at some stage. Most were also, or had been, keen performers of sabar and popular dances. It also became obvious that for all the talk about rooted-ness in the local, the contemporary genre had a much smaller and more cosmopolitan audience than the neo-traditional genre. What was it, I wondered, which led people into these choreographic experiments?

Addressing this question required me to widen the perspective beyond Senegal. In the past two decades there has been hope that African contributions would help to refresh global contemporary arts circuits, including the contemporary dance world. Through their mobility and their aspiration to take their rightful place in global cultural movements, African performers have encouraged this interest. Global circuits and the Senegalese dance world, however, have often had different agendas, which have intersected at the desire on both sides to create something new. In this chapter, I look at the transnational genesis of the so-called 'African contemporary dance' genre of which individualized choreography in Senegal forms a part. I suggest that this movement has been driven by a growing global interest in African 'contemporary arts', French foreign policy, and a desire on the part of performers to bypass age hierarchies in the creative process. Ultimately, the rise of contemporary choreography in Senegal is yet another instance of appropriation and mutual engagement: just as neo-traditional performance has been appropriated to serve regional, local and individual agendas, so the transnational resources of contemporary performance have been appropriated to develop fast-track pathways to success for youths with creative aspirations.

'African contemporary dance': African innovation or European invention?

Since the early 1960s, dancers in North America, and later in Europe, have developed a range of choreographic experiments aimed at disrupting the codes of classical ballet and modern dance. In the earliest movements, like the Judson Dance Theater in New York (1962–64), performers chose the term 'postmodern dance' to mark their distance from the modern dance innovations of the previous decades. Often trained in the techniques of Merce Cunningham, Martha Graham or José Limón in the US, they explicitly rejected the hierarchies and codification of American modern dance, which had itself emerged as a reaction against classical ballet in the early twentieth century. In their search for new ways of making dance, the Judson artists sought to challenge the boundaries between dancers and choreographer, between dance and non-dance, between professional dancers and ordinary individuals, and between performers and audience. They experimented with serendipitous movement, with bodies reacting to other surfaces than a stage (roofs, stairs, fabric, water . . .), and most importantly, to each other (Burt 2006). They sought to involve all the senses by using their voices, the sounds of their bodies or silence instead of music. They collaborated with musicians – in the Judson Dance case this was Robert Dunn, a student of John Cage – but also with visual artists to develop new ways of 'making' space (Guigou 2004). In short, postmodern dance was about dissolving all the traditional boundaries of choreographic spectacle.

The Judson Dance group was not unique in its search for innovation, for similar experiments were taking place throughout the US and Europe in the 1960s and 1970s. Some of this work took place under the impulse of former Judson Dance people, most famously Steve Paxton, who led the early Contact Improvisation Movement (Novack 1990). Yvonne Rainer, Trisha Brown, Lucinda Childs and Meredith Monk, for example, were all Judson Dance members who went on to lead their own choreographic movements. Over time, the principles of postmodern dance and contact improvisation were in turn challenged by new generations of performers who charged the pioneers with codifying experimental matter into genres, and reproducing the hierarchies they had worked so hard to dissolve (Novack 1990). Gradually, the term 'contemporary dance' was preferred to capture the diversity of styles and places of origin in individualized choreography. The European and North American strands both, however, identify themselves as a reaction against pre-1960s choreographic traditions.

The choreographic experiments which have come to be subsumed under the term 'African contemporary dance' position themselves in relation to neo-traditional performance, but this is not necessarily antagonistic. As we have seen in the previous two chapters, this was the genre that came to define modern spectacle in West Africa during the colonial period. When looking for ways to unsettle the codes of the genre, artists in Senegal and other parts of West Africa appropriated aspects of the American and European experiments. This happened through the training of young performers outside the continent and the impact of major French-funded events. Indeed, I suggest here that the crystallization of choreographic experiments carried out throughout Africa into a genre is intimately connected to French foreign policy, as exercised in the patronage of pan-African choreographic competitions, festivals, workshops and venues. It was initially dance people in Senegal who alerted me to this connection. As one informant put it, the very concept of 'African contemporary dance' was in many respects a French invention:

It was an idea of the French to create African contemporary dance. They've put a lot of money into it [. . .]. They talk about 'globalization'. But in truth they want to civilize us because our African dances disturb them. Our culture disturbs them . . . There's a lot of money in it, so the dancers throw themselves into it without thinking.[3]

This informant alluded to the fact that it was French funding that crystallized disparate choreographic experiments into a genre. As funders, the French state agencies involved also had the power to name it: 'African contemporary dance'.

In retrospect it is difficult to say whether the French cultural authorities planned to create a genre or whether this happened as an outcome of promotion. Informal conversations I had with French civil servants involved suggest that it was the latter, and that the early objectives of the patronage policy were twofold: first, to maintain a strategic presence in Africa over the longer term, and second, to raise the profile of the local performing worlds so as to discourage migration to Europe. In other words, investing in cultural innovation for the African youth was about a combination of political alliance and migration 'containement'.

The biennial choreographic competition initiated in 1995 for the continent as a whole, the Rencontres chorégraphiques de l'Afrique et de l'Océan Indien (hereafter 'Rencontres'), was to play a leading role in this process. The timing was due in equal measure to foreign policy, to the co-option of former contemporary dancers into French funding agencies, and to the influence of well-established African dancers like Germaine Acogny and Ivorian, Alphonse Tiérou. The first Rencontres were thus organized in 1995 in Luanda by the French programme, Afrique en Créations, a state-funded arts agency created in 1991 under the auspices of the French Cooperation Ministry. The programme was later integrated into the bigger state agency AFAA (Association Française d'Action Artistique), itself restructured as Cultures France in 2006, and finally the French Institute in 2011, under the Ministry of Foreign Affairs. The French Institute, now the main funding body and organizer of the Rencontres, is presented as 'a new actor in charge of implementing France's cultural diplomacy'.[4] The anchoring of the Institute and its preceding agencies in French diplomacy is evident in their leadership by high-ranking civil servants and diplomats. In 2013, the French Institute President, Xavier Darcos, is thus a politician who has held successive posts since 2002 as a Minister for Cooperation and Development, an Ambassador with the Organization for Economic Cooperation and Development (OECD), a Minister of National Education and a Minister of Labour. Indeed the political dimension of arts patronage has become more visible over the years, and is now explicitly linked to French foreign policy in Africa. In 2010, this link was thus discernible through the slightly convoluted diplomatic language on the Cultures France website:

Afrique et Caraïbes en Créations: strategic objectives
Drawing on a long and fruitful experience in cultural cooperation with the countries of the Priority Solidarity Zone, France now faces new challenges in a competitive economic environment: continuation of a policy of solidarity towards those countries; preservation of a strategic position as a historic partner with an original cultural vision aimed at promoting economic and human development; anticipation and promotion of innovation through methods and tools implemented towards a sustainable cultural development.[5]

Officially, the first competition was held in Luanda at the invitation of the Angolan government. Reports by professional participants which I had the opportunity to read at the French Institute's archive, however, suggest that there were political reasons for this choice. This is all the more likely as the first Rencontres coincided with a period during which France was attempting to strengthen its presence in Southern Africa, and nursing its oil interests in Angola. It is certainly no coincidence that among the Angolan state officials present at the opening in November 1995 was Albina Assis, then chairwoman of state oil company Sonangol. Nor was it accidental that one of the main sponsors of the event was Elf Exploration Angola. Given France's history of coupling foreign policy with arts sponsorship, there is little doubt that the Rencontres formed part of France's political playground in Africa. The second event was held in Luanda in 1997. The third was cancelled and moved to Antananarivo, Madagascar, in 1999. The Malagasy authorities made their mark on the event by renaming it 'Sanga', 'the summit' in Malagasy. The official reason given by the French authorities was that the civil war had resumed in Angola. But the fact that the change also coincided with the souring of French-Angolan relations over oil is unlikely to have been a coincidence. France had wanted to make its mark on the region for its oil and mineral wealth, and it is in this light that the choice of Johannesburg for the 2012 biennale should be understood.[6]

The initial objective of the event, as stated by Afrique en Créations, was to promote the development of creative choreography in Africa through financial support, the organization of international tours, administrative support towards professionalization and media exposure. Financial support was meant to encourage high-quality work by granting individual performers an income during the gestation of a piece. In 2003 for example, each pre-selected group received 3,000 Euros towards preparation for the competition. The winners of the first prize received a fully paid tour together with a daily amount towards living expenses, the attractive per diem. The second prize winners received 5,000 Euros towards a new creation, and the group selected for the Trophée RFI-Danse, sponsored by French state radio station Radio France Internationale, received 3,500 Euros. The touring aspect is by far the most attractive to performers. For the first seven occurrences of the biennale, Afrique en Créations organized European tours for the first three prizes, and for a few years an African tour was arranged for the first prize and the Trophée RFI-Danse. Limited to France until 2001, after 2003 the European tours were extended to Spain, Italy, Germany and the UK among others. Media exposure and 'professionalization' are also presented as beneficial side effects: the process of application, which requires candidate groups to submit photographs, a video and a written description of their work, encourages candidates to promote their work in accordance with international standards.

The biennale has grown substantially to become, in the eyes of many professionals, the most important choreographic event on the continent. The competitive dimension was abandoned in 2012 for a variety of reasons,[7] and it is now explicitly a 'market' where presenters come looking for new talent to showcase around the world. It is also, of course, an opportunity for the hosting country to display its capacity to organize high-calibre events. Given the political significance of the event, it probably became obvious that it could not remain the prerogative of Madagascar. In 2003, therefore, it was decided that the biennale would be hosted in a different African country every time. The 2006 biennale took place in Paris after the failure of a French bid to host it in South Africa, thus making it plainly obvious where the real decision-making power lay.

Though the French Institute works as the main gatekeeper, French sponsorship is actually spread across several, at times competing institutions. This includes the Organization Internationale de la Francophonie (OIF), established since 1970 as a cultural and political gathering of seventy nations which recognize French as one of their languages to some degree. The OIF presents itself as organizing 'political activities and actions of multilateral cooperation that benefit French-speaking populations'.[8] Though the French Institute and the OIF are officially independent of each other, they invoke a strikingly similar discourse of 'cultural diversity'. Both, it is said, fight for the preservation of cultural diversity, and the promotion of the local arts worldwide is an essential part of this salvation project.

This is eerily reminiscent of the debates over the preservation of local cultures in the colonies that took place in France during the colonial period, and which culminated with the 1937 Paris Congress (Chapter 1). There is also clear continuity with UNESCO's 2005 stated objective of protecting cultural diversity, via its recognition of 'cultural heritage', which the OIF also explicitly supports. UNESCO was already involved in promoting contemporary choreography in Africa through partly funding Mudra Afrique, and it is one of the sponsors of Mrs Acogny's choreographic centre in Tubaab Jallaw. All these institutions have adopted policies that resonate with a Francophone-dominated discourse on 'cultural diversity' and 'culture as an actor in development'. This is in striking continuity with an enduring tension between the France's desire to expand French culture on the one hand, and a lingering fear of being accused of neo-colonialism on the other hand.

France is not the only state involved in supporting the contemporary arts in Africa, but there is a Francophone convergence since the other important player is Belgium, albeit with a slightly less ambitious role. Thus in March 2003, a four-day festival of contemporary African performance, Africalia, was held in Brussels. This was the third in a series of events initiated in 2001 by Eddy Boutmans, the Belgian Secretary of State for Development and Cooperation. Thirteen contemporary dance companies from eleven African countries took part, including three Senegalese dancers from Mrs Acogny's Jant bi Company, and several Senegalese drummers. Most of the individuals invited had also been participants at the previous Rencontres in Antananarivo. Like the Rencontres, the objectives of Africalia, also one of the sponsors of the Kaay Fecc festival at the time, were described in terms of 'professionalization', 'structural development' and partnership, and the underlying political dimension was equally perceptible:

> [Africalia is] an innovative first time happening that stems from a real desire
> on the part of the Belgian federal government to place south-south and
> north-south culture exchanges at the centre of its sustainable development

co-operation efforts. Africalia is not a cultural promoter; neither is it just another provider of funds intervening directly in Africa. Africalia is a partner, attentive to the needs of African cultural operators. (Africalia 2003)

Just like France, Belgium, another former colonial nation, was repositioning itself as a partner concerned with respecting the aspirations of Africans, rather than as a giver of international aid. But for all the talk of cultural diversity and sustainable development, there has been widespread criticism among West African performers that the Rencontres and other major events of this kind have had a standardizing effect on choreographic production in Africa. If this is true, this is an ironic, and unexpected outcome of policies which may not have been as concerned with cultural diversity as they claimed to be. It may not be possible to answer the question fully in this book, but we may begin to get a sense of the impact of the biennale by looking at the ways in which it has shaped choreographic expression in Senegal.

French-funded events and the Senegalese performing world

In the Senegalese dance world, every African dance biennale raises both hope and resentment. Contemporary dancers follow the event closely, and the links tying the event to the Senegalese scene mean that it is experienced by some as socially close if geographically remote: Mrs Acogny was simultaneously the director of the event and the director of the dance section at Afrique en Créations between 1997 and 2000. More importantly, the professional workshops she has held in Tubaab Jallaw since 1998 with dancer-choreographers from all over Africa have been a major 'breeding ground' for the competition. In 2003 for example, four choreographers among the eleven selected had attended a workshop at her centre at some stage. In 2012, probably two-thirds of the forty-four participating companies had been through the Tubaab Jallaw centre.

Senegalese performers, though, have not always been as successful as the presence of the Ecole des Sables may suggest. In 2003, four Senegalese groups applied, and only one was selected. In 2006, on the other hand, the winners were Andreya Ouamba's Dakar-based company, Premier Temps, who presented a duet by Ouamba himself with Fatou Cissé. Ouamba is a Congolese dancer-choreographer who grew up in Brazzaville and came to the dance world through American-style street dances first, then moved on to a neo-traditional dance troupe set up by a young dancer in Brazzaville in the early 1990s. Fatou Cissé, daughter of Ousmane Noël Cissé, is one of the most experienced women performers in the Dakarois dance world. In 2008, La 5ᵉ Dimension dancer Mustapha Guèye was shortlisted with a solo for the seventh biennale in Tunis, but did not win. The winner in the solo category that year was another Senegalese dancer, Kaolack. Whether or not they returned with awards, returning candidates and other participants (company managers, festival organizers, journalists) have had a significant impact in diffusing the prestige and style of the competition. Those who returned with touring opportunities were looked upon with a mix of admiration and envy, both in the regional dance world and among relatives and friends. In short, participants have acted as intermediaries between the transnational circuits present at the biennale and the Senegalese dance world. This has happened through both face-to-face interaction and visual media.

Performances and workshops held by Rencontres winners have been the most significant factor due to the personalized nature of the interaction among dancers on these occasions. The Africa-wide network of French Cultural Centres[9] has played a crucial role in promoting the talents who have come through via the biennale, and the Centre in Dakar has been an important step in pan-African tours.[10] Malagasy dancer-choreographer, Ariry Andriamoratsiresy, who won both the RFI prize and the second prize at the biennale in Antananarivo in 2001, has performed in Dakar several times, both solo and with his company, Rary. On every occasion the audience included a significant proportion of local dance people and journalists. However the entrance fee at the French Centre, between 1,000 and 3,000 FCFA, is an obstacle and performers tend to select those occasions when free tickets are made available to them. Although the French Institute has been generous in this respect, its location in the city centre requires people to pay for transportation and food, which adds up to significant amounts. This is particularly problematic for young women, whose reputation would be at risk if they were seen coming home from the city centre on their own, late at night. For city dwellers, such autonomous coming-and-going at night is associated with young women who go to bars and night clubs to find foreign partners. There are always complaints, therefore, that too little is done to make contemporary performances accessible to all. For this reason, between 2001 and 2005 the Kaay Fecc festival offered an entire programme with free entrance to the public, and has attempted to collect funds for a mobile stage to bring contemporary dance to the *quartiers*. But funding has dwindled dramatically since 2005, and though early festivals included a few events in the suburbs, the mobile stage project has been filed for now.

Workshops with former participants in the biennale take place less often, but many dancers prefer them over the performances because they allow for more personalized interaction and are more effective in stimulating creativity. In June 2007, during the Kaay Fecc festival, Ariry Andriamoratsiresy and his group thus held a two-day contemporary workshop for professional performers. Andriamoratsiresy himself had discovered contemporary dance during a workshop in Kenya in 1994, the same in which Linyekula and Okach had taken part before setting up the Gàara Company. Most participants in his Dakarois workshop had been trained in the neo-traditional genre, and his emphasis on choreographic structure and improvisation was new to them. A few had prior training in improvisation techniques, but were unfamiliar with the Rary style. A drummer from a Saint-Louis-based troupe joined the Malagasy musicians, and worked on the musical aspect of choreographic production.

Similarly, in Tubaab Jallaw in May 2007, an African Diaspora event, Projet Diaspora, was held at the school under Mrs Acogny's leadership. Over two weeks, some forty dancers and musicians from various African countries, as well as from Brazil and Haiti, engaged in choreographic creation, discussions and daily workshops led alternatively by the participants themselves. When I visited the event, Nigerian dancer-choreographer, Adedayo Liadi, who won the first prize at the Rencontres in 2003 with his company, Ijodee, was initiating the other participants into his style in an hour-long session. The dancers were gathered at the centre's distinctive sand floor 'dance room', a 400 square metre open space facing the nearby lagoon, covered by a tent-style dome. Liadi stood in front of the dancers, who had lined up behind him. He demonstrated a sequence of his, an energetic piece which the dancers repeated over and over. He provided little by way of correction, the whole idea being to encourage individuals to find their own style within a set sequence. Also, Liadi's original training was in Nigerian dances, transmitted through imitation rather than verbal explanation, and this was clearly the teaching style he felt most comfortable with. Exhausted by the high energy level of the sequence, which involved a lot of jumping on soft sand, the dancers eventually sat down in a circle. Speaking in English followed by translation into French by Mrs Acogny's son, himself a choreographer and workshop participant, Liadi explained that this was part of a piece he had choreographed for Nigerian band, Infinity. The piece, he said, had become so popular in Nigeria that people attributed the success of the band to his choreography. He had drawn on the 'traditional' styles he knew, and refashioned them to suit Nigerian pop music. At Mrs Acogny's request, Liadi also spoke about how he had been initiated into Yoruba traditional religion at a young age. The dances he had learned as part of his initiation, he said, still formed the basis of his choreographic practice. Although not everyone understood English, the other dancers listened attentively. The afternoon workshops were framed as moments of 'transmission'. Several of the participants had taken part in the biennale in previous years, and things were coming back full circle since Liadi himself had taken part in several workshops at the Ecole des Sables since 1998. Although few Senegalese dancers were present, this was an important forum during which movement styles which had been successful at the Rencontres were being passed on.

Another significant way in which what takes place at the biennale affects the local dance world is through the use of visual media and the internet. In Chapter 1, for example, I mentioned how the students and staff at the National School of Arts had been watching video recordings of the 2001 Rencontres. Watching dance recordings has now become an integral part of the daily programme at the Ecole des Sables workshops. In Dakar, individual companies like La 5e Dimension also get together at the home of members who own DVD players or laptops – or VCRs, still in use when I started fieldwork – and watch recordings of the biennale and any choreographic piece people pass on to each other during festivals and workshops. Now that broadband internet is widely available, YouTube is used to the same end.

Despite the inspiration these exchanges may lead to, not everything about the biennale is perceived in a positive light by the local dance people, and the biennale also serves as an idiom through which issues of morality, and of African and European agency, are discussed. Some of the performers I knew in Dakar were unreservedly positive and described the event as a motivation to work harder. Were the Rencontres not a place, one choreographer asked, where one could show the rest of the world that young Africans could do 'art' rather than 'African art' as they had always been expected to? Others, however, were much more ambivalent about the event. They recognized that the competition provided a unique window into a wide range of choreographic works of the continent, but they also denounced what they saw as the re-appropriation of African arts by Europeans. Some complained about the competitive side of the event (until 2012), seeing it as a European invention which they felt stifled creativity. 'Everybody is doing the same all over Africa now, because they have seen what works in Tana and they want to please the jury'[11] one informant said. When I pointed out that the jury had always included African artists,[12] he replied that this was a window-dressing exercise and that these artists had in effect little power to shape the event. Some also complained about the formal rules of the competition, such as the restricted length of the pieces and number of performers (no more than five per group), a straightjacket in their view. One informant elaborated further on these complaints:

> For Tana, everything is biased. As long as we Africans do not put our own systems in place to evaluate our own works, we will only be able to watch and put up with it. Unfortunately it is once more the law of the richest, and the results of this competition are open to discussion, to say the least. Whose interests do they serve in the end? [. . .]
>
> The danger is also that we are forced into a certain rhythm which has an impact on the creation process. You don't become a good artist in two years! They glorify young artists who do not necessarily have the creative maturity, and who are still 'searching'. The other danger is that the artists begin at the wrong end: [the competition] favours the product but not the creation process. [. . .] In 2003, everybody had lots of props, stage effects which tried, unsuccessfully, to hide the lack of sophistication. We must [. . .] concentrate on the substance and possibly evaluate it later, if necessary. Is it so necessary to compete? The good thing is that the creation of all these festivals in Africa will make it possible for artists to present their work in a healthier environment, without all this pressure.
>
> But at least, Tana is a means for people to see what is going on in the dance scene in Africa. It was the first event to show African 'contemporary' dance, and in a way it's inspiring for African artists, given the conditions of creation and diffusion they are facing back home. And it has launched a good number of companies on the international stage.[13]

The French Institute has indeed shaped individualized choreographic work on the continent by setting up competition rules, funding the biennale and organizing international tours for the winners. It has also encouraged artists to present their work in a particular format, re-writing the texts produced by the artists when this was deemed necessary for promotion purposes. This is a legitimate practice from the point of view of an agency working with the stated aim of encouraging the 'professionalization' of choreographic production, and with its own requirements in terms of consistency of style for its written productions. From the perspective of some of the participants, however, this is a direct interference with the contents of their work, as well as a suggestion that African artists are incapable of writing decent texts. This is especially sensitive since the verbal articulation of choreographic work is becoming increasingly important in determining which artists will be promoted onto the worldwide stage. Performers are usually grateful for the financial support, but there is a widespread perception that they are paying the price of this 'aid' by losing some of their artistic agency. The critique has also become too widespread to be dismissed as an expression of resentment by those who have not been awarded prizes at the Rencontres, even though the fact that young performers may be rewarded ahead of their more experienced 'mentors' does generate substantial tensions.

The French Institute has taken some of the criticism to heart by removing the competitive element of the biennale, as mentioned earlier. But it has not been keen to address the issue of a normative framework. I discussed this in an interview in July 2009 with one of the Dance Officers at, what was then, Cultures France. When I put the 'standardization' critique to her, she replied in a defensive tone that she had heard this misconception many times before, but that the agency did 'not intervene in the creative process.' In reality, she said, this came from a tendency by some of the performers to work within a style they imagined would please the jury. This was a mistaken view, however, since the jury would always look for original and personal work. She added that the number of performers was limited by the funding available for touring, hence the restriction to five per piece. The removal of the competitive dimension has not removed the criticism, however, and at the 2012 event, conversations were buzzing with questions about the opacity of the criteria used to select the participants. The selection, it appeared, had been centralized in Paris, on the basis of video material and artists' reputations, but with concern to include both experienced choreographers and young, upcoming talents.

Black bodies on stage and choreographic agency

There is often a problematic relationship between patrons and artists. In the classical ballet world, Wulff (2012) describes an uncomfortable relationship between dancers and corporate patrons. Although many Senegalese artists now look back to the Senghor period with nostalgia, there was plenty of critique of state control of the arts then, as evident, among other things, in the endless controversies over the 1966 World Festival of Negro Arts (Chapter 1). Critique is now directed both at the Senegalese state's lack of commitment to the arts and the heavy-handed French patronage, sometimes perceived as thinly veiled neo-colonialism. Whilst there is no doubt that the French state uses patronage of the arts as an essential tool in its diplomatic strategy in Africa, the charge of 'neo-colonialism' is probably exaggerated. Its undoubtedly remains strategically important for France to maintain a presence in Africa, in part to protect access to the continent's natural resources, and its arts policy, I suggest, is aimed at legitimizing this presence rather than controlling whole nations. But what is significant for the purpose of this study, is that the controversies that erupt on a regular basis around the location of choreographic agency serve as a space within which people can reflect on issues of authenticity, power, and changing perceptions of embodied morality. This was nowhere as evident as during the 'Mozambican affair' at the Malagasy biennale in November 2003.

While the first prize was awarded to Adedayo Liadi's Ijodee group for its piece *Ori*, the second prize went to Mozambican, Augusto Cuvilas' Projeto Cuvilas for *Um solo para cinco*. The piece featured five women who, in the words of journalist Ayoko Mensah (2004), brought the audience 'into a playful female world, intimate, on the edge of dream and reality.' After performing a game of musical chairs, the dancers left the stage, only to return shortly after with metal buckets. This time, however, they were fully naked. Each of them performed a solo, and the piece ended up with the women throwing themselves into a metallic bath tub filled with mud. A diplomatic crisis ensued, with the Malagasy authorities accusing the jury of deliberately ignoring the national law forbidding nudity in public. Indeed the winners were scheduled to perform at the closing ceremony in the presence of Malagasy President, Marc Ravalomanana, and with the national TV channel broadcasting the event live. After much negotiation between the organizing committee and the government, Cuvilas was asked to 'cover his dancers lightly' (Mensah 2004). But he refused, arguing that this would compromise the integrity of the piece. The Malagasy government then cut the piece from, what ended up being, a very tense closing ceremony. This did not prevent Cuvilas and his group from embarking on a European tour over the next couple of years. The Mozambican government allegedly begged him to dress his dancers to avoid national embarrassment, but Cuvilas never relented. Sadly, however, the Projeto Cuvilas adventure ended abruptly when the choreographer was shot dead by police at his home in Maputo in December 2007, in mysterious circumstances. None of the police officers involved were charged, and whether Cuvilas' death was related to his defiance of his own government was never established.

When I returned to Dakar in December 2003 after a short period of absence, the dance world was in a state of frenzy over the affair. One dancer said he was thrilled by what he saw as a sign of the emancipation of African choreographers, thus echoing the view of a number of French journalists present at the biennale.[14] On the whole, however, comments by Senegalese dance people ranged from puzzlement to anger. Most were unimpressed by what they regarded as a form of European voyeurism of naked African bodies. The most radical voices spoke about manipulation, and insisted that 'Africans would never make people dance naked on stage' if not 'strongly incited' by Europeans. The agency of the Mozambican choreographer, who seemed quite surprised to have won a prize, seemed irrelevant in this debate. By making his dancers go naked on stage, he had positioned himself firmly on the European side. Therefore his view, it was said, could not be taken seriously. It would be easy to dismiss the debate as a discussion pitting a conservative, essentialist view of 'African traditions' and 'African bodies' against a more progressive view of artistic freedom. After all, Cuvilas' gesture could be seen as a statement of freedom from the burden of having to stage 'African identities', a view that was came through in his interventions at the 2004 panel in Durban:

When I'm creating a piece, I'm not trying to say that I'm African. I know I'm African. So claiming an African identity is not my purpose really. My identity's there and there's no way I can lose it. What I'm really interested in today and here, is my artistic identity and trying to find my space in a context, in a society. And to try and face the problems that face me, which brings me to the question of the role of an artist. As an artist, I always strive to make visible, things that are not clearly visible. (Augusto Cuvilas in Douglas et al. 2006: 109)

It is also true that Cuvilas' dance training included years in Cuba (1985–1994) and in France (1997–1999), and that one could therefore reasonably assume that Euro-American stage techniques have had an impact on his work. Indeed nudity has been a common way of commenting on the self and the modern body in Euro-American dance since the 1960s.[15] It is more relevant, however, to ask what debates of this kind say about local notions of dance, body and morality. Indeed this was not an isolated occurrence. When I returned to Dakar in late 2005 after a year of absence, the dance world was still buzzing with outraged comments on some of the contemporary performances that had taken place during the third Kaay Fecc festival held earlier that year. There remained a frisson about a solo performed by Sophiatou Kossoko, a French dancer and choreographer originally from Benin, and choreographed by South African, Robyn Orlin. The piece, *Although I live inside . . . my hair will always reach towards the sun*, featured Kossoko dressed in a tight golden leotard, wearing high heels and a flamboyant light-brown afro wig. Some talked about the performance as a pointless provocation and an exercise in indecency, a perspective which was echoed in some of the local press reviews. Clearly, the choreographer's attempt to involve the audience and to displace the classical conventions of spectacle was lost on much of the local audience, who saw this as exhibitionism disguised as 'art'. This was reflected in the ambivalent character of reviews in the Senegalese printed press:

> Perched on high heels, full of temerity that works with improvisation, she asks her audience to fill in the gaps in her memory to finish her text. [. . .] This Beninese dancer living in France is a danger for the performing market. You buy your ticket to see dance. Contemporary dance. In the end you get none of this. [. . .] After Sophiatou's performance, one is concerned with knowing from which planet the woman has escaped. With a wig as an antenna and a golden 'leotard', she looks like a magician's assistant who got lost in a dance show. [. . .]
>
> The piece is meant to show how 'a white woman who lives in Africa and a Black woman who lives in Europe work together'. On stage, Kossoko uses the audience to bear witness to the choreographic aberration of her boss [the choreographer]. (Mbengue 2005)

A young Senegalese dancer who presented a solo of his for the first time was equally criticized for wearing nothing but tight shorts, and performing suggestive forward-thrusting movements of the pelvis. This had been so inappropriate, I was told, that the Culture Minister at the time, Safiatou Ndiaye Diop, had walked out of the performance. Although I did not have the opportunity to verify whether this was indeed the reason why she walked out, it was significant that people made an immediate connection with what they regarded as the immorality of the performance. In both cases the dancers were dressed, and yet people saw their minimalistic costumes as very close to nudity.

Local debates on the morality of the performing body also point to the enduring importance of 'race' matters in people's perception of their place in the world. Nudity on stage reminds Senegalese performers and audiences alike of a long history of objectification of Black African bodies on European stages, a history to which I alluded in the first chapter. There is a strong sense in which 'making people dance naked on a stage' is regarded as pandering to White people's insatiable desire to be titillated by Black bodies. The question of objectification of the body on stage, therefore, is never far beneath the surface of performers' more materialistic concerns. This was brought home to me when I visited a young woman dancer I knew in Dakar at her family home. During the conversation, she offered to show me a dance video in which she featured. The five-minute long opening sequence was striking. Lying on white sand against a dark background, wearing only shorts and a bra, she was rolling slowly to one side. Shot in close-up, she seemed to be discovering her own body as her hands moved across her neck, face, shoulders and legs. Her perfect skin shone in the light. This was a moving, sensual scene performed in silence. She spontaneously told me how difficult it had been for her to do this in front of the camera. She was afraid that people would deem her performance indecent, even shameful. She only reconciled herself with these images when Mrs Acogny reassured her that the scene was beautiful. After the film had been viewed by professionals in France, however, she began receiving phone calls inviting her to audition for new shows. She went to the auditions, and then the shock came: people wanted her to dance naked! She recalled a particular occasion when the choreographer had said that the 'raw energy' emanating from her body would be a huge success if she was naked. She was deeply frustrated with the fact that although she told the choreographers about the consequences this would represent for her social life in Senegal, they did not seem interested in considering her perspective.

Around the same period, there were (quite possibly unfounded) rumours that French-Algerian choreographer, Heddy Maalem, had wanted his dancers to perform naked for his version of 'The Rite of Spring'. He had recruited dancers across West Africa for a global tour, including several women dancers in Senegal. They had refused, I was told, and so he had staged the piece with the women dancers wearing bikinis, and the men wearing tight shorts. The aesthetic of the piece was based on the striking effect produced by the muscular bodies of the dancers, men and women alike, and they were recruited with this aesthetic in mind.[16]

In some ways this is not far removed from the fascination with the bodies of Black performers like Féral Benga and Habib Benglia in Paris in the 1930s.[17] Even further back in time there are echoes of the plight of Saartjie Baartman, the 'Hottentot Venus', in the early nineteenth century. It is this history of objectification that the young woman in the film reacted against by only making her body 'available' for display under conditions which satisfied notions of morality in her own social environment. Some of the more articulate dance people phrase this explicitly in terms of resistance, saying that economic power may not be in their hands but that they still have control over their bodies. And yet this turns out to be only part of the story, in a globalized world of spectacle which privileges particular body shapes at the expense of others. I have written elsewhere about the anxieties this generates in a society in which young women may be not regarded as attractive marriage partners, or good wives for that matter, if too thin (Neveu Kringelbach 2007b).

In addition to a genuine concern about the ways in which Black bodies are offered to the global gaze, local debates on decency on stage also point to the ambiguous social position of the dancer in urban Senegal. In earlier chapters we have seen how often the figure of the dancing woman, and that of the dancing male youth, were subjected to suspicions of low morality. Dance is at the heart of everyday discourses on morality, and women dancers, in particular, are all too aware of this. A young woman's reputation is a valuable resource which can be easily destroyed, with unpredictable consequences for her family as a whole.

New techniques of transmission

Issues of morality in contemporary performance are all the more important as the genre encourages forms of individualism which can be difficult to combine with the social environment of the performers. Of course, individualism, the space to make and reflect on the self as a unique entity, is also very present in regional traditions like the sabar genre, and in neo-traditional performance. There is also a growing literature which indicates that the way in which 'African art' has been conceptualized has obscured local appreciations of individual skill. Robert Farris Thompson (1974: 1) was one of the first scholars to highlight the existence of regional traditions of criticism in performance, which included the evaluation of individual skill:

> In 1912 Robert Schmitz noted artistic evaluation of dancing among the Baholoholo of Central Africa: 'the spectators commented, one to the other, on the aesthetic qualities of the dancers, and upon the choreographic expertise of each person'. In 1938 Jomo Kenyatta showed Kikuyu children in Kenya were subject to close scrutiny by their parents when they danced. [. . .] As to the Kan, Kwabena Nketia discovered distinct qualities lauded in dancing, especially creative self-absorption. The ideal dancer, Akan say, never seeks applause while dancing, but spontaneously incites enthusiasm through total commitment to his footwork and kinetic flair. It is never to be said, in Akan culture, that a dancer performed 'throwing glances at people', i.e., disgracefully begging support or praise. Nor will Akan connoisseurs tolerate the one-style dancer.

In Dakar, the sabar genre provides a space in which individual skill, innovation within the established rhythmic structure and the capacity to use movement as irony or parody are highly valued. The guéew, the circle in which people take turns to dance solo or in pairs in front of the musicians, is a near-perfect image of the inter-play between the individual and the collective.

Nevertheless contemporary performance introduces additional layers of indi-vidualism in two important domains of practice: transmission and the choreographic process. I will return to the latter in the next section. Transmission has to do with the way in which people learn to become skilled dancers, as well as the way in which tools for choreographic innovation are taught and learned. It is perhaps in transmission that the contrast between the neo-traditional and the contemporary genre is most significant. A vignette from a Kaay Fecc workshop in 'dance and theatre' will help to illustrate this.

Kaay Fecc workshop, Dakar, late December 2003
At the Centre Culturel Blaise Senghor, some twenty dancers are gathered for the Kaay Fecc 'dance and theatre' workshop. Coming from the bright sunshine outside into the big dark room with the centre's single stage feels like walking into a cave. The dancers' faces look concentrated, and there is tension in the air; nothing like the joyful atmosphere I had experienced during the Kaay Fecc 'traditional dance' work-shop the year before. The participants are here by choice, and they are paid a small fee to participate. Most of the dancers belong to neo-traditional troupes, and a few are also involved in contemporary companies.

The workshop is led jointly by Sandra Laye, a French stage director, and Andreya Ouamba. Laye works with the idea of encouraging dancers to 'search for the balance centres in the body in order to arrive at a control of expressiveness and liberation of the imagination' (Wane 2004). Ouamba's role is to design practical exercises to put this into practice. The previous day, the group has experimented with ways of walk-ing, running, and with the use of space. Now they must begin to do choreographic work properly, and things do not go smoothly. Ouamba has asked the participants to improvise individually, working with changes in movement style and source of energy. They must try to access different feelings within themselves and express them in movement. Some of the dancers seem comfortable with the task and soon begin to move on their own. Their faces are expressionless, withdrawn. Others, by contrast, seem reluctant to engage in the exercise. Because I have seen them in other training contexts, the contrast is obvious. Some of the young women giggle, and Ouamba asks them to concentrate. He says that part of the objective of the workshop is to teach people to concentrate, to find inspiration. But this does not come easily to all. Eventually, the last ones begin to move in the styles they are most comfortable with, mostly Mandinka and Jola styles, a bit of sabar, some contemporary dance. Ouamba looks at each dancer in turn, shouting words of encouragement in French, correcting a posture. Occasionally he follows the movement, standing right behind the dancers and moving so close as to touch their bodies. He pushes them to expand the scope of the movements, pushing a leg here or stretching an arm there to make it reach further. He tells them to take risks, to work with the floor rather than against it, to be prepared to fall when a movement is taken to its limits. He tells them to experiment with changes in the quality of the energy deployed to perform familiar routines; this is one possible way of transforming the movement entirely. Before long, some of the women dancers, in particular, end up with sour faces. They are visibly upset to have their bodies literally pushed around. They say nothing but turn their back to Ouamba, slowly walking away from him and back to the corner from where they will have to start all over again. The silence, the sloppiness of the movement, the way they avoid his eyes when he is looking straight into theirs are not habitual for some of these dancers.

During the second part, the dancers are asked to split into smaller groups of three or four to create a short choreography on the theme of 'initiation'. Their task is to think about initiation in a broad sense, and to create their own ritual. Later, they will be asked to explain the ideas underlying the performance. In every group it is a male dancer who is chosen to speak, while the women remain behind their wall of silence. One of them, a dancer in her mid-twenties, even lies with her back on the floor when it is her group's turn to perform. She invokes pain, fatigue and refuses to move for a while. It takes much persuasion from Ouamba to get her to stand up. Although clearly tired, she is also frustrated with the process. On different occasions I have seen her dance through much more demanding routines for hours. It is only when the workshop ends that the dancers seem to return to their usual selves. Some of the women later tell me that they do not understand why they have to do everything, why they have 'not been given any steps'.

This workshop formed part of the Kaay Fecc training programme for professional performers, a series mostly led by Senegal-based dancers, choreographers and stage directors. Whereas shorter workshops were held during the biennial Kaay Fecc festival, longer ones, lasting three to four weeks on a daily basis, took place between festivals. In total, twelve professional workshops were held between 2002 and 2006, in addition to in-festival training. Ten of these twelve 'modules' were entirely or partly focused on aspects of contemporary performance: choreographic writing (January 2002 and 2006), contact improvisation (April 2002), modern dance (January 2003), dance and theatre (December 2003), contemporary dance (March 2004), improvisation (June 2004 and July 2006), 'techniques of the body' (December 2006) and the use of visual installations (September 2003). Other aspects of the workshops included hip-hop, capoeira, jazz, Afro-Caribbean dances, sabar, Casamançais *gambacc*, oral histories of regional dances, voice work, and training for disabled dancers. The Kaay Fecc workshops have served as one of the four main pathways for contemporary dance training in the region. The other three are Mrs Acogny's Ecole des Sables, workshops held by visiting European or American performers in Dakar, and international workshops, such as the Association Française d'Action Artistique (AFAA)-funded Atelier du Monde held during the Montpellier dance festival in 2002. Andreya Ouamba and Simone Gomis, a former dancer with La 5ᵉ Dimension Company, were among 180 participants from around the world. There they attended a choreography workshop led by American choreographer Susan Buirge, alongside individuals who have since become well-known choreographic figures across of the continent, like Auguste Ouedraogo from Burkina Faso and Jean-Michel Moukam Fonkam from Cameroon (Wern 2002).

In order to draw the contrast between transmission in the neo-traditional genre and in contemporary performance, I shall first attempt to give a sense of the former. Learning to become a dancer or a dancer-drummer in the neo-traditional genre often follows the principle of apprenticeship. This is a guiding principle in many skilled occupations across the region, and in this sense apprenticeship is closely associated with ñeeño and similar 'men-of-skill' status groups (Dilley 2004). Although they do not recognize such groups, Jola troupes in Dakar follow the same principle. In neo-traditional performance, one learns by joining a troupe as a junior member and precisely imitating the more experienced performers. Precision in the timing of the movement is essential, and it is also important to emulate the style of the troupe master or the more experienced dancers. In sabar drumming, this process of emulation usually goes on for years before the lead drummer may deem an apprentice to be worthy of playing solo (Tang 2007). For dancers the process is slightly shorter, perhaps because waiting for too long would risk wasting people's best years as dancers, when energy is at its highest and the body is able to endure intense physical work on hard, often concrete or tiled surfaces. Whereas experienced drummers can continue to play a leading role in an ensemble until an advanced age, lead dancers are often in their twenties and thirties, and rarely beyond their mid-forties. Still, the process of apprenticeship may be long and arduous, with dancers moving between troupes and training with several at a time in order to learn their craft. Most of the experienced dancers I knew had worked with several troupes by the time they reached their late twenties. This may be done in an opportunistic way, usually through neighbourhood friends or relatives already in a troupe. Increasingly however, this is done strategically so as to acquire a wider repertoire of styles and techniques. Several of the contemporary dancers I knew, for example, had received training with Bakalama for several months in order to learn the Jola dances that would make a useful addition to their personal knowledge. Conversely, several of the Bakalama women dancers had trained with other troupes, such as the large Dakar-based (now disbanded) Ballet Mansour Guèye,[18] all while remaining loyal to Bakalama. Apprenticeship does not imply complete mimicry, and in practice transmission in the codified neo-traditional genre involves 'kinaesthetic empathy' (Foster 1996), so that the individual needs to imagine how a particular movement feels in the body of a more experienced dancer in order to reproduce it with appropriate flow and texture. A simple mechanistic imitation is unlikely to produce a texture that is worth watching, because it lacks 'presence'. Yet the spoken ideal of apprenticeship is one of imitation, a transmission process in which the receiving dancer strives towards mimicry without ever achieving it completely.

As illustrated in the workshop vignette, transmission within the contemporary genre is of a different character. There the focus is on mobilizing the body's creative potential rather than creating specific figures. This is similar in European contemporary dance where, as Joëlle Vellet (2006: 88, translated from French) puts it, 'it is not a figure, rather a work of the body that is being referred to'. Neither is the focus on the transmission of a movement style. Nevertheless style gets carried over with kinaesthetic empathy, through the physical proximity among dancers working

together. I suggested this earlier in relation to the impact of the African dance biennale on the Senegalese dance world. Whereas movement style could be described as
a kind of *habitus* transmitted over time without full consciousness of it (Bourdieu
1972), the creative process, on the other hand, involves complete self-consciousness
on the part of the participants. Dance scholars have written about transmission in
contemporary dance in relation to particular choreographers: Guigou (2004) on
Dominique Bagouet and the choreographers of the 'new French dance' generation
in the 1970s to early 1990s, or Vellet (2006) on the work of Odile Duboc. Guigou,
for example, focuses on non-verbal aspects of transmission and the role of choreographers' charisma in fostering creativity in their dancers. Vellet's work, which is
also closer to the everyday work of Duboc, takes an ethnographic perspective to
show how Duboc's transmission of a short variation to dance teachers involves a
verbal explanation of the intention motivating every movement. This, she suggests,
generates kinaesthetic empathy. She also demonstrates the essential role of physical presence by comparing a live workshop with the participants' previous efforts
to learn the variation from a video recording. In other words, the transmission of
contemporary dance in this context is both kinaesthetic and verbal, in what seems
to perfectly capture Parkin's (1985) notion of performance as the 'moving together'
of reason, emotion and body.

In Senegal, choreographers like Germaine Acogny, Jean Tamba and Andreya
Ouamba, all rely on their charisma, experience and capacity to articulate what
they do to wrestle innovative movement out of their dancers. The capacity to
articulate choreographic work verbally is indeed an important factor of distinction
from the neo-traditional genre. In the vignette above I mentioned that the dancers were required to speak about how they had arrived at their short variation.
'Speaking' about movement means reflecting on it in ways different from what
is encouraged in the apprenticeship tradition, and this in turn affects movement.
This was evident during a Kaay Fecc 'choreographic writing' workshop held in
December 2005 – January 2006 at the MCDS in Dakar. The four-week long
workshop gathered thirteen dancers, all with a background in neo-traditional performance. Most were Dakarois, but the group also included two dancers from the
DRC, and two from Diourbel in central Senegal. Two of the Dakarois dancers
gave up within the first couple of days, and attendance varied a great deal over
the remaining time. The fact that many dancers lived far away in the suburbs
was compounded by the fact that Tabaski[19] was fast approaching. Most Muslims
prioritized the preparation of the festival over the dance workshop, since this was
what their families required of them. One of the young dancers, for example,
missed a couple of days so as to travel to Kaolack, 200 km southeast of Dakar,
to collect a sheep that had been kept by relatives on behalf of his mother. He did
so reluctantly, but felt that raising the idea of attending the workshop instead was
simply not an option.

The workshop was led by Jean Tamba, for whom this was the most important
training module of the Kaay Fecc series since it was aimed at 'allowing the dancers to
gain confidence in their creative capacity.' The dancers, he explained, needed to learn

to create dance for others to perform. For this they had to be able to explain their approach, both verbally and in writing. He added that this process of verbalization forced the dancers to think carefully about what they did, and why:

> When you create for someone else, you realise that if you do something today, you have to be able to do the same thing again tomorrow. Otherwise you confuse people. So you really have to think about what you're doing. (Tamba, personal communication, Dakar, January 2006)

Tamba went on to explain that learning to become a choreographer was a lengthy training. This was only a first step, during which dancers were asked to create a five-minute-long piece. Over time, they would be able to create longer pieces, and eventually the forty to forty-five-minute length that is common in the dance world.

On the first day, Tamba asked the participants to choose a move they were familiar with, and to perform it in turn in front of the group. Given their background, most of them chose a move from neo-traditional pieces they had performed with their respective troupes. I had seen several of these dancers perform on different occasions, and was therefore able to compare this work with their usual style. As they executed the moves individually, it was noticeable that the texture of the movement had changed. It even changed in front of my eyes as Tamba made them repeat the moves over and over again, at decreasing speed but with a request to be fully attentive. One of the participants, an experienced dancer from Bakalama, had chosen a fairly simple step from a Mandinka-style piece she enjoyed. The step involved a small jump on the spot, a *dégagé* (opening movement with one leg, led by the heel and without shifting the body weight on the standing leg) to the right with an accompanying milling, symmetrical movement of both arms; she then repeated this to the left. This was a step she mastered in performance, and yet here she struggled. Tamba stood very close to her, occasionally touching her arms and asking her to think about how she was using them. He asked her to repeat the step as slowly as possible, with complete clarity in every movement. The very notion of clarity in movement, which refers to clean movement performed without hesitation, is important in classical ballet and in many Asian dance traditions. But this is not the effect that is usually strived at in neo-traditional performance, even though some informants have mentioned that the search for 'clean figures' had been introduced in the genre under the influence of Russian ballet dancers working in Guinea and Mali in the 1960s. The more the dancer appeared to reflect on her movement, the less fluid it was, and the more she struggled. This is a known outcome of reflexivity in bodily work: as soon as we begin to think about what is involved in walking, we can no longer walk in a natural way. This is compounded by the fact that movement is structured according to time- and space-related elements. Changing one of these elements, for example decreasing the usual speed, thus modifies the texture of movement, and requires practice to achieve fluidity. The very capacity to perform movements that have been thought through consciously in a flowing manner requires training, and this was what Tamba was trying to achieve. Few dancers had ever been encouraged to do this, and they reacted with varying degrees of enthusiasm.

On the second day, the dancers were asked to work on their five-minute pieces. They were paired up and asked to take turns in playing the role of the choreographer, so that everyone would experience the role of subject as well as that of creator. The dancers were also asked to write a short, personal text on their piece. Tamba explained that every piece must have a text, and that choreographers must be able to communicate their ideas verbally. Although this was explained in Wolof, they were asked to write in French. The next day the dancers returned with handwritten texts. In most cases it seemed obvious that they had struggled to complete this school-like task. The texts were short, a few lines, and written in hesitant French. With very few exceptions, the themes were far from personal; rather, they stayed close to the usual themes staged in neo-traditional ballets: occult practices and village scenes, despite the fact that the dancers were all urban youths. They were scribbled on scraps of paper torn from school-type notebooks. Visibly unhappy with the result, Tamba asked them to re-write and to think carefully about what their pieces were really about, in content as well as in form. The dancers reacted with quiet respect, looking very much like children in a local classroom. Over the following days attendance diminished, but those who remained made an obvious effort to come up with more personal stories. The young man who had had to travel to fetch his mother's sheep created a minimalistic, inward-focused piece on the theme of devotion to his marabout. He was visibly pleased when Tamba praised his effort, but was momentarily thrown off balance when reminded that he had to teach the piece to his partner, a young woman. Would the significance of Muslim devotion as he knew it remain when performed by a woman? He set to the task with visible unease. After some negotiation between them, the result ended up being very different from his original idea.

Aside from the deconstruction of movement, innovation, transmission and the verbalization of ideas, Tamba encouraged the dancers to make full use of the space in which they were working. From beginning in one of the main rooms of the MCDS, he asked them to work outdoors. There were green spaces bordered with bushy areas, and the dancers were asked to work with the different surfaces. This was a similar approach to the experiments of the Judson group in New York in the 1960s, and to the way in which Mrs Acogny encouraged her dancers to work with her centre's 'sand floor' in Tubaab Jallaw. In every case the approach was similar: to find new inspiration in the interaction between the body and the surfaces it came in contact with, and to blur the boundaries between 'stage' and life.

Although the individualistic approach to choreographic production did not suit everybody, over time some of the dancers who had been exposed to it became enthralled. Simone Gomis, a young woman who came from high-level athletics and discovered a taste for dance by taking part in (and winning) the 1994 Oscars des Vacances, thus went on to work with Jean Tamba's La 5ᵉ Dimension (Figure 6.1). Encouraged by Tamba, she soon joined Mrs Acogny's first workshops in Tubaab Jallaw in 1998 and 1999. She described her discovery of the 'contemporary' approach as a discovery of the self:

Figure 6.1 Simone Gomis after a rehearsal with La 5ᵉ Dimension Company, Tubaab Jallaw, July 2002. Photograph by the author.

In contemporary (dance), you discover new sensations you didn't know. [. . .] Like standing still for a whole minute and feeling your feet, feeling that you're going to fall. In traditional dance you arrive, they send the drumming full on . . . you don't have the time to feel that. It's pure energy but you don't feel the air around you and all that. [. . .] For me it's very important because it also enables me to know my body. There were things about my body I didn't know I could do. [. . .] In contemporary dance you're taught to go even further, and that's extraordinary! (Gomis, personal communication, Dakar, June 2007)

Gomis suggested that for her, it was the fact of taking time to explore new ways of feeling in the body that opened up possibilities for innovation. Although I knew from watching her perform neo-traditional dances and sabar that she enjoyed these as well, she had obviously grown frustrated with the lack of attention to the individual body she had experienced in neo-traditional troupes. She spoke of missing out on the 'pleasure' of experiencing sensations intensely, a pleasure often achieved through an initial unsettling of the body's habitual ways of moving. This was challenging, and could even be physically painful, but ultimately, for Gomis and other dancers I spoke to, this could be an immensely rewarding experience.

For neo-traditional troupes there is no time to dwell on this: the aesthetics of the genre as it has developed historically require a fairly high number of performers on stage to achieve the desired group effect. Given the rapid turnover of performers in many troupes, individuals must be replaceable at short notice. The emphasis is therefore on training performers to fit within a type of character, a persona, rather than on bringing out the personality of individuals. The 'contemporary' approach, by contrast, uses the personality traits and experience of individuals as the creative 'raw material'. Some choreographers express this as making visible those aspects of the person which are normally hidden from view; making the private public, and blurring the boundaries between stage and 'real' life. Guigou (2004: 116, translated from French) identifies this as one of the main characteristics of French contemporary dance between the 1970s and the late 1990s. This is articulated in an implicit opposition to classical ballet:

> Whereas dance has long staged perfect bodies, removed from the materiality of everyday life, contemporary dance does not hesitate to present deformed, filthy characters who do not hide their crudest behaviour. By centering the work on the personality of ordinary individuals, contemporary dance shows gestures which normally remain private.

Undoubtedly, the reflections of dancers like Gomis draw on the 'emancipation of the self' discourse that circulates in the globalized contemporary dance world. There is also continuity with Mrs Acogny's Negritude-related discourse on the necessity for young Africans to rediscover the essence of 'African culture' in them. But discourses around the body do affect people's experience of their own bodies, and if the notion of 'African culture' discourse is highly contested in choreographic scenes across the continent, the foregrounding of individual character does affect performers' sense of their work. Having followed the same individuals over several years, I thus witnessed the more persistent dancers widen their repertoire of skills and gain confidence in their creative possibilities.

Increased individual agency, however, is not equally satisfying for everyone. There is no shortage of performers who prefer to improve their skills within a genre they are familiar with, and to follow the lead of more experienced peers. For those with a strong desire for novelty and individualism, however, choreographic workshops provide a door into new territory. This is not restricted to dancers, and some of the drummers who play for the contemporary genre report similar 'turning points'. Former La 5ᵉ Dimension drummer, Oumar Diaw, thus took part in workshops at Mrs Acogny's centre, and told me how she had taught him to relax and be more attentive to his play. This, he said, had enabled him to expand his skills well beyond what he had thought possible. He had stopped hitting away at the drum with all his strength, and had since felt more in control of his play.

One may argue that this has to do with choreographic agency rather than transmission. One of the main factors of distinction between neo-traditional and contemporary performance, however, is that in the latter, the two are inextricably linked. Contemporary performance has become globalized, not as an aesthetic but rather as a mode of creation. It is often the case that the choreographer begins with disparate elements such as a theme, an atmosphere, a movement texture, a basic structure (for example changes of speed), a piece of music, a task involving a work of imagination (for example 'think of getting in touch with your feminine/masculine side'), or a combination of several of these elements. This, of course, is in continuity with the work of pioneers like Merce Cunningham, who experimented with leaving the different elements of choreography to chance; a roll of the dice, for example, might determine how many dancers would feature in a piece. Dancers usually experiment with the task that is set to them, on their own or in small groups, and the choreographer then selects and structures this raw material into a coherent piece. Learning to become a contemporary dancer, therefore, means learning to 'do' choreography.

Making new selves in the choreographic process

There are important consequences to the emergence of these new choreographic techniques. These include the necessity for performers to master prior body techniques on which they can draw, and a reshuffling of gender and generational hierarchies in the performing world. An important question deriving from this is the extent to which this affects self-making in urban Senegal. In other words, do alternative experiences in the choreographic world affect lives outside as well?

A widespread idea in European contemporary dance circuits is that an important aspect of choreography is to show the true nature of humanity by making dancers deconstruct, even 'unlearn' their training (often in classical ballet) to reveal their naked selves. There is, among many choreographers, a sense that working with the same performers over time can enable them to reach human material that is beyond (or beneath) socialization. Writing about French choreographer, Karine Saporta, for example, Guigou (2004: 106) says that for Saporta, 'one of the characteristics of contemporary dance is the will to free oneself of determinism, the choice to make a break with the whole set of symbolic representations that make up culture'. The author goes on to remark that Saporta is aware of the utopia inherent in this project since no individual can free themselves completely from being grounded in a particular cultural context. However unattainable, this is an ideal many contemporary European choreographers strive to achieve.

In the Senegalese dance world, by contrast, the discourse of pure individualism is perceived with ambivalence, as one may have expected from the discussions of personhood in earlier chapters. It is taken for granted that there is no such thing as individual agency that is completely independent of social context. Constantly reminded of being 'African' in the world, Senegalese performers are under no illusion that pure individualism may be achieved. They do not need to have read Mauss's *Techniques of the Body* (1973 [1935]) to know that ways of moving are socially constructed; this is the image that is constantly being projected back to them. This awareness leads dancers to insist on being 'grounded' in a clearly identifiable, regional genre. As a result of the Senegalese history outlined earlier, this grounding is usually found in neo-traditional performance, in sabar and its popular offshoots, even though people may have learned these genres after beginning with Cuban dances, hip-hop or breakdancing. This is also what they feel the world expects of them, as 'African' performers. Mrs

Acogny is undoubtedly aware of this when she insists that dancers in her workshops use their own 'tradition' as raw material for their choreographic work. A term, such as 'tradition' in French, or *cosaan* in Wolof, speaks to Senegalese performers because this is a term that was widely popularized in postcolonial Senegal under the influence of Senghor and his version of Negritude. Often forceful in her approach, she insists that the 'traditions' the dancers work from must be 'African'. Those who came to dance from mbalax, hip-hop, jazz or other popular forms, therefore, are strongly encouraged to turn to the neo-traditional genre in search of a grounding that will be recognizably 'African' to the wider world. Seen in this light, the choice of Simone Gomis to learn Jola and Mandinka dances following a background in mbalax and athletics makes perfect sense, as does her interest in local ceremonies during family visits to the Casamance.

Others have made similar efforts to fashion suitably 'Senegalese' or 'African' bodies. In June 2007, one of the contemporary dancers I knew was thus training several times per week with a member of one of the neo-traditional troupes rehearsing at the CCBS. She had also joined a smaller troupe in her neighbourhood. For this she received no payment, but considered the work as a necessary process of apprenticeship. Meanwhile she still rehearsed with her contemporary group. That she took this very seriously was evident in the numerous hours she spent every day, walking and sitting in minibuses, caught up in heavy urban traffic to get from one rehearsal space to the other. With little or no time to eat, she confessed that she had resorted to taking appetite-enhancing pills to make sure she was able eat when she came home in the evening, exhausted. She and her husband had two young children, and had chosen to move closer to her parents' home in one of the suburbs so that the grandparents could help to look after the children while she was training.

Needless to say, some artists experience the 'market-led' requirement to construct a scripted Africanity as a straightjacket. This was expressed accurately by Ayoko Mensah (2001: 6, translated from French), one of the first to write extensively on 'contemporary African dance':

> Nothing is easy for these choreographers, neither materially nor artistically. If they stay too close to the traditional forms, they are blamed for not innovating; but if they turn their back on them, they are accused of being uprooted.

This was also reflected in the oft-repeated comment by a prominent Senegalese choreographer that he wanted to 'be like Merce Cunningham' if he so wished; by this he meant that he wanted people to see him as a choreographer who happened to be African, rather than as an 'African choreographer'.

The dissonance between people's sense of self and the requirements of the 'market' were also perceptible in the unease with which dancers often struggled to talk about questions of identity. Many insisted that they were 'African' dancers and could not escape this fact, but the question of what made their dance 'African' or even 'Senegalese' generated anguished or scripted answers. Gomis (personal communication, Dakar, June 2007, translated from French), otherwise articulate when talking about her trajectory, thus struggled when I asked her what she had gained from her training in neo-traditional performance (*danse traditionnelle*):

> It's been very useful because you need to have a traditional basis first, it's very important because I'm African, I was born with . . . you see, and it's very important for me to take this traditional dance and to carry it . . . into the contemporary. It's very important because they say 'contemporary African dance' and 'African dance'. I think it's a mix of the two . . . You can't say that contemporary dance is a culture. It's African culture that is introduced into today's dance. And so the two form a *métissage*, they supplement each other.

Another performer told me that his 'body [spoke] the language of an African' and that he therefore felt compelled to 'create using African dances to have anything interesting to say'. Yet what he meant by 'African' was never clear. There are aesthetic elements in the contemporary genre which people recognize as distinctively new, such as the purposeful disconnection of music and movement, patches of silence or very slow movement. But most of the time people find it difficult to explain what is distinctively 'African' about what they do, which is unsurprising given the recent and essentialist nature of the notion of a shared 'African culture' (cf. Mudimbe 1988; Appiah 1992).

Yet as we have seen, the expectation that choreographic work be verbalized is a significant difference between the neo-traditional and the contemporary genre. As a consequence, the most successful African choreographers on the world stage are also the ones who are best able to articulate what they do, preferably in English, French or Portuguese. Contrary to many dancers' expectations when they embark on training, talent and technique are not the sole factors that will determine success on world stages. It may not even be as important as the ability to develop interesting ideas, and to demonstrate the presence of an original character. At the dance biennale in Johannesburg in 2012, several European and American presenters thus explained to me, during informal conversations, that they had come to look for interesting personalities, for artists with 'things to say' rather than for finished pieces. As the director of an American dance festival put it, when taking part in performing arts markets of this kind, she likes to 'sit at a table with a dancer and talk for three hours' to get to know them as individuals.

Performers with little formal education are thus at a disadvantage. Due to the imbalance in the formal education of girls in Senegal, young women dancers are much less likely to achieve success as contemporary artists than their male counterparts. Performers with experience in theatre, by contrast, often benefit from their capacity to articulate things verbally. One of my informants, a forty-year old male dancer who had recently married a dancer in her early twenties, told me in 2003 that his wife wished to give up dancing. She was illiterate, did not speak French and as a result, she had lost confidence in her future as a dancer. She often felt inferior to educated dancers, and did not enjoy relying on her husband to read her contracts.

*Figure 6.2 Fatou Cissé performing Gacirah Diagne's 'picc mi' at the Kaay Fecc festival, Dakar, May 2003.
Photograph by the author.*

She had also discovered that one of the most lucrative opportunities, teaching dance to Europeans, was out of her reach for the same reasons.

On the other hand, young women who take to the contemporary approach often enjoy the freedom to experiment outside the norms of a genre, and a valorisation of their individual qualities which they may not find in neo-traditional troupes. It is no coincidence that those women dancers who have led their own companies (in some cases composed only of themselves) have all worked within the contemporary genre: Germaine Acogny, Marianne Niox (who trained as a classical ballet dancer in France), Fatou Cissé, Simone Gomis, Fatou Samb, to name but a few. Gacirah Diagne, an acknowledged choreographer and Kaay Fecc director, performed for many years with New York-based Urban Bush Women. In 2003 she restaged her solo *picc mi* ('the bird') for Fatou Cissé (Figure 6.2), who performed it at the Kaay Fecc festival and on numerous occasions in subsequent years, both in Senegal and in several other African countries.

Other women dancers who have not gone as far as forming their own group have nevertheless carved out a more prominent role for themselves in everyday work. In 2003 I thus observed a gifted young dancer as she worked alternatively with one of the big neo-traditional troupes based at the CCBS and with a smaller, recently formed contemporary group. Despite being one of the most experienced and skilled dancers, with the bigger troupe she often seemed reserved during rehearsals. When she danced she livened up, but between sets she seemed respectful of the authority of the older masters, a man and a woman, and of the senior male dancers. With the smaller group by contrast, she enjoyed more of a leading status. Although she did not have a very long experience of the contemporary approach, a couple of years at most, this was longer than the others. The exception was the group leader, a young man with a background in theatre and Mrs Acogny's workshops. There were young men from diverse backgrounds, from the neo-traditional genre to theatre, sports and acrobatics. On a day when I came to see the group work, the choreographer asked the dancers to improvise on the feeling of being held captive. Focused inwards, the young woman began experimenting with her own movements in a very different style from what I had seen her do with the other troupe. Meanwhile several of the male dancers were obviously uncomfortable with the task. They kept glancing over to her, trying to follow her movements. She was too concentrated to look back at them, and yet she obviously enjoyed this. A few times she stopped to demonstrate a minimalistic move she had come up with, beaming with pleasure. This would not usually happen in her neo-traditional troupe, where men and women performed different routines and different songs. She has since become a successful contemporary dancer and choreographer in her own right.

But this momentary reshuffling of gender hierarchies does not always happen smoothly, and internal conflict sometimes erupts when men feel that their masculinity is being challenged in front of women. In one woman-led group I watched several times as they were working towards a big show, the approaching premiere put everybody under pressure, and an argument erupted between the female choreographer and dancers of both sexes. It was an argument over authority and work discipline, with which the choreographer was dissatisfied. The tone rose, and two of the girls stormed out. One of the male dancers threw himself to the floor, the whole body nervously contracting in what looked like a kind of seizure. It was obvious from the calm attitude of the others that they had seen this before. A friend I reported the incident to, commented that this was a common expression of anger among young men from the Senegal River Valley. Although I did not know the young man's background, this seemed a plausible explanation for what I had witnessed. I had a strong feeling that the situation would not have generated this level of anger if the choreographer had been a man.

Conclusion

In this chapter I have introduced 'contemporary choreography' in Senegal as a field of practice and a working process, rather than established choreographic genre. A genre is gradually emerging, however, shaped as much by regional neo-traditional performance, sabar, popular dances and popular theatre as it is by French-funded events on the continent. But young performers are not passively copying a genre developed in Europe and North America throughout the twentieth century. Not only have performers from Africa contributed to this history in important ways, as we have seen in Chapter 1, but also, contemporary choreography is being appropriated by urban youths to shape new ways of being creative, and promoting individual autonomy without having to wait for full social maturity. In his analysis of beauty pageants in Belize, Wilk (1995) suggests that the globalization of cultural forms works as the superficial expression of diverse local agendas. Here too, beyond the globalization of 'contemporary dance', choreographic experimentation enables those searching for new forms of expression to explore the possibilities afforded by their own bodies and verbal skills. For the most persistent, this becomes an exploration of new forms of sociality and mobility, which include social spaces far beyond the confines of Senegal. Making choreographic work, here, is about making the self.

But the transition from distributed agency to autonomous work in choreographic production is not welcome by all, as evident in the workshop scenes described in this chapter. This unease is culturally determined in part, and Senegalese women dancers are sometimes reluctant to promote themselves in individualistic ways, at least initially. Those who struggle with the individualistic process involved in the contemporary genre often find relief in continuous engagement with the neo-traditional genre, and sometimes also with sabar and popular dances. This should also be understood in the light of ideas of feminine morality as outwardly compliant with the authority of men and more experienced women, as discussed in earlier chapters. Also, the intimacy with dancers of the other sex that is often involved in contemporary choreographic work may put reputations at risk.

Contemporary performers are also concerned with the contents of their art. Morality is particularly at stake for women dancers, who must navigate the fascination of global audiences with Black bodies whilst simultaneously maintaining their reputations at home. For men, morality is at stake too, but in different ways: they are expected to earn a living from their practice, and to make it both 'here' and 'there', whilst maintaining complete creative autonomy, despite the dominance of French and Francophone sources of funding.

Notes

1. I had illuminating conversations with Adrienne Sichel during the 2012 biennale in Johannesburg, and I have greatly benefited from her erudite insights into the histories of dance in South Africa in the twentieth century.
2. Jazz pirouettes are similar to turns in classical ballet, but may be executed on a bent rather than straight supporting leg, and with more freedom in the position of the arms.
3. E-mail communication with Dakar-based performer, August 2004.
4. www.institutfrancais.com/fr/faites-notre-connaissance, accessed 01.09.2012. Translated from French.
5. www.culturesfrance.com/afrique-caraibes-en-creation/presentation/de4.html, accessed 05.11.2010. Translated from French. The Priority Solidarity Zone was defined in 1998 as the countries towards which French aid should be directed. It includes the quasi totality of Africa, with the exception of Libya, Egypt, Somalia, Botswana, Zambia, Malawi, Lesotho and Swaziland.
6. It is significant in respect of France's interest in southern Africa and its resources that the main sponsors of the 2012 dance biennale were the French Institute and the French oil company, TOTAL.

7. Participating dance companies are still selected by the French organizers, but the competitive element was abandoned with the 2012 biennale, officially because it was said that the competition had achieved its objective of fostering contemporary dance on the continent. Additional factors, however, include the growing difficulty of finding presenters willing to schedule a 'bouquet' of three winners, and sustained criticism from African artists. In 2010 the biennale was renamed Danse l'Afrique Danse, with no official translation into English so as to continue marking the role of France in the event.

8. www.francophonie.org/English.html

9. The French state-funded network of 'cultural centres' covers most of sub-Saharan Africa.

10. The French Cultural Centre in Dakar was renamed Institut Français Léopold Sédar Senghor in 2004, and simply Institut Français (French Institute) in 2011.

11. The choreographic competition was nicknamed 'Tana' while held in Madagascar.

12. African artists in the jury have included Mrs Acogny, choreographer Salia Sanou from Burkina Faso, Alphonse Tiérou from Côte d'Ivoire or film director Abderhamane Sissako from Mauritania.

13. E-mail communication with Senegal-based choreographer, October 2004, translated from French.

14. See, for example, 'Pas à pas, la danse contemporaine séduit l'Afrique', *Le Monde*, 18 November 2003; 'Mouvements de fond en Afrique', *Libération*, 8 April 2004, by Marie-Christine Vernay (www.liberation.fr/culture/0101484752–mouvements-de-fond-en-afrique, accessed 01.11.2012).

15. See, for example, Lepecki (1999).

16. See www.heddymaalem.com/unecreation.php?id=5.

17. When Benglia appeared at the Théâtre de l'Odéon in 1923 in Gaston Baty's 'L'Empereur Jones', René Wisner wrote in *Le Carnet*, 11 November 1923: 'His whole body bends, straightens up, leaps and falls back. Of his black nudity ['de sa noire académie'], he makes a poem which expresses distress or hope. An actor plays with his brain and his face. Mr Benglia plays with his muscles. [. . .] Sweat drenches him, makes his tanned torso glisten, and proves that he does indeed suffer the torment of the Emperor Jones. One could not be more sincere, closer to animality, and more artistic (Chalaye 2003: 99, translated from French).

18. Francesca Castaldi writes about the Ballet Mansour Guèye in her monograph on the National Ballet (2006).

19. This is the Senegalese version of the Eid el-Kebir or Eid el-Adha, one of the main Muslim festivals, during which each household must sacrifice a sheep in remembrance of Ibrahim's (Abraham) sacrifice of a sheep in place of his son.

Chapter 7

Contemporary Trajectories

In this chapter I focus on individual trajectories to illustrate the ways in which people mobilize various forms of creativity to shape their lives. I also examine the broader question of the social status of the performer in light of the transformations in choreographic production described in the previous chapter. Given the individualistic nature of creative agency in contemporary choreography, and given the prominent role of European funding in shaping the genre, local audiences have come to view this as a European phenomenon. Performers, by contrast, think of what they do as embedded in local life. For them, external funding and globalized approaches to choreographic production only serve to comment on local lives. While keeping an eye to international audiences and funding bodies, they are also concerned with the approval of relatives, friends and fellow performers. In order to navigate the fine line between the scorn and approval of their peers, contemporary performers invoke the idiom of 'tradition' and their role as social critics. Making the hidden visible thus enables them to carve out an acceptable status for their production.

I illustrate this through the trajectory of a group already mentioned in previous chapters, La 5ᵉ Dimension. Contemporary pieces are explored, showing the recurrent theme of marginal figures such as the homeless or the mad during the first half of the 2000s. Individual pieces shed light on the ways in which creators transform the 'movement material' generated by individuals into a mirror of social ills. Performers and choreographers are also concerned with their engagement with global circuits on an equal basis with peers from elsewhere. Through transnational collaborations, for example, they use their own bodies to imagine a more egalitarian world order.

The contemporary uses of 'tradition'

The interaction of the Senghorian project of developing a local art world based on regional 'traditions' (Chapter 1) and Euro-American constructions of dance and music in Africa (Introduction) have fostered an enduring concern with 'tradition' in the Senegalese performing scene. What artists understand as 'tradition', however, varies greatly. It is not so much actual histories as it is a discourse that is invoked differently to claim moral authority in various contexts: to distinguish choreography from the popular dances, for example, or to claim the moral high ground over another genre of performance. Interestingly, the same performers who claim to be going back to traditional expression when working within the neo-traditional genre may make the exact same claim when working within the contemporary approach, and see no contradiction in this. In practice, whereas both genres make use of regional performative practices, they differ in the consciousness with which they work with them: whereas neo-traditional choreographers take it for granted that what they are doing is inspired by 'tradition', contemporary choreographers have to articulate their use of local life as inspiration for their work. Not only is this expected by international audiences and presenters, it also enables artists to claim a moral high ground in spite of the problematic status of performers in society.

Choreographers often address this concern by 'researching tradition', preferably in the rural areas. This is by no means restricted to Senegal, and Kwabena Nketia (1996) identified a similar phenomenon elsewhere on the continent. Simone Gomis, who grew up in Dakar, explained how she had spent time in her parents' Manjaco-speaking village of origin in the Casamance, watched ceremonies and learned some of the local dances. This meant so much to her that her first creation, *Tenane*, was a contemporary piece that was meant to convey the courage of rural Manjaco women in the face of hard every-day labour. In 2003 Djibril Diallo, a young Dakar-based choreographer, made plans to travel throughout Senegal for two months to present his work and learn about regional dances, but the project was never completed due to a lack of funds.

Similar obsessions with 'tradition' have been documented by anthropologists working in other contexts. In Ireland, Wulff (2007) suggests that interpretations of Irish 'tradition' are as important in competitive dancing, *sean-nós* and Riverdance as they are to cutting-edge dance theatre, and that these reveal an obsession with what constitutes Irishness. Although concerns with the past are found in all dance worlds, they are perhaps particularly salient in postcolonial contexts given their central concern with retrieving the histories that were obscured by colonialism.

Broadly speaking, there are two aspects of the discourse on the 'modernity of tradition' in the Senegalese choreographic world: tradition as 'language', and tradition as 'social criticism'. The first aspect is the widespread notion that what makes 'contemporary dance' in Africa interesting and 'authentic' is the innovative use of regional techniques of performance to create something new. 'Traditional' performance is viewed as a kind of language from which syntax and a vocabulary can be extracted to create a new language. This is in direct continuity with the way in which Senghor (quoted in Acogny 1994 [1980]) described the Mudra Afrique project in the late 1970s:

> Before going further, I would like to call attention to Madame Acogny's vocabulary, since it characterizes the négritude of her dance. The purpose of African dance is to ensure that students correctly perform certain dance

figures which Madame Acogny invented, based on Black African folk dances. In doing so, her procedure is the same as that of European choreographers who invented the figures of classical ballet.

Given the dominant role played by Mrs Acogny in training contemporary chore-ographers from a wide range of African countries, it is not surprising that the same discourse should have been appropriated by Tubaab Jallaw-trained artists across the continent. Nigerian, Adedayo Liadi (quoted in Douglas et al. 2006: 106), whom I mentioned in the previous chapter, also spoke about his work in terms of using 'tradition' as a language:

> What we're doing now in contemporary African dance is showing ourselves on stage as we are, not imitating Western culture. Having learned a lot in Europe, I discovered that I needed to develop a strong language – personal body language – for Nigerian audiences and Africa, if possible. I started learning a lot about what it takes to be a very strong traditional dancer. From traditional to contemporary, then back to traditional because working in Europe has really affected my way of moving on stage. The tools that I'm making use of are from Europe and that experience has broadened my mind but not changed who I am.

The words of Nganti Towo, one of the Kaay Fecc directors in 2003, echo a similar discourse as she speaks to the press about the rationale behind the central presence of 'traditional dance' in the Kaay Fecc training workshops:

> We use tradition to create different stories, another kind of writing. We don't have to appropriate the Western techniques. We can use our own techniques. If we isolate tradition, we can create an alphabet to write our own dance. [. . .] We don't want to devaluate or ignore tradition. [. . .] We simply want to allow the youth to use a different kind of writing, to learn about traditional dance and take from it what can be sold internationally, so that they may be able to earn a living. (Walfadjri 2002)

The notion that dance may be codified into sets of 'techniques' is, in fact, a Eurocentric idea. It is no coincidence that classical ballet, to which Senghor refers explicitly, was codified at a historical time when the industrial revolution was taking off. This was a time when European societies became concerned with technique and efficacy. The professionalization of ballet, which introduced increased performance into a court dance, resonated well with this. By appropriating the discourse of a 'language' or a set of 'techniques', however, Senegalese dance people attempt to reaffirm their ground-ing in local life. It is their way of saying: 'we may be using tools from elsewhere, but we are still ourselves when we do this.'

The second aspect is the idea that what makes performance 'traditional' is its capacity to comment reflexively on social life. Similar claims are made by rap artists, who routinely trace their inspiration to local oratory genres, such as women's *taasu* and men's *taaxuraan*, and not exclusively to American rap. In choreography, people invoke inspiration from regional forms of total theatre, such as the Malian *koteba*, which mixes song, dance and theatre in a bittersweet farce. In this view, contemporary performance is at least as locally grounded as the neo-traditional genre. The latter is even presented as obsolete by some because it has become detached from people's everyday lives, as evident in the words of La 5ᵉ Dimension's Papa Sy and Jean Tamba:

> We no longer live in huts, do we? Our parents and grandparents did, but our lives are different. So we need to develop a dance that will talk about living in the city, about our lives today. (Sy, personal communication, Dakar, September 2002)

> Our tradition is to dance what people do in life. So what we do is tradition, isn't it? In thirty years people will say that what we are doing today was tradition. But tradition is not fixed, it's moving all the time. (Tamba, personal communication, Dakar, April 2003)

Tamba also insisted that what neo-traditional dance troupes were doing was 'folklore' and not 'tradition', and compared Senegambian tradition to classical ballet, which he thought had authority in Europe by virtue of its long history:

> People talk about tradition [in dance], but the first ballets in Africa go back to Fodéba Keita in 1950. If you compare that with the classical ballet tradition in Europe, which goes back to Louis XIV, it's very recent. Our traditional dances are 100, maybe 200 years old . . . That's nothing! (Tamba, personal communication, Dakar, April 2003)

On a different occasion Papa Sy, a performer and choreographer who had worked with Tamba since 1995 and had his own company in Dalifort, showed me how he had worked with a transformed version of the Lebu *ndëp*. One simple sequence of the ndëp is based on the repetition of small jumps on alternate legs while the other leg is extended in front, heel touching the ground. It is performed to sabar drumming. Papa Sy had retained the basic structure while widening the scope of the jumps, making them higher and more athletic, legs thrown higher. The result was an entirely new movement, both visually and in terms of the energy deployed. The novelty also came from the fact that he was a male performer, whereas the 'real' ndëp is usually performed by women. The way in which he commented on the innovation indicated that he was conscious of having to modify the ritual practice in order not to interfere with a domain that is known to be both powerful and inappropriate to stage for public display:

> You see, this is a ndëp step [performing the step]. Now, if I do this [throwing the legs higher] . . . Is it still the ndëp? Of course it's not. Have I got the

right to do this? I do, because I am creating something new, but I use tradition to do that. And I'm saying something that is closer to me. (Sy, personal communication, Dakar, September 2002)

There are indeed limits to the degree of manipulation of ritual practices which people find acceptable for purposes of commercial production, a point Castaldi (2006) also noted with the National Ballet. The case of a young dancer-choreographer who suffered a severe bout of mental illness illustrates this point. An articulate young man who had studied philosophy at the University of Dakar for a couple of years while also doing drama, he had been noticed by Mrs Acogny during a theatre performance in Tubaab Jallaw. He attended workshops at her centre, trained intensively to build up a muscular body, and later began working with neo-traditional troupes so as to infuse his choreographic work with locally grounded spirituality. Within a few years he was touring with Mrs Acogny's Jant-bi Company, had his own group and was awarded a studentship to pursue his studies at an arts school in Europe. Ambitious in his desire to draw on regional ritual practices, he spent time listening to oral historians, and reading texts on regional rituals. In 2003 he performed a solo at the French Cultural Centre, which explicitly drew on his research. One particular sequence involved him moving slowly across a wooden tablet of the type used in Quranic teaching, his bare feet touching the inscriptions in black ink. By his own admission a pious Muslim, he did not see this as a problem, but the sequence generated a palpable stir in the tightly packed open-air space by a massive baobab tree. When the dancer later came down with what looked like depression, everyone I spoke to was certain of it: he had carried his 'research' too far, and had interfered with forces beyond his control without proper initiation. But this was, in effect, only a slight shift of idiom from what people had expressed only a couple of years earlier, when he seemed to go from strength to strength: that he was attempting to fast-track his way to success rather than work patiently to develop his skills. This critique, which was often formulated by more experienced performers, was particularly damning in a context in which moral standing rises with the strength to undergo lengthy training and a degree of self-sacrifice.

Beyond the discourse according to which contemporary choreographic production blurs the boundaries between life and stage, therefore, some boundaries remain salient, and crossing them is perceived as carrying potentially serious consequences. The younger the individual, the more dangerous this is likely to be. This is a reminder that the globalization of cultural forms does not necessarily entail a radical reshuffling of local hierarchies. The moral domain still offers powerful ways of keeping the youth 'in their place'. To counter this, many younger artists in contemporary Senegal consciously position themselves as social critics.

The burden of engagement

For a few decades there was a widespread view, sometimes echoed in scholarly work, that African theatrical production was no longer meaningful because it was no longer embedded in social life. This view is thus reflected in Nicholls' (1998: 53) contribution to an edited volume on African Dance, in which the author establishes a direct link between this cultural impoverishment and the transformation of artistic forms:

> The separation of form and function is observed in the process of artistic trivialization that is occurring throughout Africa, from Ritual Art-to-Folk Art-to-Tourist Art. Each stage represents a loss of authenticity, a loss of aesthetic quality, and a corresponding loss of historical significance and cultural relevance.

Yet contemporary choreographic production often carries more or less explicit elements of social criticism. Karin Barber (1987) makes a similar point when she suggests that the popular arts in Africa may contain social or political commentary concealed within the layers of each genre. In Senegal, the same artists who are faithful to the state-created idiom in the neo-traditional genre may also enjoy being scathing about social ills through more individualized choreography. It is thus understood that creativity should be used to celebrate as well as criticize, and that it takes different genres to express different things.

The critical character of contemporary choreography, I suggest, comes out of the intersection between local agendas and external discourses. In the local context, positioning themselves as those who hold a mirror to society so that it may see its own ills, and so that people may 'cleanse' it, enables young dancer-choreographers to claim the moral high ground. This may later be turned into actual power of course, but I would like to suggest that moral authority and social recognition are also sought after for their own sake. Aspirations to moral authority will be illustrated more concretely with the trajectory of La 5ᵉ Dimension Company, in the next section.

External discourses which romanticize certain forms of engagement are mediated through international funding agencies and presenters. Many of the presenters I met at the 2012 biennale in Johannesburg thus had expectations that the works presented would contain political messages, or at least comment on the burning social issues faced by the continent's populations. In this context, Fatou Cissé's solo on the plight of women, 'Regarde-moi encore', was well received, and so was Saint-Louis-based Diagn'Art's 'Banlieue', a piece for three dancers on the betrayal of the youth by African elites. There was also widespread acclaim, for example, for Mozambican Panaibra Gabriel Canda's 'Time and space: the Marrabenta solos', described in the programme as calling into question 'all the ideas that the Mozambican body has absorbed in the course of its history: nationalism, socialism, communism, militarism and finally, individual freedom.'[1] On the other hand, the selection featured very few pieces explicitly concerned with formal experimentation rather than taking on the world's issues, and those that were scheduled did not draw much attention. In the contemporary genre, experimenting with form, or simply creating entertainment, is simply not a viable option.

The romanticization of political engagement also comes across in the body of texts produced around contemporary pieces from Africa: programmes (usually written or heavily edited by the funding agencies or producers), webpages, and media reviews. Senegalese dancer, Pape Ibrahima Ndiaye (a.k.a. Kaolack), thus won the first solo prize at the 2008 biennale in Tunis for his piece, *J'accuse*. Whenever I have heard someone talk about the piece in subsequent years, it was usually the political message that was discussed, and seldom the aesthetics. The piece had been inspired by Kaolack's traumatic experience of racism and detention in a North African country, and presenters (some of whom I have met) were undoubtedly fascinated by the idea that the artist they were promoting had suffered the violence of incarceration in his own flesh. London's Dance Umbrella festival scheduled the piece in 2009, and the promotional text made much out of its critical content:

> *J'Accuse*, Danse L'Afrique Danse prize-winner (2008), is a physically and emotionally charged solo which asks important questions about the condition of the African person in a global context. Based on personal experiences of prejudice, travel restrictions and ignorance, Kaolack has created a polemical response which celebrates an African identity and confident stance in the face of an unfair world.[2]

There is thus a similarity between the 'romance of resistance in world music discourse' and that in the choreographic world, which equally leads choreographic artists to 'stress their antiestablishment credentials' (Stokes 2004:61). This is not to suggest that African creators are not genuinely concerned with social and political critique, and indeed many of them are. But what I want to suggest, here, is that the way in which this concern is expressed in choreographic work is heavily shaped by the Euro-American gaze.

As one might expect, treating choreography as a political gesture is not without consequences for the lives of those involved. Indeed, artists who comment openly on their society's shortcomings may find themselves forced to live abroad, not necessarily because of government bans but often with a view to finding more freedom of expression. Choreographers based in Senegal on a permanent basis are often uneasy about being seen as openly political, and prefer to speak of an engagement to improve society than a political engagement. For them, the challenge is to be sufficiently critical to draw recognition for their moral qualities, while at the same time avoiding the sort of anti-establishment stance that may compromise their well-being and that of their families. They must also contend with the local bureaucracies who control the venues, permits, visas and other resources without which artists can neither work nor travel. One Dakarois choreographer I discussed this with, for example, insisted his desire was to raise audiences' awareness of the plight of the underprivileged. However, he did not wish to be seen as a politically committed artist for fear of being perceived as overestimating his power. Others by contrast, often among the younger generation now in its twenties to early thirties, were much more confident about having important things to say about their society, and about the state of the world more generally.

In practice however, the creative process does not always contain conscious engagement from the outset. Choreographic works are usually the outcome of ideas and experimentation by several individuals drawing on many different sources of inspiration, including personal experiences. Beyond an initial theme, social and political contents often come through fairly late in the process, if not entirely in retrospect. Here the global circulation of discourses of resistance plays a decisive role indeed.

To convey some of the complex ways in which choreographic pieces emerge, I will trace the trajectory of a Dakar-based contemporary group, with a focus on the creative and social processes underlying the work of the company. Individual trajectories will also bring to life the links between genres and the circulation between groups which I have mentioned throughout the book.

La 5ᵉ Dimension

The trajectory of this group is intimately linked to that of its choreographer and co-founder, Jean Tamba. Tamba was raised in Fass, a fairly small neighbourhood near the Medina. His parents were migrants from the Casamance, his father a Jola and his mother from a Creole family with links to Guinea Bissau. Tamba says he always had a passion for dancing, and went clubbing regularly as a young man in Dakar in the late 1970s and 1980s. Like many men of his generation, he is nostalgic about those days and says that as long as you were a good dancer, you could always find a way into nightclubs because women needed good dancers. Whereas many of today's young men are not keen to confess a passion for dancing unless they are professional performers, many Dakarois men from the previous generations remember the dance floors of their youth with visible pleasure. This comes across in novels set in Dakar during this period. Boubacar Boris Diop's (2009) French translation of his novel in Wolof, *Doomi Golo*, is a memoir written by eighty-year old Nguirane Faye. There is a concern with the issue of transmission running through the novel, and it is therefore framed as Nguirane writing a series of seven diaries to his grandson, who has long departed for an unknown foreign destination. Within the first two pages, Nguirane writes about the Cuban dance parties that were the happiest moments of his youth:

'When it comes to living, I made no half measure. In fact, as I write to you, a very popular tune from about sixty years ago comes back to me. [. . .] It was something about the time we spend on this earth, the days and nights so empty and uncertain that one would be a complete idiot to accept, on top of it all, to die without having been happy! We loved this tune. That and the pachangas . . . We were playing lots of Cuban music at our parties in Le Plateau [in the city centre]. These parties were hot and alcohol was flowing. I can still see us shaking our bodies in complete chaos in a burning hot, dusty warehouse. Imagine dozens of girls and boys with bodies shivering as if taken by complete madness, and shouting even louder than the tumbas and the maracas!'[3]

Sometime around 1980, Tamba was recruited as lead drummer into Ahmed Kunta's troupe, Les Ballets de Maître Kunta, where dance master, Alioune Fall, taught him dances and rhythms from across the region. As in many other 'ballets', the emphasis was on the Mandinka areas of Senegal, Mali and Guinea, as well as on Sereer dances. Like many performers of his generation, Tamba insisted that he had learned the proper 'traditional rhythms', and not a modernized version. It was with this troupe that he made his debut as a choreographer. By the late 1980s, he yearned for novelty. While still performing with various neo-traditional troupes, he joined the Sotiba Boys, with whom he performed on TV and at promotional events (cf. Chapter 1). He took classical ballet classes with Andrée Lorenzetti, a former dancer with the Ballet de Marseille who taught classical ballet at her Rue Parchappe studio for many years. He enrolled at the National School of Arts for a six-year curriculum which included classical ballet, contemporary dance, acting and other stage skills. Simultaneously, he danced with Ousmane Noël Cissé's Manhattan Dance School, and took part in workshops with visiting dancers from Europe or the US, including African American choreographer, Chuck Davis.

Meanwhile, at the Christian school where he was teaching dance classes, and where Bakalama's Landing Mané had been teaching, Tamba met Honoré Mendy, an organizer of cultural events for the youth (*animateur culturel*) originally from Ziguinchor. When Tamba graduated from the National School of Arts in 1995, they set up La 5ᵉ Dimension together. A few years later, they would form part of the small group of dance professionals who set up the Kaay Fecc association. With the company, Tamba was the main choreographer while Mendy initially looked after the administrative aspects of the group's work. Dancers and drummers were recruited from among people they knew. There were the Mané brothers from Bakalama, whom Tamba knew from the Manhattan Dance School, and fellow graduate Papa Sy. Tamba says that setting up his own group was about creating a 'free space' to experiment by, for example, mixing moves and rhythms from the regional dances with inspiration from the Euro-American jazz, modern and contemporary dance traditions. The idea came to him much earlier, he says, when hearing a radio speech by former President Senghor sometime in the mid-1980s. Senghor was discussing his cherished notions of 'rootedness and openness' and cultural creolization (*métissage culturel*). Tamba describes this moment as a turning point, a moment of revelation during which he knew this was the kind of dance he wanted to do. He did not know what it would come to look like, but the principle spoke to him. This may well be a retrospective re-writing of history since by that time Tamba had already been exposed to Ousmane Cissé's Senghorian ideas for many years. Nevertheless, like many in his generation Tamba is nostalgic about the golden days of the Senghor regime. The company's first leaflet, produced with funding from PSIC (Programme de Soutien aux Initiatives Culturelles) for its national tour in 2002, thus makes explicit reference to its Senghorian inspiration:

> If the heart of the [group's] inspiration is in Africa, Asia, India, the Middle East, Europe and America also enrich this blend. 'Metiss dance' materializes the principle of rootedness and openness dear to the President-poet L. Sédar Senghor; it is universal and capable of reaching to people of all the continents.' (Extract from *Bujuman* leaflet, 2002, translated from French)

The company's first piece, *Qui suis-je?* ('Who am I?'), was created in 1995 and performed at the French Cultural Centre in Dakar. Tamba and Mendy wrote that it dealt with 'the big questions of identity and human destiny', but I have never seen a detailed description or text of the piece. *Dina baax* ('All will be well') followed in 1997, also performed at the French Cultural Centre, in several schools and for the inauguration of the slavery memorial on Gorée Island. Centred on the spiritual quest of a man who believed in a brighter future in spite of misfortune, *Dina baax* had a resolutely optimistic outlook.

By the time I met the group in May 2002, they had recently received funding from the PSIC and a grant from Mrs Acogny's centre. This enabled the group to work regularly on a forty-five-minute piece, *Bujuman*, at least three times per week, for four hours from 10.00 am to 2.00 pm. By then the company had existed for seven years, and there had been much coming-and-going. One of the male dancers had been enrolled in a transnational company, and was touring abroad much of the time. One of the young women had travelled to Spain to teach, and had eventually married and stayed there. A second woman dancer, who worked simultaneously with Bakalama, had given up the stage after getting married. A third had taken a break from dancing after getting pregnant, and although she planned to return, she could not be involved with *Bujuman*. Landing Mané had made his way to the UK, and his brother Ousmane continued to work with Bakalama but had chosen to leave aside contemporary work. At this point, therefore, the group was composed of Tamba himself as the choreographer, drummers Oumar Diaw and Oumar Mbow, and dancers Papa Sy, Simone Gomis, Moustapha Guèye and Aliou Mané. Moustapha Guèye, who had a lifelong passion for dance, had begun with jazz dance and a best-dancer award at the 1994 Oscars des Vacances (with a choreography by Landing Mané) before learning the neo-traditional genre with several Dakarois troupes. His training in contemporary choreography came from two professional workshops at Mrs Acogny's centre, as well as work with La 5ᵉ Dimension.

The most recent recruit at the time was Aliou Mané, whose parents came from the Lower Casamance. He had aspired to a career as a football player and had attended a football school, but had eventually realized that there would be little prospect of being recruited into a major club abroad. With encouragement from a neighbourhood friend, he had then joined a neo-traditional troupe in Dakar. There he had learned a range of dances from the Casamance and Guinea. Around 1998 Mrs Acogny, who was scouting for talents for her newly opened centre, noticed Mané and encouraged him to join her three-month workshop in Tubaab Jallaw. This is where he met Tamba and the others. Since one of the drummers had also trained to become a football player and Gomis was a former athlete, the company was largely made up of people already familiar with the discipline of daily physical training. Some went running on the beach every day. The rehearsal sessions started with each performer warming up in the style each of them was used to. Choreographic work would begin with dancers experimenting with moves individually or in pairs, on a theme or an idea suggested by the choreographer. Several duets were thus included in the piece after the dancers had chosen to create sequences together. Each individual had a different training and a different movement style, and much time was spent showing the others new moves, or new ways of performing the familiar.

The PSIC funding also enabled La 5ᵉ Dimension to embark on what they had long hoped for, a 'national tour' following the *Bujuman* premiere in Dakar in October 2002. The piece was performed in Diourbel, Kaolack and Saint-Louis, with two days between each performance. Due to the difficulty of travelling inland and the lack of organizational facilities in the cities visited, the tour turned out to be exhausting. Since all the performances were free, no profit was generated, and the performers often had to advertise the show themselves. Though I was not able to follow them on tour, they reported in detail their experience of driving around with a microphone on the days of the performance. Yet they returned to Dakar exhilarated by the enthusiastic response they had received from audiences who had never before seen contemporary dance:

> There were even older people who came to see us. They had never seen anything like that, but they loved it! They came to talk to us afterwards, they encouraged us. It was incredible to meet people in this way![4]

The company took a week or two to regroup before resuming the usual routine. They had now identified the sections that needed 'cleaning up', and set to the task. In January 2003, *Bujuman* delighted audiences again at the French Centre in Dakar. Because of the prestige attached to performing in what was in effect the city's best venue, with qualified stage technicians, it was important that *Bujuman* be successful there. Christian Saglio, the director at the time and a former anthropologist, spoke of the piece as a 'revelation'.

But the group was also aware that performing for the cosmopolitan audience of the French Centre was a double-edged sword. On one hand it was a necessary step towards gaining media attention, further funding and possibly international recognition. On the other hand, it was reinforcing the widespread perception that the contemporary genre was 'white people's stuff'. There were practical implications to this: people in the ministries, they said, often found an easy excuse to turn down their requests for support, arguing that their role was to promote 'culture for the Senegalese people' and not for the European residents. On the whole however, the written press was positive about *Bujuman*. The group was also asked to perform a short sequence at a charity event organized by Senegal's First Lady, Viviane Wade, in a luxury hotel. Photographs of the piece were exhibited at the Goethe Institute in Dakar. In June 2003, *Bujuman* was shown once more at the French Centre, but this time as part of the Kaay Fecc festival. The entrance was free, and the place was packed with several hundred people of all ages, but mainly the young. Children huddled next to each other in the front rows. The group hoped that this would represent an important step towards engagements abroad. Showing *Dina baax* for the first edition of the festival in 2001 had failed to produce international touring, but there was now a strong expectation that the right time had come. Although some of the performers wished to remain based in Senegal with their families, there was a general recognition that in order to earn a living, one had to work abroad as well. The ideal situation would be to travel and return. Ultimately, gaining recognition at home was what mattered most.

Dreams of mobility

The sense of urgency in building up a transnational career was heightened by the recent experiences of several of the members, who had gained a taste of what mobility could offer. In 1999, Tamba, Guèye, Sy and Diaw had been recruited by Mrs Acogny and German choreographer Suzanne Linke to create a piece in Tubaab Jallaw, *Le Coq est mort* ('the rooster is dead'). The piece featured eight male dancers: six Senegalese, a dancer from the DRC and one from Nigeria. The dancers said the title had been inspired by a rooster waking them up every morning at dawn. There was also word-play involved, of course, since the rooster is a symbol of the French nation. Perhaps because of this, the piece turned into a commentary on the postcolonial situation. In 1998 already, Suzanne Linke, who had trained under Mary Wigman in Berlin and worked with Pina Bausch, had been invited by Mrs Acogny to be one of the leaders of her first workshop. Linke's assistant choreographer was Avi Kaiser, an Israeli dancer with a Martha Graham training, who had worked with the Tel Aviv-based Bat-Sheva Company. The music was composed of a piece by Shostakovich, live voice, djembé drumming, West African string instruments kora and rithi, bass, violin, cello, clarinet and piano, all produced by French musician Etienne Schwarcz. The eight men entered the sand-covered stage in suits and wearing suitcases, and marched in procession before breaking off into individual variations. Eventually, the jackets were shed to reveal glistening torsos.

Although the leaflet described the style of the piece as a 'symbiosis between African dance and German *Tanztheater*', this was a genuinely transnational enterprise. Most of the 'raw material', however, came from the dancers themselves. This is evident in the aesthetics of the seventy-minute long piece, which includes cut-off sabar moves as well as neo-traditional steps, breakdance moves, and glimpses of Senegalese wrestling. The international tour with the *Coq est mort* production gave the lesser experienced dancers confidence in their ability to create work of international standard. The production was sponsored by what was then the Association Française d'Action Artistique (AFAA), the Stiftung Kunst und Kultur in Düsseldorf and various French and German foundations and theatres. The show toured over two years in France, the UK, Austria, Germany, Spain, the Netherlands, Denmark, Portugal, Israel, Canada and the US, where it featured at the prestigious Jacob's Pillow Festival in Massachusetts in August 2000. In Paris, the venue was the Théâtre de la Ville, often described as one of the most prestigious for contemporary dance in Europe.

A cursory look through press reviews in different countries suggests that many of the critics felt disconcerted by the *Coq est mort*, and did not always know what to make of the postcolonial theme. There was often genuine appreciation of the physicality and talent of the dancers. Several reviewers also alluded to the fact that this was the sort of work that was helping to revitalize the Euro-American dance world. *New York Times* critic Jennifer Dunning (2000) was among them:

There are considerable intellectual pleasures to the piece. One becomes fascinated by the gradual layering and melding of everyday and modern-dance movement with African dance forms and motifs of a sort that are revitalizing American modern dance today.

By the time I met La 5ᵉ Dimension dancers almost two years later, they was still buzzing about the tour. Rehearsal sessions often ended with memories of encounters in different destinations, and the future of the group was accordingly imagined as being a continuous engagement with the world. One particular moment of the North American tour was recurrent. Apparently, upon arrival at a festival the *Coq est mort* dancers had been met with the condescending attitude of a group of American performers who were due to appear at the same venue. They described the Americans as much taller and more strongly built than they, and as having drawn admiring looks from the women present at the festival. But the *Coq est mort* performance, they said, changed everything. Having revealed their dancing skills and bare torsos, the next evening they were the talk of the town. This time it was their turn to capture women's attention, and they roared with laughter when recalling the dismayed faces of the American dancers. Travelling stories were told and retold long after the rehearsals had ended, while walking the couple of miles across the traffic-ridden city centre to the *car rapide* station. The dancers lived in the Medina, Fass, HLM, Hann, Pikine and Dalifort, and the trip home could easily take several hours. There was plenty of time to dream of mobility.

By the autumn of 2002 however, La 5ᵉ Dimension had yet to receive an engagement abroad as a group. People bitterly resented the missed opportunity of the previous year, when Mrs Acogny had the company invited to perform in Jordan. On the day of the departure, the transit visas through France were refused and the trip was cancelled. Those who had not yet travelled complained that they were tired of waiting. *Dina baax, dina baax . . . ba kañ?* ('All will be well, all will be well . . . until when?'), one of them repeated ironically. He also joked that he would leave the country by the end of the year, and would swim or take a boat if he had to. Soon after, it was decided that the group would try to establish a base in Europe. This had to be done individually to maximize the chances of success, and once several members had established themselves, it would be easier to regroup for occasional performances.

In 2003, the networks nurtured by Tamba began to bear fruit. In July the group went to France for a week and performed at an independent arts festival in Douarnenez. This was unexpected for the performers, whom Tamba had simply told that something was underway and that they had to make sure their passports were up-to-date. This is a common strategy in Dakar, where people often avoid discussing travel plans in advance. This is partly for fear of envy, and partly to avoid disappointment should visas be refused. Once in France, they were thrilled by the welcome they received. They also enjoyed performing outdoors in the Douarnenez town centre, where they said they had felt a sense of connection with the audience. They did not consider dancing in a town square degrading; on the contrary, for them the size and response of the audience were just as important as the prestige of the space.

Back in Dakar, peers from other dance groups were surprised when the whole group returned. This was unusual in a world in which tours abroad routinely end with a few performers disappearing at the first given opportunity. But this group insisted that they were 'real professionals', for whom becoming irregular migrants abroad would be utterly unattractive. Junior performers in the group were even warned against living a miserable life in Europe, with no possibility to teach or perform, before being deported back empty-handed.

Over the years the future that was imagined in 2002 has only partly materialized. There have been several more trips to France, including performances and classes for the 'Senegalese week' organized by a Senegalese workers' association in Grenoble. Performers returned from Grenoble full of enthusiasm about their experience of teaching children, and challenging their stereotypes about Africa. They had been surprised at the children's ignorance since at the same age, they knew a great deal more about Europe than these French children knew about Africa. There was also further involvement in transnational networks, including Tamba's two-week 'study tour' in Germany, organized by the Goethe Institute to promote intercultural contact between artists. Whenever possible the group also performed and taught within the neo-traditional genre, which all the performers have remained enthusiastic about.

Throughout 2004, extracts of *Bujuman* and new, shorter choreographies were presented at various events in Dakar and elsewhere in the region. There was, for example, a performance at the African American-funded Ebony Festival on Gorée Island in June. In December, *Bujuman* was shown at the Dialogues de Corps Festival in Ouagadougou. By then, two performers had already made their way to Europe, and the group had to spend time training new recruits. But the most significant moment in the travelling life of the company was probably September 2006, when they were invited to perform at the Lyon Dance Biennale. The Lyon Biennale is one of the major dance festivals in Europe, and the company was one of only two Senegalese acts featured that year; the other one was Germaine Acogny performing *Tchouraï*, a solo choreographed for her by Sophiatou Kossoko. A handful of other contemporary companies from Africa also featured in the programme: Boyzie Cekwana's Floating Outfit Project from South Africa, the Faso Danse Théâtre and Salia nï Seydou, both from Burkina Faso. Salia nï Seydou presented *Un pas de côté* ('A step aside'), a piece created jointly with avant-garde music ensemble, Ars Nova, over four evening performances. Based at the Termitière choreographic centre in Ouagadougou, Salia nï Seydou was headed by dancer-choreographers Salia Sanou and Seydou Boro. They were well known to La 5ᵉ Dimension, and I joined the group to go and see the Salia nï Seydou/Ars Nova piece performed in an imposing theatre just outside Lyon. Seeing each other's performances during festivals is indeed one of the important ways in which choreographic 'trends' circulate.

La 5ᵉ Dimension presented its newest creation, *Eau b nite*, in two sold-out evening shows and a matinee for school children at one of Lyon's theatres (Figure 7.1). Again the reviewers seemed disoriented by a genre which clearly departed from the 'African' style they were used to, for example David Tran (2006):

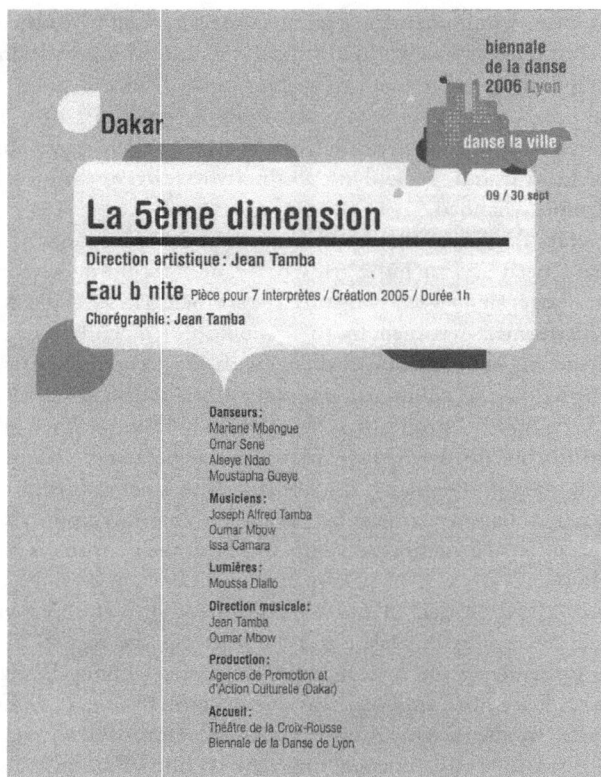

Figure 7.1 Front page of the Eau b nite *programme for the Lyon Dance Biennale, September 2006*

The four dancers (three men, a woman) seem to be born out of the sand, to emerge from a homeland ['terre natale'] which also works as a grave, to invoke the sky and the rain. Later, the children will admire the energy of a resolutely African dance. It is powerful, it shuffles in the sand and sends the grains flying in the wind. Meanwhile their parents will be thinking hard to try to differentiate the various rituals of purification running through the piece. This is an exercise all the more challenging as the eye immersed in European culture sometimes struggles to see 'beyond' ['eau-delà'][5] African folklore.

There were few reviews, but overall the response was positive if not enthusiastic. Audiences, on the other hand, seemed suitably entertained, and both evenings ended in a standing ovation. Following one of the shows there was a short conversation with the group, during which children could ask about the piece, about Senegal, and have Tamba sign their copies of the programme. This was a moment of sheer pleasure for the group. Tamba and Mbow also taught a workshop for dance students at the Lyon branch of the National Dance Centre. The week in Lyon was not only a professional highlight, it was also an intense social occasion during which it felt as if the group was brought back together again: two former dancers came to visit from their respective homes in Spain and Belgium. But some of the former members had cut off contact, and Tamba seemed ambivalent about the plan that had been laid out years earlier. A devout Christian, he attributed this momentary success to the strength of his faith, and seemed reluctant to celebrate before this opportunity led to more sustained activities. Uncertainty about the future loomed, even in this moment of joy.

The increasing engagement outside Senegal did not mean that the performers' social environment in Dakar was being neglected. Performing abroad, in fact, enhanced recognition at home, regardless of the response of far-away audiences. Being invited to perform abroad was a sign of success in itself, even more so if this happened at a prestigious venue alongside artists from other parts of Africa. One of the musicians thus told me how he used to sneak out of the house discreetly to go to rehearsals, at a time when he worked exclusively with neo-traditional troupes. But now that the company was travelling and performing in proper theatres, and not just in hotels, he had gained more status in the family. It was not just the money, although this was obviously an important part of it, it was also that this seemed like a more serious profession.

Initially, it had been difficult to convince friends and relatives to come and see the performances. But as one of the performers told me proudly, 'when they finally came, they loved it!' They were intrigued by what they saw, he continued, and made comments like 'we didn't know you were doing *this* kind of thing!' in admiring tones. Tamba was equally proud that some of his relatives in Dakar were now prepared to pay for their ticket. One of his nephews, a young boy, had said to him that he wanted to be an artist like him when he grew up. This meant a lot to the choreographer, who had told me about it without me prompting him on the topic of reception. 'If you don't create for your family, who do you do it for then?' he added.

A couple of years after Lyon, however, a feeling of exhaustion pervaded the group, as well as a sense that time was passing without a major breakthrough. Tamba and Moustapha Guèye took part in the African biennale in Tunis in 2008, where Guèye had been selected to compete in the solo category. As we have seen, though, the first prize went to Kaolack for *J'accuse*. Kaolack, a dancer with Mrs Acogny's Jant-bi Company, had originally been trained by Papa Sy in Dalifort. Was this an indication that the younger generation was now cutting the grass from under the feet of its mentors? Were years of hard work coming to little more than a few engagements abroad?

Over the years, new, younger members had been recruited from Papa Sy's company in Dalifort to replace those who had found opportunities to settle abroad. By early 2011, six of the performers who had worked with the company since 2002 had left for Europe or the US, with two or three of them coming-and-going on a regular basis. The company had taken part in the big performances organized for the Second World Festival of Black Arts in Senegal (FESMAN) in December 2010, but those left behind were demoralized. It was still a struggle to earn a regular living, and paying the expenses generated by the daily work of a company was proving increasingly difficult. Several former members now settled abroad also struggled to get by; they taught dance or percussion classes, and had to learn new trades altogether to supplement those modest earnings. As the dreams of mobility materialized they lost much of their shine, but immobility was not a desirable alternative.

Bujuman

The company's trajectory only makes full sense if one considers its choreographic production, which sheds further light on the questions of social engagement discussed earlier. It also illustrates how performers engage with 'home' and 'away' in their work.

Bujuman began at the Centre Culturel Blaise Senghor (CCBS) in Dakar, on one of the many afternoons Tamba spent there chatting and working with other dance and theatre people: performers, troupe managers, technicians, journalists, civil servants posted at the CCBS, and ordinary youths who gravitated around the troupes in the hope that it might lead to job opportunities. It was during conversations with Massamba Guèye, state culture officer Tidiane Diallo and others that the idea emerged. According to Guèye, who wrote the text for the piece, *buju* means 'to fall into poverty' in Wolof. At the studio, in early 2002, Tamba set his two drummers and four dancers to work in the usual participatory way. The idea of doing a piece on the 'bujumen', homeless city dwellers who live off scraps and urban waste, was discussed and deconstructed into themes, inner feelings and scenes of life. Could they imagine what it felt like to be a bujuman? What would the future look like? What would be the role of loneliness, love, friendship, hope, faith or substance abuse in the life of a bujuman?

The dancers were then asked to create their own sequences, sometimes with Tamba's suggestion of how to begin or how to use the space. His role was that of mentor and critic. After several months of work, the piece really came together during the summer of 2002, when the group spent six weeks of intensive work in Tubaab Jallaw. Mrs Acogny had lent the company her 'sand stage' (Figure 7.2), a house had been rented for the occasion, and a cousin of Tamba's had been recruited to cook for the group. This quiet landscape of sand and baobab trees facing the ocean was an ideal space to find inspiration, and rehearse the same sequences over and over. Evenings were enjoyable moments to relax together. During weekends, wives, friends and relatives came to visit from Dakar. This was a summer of intense bonding for the group, and in the following months they spoke fondly of the quiet respite from exhausting city life, and the simple pleasure of being able to focus on creative work without wasting vast amounts of energy on transport and the demands of everyday life.

For the premiere, the finished fifty-minute piece was presented on the outdoor stage of the CCBS. The seating consisted of metallic chairs lined up in the sand. Entrance was free, and the show was attended by some two hundred fellow dancers, musicians and actors, friends, relatives, people from the nearby neighbourhoods of Grand Dakar and Fass, a handful of journalists and a few foreign dance or drumming

Figure 7.2 Bujuman *rehearsal, Tubaab Jallaw, July 2002. Photograph by the author.*

students. It took a while to set up the décor, which had been designed by Tidiane Diallo to evoke a rubbish dump. A straw wall was hung at the back of the stage. In the afternoon the musicians and I had collected branches, discarded food tins, plastic bags and other scraps from the grounds around the centre, and hung them on the straw wall. Second-hand clothes were scattered across the floor. Some of the dancers warmed up until the last minute, while others prepared mentally by reciting *xasaids* (cf. Chapter 4).

The performance was due to begin with a twenty-six-minute film by director Mame Daour Wade, in which sequences from the piece alternated with interviews of real bujumen, but the projection was cancelled due to technical problems. The piece began in complete darkness, suddenly broken by a beam of light coming from the back right corner of the stage. Bathed in light, Moustapha Guèye sat alone, both legs stretched in front of him, looking away from the audience towards the source of light. Pushing his body backwards with both hands, he dragged himself slowly across the stage. He was wearing black trousers, a black T-shirt and a bandana. For the first minute there was only silence as he moved across the stage. This was a far cry from the loud drumming that usually introduces neo-traditional performances. Slowly, softly, Guèye reclined without moving his legs until he lay still, flat on his back. All of a sudden, as he lifted a leg slowly into vertical position, and a soundtrack with Schönberg music came on. He rolled over to one side and pushed himself into a twisted position, both feet on the floor and legs stretched. His body was folded over in two, his hands and neck on the floor. This was a position I had seen perform many times in Euro-American modern dance. It is also uncannily similar to the cover photograph on Helena Wulff's (2007) book on Irish dance, which features a scene from *Ballads* by CoisCéim. From this position, Guèye slowly kneeled, sat on his heels and raised his back to a vertical position, arms to his sides, facing away from the light beam. For a short while he seemed to be meditating, such that there was only a minor difference in mood projected between his pre-performance preparation and his concentration on stage. As Schönberg's tempo accelerated he swiftly came back to his feet in a frozen walking position, knees bent deeply, arms stretched horizontally in a front-back direction, then shifted quickly to a symmetrical position on the other side. Two *chassés*[6] to the right, arms opening sideways and closing, a roll back onto the floor, and back into the frozen walking position, arms stretched out before raising them slowly, slowly upwards. The position was reminiscent of the American jazz style but slower, more contained. Guèye's solo was a succession of changes in the quality of the energy, from complete stillness to frantic movement. With the beam as the sole source of light, the dancer seemed almost ethereal, withdrawn into a world of his own. This impression was reinforced by the dissonant notes of the Schönberg soundtrack, unrecognisable to most in the audience.

As he performed a couple of athletic jumps, one leg bent and the other stretched forward, then moved towards the back of the stage, Gomis ran onto the stage. She wore a half-open multicoloured dress, black footless tights and a green headscarf soberly tied up. She stopped abruptly in the middle of the stage and came to a standstill in a frozen walking position very similar to Guèye's a moment earlier. With her arms down to the sides, she slowly stretched a leg forward and then stood still on both legs. A chassé to the left, then to the right, arms as well as legs chasing each other. A pirouette, then several jumps backwards on one leg, arms flying as if she were a bird. She came to a halt, thrust the left leg forward and bent the knee deeply, the right leg stretched to the back. She stretched the arms horizontally in a front-back direction, right arm pointing towards the horizon. Like Guèye earlier, she had her side to the audience, and there was no eye contact. There was no contact with Guèye either. Both dancers seemed lost in their respective worlds, and yet as they continued to dance, their movement gradually took on the same quality, the same shifts in energy. As Guèye crossed the stage diagonally in wide, slow-motion steps with legs lifted high, Gomis returned to her deep plunging position and seemed to perform an intimate ritual of her own. She stroked her face from front to back with both hands in a washing-like gesture. Then Guèye seemed to perform his own ritual, gathering an imaginary load from the floor and pushing himself backwards, standing on bent knees and using Martha Graham-technique contractions of the torso to initiate a movement of the whole body. Meanwhile Gomis, still oblivious of him, seemed to be searching for something amidst the clothes on the floor. With a sudden shift of energy entirely dissonant with the music's low tempo, she launched into a Mandinka variation, a series of symmetrical sideways jumps with flying movements of the arms. Still lost within herself, she stopped to pull at an imaginary strand of hair.

She performed the variation again, giving it wider amplitude. As she moved back and forth between vigorous dancing and a quiet, intimate concentration on her hair strand, Mané entered the stage from a back corner. He moved forward diagonally and in slow motion, following the same pattern as Guèye. He wore army trousers and a green T-shirt.

Shortly after, as Gomis and Mané gradually glided into synchronized movements, still seemingly oblivious of each other, Guèye turned on the spot, following his own pointed finger round and round in circles. A shopping trolley, like those used by bujumen, stood at the back of the stage.

Later, Mané acted a bujuman trying to rise above the grim reality of his wasteland by climbing into the trolley. He asked Papa Sy, who was wearing women's high-heel shoes, to push him around. But the unlucky bujuman fell when the trolley got stuck on the floor, in a theatrical moment which drew laughter from the audience. During a pas-de-deux between Guèye and Gomis the voices of the two musicians rose from the back of the stage. They entered and walked to the front of the stage, occasionally beating the drums strapped in front of them and taking turns to speak in Wolof, in the emphatic manner used by the géwël. This two-voice dialogue, a succession of short announcements of events due to take place in an imaginary urban neighbourhood, was undoubtedly the moment that elicited most laughter from the audience. The first announcement was an appeal for people to come and support a meeting of the 'party for the revolution of the disenfranchised artists' scheduled the same evening at the Maison de la Culture Douta Seck (MCDS). It was followed by the announcement of a *simb*, a short story about a woman who had been caught by the spirits (*ràb*), and an appeal to join a protest march to the presidential palace, organized by the 'bujuman union of the Cap Vert region'. Naturally, such a union does not exist, only in the piece. Later, two drunkards – the two musicians – crossed the stage, holding on to each other and laughing at each other's misery.

Throughout the piece the music shifted from Schönberg to James Brown's, 'I feel good', djembe drumming and *kasa* rhythms played live on a tree trunk. At the end, all six performers came together to sing a Jola song of hope composed by an actor in a Dakarois theatre troupe. There were patches of silence, too, a device common in the Euro-American contemporary genre but a radical departure from regional traditions. Silence, some choreographers say, may evoke imaginary soundtracks in the minds of dancers and audiences alike.

There are many possible interpretations of this piece, and although mine is subjective, it is nevertheless informed by sustained interaction with the group over several years. The performers themselves were always reluctant to discuss possible interpretations since contemporary work is meant to remain somewhat open to interpretation. Aesthetically, however, the piece revelled in the wide range of genres it drew on. The comical dimension made obvious reference to Senegalese popular theatre, and the textual elements drew on the Wolof tradition of praise-oratory. The aesthetic of Euro-American contemporary dance was mixed with moves from jazz dance, sabar, and Mandinka, as well as Sereer and Jola dances. The neo-traditional genre was used as raw material and subverted at the same time. Thus the strict gender differentiation that is characteristic of the genre was subverted when the male dancers shifted between movements that emphasised their masculinity and sequences in which it was consciously erased. In one scene, for example, Mané and Sy performed a parody of tango, dressed up in the women's clothes they had collected from the floor. Gomis played the same role as the male performers. Her clothes were as shabby as theirs and she wore no make up. Though she had her own style and experience as a dancer, she did not move in a particularly feminine way by local standards. When she stepped into high heels shoes, so did the three male dancers. When five of the six performers changed into several layers of rags towards the end of the piece, there was no difference between the clothes she and the men collected. The bottom of society is equally miserable to all, they seemed to say.

With the inclusion of second-hand clothes and other artefacts into the choreography, the stage design seemed to make reference to a widespread trend in West African visual arts in the 1980s and 1990s: the incorporation of used materials and things from everyday life into artworks. [7] Although this is not always a conscious association, ideas and styles circulate between artistic fields, and one of the features of contemporary choreography is indeed the breakdown of boundaries between art forms. The use of different surfaces is also a recurrent feature of contemporary choreography. In *Bujuman*, this was exploited in the use of clothes on the floor and an acrobatic sequence in the shopping trolley. The form, therefore, drew on a repertoire of local, regional and Euro-American genres. At the same time the piece worked well as a celebration of the diversity which characterized the performers: these were city dwellers with family connections across Senegal, Christians as well as Muslims.

In terms of the contents this was very much a local story, albeit one which resonated with the broader theme of social exclusion. The piece could be interpreted as a sideways critique of an urban society which spits out lives on the margins. There was nothing to distinguish the performers from ordinary citizens, and so *Bujuman* seemed to suggest that all were at risk of ending up at the bottom of society, where poverty and loneliness are the daily fare. The political dimension of the piece was more ambiguous, but it was present in the references to trade unionism, which has a long history of political involvement in Senegal. It was also evident in the references to a march towards the presidential palace and a mobilization meeting at the MCDS, a symbol of state-controlled culture. Yet the seriousness of these references was transformed by their insertion into the speech of géwël. Exposing the ills of society is part of what they do in real life, but this is done within a traditional genre that is malleable, open to multiple interpretations. One can never tell for sure whether the géwël speak for themselves or on behalf of others. Their speech style is metaphorical, at times coded, and therefore its appropriation in performance introduces a metaphorical dimension. The géwël are known to comment on social life, but what happens when performers who are not géwël in everyday life play their role in a show? What are they actually commenting on, and for whom? How seriously is the audience to take their plea to do something about exclusion? Can they be taken seriously when announcing, from the bottom of a rubbish dump, a name-giving ceremony at which food will be served in abundance?

At the same time it was no coincidence that the role was played by two musicians. The audiences did not know whether they were real géwël, but being drummers placed them within a similar social role, and framed their performance as potentially serious despite the derision. How seriously the message would be taken would depend on individual knowledge of the conventions of géwël speech, and on the context. Back stage, the making of pieces like *Bujuman* adds further complexity to their political significance. Just as the Jola troupes discussed in Chapter 5 included individuals who actively participated in the nation-building project while also pursuing regionalist agendas, so the multiple layering of roles in contemporary choreographic production renders a simple 'political resistance' analysis obsolete.

The social lives of performances

Since Appadurai's (1986) influential volume, the notion that the social significance of things changes over space and time has been applied to performance (cf. De Jong 1999), albeit not as widely as to material culture. This is perhaps because transformation over time is an inherent characteristic of performance. Whereas objects may travel through time and remain fairly stable in their materiality, dance, theatre and music change from one performance to the next, even with the same performers. Applying the same analytical approach to objects and performances is therefore problematic. Yet the diachronic perspective contained in the 'social life of things' may be fruitful. In the dance world, change comes not only from the fact that it is impossible for individuals to perform in exactly identical ways each time, but also from individual performers being replaced by new ones. This raises problems of continuity and transmission for dance troupes. In the worst cases, untimely departures may irremediably destroy a repertoire, or even a group.

With *Bujuman*, both factors account for the ways in which the piece changed over the course of just a few years. By the time it was performed during the Kaay Fecc festival in 2003, some elements had already changed in less than a year. The transformation was not only aesthetic, it also had to do with the experience of the dancers, and this in turn affected the texture of the performance. When I went to see the dancers rehearse in the weeks leading up to the show, they told me how they felt that the choreography had now made its way into their bodies. By contrast, at the premiere it had been 'outside', they confessed. This is part of the creative process in dance. Choreographic work is as much about individuals making movement their own through endless repetition, as it is about coming up with ideas and sequences. Making movement one's own translates into improved flow between sequences as the body takes action before one is fully aware of it. This in turn produces 'presence' on stage and a thrilling texture for spectators.

There were also aesthetic changes to the music and the décor. Schönberg had been replaced by avant-garde jazz music by Danish composer, Pierre Dørge, whom Tamba had met at an event abroad. He had liked the music, and also the idea of including a piece created by someone he had met. Also, the new soundtrack fitted more harmoniously with the choreography. For the stage design, the background wall had become filled with more waste and the objects hanging had been sourced in advance, rather than collected randomly on the day of the performance. A whole collection of second-hand shoes had been acquired and brought prominently to the front of the stage (Figure 7.3). Gomis had traded her black tights for yellow ones, which created an incongruous contrast with her dress, and reinforced the impression that her outfit had been put together haphazardly in a rubbish dump.

Aesthetic changes, in turn, affect the experience of the performers in various ways. The shoes on the floor, for example, now gave them a different experience to those sequences in which they wore shoes. They were acutely aware that the multiplication of shoes on stage would draw the spectators' attention to their own feet. This was visible in the increased clarity of the shoe-laden movements.

Other transformations in the texture of a piece are forced by the materiality of the space. There was an instance of this when the company presented *Eau b nite* in Lyon. This was a piece performed on a thick layer of sand, a conscious reference to the profound relationship between man and soil. It was also a reference to the dominance of sand in the Dakarois landscape. The piece began with the four dancers lying buried under small mounds of sand, only their heads emerging. Lying still as the music rose, they emerged one by one and began to move. The slow pace of the sequence meant that the dancers remained lying still in the sand for up to several minutes before moving. While pleasant in Dakar where the sand was warm, in Lyon in late September, this was a different experience altogether. The Biennale had sourced a couple of tons of sand locally, which was coarser, and much colder. By the time the dancers emerged from their mounds, they were so cold that they could hardly move. One of the press reviewers mistakenly interpreted this as the dancers being petrified by stage fright (Tran 2006). The next day they tried to compensate

Figure 7.3 Bujuman *performed at Kaay Fecc festival, Institut Français, Dakar, June 2003. Photograph by Marie-Laetitia Dumont.*

for this by warming up even more intensely, and the expectation of the cold sensation also helped. The materiality of the space affected the sensual experience of the dancers, and therefore also the quality of their movements.

Performances also change, of course, with the turnover of performers. Whereas the perfection of movement over time is experienced positively, this is often a serious problem dance groups must contend with. In contemporary choreography, the timing people may choose to leave is even more critical than in the neo-traditional genre due to the individualized nature of the choreography. A performer leaving during a tour abroad after months of work on a piece in which all individuals have contributed sequences can result in curtailing of the tour. For the remaining performers, this means losing out on both earnings and credibility for future engagements. This can also compromise their chances of getting visas, since many embassies have taken to 'blacklisting' troupes known as having a habit of 'losing' members abroad. When departure does not happen in the middle of engagements, however, choreographers are in a better position to include new performers into existing pieces. Those pieces are then transformed by the individual qualities the new performers bring with them. In fact, there is often an attempt to find similar 'body types' as replacement. With *Bujuman*, for example, when one of the performers left following his marriage to a visiting dance student, he was replaced with a young man from Papa Sy's junior Pastëf Company. He was chosen, in part, because his movement style and muscular body were the closest to the dancer who had left. An important distinction between contemporary choreography and neo-traditional performance is thus the value attached to the individual qualities of the creators of a piece.

Given the current search for mobility at all cost among many youths, however, trust has come to matter as much as creative and technical skills. Given the choice, dance people prefer to recruit among performers already known to them. These may be relatives or friends with little experience, and who will have to be trained by the group. In this sense, dance groups operate in similar ways to other forms of association in Senegal, from rotating credit associations and neighbourhood groups to youth clubs, hometown and religious associations.

Cross-cultural collaborations

Dance people from other parts of the world have become a central point of focus as a key to an increased engagement with transnational arts circuits. Dancer-choreographers from Europe, America, the Caribbean and, more recently, the Asia-Pacific region, for their part, have become increasingly keen on collaborative projects with African performers. Such collaborations are perceived as having the potential to rejuvenate choreographic scenes elsewhere. In Senegal, these projects have played an important role in the development of the contemporary genre through the exchange of ideas and choreographic practices. They have in fact become an essential part of what makes the contemporary genre attractive. This is because cross-cultural collaborations embody the widely shared aspiration, among contemporary African artists, to participate in global cultural production in partnership with peers from other parts of the world. In other words, cross-cultural choreographic collaborations are sought after for two main reasons: first, because they increase individual chances of mobility, and second, because they are regarded as having the potential to reverse the colonial world order.

In practice these projects set complex relationships in motion, and continue to affect the lives of those involved long after the completion of a piece. Differences in expectations may result in frustration on both sides. On the Senegalese side there is nearly always an expectation that joint work will eventually result in increased touring opportunities, choreographic residencies and workshops abroad. Disappointment can turn into bitterness when this fails to materialize, or when some individuals benefit while others in the same group are left behind. As I have alluded to in Chapter 5, the sense of being 'left behind' is prevalent in the local performing scene, particularly among men. Although this is not restricted to artistic circles, expectations of travel are very high there because mobility is a necessary part of a performer's life.

From isolated cases in the 1960s to 1980s, choreographic collaborations have gained momentum since the early 1990s. I already mentioned the *Coq est mort* project with Suzanne Linke in 1999–2001, while French choreographer, Bernardo Montet, created parts of *O More* in Tubaab Jallaw in 2001–02, before embarking on an international tour. But the turning point came a decade earlier, when the small elite of dancers already established in Europe became influential enough to facilitate contacts.[8] In 1993, French choreographer, Mathilde Monnier, went to Burkina Faso to create a new piece loosely based on Sophocles' classic *Antigone*. Monnier's *Pour Antigone* included a mix of dancers from her own company in Montpellier and dancers from neo-traditional troupes in Burkina Faso. What distinguished this production from previous experiences in West Africa was its scale. As the director of a National Choreographic Centre (CCN) in France, Monnier was a well-established choreographer with access to significant resources. The piece was billed over several years at prestigious theatres and festival around the world, including the Lincoln Center Festival in New York in 2000.

In Ouagadougou, Mathilde Monnier recruited two gifted dancers into her company: Seydou Boro and Salia Sanou. Both were trained in the neo-traditional genre (Sanou and Tempé 2008). As we have seen briefly, they went on to set up their own choreographic centre and dance festival in Ouagadougou, Dialogues de Corps, with substantial funding from the French Institute. Since *Pour Antigone* many European, American and even Japanese performing artists have travelled to Senegal, Mali and Burkina Faso, in particular, to work with dancer-choreographers and musicians.

I came across eight collaborative choreographic pieces in 2002–03 alone, ranging from creations of a few minutes to full-evening performances. In a couple of cases I was able to record rehearsals and final performances, at the request of the participants. Among others, Djibril Diallo and American dancer-choreographer and scholar Esther Baker jointly created *Bul Faalé*, a full-evening piece which was shown at the CCBS and at the French Institute. US-based choreographer, Onyekwere Ozuzu, created *Lu tax/Why?* with Mamadou Diagne. Austrian, Editta Braun's *Manifest* featured Ibrahima Sène, a Senegalese martial arts expert. *Stück* was a contemporary duet choreographed by Togolese, Pierre Sanouvi, and German, Annette Vogel, and *Fagaala* was created jointly by Mrs Acogny's Jant-bi Company and Japanese choreographer, Kota Yamazaki. This full-evening performance for seven male dancers was inspired by Boubacar Boris Diop's (2000) novel on the Rwandan genocide, *Murambi, Le Livre des Ossements*. Following a premiere in Tubaab Jallaw in January 2004, *Fagaala* was performed at several prestigious venues in the US, and shots from the piece featured in the film on contemporary African dance, *Movement (R)evolution Africa*.[9]

Choreographic artists in Senegal discuss these collaborations in two different ways. In the first perspective, collaborative work with Europeans and others is viewed as a form of artistic exploitation, a process through which those with the resources to travel come to look for inspiration and work with movement styles unfamiliar to them. The second perspective is much more optimistic, and views collaborations as an exchange in which all parties find inspiration, develop new skills, promote their individual careers and affirm their membership in transnational communities of artists. In this view, the face-to-face interaction over prolonged periods of time allows people to try out new ideas, learn new techniques and use the partner's eyes as a mirror of their own work. A particular instance of a collaborative project will illustrate both perspectives.

A neo-traditional dancer I knew in Dakar had come to the contemporary genre through the Kaay Fecc workshops. The prospect of working on collaborative projects with foreign choreographers had been an important part of his motivation, and less than two years after his first workshop, he felt ready. While still working as a dancer in a neo-traditional troupe, he asked a visiting American choreographer to do a joint piece with him for the upcoming Kaay Fecc festival. They recruited another American dancer who had travelled with her, two Senegalese dancers and two drummers he knew, and set to work. The two choreographers had different perspectives on virtually every aspect, from the speed of the movements to the appropriateness of having a long sung sequence in English, or the costume design. The two Americans spoke English to each other, and the Senegalese choreographer did his best to retain authority over the Senegalese performers by giving them instructions in Wolof. Tensions over creative authority grew over the two months of genesis, and by the time the performers were getting dressed for the final show, the choreographers barely spoke to each other. Despite the tensions, the Dakarois choreographer expected to be offered opportunities by some of the dance people who had travelled from abroad to attend the festival. He had also performed a few days earlier with his neo-traditional troupe, but had higher expectations to be singled out in the contemporary piece due to the more individualized nature of the choreography. When contacts failed to materialize, he was bitterly disappointed. He also resented the fact that the American choreographer had chosen to take one of the drummers back home with her. He felt unfairly 'left behind' at the end of a project which he felt had come about at his initiative in the first place. Yet the American choreographer had promised nothing beyond the completion of the show. From her point of view, she had respected her engagement. But the Senegalese dancer's disappointment was compounded by his perception of having been 'exploited' in the past, both by foreign dance students and by his own troupe leaders.

The performers he had recruited, however, had a different take on the situation. Their ambitions had not yet matched his own, and for them, this was a welcome opportunity to present small-scale contemporary work to which they had contributed, in a prestigious venue. One of them, a young woman, was recruited to take part in one of Heddy Maalem's transnational productions not long after, and the collaborative experience had undoubtedly given her confidence in her capacity to perform 'contemporary' work. The project had also enabled her to try her hand at the sort of intimate, body-to-body work which Maalem required of his dancers.

The first perspective should thus be understood in relation to local as well as global hierarchies. The issue of exploitation arises from very real inequalities in global artistic circuits; as we have seen, funding mainly comes from Europe and North America, and this is compounded by the difficulty for African artists to get visas to present their work abroad. The way in which people experience transnational collaborative work, however, is heavily shaped by their own experience in the local dance world. Those who have accumulated a sense of being 'left behind' in spite of hard work, and who fear the decrease of opportunities with ageing, may thus be more resentful in the face of the inevitable tensions that come with collaborative work.

In the best cases, by contrast, collaborative projects make the desired engagement with global circuits tangible, and enables people to work actively to fulfil their aspirations without being burdened by the abstraction of the 'global'. This form of intimacy with the 'remote' is so attractive that some dancers move into choreography in order to have access to collaborative opportunities. Indeed a wider repertoire of skills makes one more attractive as a choreographic partner. In short, collaborations embody aspirations by young Africans to act upon the world with the resources that they have.

Conclusion

As I suggested in the previous chapter, the individualized nature of the creative process has played an essential role in fostering interest in contemporary choreography throughout Africa. In Senegal, experimenting with new bodily techniques to explore the self, the thrill of novelty and the perspective of by-passing the hierarchies of age and gender prominent in the neo-traditional genre have attracted young performers to this creative *bricolage* of movement styles and working methods. This could be described as the inward-looking dimension of contemporary performance. But an equally important dimension has been the aspiration to engage with global artistic circuits on equal terms with artists from other parts of the world. As we have seen, this has been manifest in the value placed on cross-cultural collaborations, but also on performing in prestigious venues rather than being confined to 'African' or 'folklore' festivals.

In addition, economic considerations have played an important role in attracting artists to the genre. Although the privilege of a few, being successful with contemporary choreography generates opportunities to earn more from international touring than is usually the case with the neo-traditional genre. This is partly because the venues and funding sources are different, and partly because the fees are distributed among fewer performers, often three to seven as opposed to the fifteen or more in neo-traditional troupes. Moreover smaller groups tend to have fewer 'apprentices' waiting for their turn to go on tour, and to whom a small fee must be redistributed. Crucially, getting visas to travel abroad is easier for smaller groups since embassies are less suspicious that they may serve as a cover for 'migration candidates'.[10]

The diversification of choreographic practices has important consequences for the status of performers in Senegal. Whereas mbalax or sabar performed in music videos remain associated with ñeeño status and compromised morality, 'contemporary' choreography is regarded as closer to theatre, and therefore further removed from ñeeño status, as well as less compromised on moral grounds. This is therefore a more acceptable practice in the eyes of many géér families. The neo-traditional genre is perceived as somewhere in-between, and status there is shaped by people's earnings and travel opportunities. As a result, the status and moral standing of performers may be even more contextual than in the past, shifting as it does depending on genres, destinations, venues and types of audiences. Within both neo-traditional and contemporary performance, invoking the mastery of 'tradition' helps to distinguish oneself from the domain of popular dances, even though these dances often form part of people's trajectories.

Paradoxically, an important concern to dance people in Senegal and elsewhere in Africa is also whether the current interest in choreographic production on the continent may be compromising the future. Dance people worry that this may be a momentary fashion from a 'market' in search of novelty, and that it may be over before African artists have been able to gain more control over the circulation of their work. The multiplication of locally organized dance and music festivals across Africa suggests that this cannot be reduced to an economic issue; there is also a genuine urge to break away from the control that comes when organizational power is located elsewhere. But artists do not aspire to isolation, either, and there is growing confidence that they have the skills to make important contributions to world culture.

Yet making it into the world through choreographic work is a double-edged sword. Accusations of pandering to the desires of Europeans are common expressions of resentment aimed at those whose international careers are picking up. This is in continuity with the ambiguous position of migrants in Senegalese society: whilst young men (and increasingly, young women) are expected to spend time abroad as a step toward social adulthood as well as to send back remittances, resentment quickly follows if they are too successful too quickly. The status of performers may be rising with the transformation of the profession, but 'contemporary' performers are more exposed to criticism than others because what they do is regarded as 'tainted' by European control. Their morality is compromised as well, but in different ways than when they practise other genres. In this context, artists often seek redemption by infusing the content of their work with postcolonial critique.

Notes

1. *Danse l'Afrique Danse* – 9th edition programme. Paris: Institut Français.
2. Dance Umbrella 2009 'A brief encounter with . . . Kaolack (Senegal) – *J'Accuse*'. Retrieved from www.danceumbrella.co.uk/page/3113/JACCUSE/110 on 01.05.2012.

3. 'Pour ce qui est de vivre, je ne me suis pas gêné, moi. D'ailleurs, au moment où je t'écris ces lignes, un air de musique très populaire il y a une soixantaine d'années me remonte à la mémoire. [. . .] C'était quelque chose à propos du temps que l'on passe sur cette terre, des journées et des nuits si vides et incertaines qu'il faut vraiment être con pour accepter, en plus, de mourir sans même avoir été heureux! Nous aimions cet air-là. Ça, et aussi les pachangas . . . Nous mettions beaucoup de musique cubaine lors de nos soirées du Plateau, chaudes et plutôt bien arrosées. Je nous revois en train de nous trémousser dans le plus grand désordre sous un hangar surchauffé et poussiéreux. Imagine des dizaines de filles et de garçons faisant trembler leurs corps comme des fous furieux et criant encore plus fort que les tumbas et les maracas!' (Diop 2009: 14).

4. 5ᵉ Dimension dancer, Dakar, October 2002.

5. This is a wordplay in French, the word 'au-delà' (beyond) sounding exactly the same as 'eau de là' (water from there).

6. This is a term borrowed from classical ballet vocabulary, but which is used in other dance forms as well. A *chassé* is a shuffling step, usually performed sideways, in which the leg that moves second 'chases' the other.

7. See for example Elizabeth Harney's (2004) monograph on contemporary Senegalese artists.

8. There were, for example, Germaine Acogny; former Mudra Afrique student, Irène Tassembedo, from Burkina Faso; Ivorian, George Momboye, in France; or Nigerian, Peter Badejo, in the UK.

9. *Movement (R)evolution Africa,* by Joan Frosch and Alla Kovgan, USA, 2007, 65 minutes.

10. In several cases I encountered, visa applications for a big group were returned to the organizer with the specific request to send them back for a second round when all 'migration candidates' had been removed from the list.

Chapter 8

Movement, Imagination and Self-Fashioning

This book is an ethnographic attempt to demonstrate that performance, as dance, music and drama performed together in integrated ways, is the stuff of which social life in urban Senegal is made. For the participants at the centre of this study, moving through life, from one status to the next or from one field of practice to the next, means acquiring new skills: new ways of being attentive to the world, of dancing, of imagining movement, of speaking about dance, and new ways of 'making work'. This is why several genres are included in this study, and it is often the same people who engage in sabar, mbalax, neo-traditional performance and contemporary choreography. They may do this simultaneously, or at different life stages. But performance also 'makes' social life by creating a space in which sociality is experienced anew every time. It is a space in which people enjoy the pleasure of being together while also competing, and excluding others. It is in dance events that social hierarchies are made visible, defended and contested. In its diverse forms, performance constantly displays the tension between the individual and the collective, while enabling performers to navigate this tension without being explicit about it. It is also through performance that the past is imagined and brought to bear on the present.

In this study, I have attempted to move away from stereotypical perceptions of dance in Africa as pertaining to either ritual or spontaneous expressions of joy. Though there is often a ritualistic dimension to the genres discussed here, I want to suggest that the social significance of dance and music in urban Senegal go beyond ritual or fun. They also play a central role in the making of urban personhood, which involves different ways of moving depending on gender, 'caste', class, age and marital status. In practice there is a great deal of fluidity, of course, nevertheless there are ideal categories according to which people judge the quality and appropriateness of individual performances, particularly in the sabar genre. Performance is also central in the fashioning of urban youth identities, often centred on the neighbourhood, but also with an eye to rural localities elsewhere in the region. Neighbourhood identities are constructed around school, which may be replacing the old age-set categories; youth clubs, which often combine competitive sports practice with competitive dancing; neighbourhood women's gatherings; and local religious associations. Dance is present in one form or another in all these social spaces, with the exception of the Muslim associations (though in some cases, dance is involved there as well). It is in this sense that urban dances constitute a form of popular culture which calls new identities into being (Barber 1997).

Dance, music and drama have also fostered the imagination of regional identities in a migration context. Hometown associations from the Casamance and the Siin and Saalum, in particular, have played a crucial role in the development of the neo-traditional performing scene in Senegal. This is because with mass migration to Dakar since the 1950s has come the urge to preserve a sense of belonging to the Casamance, and the need to ensure younger generations would remain emotionally attached to the region. Given the promotion of musical theatre in colonial and postcolonial Senegal, this was the form of expression many migrant associations turned to. The result was not only a lively theatrical scene with strong networks between Dakar and those parts of Senegal from where many migrants came, but also a toolkit with which to articulate regional and local identities. In the case of the Lower Casamance, one may even speak of dance and theatre as being put to use in the fashioning of 'Jola bodies' away from the region.

The tension between individuality and the collective in urban Senegal is magnified in the dual structure of the professional dance scene, which consists mainly of two overlapping fields of practice: a neo-traditional genre which emphasizes collective identities, and a contemporary choreographic genre in which individual creativity is valued above all else. Looking at both fields simultaneously sheds light on how young Dakarois men and women, in particular, put their bodily skills to use in different ways according to the social world they wish to engage with. These social worlds have a global reach, and this is what makes the professional performing scene particularly attractive. Acquiring a wide repertoire of performing skills, therefore, may offer opportunities to increase one's status locally while simultaneously carving out a space for oneself in transnational artistic circuits. But this also leads to unfulfilled dreams of mobility, since only a small minority of performers achieve successful careers both at home and abroad. Aspirations often end up in what is experienced as forced immobility (cf. Carling 2002), with people 'left behind' imagining what might have been. Watching one's younger peers 'make it' abroad while one is ageing, then, is a source of immense resentment. In this sense, the same vivid imagination that stimulates creativity also contains the seed of its own destruction.

One of the main points in this book, therefore, is that performance is flexible enough to help people to pursue individual and collective agendas simultaneously, without having to compromise on either. A dance troupe may thus serve as a surrogate family or as the embodiment of local, ethnic or national identities, while also helping individuals to achieve social and spatial mobility. Individual ambitions are by no means a new phenomenon, and the importance of the individual in African societies may have been underestimated in anthropology. But from the local point of view, individualism has become more problematic with people's increasing mobility because mobility renders control of the moral community more difficult. Performers who achieve international careers but who see their moral standing compromised in their Dakarois circles often feel that they have lost what they were searching in the first place. I now turn in more detail to some of the additional themes this study addresses.

Dance and imagination

Embodied practices such as dance are not often thought of as involving imagination. Yet in their review article on 'culture-as-performance', Palmer and Jankowiak (1996) argue for the central role of imagination in performance more generally. They suggest that 'performers project and register images and interpretations of themselves, of others, and of the life of the community itself' (Palmer and Jankowiak 1996: 240). Though it is not possible to know with certainty what people have in mind while dancing or watching a performance, years of experience with dancers, as a participant and as a spectator, have convinced me that imagination is at the heart of choreography. Imagination, here, is both a cognitive process and a socially determined phenomenon.

It is in contemporary choreography that the role of imagination in motivating movement is most evident because this is articulated verbally in the choreographic process: dancers are often asked by choreographers to work with images in mind, to imagine situations and feelings that will make their way into the body. Contemporary choreography, like drama, draws on the 'raw material' that is individual performer's imagining of the lives of others. This was the case, for example, when La 5ᵉ Dimension performers attempted to imagine what it might feel like to live off scraps and urban waste. It also draws on the performers' own memories, whether invoked spontaneously or prompted by verbal guidance. When working on *Eau b nite,* Jean Tamba thus asked his dancers to remember what it had felt like, as children, to drench themselves in the first showers of the rainy season. The movements they initiated were then used in a scene of 'purification' in which the dancers washed off the sand from their bodies through a curtain of water released from the top of the stage. Memory is also mobilized when performers draw inspiration from other choreographic works witnessed in the past. Memories find their way into movement in unexpected, not always conscious ways. Thus when I remarked to Jean Tamba that I found similarities between his 1995 piece *Qui suis-je?* and some parts of Alvin Ailey's now classic, *Revelations,* created in New York in 1960, he simply replied that though this had not been conscious, it might well be the case since he had watched a recording of Alvin Ailey's piece in the 1980s, and performed parts of it. Ousmane Noël Cissé, one of Tamba's mentors at the time, also acknowledged his debt to *Revelations.* This fits well with Palmer and Jankowiak's (1996: 241) notion of creativity in performance: drawing on Bruner's (1986) work, they characterize creativity as referring to 'enactments of new scripts and novel combinations', and suggest that 'the recombination of schemas is a function of imagery'.

Imagination also comes into play in the neo-traditional genre, in sabar and in the popular dances. In all these forms, dancers acknowledge that they perform with ideal images of movement, life situations, videos or memories of previous performances in mind. The old cliché that dance in Africa is the movement of bodies responding to rhythm is therefore terribly inaccurate. The minds of individual performers are always charged with memories and images of movement. When encouraged to reflect on this, for example during the contemporary choreographic process, dancers acknowledge that the nature of the images they invoke affects the texture of their movement. Mastering a choreographic sequence often involves learning to mobilize those images that will inspire the best quality of movement. This is true of set choreographies as well as of the more improvised sabar sequences.

Dance is almost always performed for someone, and imagination is also central to the experience of spectators and participants.[1] Spectators experience performance differently depending on their knowledge of the genre, and their imagination of what 'good performance' is. But there is an even more important way in which imagination is invoked: it is that to which the performance refers. I find it useful here to draw on the sophisticated body of literature which has emerged in the past two decades on the power of that which is hidden. This is particularly developed in studies set in West and Central Africa. In an illuminating paper on political cartoons in Cameroon, Mbembe (1996) thus suggested that in the societies of southern Cameroon which he was familiar with, the most significant epistemological rupture was not between that which was seen and that which was read, but between the world of the visible and that of the invisible. Images, Mbembe (1996) argued, drew their power from their capacity to suggest the reality they were a metaphor of. But this happened in oblique ways, so that one was always reminded of the multifaceted, elusive and therefore powerful nature of the reality images alluded to. Ferme (2001) makes similar points in her dense study of sources of power among the Mende of Sierra Leone. Drawing on Simmel (1950 [1908]), she argues that secrecy and power share the same dynamic in that 'they are both predicated on the relationship between the subject's concealed aims and their visible manifestations in the external world', and that 'they are both strategies for magnifying reality through the aesthetic display of the body and through the expansion of its boundaries' (Ferme 2001: 161). I want to suggest that spectators' and participants' assessment of performance in Dakar also hinge on the capacity to suggest things concealed in everyday life in aesthetically pleasing ways. This 'capacity to suggest' puts the imagination to work in thrilling ways, and it is in this sense that imagination is also social, and not simply individual.

The sabar genre is exemplary in this respect. As described in Chapter 3, its attractiveness relies heavily on the performers' and participants' skilful suggestion of vitality, powerful sexuality, social standing and economic resources. The qualities of performance are perceived differently by different people, of course, but there is a shared emphasis on suggestion rather than outright display. This is why a woman who gradually reveals the inner layers of her outfit in a dance without ever showing the full extent of her anatomy, and whose waist beads are heard or glimpsed through the fabric is usually considered a better dancer than a young girl who displays everything at once. Women who remain seated, motionless, are also part of the performance in that the juxtaposition of their stillness with the exuberant dancing of others intensifies the status of the still participants by hinting at the social position that makes it inappropriate for them to dance.

The suggestion of things hidden is also important in the neo-traditional genre, where regional stereotypes are played out. When Jola troupes in Dakar perform staged versions of rituals, it is not only because of the skilful dancing that Dakarois audiences are thrilled; it is also because this type of performance alludes to what city dwellers imagine to be metaphors of powerful practices, inaccessible to most of them. Were there not a pre-existing fascination with the power of fertility, initiation and healing from the Casamance, the performance of troupes like Bakalama would be experienced in more detached ways. Conversely, Casamançais theatrical performance is the main vehicle through which images of the region as a bastion of powerful occult practices are disseminated at a national level. In all these genres, it is the participants' imagination of what lies 'behind' which determines the texture and success of every performance.

Professional performance and 'caste'

As I have discussed early on in the book, being a professional dancer or musician in Senegambia has long been strongly associated with Griot (géwël), or at least ñeeño status. Since the late 1980s, however, the performing profession has grown increasingly attractive to several generations of urban youth. This was in continuity with the development of school theatre in the colonial period, and with President Senghor's generous patronage of the arts in the 1960s and 1970s. But the phenomenon has been accelerated by the global success of African music and dance on the one hand, and by the lack of alternatives in formal employment on the other. Becoming a performer, at least for a few years in the late teens and early twenties, has therefore become a valued option for many youths who do not do belong to ñeeño families, but who discovered the pleasure of dancing (and in some cases drumming, too) through neighbourhood dance events or youth clubs. High-status families often resist the choice of what is regarded as a tainted profession. Many performers, therefore, find themselves caught up in dilemmas that continue to shape the rest of their lives, between the importance of maintaining social respectability and good relationships with relatives on the one hand, and the desire to pursue an attractive, transnational career on the other hand. In some cases the tension gets resolved over time as performers begin to earn a decent living, build up good reputations and tour abroad. But many family conflicts never get resolved, and dancers often feel that they must constantly compensate for their choice. There is a multitude of strategies to achieve this, from claiming the moral high ground through assiduous religious practice to maintaining other jobs and showing generosity to needy relatives and friends.

Some ways of dealing with the moral risks involved in public performance find a resolution within the practice itself: by performing different genres in different contexts, or by cultivating the identity of a choreographer rather than a dancer, in other words making others dance. Contemporary choreography, in particular, has enabled some dancers to distance themselves from Griot skills, and to present themselves as entrepreneurs engaged in a globalized practice. The fact that they may continue to practice the neo-traditional genre and to have fun with popular dances does not affect their main identity as contemporary artists/cultural entrepreneurs. Creative autonomy, higher average earnings than with the neo-traditional genre, the possibility to do collaborative work with foreign artists and opportunities to perform in prestigious venues abroad all contribute to this refashioning of the image of the artist. There are obvious continuities in the ways in which contemporary dancers appropriate the role of the Griot as a commentator of social ills. An important difference, however, is that dancers do not regard their trade as involving the praise of patrons. On the contrary, they make much out of their autonomy, and try to avoid or hide their involvement in patron-client relationships altogether.

An important question that follows is whether these transformations may indicate a broader challenge of the traditional status hierarchies. In the 1960s, scholars were divided about the future of 'caste' amidst the egalitarian discourse that followed Independence. In his classic text on Haalpulaar society, Wane (1969) argued that the compromises people made in practice did not affect the ideology of the 'caste' hierarchy since this ideology remained prevalent in such important matters as marriage and political office. By contrast, Silla (1966), closer to Senghorian ideals, predicted that the 'caste regime' would soon become obsolete. The picture that emerges from looking at musical and choreographic performance is neither one of radical change, nor a static one. The history of West African 'castes' is one of constant transformation and this is no exception, albeit at a faster pace than in the past. I suggest that what is happening in urban Senegal is that the skills traditionally associated with men-of-skill categories, all transformative skills of some sort, are becoming increasingly detached from the specific power they used to release. Rather than sources of ambiguous – and dangerous – forms of power (cf. McNaughton 1988), they have become the raw material from which different occupations can be fashioned. The status of those who transform this raw material into something lucrative depends on the social contexts they become part of. The social status of a musician trained in sabar drumming, for example, will not only depend on his genealogy, his age, marital status and financial autonomy, but also on the contexts in which these skills are deployed: sabar events, pop music bands, concerts and teaching abroad. For many, the best strategy is to treat these contexts as a repertoire of potentialities. A successful artist is someone whose repertoire spans the widest range along a continuum of practices that begins with traditional performing skills. Skills acquired through lengthy training, upon which one builds different kinds of innovations in different contexts, are a sign of complete mastery.

At a more prosaic level, ideas of 'pollution' relating to the bodies of ñeeño have become largely irrelevant in the performing scene as people inevitably come into close physical contact with each other, particularly in contemporary choreography. In this context, the géér-ñeeño dichotomy is not only irrelevant; it is counter-productive. Social change, however, is neither a linear process nor a phenomenon that affects all individuals and contexts equally. It is also fraught with competition; in this case, performers from ñeeño families often claim superior expertise by virtue of their genealogy and upbringing. This creates tensions with other artists, but it is often left unspoken, and such tensions only come to the surface in moments of crisis.

Moralities across gender and generation

Issues of gender and generation are essential dimensions in the transformation of social relations. I want to suggest that these are renegotiated in different ways through the different dance forms: whereas sabar events have become dominated by women, and more recently young men, the professional world tends to be dominated by more experienced men. At the same time, younger men and women have an advantage over their senior peers by virtue of their energy, virtuosity and appeal to foreign choreographers. Those who do not yet have their own households may also be perceived as more available to travel for longer periods of time. The world of popular dances performed in youth clubs, music videos and TV competitions lies somewhere in-between, mainly dominated by younger men but with powerful female figures in successful girl groups. In all these genres, however, it may be more useful to speak of a dynamic of inclusiveness and exclusiveness that is contextual, rather than of a simple notion of dominance.

In the sabar genre, for example, the circle structure allows for inclusion on the organizers' terms, whether these are women of various age groups, or increasingly, young male dancers with their own male 'fans'. This was the case of Pape Ndiaye in the first half of the 2000s, whose popularity was eclipsed more recently by Bouly Sonko's son, Pape Moussa Sonko. While these events are a celebration of sociality among women friends or youths in a particular neighbourhood, they also serve as moments of intense competition over popularity and sexual desirability. In other words, sabar events may be controlled by women while being about men, and vice-versa. Men who do not take part in sabar events also compete indirectly through their wives, even though they are not keen to admit that they know what goes on in their absence. The dance is not a by-product of competition: it is social competition, and agency in the dance circle participates in the construction of power in various forms.

Meanwhile, women often maintain a façade of compliance to the discourse which places married men as the moral authorities of households. This outward compliance does not mean that gender relations remain unchanged, rather that they do not change through open confrontation. Many men find it increasingly difficult to provide for their families on a regular basis, and resent women's newly gained economic power as well as their control over ceremonial life. Women always kept their own income for ceremonial purposes in the past, but the drying up of the waged sector in the 1980s has given their share a new weight. This, in turn, increases their moral authority. Such gendered tensions are not often made explicit, but they are visible in the social organization of dance events. This is different in the professional world, where women dancers have no means of excluding men. There, women may become excluded or exclude themselves upon marriage, and their dancing careers are often shorter than men's. However, marriage may also become enabling: a woman performer whose spouse is also in the performing world is more likely to continue performing after marriage, and the position of her husband in the dance world may even boost her career. Women's position differs across genres: in contemporary choreography, for example, the importance of articulating artistic work both verbally and in writing means that women with at least secondary education are the most likely to be successful. Diane Barthel (1975) showed long ago that the post-independence female elite were often the daughters of men who were already educated and held posts in the colonial administration. The contemporary arts scene seems to reproduce similar features.

The flip side of social change is continuity, however, and dance practices also contain enduring aspects of social life. Because the materiality of life in African cities has changed in profound ways since 1945, urban studies are always at risk of overemphasizing change at the expense of continuity. Yet understanding continuities helps to understand what is meaningful in a given social context. An enduring aspect of life in urban Senegal is the construction of gendered selves as a process involving elements of both sexes. This is why dance events like the sabar play such an important role in the process: they provide a space in which girls can act out male attitudes, and boys may perform parodies of the female without further consequences. Performance, here, participates in the gendering of selves, not only through differentiation but also through experimenting with the possibilities of the other sex.

One is also reminded of spirit possession in what goes on in the sabar circle. The transgression of everyday boundaries, for example in the form of 'inappropriate', highly sexualized dancing, is rendered acceptable by the invocation of forces outside individual control. This makes space for fun, for imagining alternative life scenarios without comprising one's moral standing. Sometimes however, moral standing does become compromised, particularly when this takes place in a public space such as TV or the internet.

An enduring aspect of humanity anywhere is that each generation tries to challenge the previous one. In the Dakarois dance world in the 1990s and early 2000s, contemporary choreography enabled young performing artists to develop new 'techniques of the body' and to engage with global circuits without having to undergo the lengthy apprenticeship that was still the norm within the neo-traditional genre. Some of these youths came from sports or the theatre world, and were keen to achieve individual success quickly. The new choreographic practices represented a possible avenue to by-pass previous ways of acquiring moral authority, which had to do with maturity as well as knowledge, experience, and the capacity to maintain large numbers of dependents. By the early 2010s, a new generation of youths is taking on the choreographic scene. There is a similar concern with achieving success faster than ever before, but rather than new bodily skills, it is the skilful use of visual media and digital technologies that is seen as the way forward: a successful dancer is not just someone with a wide repertoire of bodily techniques and skills, but also someone whose image circulates widely through TV, music videos and on the internet, reaching beyond the national boundaries and into the expanding diaspora.

Through the lens of dance in Senegal, this book is a case study of how young urban citizens in Africa use their bodies to construct livelihoods, combining income with enjoyment, and local status with engagement with the wider world. Though this may not always be planned from the start, once young people have trained their bodies and worked hard to develop their performing skills, they are likely to put them to use in different contexts. Similar strategies are deployed in the sports world, and it is no coincidence that there is a great deal of overlap between the performing scenes and sports across Africa. Indeed for many urban youths, the body is a precious resource with a wide range of potentialities.

These potentialities have the capacity to transform the self. According to Jackson (1989: 42), 'pathways' exist 'within the human body as well as between self and society and between society and the wilderness' and the 'key to well-being lies in a person's ability to control traffic along these pathways'. I would like to suggest that the participation of dancers in global artistic circuits, while also continuing to engage with performance locally, is indicative of an ambivalent relationship between individual autonomy and the desire to be recognized as a fully socialized person.

Choreographic artists and the global order

This book thus highlights the complexities of cultural 'globalization' processes. Though many studies of globalization since the 1980s have focused on the circulation of objects, capital or the consumption of goods and cultural products, the globalization of creative practices affects social life in different ways. This is not a new phenomenon in the region: as we have seen, the Senegalese choreographic world has a cosmopolitan history. How, then, is the recent engagement with global circuits different from before? What is different, I suggest, is that through the contemporary genre, young performers claim the right to contribute to world artistic production on an equal footing with peers elsewhere. They resent having to label what they do in terms of identity when this is not expected of their European or American counterparts. Like many of the young generations of writers and visual artists across Africa, they increasingly see themselves as artists who happen to be African rather than 'African artists'. Yet they are also concerned with the images of Africa their work projects onto world stages.

This is why there is unease about the way in which contemporary choreographic work across the continent is crystallizing into a genre with European, and particularly French, patronage. But alternatives are few since most African states are reluctant to invest precious resources in supporting the arts, and paying audiences are too small. There is recognition that funding, whether it is from the local government or from international sources, comes with an agenda. There is also concern that the current interest in 'contemporary African arts' may be a momentary fashion. Global arts markets, performers know, can be elusive. Will this enthusiasm turn out to be a new ghetto for African performance, or is this a genuine opportunity for Africa's talents to make their voices heard louder than ever before?

Note

1. In the case of dances taking place at the centre of a dance circle, a guéew, the term 'participant' is more fitting since every person present is potentially a performer at some point in the event.

Bibliography

Acogny, G. 1994 [1980]. *Danse Africaine*. 4th edition. Frankfurt: Weingarten.

Adjamagbo, A., P. Antoine, and F.B. Dial. 2004. 'Le dilemme des dakaroises: entre travailler et "bien travailler"', in Momar-Coumba Diop (ed), *Gouverner le Sénégal – Entre Ajustement Structurel et Développement Durable*, Paris: Karthala, pp. 248–272.

Africalia. 2003. Africalia programme. Brussels.

Alexander, C. 1996. *The Art of Being Black: The Creation of Black British Youth Identities*. Oxford: Oxford University Press.

Anderson, B. 1983. *Imagined Communities. Reflections on the Origin and Spread of Nationalism*. London & New York: Verso.

ANSD. 2006. *Résultats Définitifs du Troisième Recensement Général de la Population et de l'Habitat – 2002*. Dakar: Ministère de l'Economie et des Finances.

———. 2008. *Situation Economique et Sociale de la Région de Dakar de l'Année 2007*. Dakar: Ministère de l'Economie et des Finances.

———. 2011. *Situation Économique et Sociale du Sénégal en 2010*. Dakar: Agence Nationale de la Démographie et de la Statistique.

Appadurai, A. 1986. *The Social Life of Things: Commodities in Cultural Perspective*. Cambridge: Cambridge University Press.

Appiah, K.A. 1992. *In My Father's House: Africa in the Philosophy of Culture*. London: Methuen.

Apter, A. 2005. *The Pan-African Nation: Oil and the Spectacle of Culture in Nigeria*. Chicago: University of Chicago Press.

Archetti, E. 1997. 'The moralities of Argentinian football', in Signe Howell (ed), *The Ethnography of Moralities*, London and New York: Routledge, pp. 98–123.

Argenti, N. 2006. 'Remembering the future: slavery, youth and masking in the Cameroon Grassfields'. *Social Anthropology* no. 14 (1): 49–70.

———. 2007. *The Intestines of the State: Youth, Violence, and Belated Histories in the Cameroon Grassfields*. Chicago: University of Chicago Press.

Askew, K. 2002. *Performing the Nation: Swahili Music and Cultural Politics in Tanzania*. Chicago: University of Chicago Press.

Aubin, H. 1951. 'Réflexions psychologiques'. *Tropiques* no. 337: 38–46.

Augis, E.J. 2002. *Dakar's Sunnite Women: The Politics of Person (Senegal)*, Chicago: University of Chicago.

Bakalama. 2007. Interview with Bakalama performers, Dakar, June.

Baller, S. 2007. 'Etre jeune, masculin et sportif. Représentations urbaines de la masculinité au Sénégal', in Odile Goerg (ed), *Perspectives Historiques sur le Genre en Afrique. Cahiers Afrique no.23*, Paris: L'Harmattan, pp. 165–190.

Bancel, N., P. Blanchard, G. Boëtsch, and E. Deroo (eds) . 2004. *Zoos Humains: Au Temps des Exhibitions Humaines.* Paris: La Découverte.

Barber, K. 1987. "Popular arts in Africa." *African Studies Review* no. 30 (3):1–78.

———. 1991. *I Could Speak Until Tomorrow: Oriki, Women and the Past in a Yoruba Town.* Edinburgh: Edinburgh University Press.

———. 1997. "Introduction", in Karin Barber (ed), *Readings in African Popular Culture,* London & Oxford: The International African Institute & James Currey, pp. 1–12.

———. 2000. *The Generation of Plays: Yoruba Popular Life in Theater.* Bloomington: Indiana University Press.

———. 2007. *The Anthropology of Texts, Persons and Publics.* Cambridge: Cambridge University Press.

Barry, A. 1987. "Fanghoumé, Village-Ecole", *Le Soleil,* 23 January, p. 11.

Barry, B. 1988. *La Sénégambie du XVe au XIXe Siècle.* Paris: L'Harmattan.

Barth, F. 1969. *Ethnic Groups and Boundaries. The Social Organization of Culture Difference.* Bergen: Universitetsforlaget, London: Allen & Unwin.

Barthel, D. 1975. "The rise of a female professional elite: the case of Senegal." *African Studies Review* no. 18 (3):1–17.

Battaglia, D. (ed) 1995. *Rhetorics of Self-Making.* Berkeley and Los Angeles: University of California Press.

Bayart, J.-F. 1999. "L'Afrique dans le monde: une histoire d'extraversion." *Critique Internationale* no. 5:97–120.

Béart, C. 1937. "Le théâtre indigène et la culture franco-africaine." *L'Education Africaine, numéro spécial*:3–14.

Behrman, L. 1970. *Muslim Brotherhoods and Politics in Senegal.* Cambridge, Mass.: Harvard University Press.

Benga, A.N. 2002. "Dakar et ses tempos: Significations et enjeux de la musique urbaine moderne (c.1960–années 1990)", in Momar C. Diop (ed), *Le Sénégal Contemporain,* Paris: Karthala.

Bingo. 1953. "Les Ballets de Keita Fodéba", *Bingo,* April, p. 18.

———. 1954. "Dans le monde", *Bingo,* June, p. 18.

Blacking, J. 1967. *Venda Children's Songs: A Study in Ethnomusicological Analysis.* Johannesburg: Witwatersrand University Press.

Boilat, A.P.-D. 1853. *Esquisses Sénégalaises.* Paris: Bertrand.

Boone, C. 1992. *Merchant Power and the Roots of State Power in Senegal, 1930–1985.* Cambridge: Cambridge University Press.

Bourdieu, P. 1972. *Esquisse d'une Théorie de la Pratique.* Genève: Droz.

Brinkley, J. 1964. "On a Culture Safari." *New York Times,* 26 January, p. X15.

Brown, S., M.J. Martinez, and L.M. Parsons. 2006. "The neural basis of human dance." *Cerebral Cortex* no. 16:1157–1167.

Bruner, E.M. 1986. "Experience and its expressions", in Victor W. Turner and Edward M. Bruner (ed), *The Anthropology of Experience,* Urbana: University of Illinois Press, pp. 3–30.

Buggenhagen, B.A. 2004. "Domestic object(ion)s: the Senegalese Murid trade diaspora and the politics of marriage payments, love, and state privatization", in Brad Weiss (ed), *Producing African Futures: Ritual and Reproduction in a Neoliberal Age,* Leiden: Brill, pp. 21–53.

Bugnicourt, J., and A. Diallo. 1991. *Set Setal: des Murs qui Parlent. Nouvelle Culture Urbaine à Dakar*. Dakar: ENDA.

Burt, R. 2006. *Judson Dance Theater: Performative Traces*. London: Routledge.

Cadilhac, P.-E. 1931. "L'heure du ballet." *L'Illustration*, 22 August, p. 13.

Carling, J. 2002. "Migration in the age of involuntary immobility: Theoretical reflections and Cape Verdean experiences." *Journal of Ethnic and Migration Studies* no. 28 (1):5–42.

Castaldi, F. 2006. *Choreographies of African Identities: Négritude, Dance, and the National Ballet of Senegal*. Urbana: University of Illinois Press.

Chapman, M. (ed) 1989. *Edwin Ardener: The Voice of Prophecy and Other Essays*. Oxford: Basil Blackwell.

Charry, E. 1992. *Musical Thought, History and Practice among the Mande of West Africa*. PhD dissertation, Princeton University.

Ciss, M. 2007. "Verdict de l'affaire 'Goudi Town': Ndèye et compagnie libres, mais mises à l'épreuve pour six mois. . . ." *Le Soleil*, 28 September.

Cohen, A. 1993. *Masquerade Politics*. Oxford: Berg.

Cohen, J. 2012. "Stages in Transition: Les Ballets Africains and Independence, 1959 to 1960." *Journal of Black Studies* no. 43 (1):11–48.

Comaroff, J. 1985. *Body of Power, Spirit of Resistance: The Culture and History of a South African People*. Chicago: University of Chicago Press.

Corbey, R. 1993. "Ethnographic Showcases, 1870–1930." *Cultural Anthropology* no. 8 (3):338–369.

Coutelet, N. 2008. "Habib Benglia et le cinéma colonial." *Cahiers d'Etudes Africaines* no. 191:531–547.

———. 2012. "'Féral Benga': De la danse nègre à la chorégraphie africaine." *Cahiers d'Etudes Africaines* no. 1 (205):199–215.

Cowan, J. 1990. *Dance and the Body Politic in Northern Greece*. Princeton: Princeton University Press.

Crais, C., and P. Scully. 2008. *Sara Baartman and the Hottentot Venus: A Ghost Story and a Biography*. Princeton: Princeton University Press.

Cruise O'Brien, D. 1998. "The shadow-politics of wolofisation." *Journal of Modern African Studies* no. 36 (1):25–46.

Csordas, T. 1999. "The body's career in anthropology", in Henrietta Moore (ed), *Anthropological Theory Today*, Cambridge: Polity Press, pp. 172–205.

Dahou, K. 2004. "Les nouvelles formes de groupements en Afrique de l'Ouest: l'action collective en postcolonie", in Sophia Mappa (ed), *Forum de Delphes: les Métamorphoses du Politique au Nord et au Sud*, Paris: Karthala.

Dakar-Matin. 1961a. "Les Ballets du Sénégal vers leur centième représentation." *Dakar-Matin*, 15 June, p. 3.

———. 1961b. "Les Ballets Sérères ont remporté le trophée Bayard." *Dakar-Matin*, 10 May, p. 3.

Darbon, D. 1985. "La voix de la Casamance . . . une parole diola." *Politique Africaine* no. 18:125–38.

De Jong, F. 1999. "Trajectories of a mask performance: the case of the Senegalese 'kumpo'." *Cahiers d'Etudes Africaines* no. 53: 49–71.

———. 2002. "Politicians of the sacred grove: citizenship and ethnicity in Southern Senegal." *Africa* no. 72 (2):203–220.

————. 2007. *Masquerades of Modernity: Power and Secrecy in Casamance, Senegal*. Edinburgh: Edinburgh University Press for the International African Institute.

De Jong, F., and V. Foucher. 2010. "La tragédie du roi Abdoulaye ? Néomodernisme et renaissance africaine dans le Sénégal contemporain." *Politique Africaine* no. 118:187–204.

De Saussure, F., C. Bally, A. Sechehaye, and A. Riedlinger. 1916. *Cours de Linguistique Générale*. Lausanne and Paris: Payot.

Décoret-Ahiha, A. 2004. *Les Danses Exotiques en France (1880–1940)*. Paris: Centre National de la Danse.

Diagne, S.B. 2002. "La leçon de musique", in M.-C. Diop (ed), *Le Sénégal Contemporain*, Paris: Karthala, pp. 243–259.

Diallo, N. 1975. *De Tilène au Plateau. Une Enfance Dakaroise*. Dakar: Nouvelles Editions Africaines du Sénégal.

Dilley, R. 2004. *Islamic and Caste Knowledge Practices among Haalpulaar'en in Senegal: Between Mosque and Termite Mound*. Edinburgh: Edinburgh University Press for the International African Institute.

Diop, A.-B. 1981. *La Société Wolof: Systèmes d'Inégalité et de Domination*. Paris: Karthala.

————. 1985. *La Famille Wolof*. Paris: Karthala.

Diop, A.O. 1990. *Le Théâtre Traditionnel au Sénégal*. Dakar: Nouvelles Editions Africaines du Sénégal.

Diop, B.B. 2000. *Murambi, Le Livre des Ossements*. Paris: Stock.

————. 2009. *Les Petits de la Guenon*. Paris: Philippe Rey.

Diop, M.-C., and M. Diouf. 1990. *Le Sénégal sous Abdou Diouf*. Paris: Karthala.

Diouf, M. 1992. "Fresques murales et écriture de l'histoire: le Set/Setal à Dakar." *Politique Africaine* no. 46:41–54.

————. 2002. "Des cultures urbaines entre traditions et mondialisation", in Momar C. Diop (ed), *Le Sénégal Contemporain*, Paris: Karthala, pp. 261–288.

Diouf, M., and M.A. Leichtman. 2008. *New Perspectives on Islam in Senegal: Conversion, Migration, Wealth, Power, and Femininity*. New York: Palgrave Macmillan.

Douglas, G., et al. 2006. "Under fire: defining a contemporary African dance aesthetic – can it be done?" *Critical Arts* no. 20 (2):102–115.

Douglas, M. 1969. *Purity and Danger: an Analysis of the Concepts of Pollution and Taboo*. London: Routledge & Kegan Paul.

Drewal, M.T. 1991. "The state of research on performance in Africa." *African Studies Review* no. 34 (3):1–64.

Dumas, H. 2002. "Réflexions sur la danse au Sénégal: la danse traditionnelle comme moteur de création." *Le Soleil*, 10 October.

Dunning, J. 2000. "From man to ape: troubling images from Senegal." *New York Times*, 14 August.

Duran, L. 1989. "Key to NDour: Roots of the Senegalese star." *Popular Music* no. 8 (2):275–84.

Ebron, P.A. 2002. *Performing Africa*. Princeton, NJ: Princeton University Press.

Edmonson, L. 2007. *Performance and Politics in Tanzania*. Bloomington: Indiana University Press.

Ellis, S. 1999. *The Mask of Anarchy: the Destruction of Liberia and the Religious Roots of an African Civil War*. London: Hurst & Company.

Evans-Pritchard, E.E. 1928. "The dance." *Africa* no. 1:446–462.

Fair, J. 2003. "Francophonie and the national airwaves: a history of television in Senegal", in L. Parks and S. Kumar (eds), *Planet TV: A Global Television Reader*, New York: New York University Press, pp. 189–210.

Fall, S. 1998. *Séduire: Cinq Leçons Sénégalaises*. Paris: Editions Alternatives.

Farnell, B. 1999. "Moving bodies, acting selves " *Annual Review of Anthropology* no. 28:341–373.

Fassin, D. 1987. "Rituels villageois, rituels urbains. La reproduction sociale chez les femmes joola du Sénégal." *L'Homme* no. 27 (4):54–75.

Faye, A. 1996. *Les Associations de Développement de Quartier, 1985–1995*. Dakar: ENDA Tiers-Monde Jeunesse Action.

Faye, O. 1994. "L'instrumentalisation de l'histoire et de l'ethnicité dans le discours séparatiste en Basse Casamance." *Afrika Spectrum* no. 29 (1):65–77.

———. 2000. *Une Enquête d'Histoire de la Marge: Production de la Ville et Populations Africaines à Dakar, 1857–1960, thèse de Doctorat d'Etat, vol. I & II*. Dakar: Université Cheikh Anta Diop, Département d'Histoire.

———. 2002. "Sport, argent et politique: la lutte libre à Dakar (1800–2000)", in Momar C. Diop (ed), *Le Sénégal Contemporain*, Paris: Karthala, pp. 309–340.

Ferguson, J. 1999. *Expectations of Modernity: Myths and Meanings of Urban Life on the Zambian Copperbelt*. Berkeley: University of California Press.

Ferme, M.C. 2001. *The Underneath of Things: Violence, History, and the Everyday in Sierra Leone*. Berkeley: University of California Press.

Foster, S.L. 1996. *Corporealities: Dancing, Knowledge, Culture, and Power*. London: Routledge.

Foucher, V. 2002. *Cheated Pilgrims: Education, Migration and the Birth of Casamançais Nationalism (Senegal). Unpublished Ph.D. thesis*. London: SOAS.

———. 2005. "La guerre des dieux? Religions et séparatisme en Basse Casamance." *Canadian Journal of African Studies* no. 39 (2):361–388.

Fuller, H.W. 1966. "World Festival of Negro Arts." *Ebony*, July, pp. 96–106.

Garrison, L. 1966. "Debate on 'Negritude' splits festival in Dakar." *New York Times*, 24 April, p.17.

Gaye, I. 1977a. "Encourager et inspirer le peuple noir." *Le Soleil*, 17 January, p. 6.

———. 1977b. "Festac 77. Alioune Sène s'élève contre l'Anti- Négritude. Premier accrochage entre la Guinée et le Sénégal." *Le Soleil*, 21 January, p. 9.

Gilman, L. 2009. *The Dance of Politics: Gender, Performance, and Democratization in Malawi*. Philadelphia: Temple University Press.

Goerg, O. 1989. "Les mouvements de jeunesse en Guinée de la colonisation à la constitution de la J.R.D.A.", in H d'Almeida-Topor and O. Goerg (eds), *Le Mouvement Associatif des Jeunes en Afrique Noire Francophone au XXe Siècle*, Paris: L'Harmattan, pp. 19–51.

Gore, G. 1999. "Traditional dance in West Africa", in J. Adshead-Lansdale and J. Layson (eds), *Dance History: An introduction, 2nd ed.*, London: Routledge, pp. 59–80.

———. 2001. "Present texts, past voices: the formation of contemporary representations of West African dances." *Yearbook for Traditional Music* no. 33:29–36.

Gorer, G. 1935. *Africa Dances: A Book About West African Negroes*. London: Faber & Faber.

Greenhalgh, P. 1988. *Ephemeral Vistas: The Expositions Universelles, Great Exhibitions and World Fairs, 1851–1939*. Manchester: Manchester University Press.

Guèye, C. 2002. *Touba: la Capitale des Mourides*. Paris: Karthala.

Guigou, M. 2004. *La Nouvelle Danse Française*. Paris: L'Harmattan.

Hale, T. 1999. *Griots and Griottes*. Bloomington: Indiana University Press.

Hamer, A. 1981. "Diola women and migration: a case study", in Lucie Colvin Phillips (ed), *The Uprooted of Western Sahel*, New York: Praeger, pp. 183–203.

Harney, E. 1996. "'Les chers enfants' sans papa." *Oxford Art Journal* no. 19 (1):42–52.

———. 2004. *In Senghor's Shadow: Art, Politics and the Avant-Garde in Senegal, 1960–1995*. Durham: Duke University Press.

Hastrup, K. 1995. *A Passage to Anthropology: Between Experience and Theory*. London and New York: Routledge.

———. 2004. *Action: Anthropology in the Company of Shakespeare*. Copenhagen: Museum Tusculanum Press.

Havard, J.-F. 2001. "Ethos 'bul faale' et nouvelles figures de la réussite au Sénégal." *Politique Africaine* no. 82:63–77.

Heath, D. 1990. "Spatial politics and verbal performance in urban Senegal." *Ethnology* no. 3:209–223.

———. 1992. "Fashion, anti-fashion and heteroglossia in urban Senegal." *American Ethnologist* no. 19 (1):19–33.

———. 1994. "The politics of appropriateness and appropriation: recontextualizing women's dance in urban Senegal." *American Ethnologist* no. 21 (1):88–103.

Holmes, R. 2007. *The Hottentot Venus: The Life and Death of Saartjie Baartman*. London: Bloomsbury.

Hough, C.A. 2008. "Re/producing mothers: structure and agency in Gambian Kanyaleng performances." *Ethnology* no. 47 (4):257–269.

Howell, S. (ed) 1997a. *The Ethnography of Moralities*. London & New York: Routledge.

———. 1997b. "Introduction", in Signe Howell (ed), *The Ethnography of Moralities*, London & New York: Routledge, pp. 1–22.

Irele, A. 1965. "Negritude: literature and ideology." *Journal of Modern African Studies* no. 3 (4):499–526.

Irvine, J.T. 1974. *Caste and Communication in a Wolof Village. Unpublished Ph.D. Dissertation*, Anthropology Department, University of Pennsylvania.

———. 1989. "When talk isn't cheap: language and political economy." *American Ethnologist* no. 16 (2):248–267.

Jackson, M. 1983. "Knowledge of the body." *Man* no. 18:327–345.

———. 1989. *Paths Toward a Clearing: Radical Empiricism and Ethnographic Inquiry*. Bloomington: Indiana University Press.

James, D. 1999. *Songs of the Women Migrants*. Edinburgh: Edinburgh University Press for the International African Institute.

James, W. 2000. "Reforming the circle: fragments of the social history of a vernacular African dance form." *Journal of African Cultural Studies* no. 13 (1):140–152.

———. 2003. *The Ceremonial Animal: A New Portrait of Anthropology*. Oxford: Oxford University Press.

Jezequel, J.-H. 1999. "Le 'théâtre des instituteurs' en Afrique Occidentale française (1930–1950): pratique socio-culturelle et vecteur de cristallisation de nouvelles identités urbaines", in O. Goerg (ed), *Fêtes Urbaines en Afrique: Espaces, Identiés et Pouvoirs*, Paris: Karthala, pp. 181–200.

Jola, C., F.E. Pollick, and D. Reynolds. 2011. Special issue on Dance and Neuroscience. *Dance Research* 29 (2), www.eupjournals.com/drs.

Journet, O. 1981. "La quête de l'enfant: représentation de la maternité et rituels de stérilité dans la société diola de Basse-Casamance." *Journal des Africanistes* no. 51 (1–2):97–115.

Jules-Rosette, B. 1998. *Black Paris: The African Writers' Landscape.* Urbana: University of Illinois Press.

Kaay Fecc Association. 2005. Rapport Festival Kaay Fecc. Dakar: Association Kaay Fecc.

Kaba, L. 1976. "The cultural revolution, artistic creativity, and freedom of expression in Guinea." *Journal of Modern African Studies* no. 14 (2):201–218.

Kaeppler, A. 1978. "Dance in anthropological perspective." *Annual Review of Anthropology* no. 7:31–49.

Keita, F. 1952. *Le Maître d'école - suivi de Minuit.* Paris: Pierre Seghers.

———. 1955. "Les Hommes de la Danse." *Trait d'Union* no. 39:53–56.

Konté, F.B., and K.M. Kossi. 2006. "Ndèye Awa Guèye, danseuse: mes relations avec Oumou Sow, mon premier mari et mon allure sexy." *L'Observateur*, 5 August.

Kringelbach, M.L. 2007. "Emotion, feelings and hedonics in the human brain", in H. Wulff (ed), *The Emotions: A Cultural Reader*, Oxford: Berg Publishers, pp. 37–60.

Laban, R. 1970. *Principles of Dance and Movement Notation.* New York: Dance Horizons.

Labouret, H., and M. Travélé. 1928. "Le théâtre mandingue (Soudan Français)." *Africa* no. 1 (1):73–97.

Lambert, M.C. 1998. "Violence and the war of words: ethnicity v. nationalism in the Casamance." *Africa* no. 68 (4):585–602.

———. 1999. "Have Jola women found a way to resist patriarchy with commodities?" *Political and Legal Anthropology Review* no. 22 (1):85–93.

———. 2002. *Longing for Exile: Migration and the Making of a Translocal Community in Senegal, West Africa.* Portmouth, NH: Heinemann.

Lamiral, D.H. 1789. *L'Afrique et le Peuple Afriquain.* Paris: Dessenne.

Lassibille, M. 2004. "'La danse africaine', un catégorie à déconstruire: une étude des danses WoDaaBe du Niger." *Cahiers d'Etudes Africaines* no. 44 (175):681–690.

Lepecki, A. 1999. "Skin, body, and presence in contemporary European choreography." *TDR* no. 43 (4):129–140.

Leymarie, I. 1999. *Les Griots Wolof du Sénégal.* Paris: Maisonneuve & Larose.

Linares, O. 1992. *Power, Prayer, and Production: The Jola of Casamance, Senegal.* Cambridge: Cambridge University Press.

———. 2003. "Going to the city . . . and coming back? Turnaround migration among the Jola of Senegal." *Africa* no. 73 (1):113–132.

Lindfors, B. 1999. *Africans on Stage.* Bloomington: Indiana University Press.

Lock, M. 1993. "Cultivating the body: anthropology and epistemologies of bodily practice and knowledge." *Annual Review of Anthropology* no. 22:133–155.

Ly, B. 2009. *Les Instituteurs au Sénégal de 1903 à 1945. Tome 3: La Formation au Métier d'Instituteur.* Paris: L'Harmattan.

Mamdani, M. 1996. *Citizen and Subject: Contemporary Africa and the Legacy of Late Colonialism.* Princeton, N.J.: Princeton University Press.

Mark, P. 1977. "The rubber and palm produce trades and the Islamization of the Diola of Boulouf (Casamance, 1890–1920)." *Bulletin de l'IFAN* no. 39B (2):341–361.

———. 1994. "Art, ritual and folklore: dance and cultural identity among the peoples of the Casamance." *Cahiers d'Etudes Africaines* no. 136:563–584.

Marshall, K. 2001. *Changing Gender Roles in Sabar Performances: A Reflection of Changing Gender Roles for Women in Senegal. Unpublished BA Thesis*, University of Washington.

Martin, J. 1959a. "Dance: 'Ballets Africains'." *The New York Times*, 17 February, p. 28.

———. 1959b. "Dance: Africana. Lively and handsome 'ballet' arrives from the dark continent via Paris." *The New York Times*, 22 February, p. X10.

———. 1959c. "The Dance: notes." *The New York Times*, 1 February, p. X11.

———. 1959d. "The Dance: notes." *The New York Times*, 1 March, p. X10.

Mauny, R. 1955. "Baobabs, cimetières à griots." *Notes Africaines* no. 67:72–6.

Mauss, M. 1973 [1935]. "Techniques of the body." *Economy and Society* no. 2 (1):70–88.

Mbaye, A. 2004. "L'autre théâtre historique de l'époque coloniale: le 'Chaka' de Senghor." *Ethiopiques* no. 72.

Mbembe, A. 1996. "La 'chose' et ses doubles dans la caricature camerounaise." *Cahiers d'Etudes Africaines* no. 36 (141/142):143–170.

———. 2001. *On the Postcolony*. Berkeley: University of California Press.

Mbembe, A. and S. Nuttall. 2004. 'Writing the world from an African metropolis.' *Public Culture* no. 16 (3):347–372.

Mbengue, A.R. 2005. "Kaay Feec. Danse contemporaine à l'Institut Français: Kossoko, du solo tout chaud." *Le Quotidien*, 5 June.

Mbow, P. 2000. "Démocratie, droits humains et castes au Sénégal." *Journal des Africanistes*, *"L'Ombre portée de l'esclavage"* no. 70 (1–2):71–91.

McLaughlin, F. 1997. "Islam and popular music in Senegal: the emergence of a 'new tradition'." *Africa* no. 64 (4):560–81.

McNaughton, P. 1988. *The Mande Blacksmiths: Knowledge, Power and Art in West Africa*. Bloomington: Indiana University Press.

McNee, L. 2000. *Selfish Gifts: Senegalese Women's Autobiographical Discourses*. Albany: State University of New York Press.

Melly, C. 2010. "Inside-out houses: urban belonging and imagined futures in Dakar, Senegal." *Comparative Studies in Society and History* no. 52:37–65.

Mensah, A. 2001. "Danses en révolution." *Africultures* no. 42:3–8.

———. 2004. "5èmes Rencontres chorégraphiques de l'Afrique et de l'océan Indien: Tana en crise." *Africultures* no. 58:Published 1st March 2004 on http://www.africultures.com/index.asp?menu=affiche_article&no=3323.

Ministère de l'Economie et des Finances du Sénégal. 2004. *Situation Economique et Sociale 2004 – Région de Dakar*. Dakar: Service Régional de la Prévision et de la Statistique.

Mitchell, J.C. 1956. *The Kalela dance: aspects of social relationships among urban Africans in Northern Rhodesia. Rhodes-Livingstone Institute Papers no.27*. Manchester: Manchester University Press.

Mouralis, B. 1986. "William Ponty Drama", in Albert S. Gérard (ed), *European-language Writing in Sub-Saharan Africa*, Budapest: Akadémiai Kiadó, pp. 130–140.

Mudimbe, V. 1988. *The Invention of Africa: Gnosis, Philosophy and the Order of Knowledge*. Bloomington: Indiana University Press.

Mustafa, H.N. 2002. "Portraits of modernity: fashioning selves in dakarois popular photography", in Paul S. Landau and Deborah D. Kaspin (ed), *Images and Empires: Visuality in Colonial and Postcolonial Africa*, Berkeley: University of California Press, pp. 173–192.

Nankasse, F. 2005. "Aziz Samb, animateur de 'Oscars des Vacances': j'ai peur d'arrêter un jour." *Le Soleil*, 6 August.

Ndao, O. 2008. Le théâtre privé au Sénégal. *www.wootico.com*.

Ndiaye Sylla, S. 2001. *Femmes et Politique au Sénégal. Contribution à la Réflexion sur la Participation des Femmes Sénégalaises à la Vie Politique de 1945 à 2001. Mémoire de DEA*, Faculté d'Etudes Internationales et Européennes, Université de Paris I.

Ndoye, Y.N. 2007. "Libération après 13 jours de détention: Ndèye Guèye retrouve la liberté sous une pluie fine." *Le Quotidien*, 28 September.

Ness, S.A. 1992. *Body, Movement, and Culture: Kinesthetic and Visual Symbolism in a Philippine Community*. Philadelphia: University of Pennsylvania Press.

Nettali.net. 2011. Revue de presse: Maitre Wade contre le 'taatou laobé' et autres danses obscènes à la télévision. *Nettali.net*, http://www.rewmi.com/Revue-de-presse-Me-Wade-contre-le-taatou-laobe-et-autres-danses-obscenes-a-la-television_a37921.html

Neveu Kringelbach, H. 2005. *Encircling the dance: social mobility through the transformation of performance in urban Senegal*, Unpublished doctoral thesis. University of Oxford, Oxford.

———. 2007a. "Cool play: emotionality in dance as a resource in Senegalese urban women's associations", in H. Wulff (ed), *The Emotions: A Cultural Reader*, Oxford: Berg, pp. 251–272.

———. 2007b. "Le poids du succès: construction du corps, danse et carrière à Dakar." *Politique Africaine* no. 107:81–101.

———. 2012. "Moving shadows of Casamance: performance and regionalism in Senegal", in Hélène Neveu Kringelbach and Jonathan Skinner (eds), *Dancing Cultures: Globalization, Tourism and Identity in the Anthropology of Dance*, New York and Oxford: Berghahn, pp. 143–160.

New York Times, The. 1959. "'Nudity' in ballet is halted by city." *The New York Times*, 20 February, p. 19.

Ngaïde, A. 2003. "Stéréotypes et imaginaires sociaux en milieu haalpulaar: Classer, stigmatiser et toiser." *Cahiers d'Etudes Africaines* no. 172:707–738.

Niang, Mor Sadio. 1961. "La jeunesse de Coki en marche dans la voie du progrès." *Dakar-Matin*, 2 May, p. 3.

Nicholls, R.W. 1998. "African dance: transition and continuity", in Kariamu Welsh Asante (ed), *African Dance, 2nd ed*, Trenton/NJ & Asmara: Africa World Press.

Nketia, J.H.K. 1996. The Arts in contemporary contexts: an overview. In *Inroads into Africa Arts International conference 5th-8th June 1996*. New York.

Nouvel Horizon, Le. 2003. "Profession: Danseurs – Une société encore réticente." *Le Nouvel Horizon*, 3 April, pp. 39–40.

Novack, C. 1990. *Sharing the Dance: Contact Improvisation and American Culture*. Madison: University of Wisconsin Press.

Nyamnjoh, F., and J. Fokwang. 2005. "Entertaining repression: Music and politics in postcolonial Cameroon." *African Affairs* no. 104:251–274.

Palmer, G.B., and W.R. Jankowiak. 1996. "Performance and Imagination: Toward an Anthropology of the Spectacular and the Mundane." *Cultural Anthropology* no. 11 (2):225–258.

Panzacchi, C. 1994. "The livelihood of traditional griots in modern Senegal." *Africa* no. 64 (2):190–210.

Paris-Dakar. 1947. "Une belle soirée artistique." *Paris-Dakar*, 2–3 March, p. 2.

———. 1961a. "Les ballets guinéens sont passés à Dakar." *Paris-Dakar*, 14 March, p. 3.

———. 1961b. "Les Ballets sénégalais préparent leur tournée européenne." *Paris-Dakar*, 20 February, p. 3.

————. 1961c. "Bagarre dans la région de Thiès pour une question de cimetière entre griots et non griots. Un mort, plusieurs blessés." *Paris-Dakar*, 22 February, p. 3.

Parkin, D. 1985. "Reason, emotion and the embodiment of power", in J. Overing (ed), *Reason and Morality. ASA monograph no. 24*, London: Tavistock, pp. 135–15.

————. 1996. "The power of the bizarre", in David Parkin et al. (eds), *The Politics of Cultural Performance*, Oxford: Berghahn, pp. xv-xl.

Penna-Diaw, L. 2005. "La danse sabar, une expression de l'identité féminine chez les Wolof du Sénégal." *Cahiers d'ethnomusicologie* no. 18.

Pratten, D. 2007. *The Man-Leopard Murders: History and Society in Colonial Nigeria.* Edinburgh: Edinburgh University Press for the International African Institute.

Rabine, L.W. 2002. *The Global Circulation of African Fashion.* Oxford: Berg.

Radcliffe-Brown, A.R. 1922. *The Andaman Islanders.* Cambridge: Cambridge University Press.

Ralph, M. 2006. "'Le Sénégal qui gagne': soccer and the stakes of neoliberalism in a postcolonial port." *Soccer and Society* no. 7 (2–3):300–317.

————. 2008. "Killing time." *Social Text* no. 26 (4):1–29

Ranger, T.C. 1975. *Dance and Society in Eastern Africa 1890–1970: Beni ngoma.* London: Heinemann.

Rasmussen, S.J. 1992. "Ritual specialists, ambiguity and power in Tuareg society." *Man* no. 27:105–128.

————. 1995. *Spirit Possession and Personhood Among the Kel Ewey Tuareg.* Cambridge: Cambridge University Press.

Richter, D. 1980. "Further considerations of caste in West Africa." *Africa* no. 50:37–54.

Sanou, S., and A. Tempé. 2008. *Afrique Danse Contemporaine.* Paris: Cercle d'Art et Centre National de la Danse.

Sarr, F. 2002. *L'Entrepreunariat Féminin au Sénégal.* Paris: L'Harmattan.

Sarr, M. 2007. "Gouddi Town: Ndèye Guèye et compagnie retrouvent la liberté." *Walfadjri*, 28 September.

Sarró, R. 2009. *The Politics of Religious Change on the Upper Guinea Coast. Iconoclasm Done and Undone.* London & Bloomington: International African Institute & Indiana University Press.

Schieffelin, E. 1998. "Problematizing performance", in F. Hughes-Freeland (ed), *Ritual, Performance, Media. ASA Monograph no.35*, London: Routledge, pp. 194–207.

Schulz, D.E. 2001. "Music videos and the effeminate vices of urban culture in Mali." *Africa* no. 71 (3):345–372.

Seck, A. 2005. *Sénégal: Émergence d'une Démocratie Moderne (1945–2005).* Paris: Karthala.

Sénégal d'Aujourd'hui. n.d. "Banc d'essai pour un théâtre total."

Senghor, L.S. 1956. *Chants d'Ombre.* Paris: Le Seuil.

Shain, R. 2002. "Roots in reverse: Cubanismo in twentieth-century Senegalese music." *International Journal of African Historical Studies* no. 35 (1):83–101.

————. 2009. "The Re(public) of Salsa: Afro-Cuban music in fin-de-siècle Dakar." *Africa* no. 79 (2):186–206.

Sharp, R. 1994. *Senegal: A State of Change.* Oxford: Oxfam.

Shay, A. 2002. *Choreographic Politics: State Folk Dance Companies, Representations and Power.* Middletown: Wesleyan University Press.

Silla, O. 1966. "Persistance des castes dans la société wolof contemporaine." *Bulletin de l'Institut Français de l'Afrique Noire* no. 28 (3–4):731–770.

Simmel, G. 1950 [1908]. *The Sociology of Georg Simmel. Edited and translated by K. Wolff.* Glencoe, IL: The Free Press.

Snipe, T.D. 1998. *Arts and Politics in Senegal 1960–1996.* Trenton: Africa World Press.

Soleil, Le. 1977a. "Festac 77: De Dakar à Lagos un itinéraire heurté." *Le Soleil,* 18 January, p. 7.

———. 1977b. "Second Festival mondial des arts et de la culture négro-africaine. Réflexions sur le colloque." *Le Soleil,* 5 March, p. 6.

———. 1987. "Festival de la Petite Côte – Un succès malgré tout." *Le Soleil,* 14 January, p. 11.

Sonar Senghor, M. 2004. *Souvenirs de Théâtres d'Afrique et d'Outre-Afrique.* Paris: L'Harmattan.

Spencer, P. 1996. "Dance and the cosmology of confidence", in David Parkin et al. (eds), *The Politics of Cultural Performance,* Oxford: Berghahn, pp. 181–197.

Stokes, M. 1992. *The Arabesk Debate: Music and Musicians in Modern Turkey.* Oxford: Clarendon Press.

———. 1997. "Voices and places: history, repetition and the musical imagination." *Journal of the Royal Anthropological Institute* no. 3 (4):673–691.

———. 2004. "Music and the global order." *Annual Review of Anthropology* no. 33:47–72.

Straker, J. 2009. *Youth, Nationalism, and the Guinean Revolution.* Bloomington: Indiana University Press.

Sylla, A. 1994. *La Philosophie Morale des Wolof.* 2nd ed. Dakar: IFAN. Original edition, 1978.

Tall, S.M. 2009. *Investir dans la Ville Africaine. Les Emigrés et l'Habitat à Dakar.* Paris: Karthala.

Tamari, T. 1997. *Les Castes de l'Afrique Occidentale.* Nanterre: Société d'Ethnologie.

Tang, P. 2007. *Masters of the Sabar: Wolof Griot Percussionists of Senegal.* Philadelphia: Temple University Press.

Thioub, I., M.C. Diop, and C. Boone. 1998. "Economic liberalization in Senegal: shifting politics of indigenous business interests." *African Studies Review* no. 41 (2):63–89.

Tholon, M.S. 2009. *Du Sable à la Scène. Circulation des Danses Sabar et Ballet Manding au Sénégal, entre Gueew et Ballet. Thèse de Doctorat non publiée,* Département Danse, Université de Nice Sophia-Antipolis.

Thomas, L.-V. 1965. "Bukut chez les Diola-Niomoun." *Notes Africaines* no. 108:97–118.

Thompson, R.F. 1974. *African Art in Motion: Icon and Act.* Berkeley: University of California Press.

Tiérou, A. 2001. *Si Sa Danse Bouge, l'Afrique Bougera.* Paris: Maisonneuve & Larose.

Tran, D. 2006. "Biennale de la danse. Eau-delà du Sahel." Le Progrès, 28 September.

Turino, T. 2002. *Nationalists, Cosmopolitans and Popular Music in Zimbabwe.* Chicago: Chicago University Press.

Turner, V.W. 1982. *From Ritual to Theatre.* New York: PAJ Publications.

Vaillant, J. 2006. *Vie de Léopold Sédar Senghor: Noir, Français et Africain.* Paris: Karthala.

van Gennep, A. 1960 [1909]. *The Rites of Passage.* Chicago: Chicago University Press.

Van Nieuwkerk, K. 1995. *A 'Trade Like any Other:' Female Singers and Dancers in Egypt.* Austin: University of Texas Press.

Vellet, J. 2006. "La transmission matricielle de la danse contemporaine." *STAPS* no. 72 (2):79–91.

Vidal, H. 1955. "Nos victoires dans les compétitions théâtrales." *Traits d'Union* no. 8.

Wacquant, L. 1998. "A fleshpeddler at work: power, pain and profit in the prizefighting economy." *Theory and Society* no. 27 (1):1–42.

Wade, O. 2007. *La Force du Verbe dans la Tradition Orale Wolof: l'Exemple des Chants du Cercle de la Jeunesse de Louga. Mémoire de DEA*. Dakar: UCAD.

Walfadjri. 2002. "Association Kaay Fecc: Une formation en danse traditionnelle." *Walfadjri*, 26 October.

Wane, I. 2004. "Stage Kaay Fecc: les jeunes des ballets à la rencontre de la danse moderne." *Taxi*, 15 January.

Wane, Y. 1969. "Les Toucouleur du Fouta Tooro, stratification sociale et structure familiale." *Initiations et études africaines (IFAN)* no. 25.

Waterman, C.A. 1990. *Juju: A Social History and Ethnography of an African Popular Music*. Chicago: The University of Chicago Press.

Weil, P.P. 1976. "The staff of life: food and female fertility in a West African society." *Africa* no. 46 (2):182–195.

Welsh Asante, K. 1996. *African Dance: An Artistic, Historical and Philosophical Inquiry*. Trenton, NJ Asmara: Africa World Press.

Wern, V. 2002. "Udfordringen." *Berlingske Tidende*, 8 July.

White, B.W. 2008. *Rumba Rules: The Politics of Dance Music in Mobutu's Zaire*. Durham: Duke University Press.

Wilder, G. 2005. *The French Imperial Nation-State: Negritude and Colonial Humanism between the Two World Wars*. Chicago: Chicago University Press.

Wilk, R. 1995. "Learning to be local in Belize: global systems of common difference", in D. Miller (ed), *Worlds Apart. Modernity through the Prism of the Local*, London: Routledge, pp. 110–133.

Williams, D. 1982. "Semasiology", in D. Parkin (ed), *Semantic Anthropology, ASA monograph no. 22*, London: Academic Press, pp. 161–182.

Wright, B. 1989. "The power of articulation", in W. Arens and Ivan Karp (eds), *Creativity of Power: Cosmology and Action in African Societies*, Washington: Smithsonian Institution Press, pp. 39–57.

Wulff, H. 1998. *Ballet across Borders: Career and Culture in the World of Dancers*. Oxford: Berg.

———. 2001. "Anthropology of dance", in N.J. Smelser and P.B. Bates (ed), *International Encyclopedia of the Social and Behavioral Sciences*, Oxford: Pergamon, pp. 3209–3212.

———. 2007. *Dancing at the Cross Roads: Memory and Mobility in Ireland*. Oxford: Berghahn.

———. 2012. "Ballet culture and the market: a transnational perspective", in H. Neveu Kringelbach and J. Skinner (ed), *Dancing Cultures: Globalisation, Tourism and Identity in the Anthropology of Dance*, Oxford: Berghahn.

Recordings

Kiné Lam (1991) *Balla Aïssa Boury*, cassette, Senegal

Thione Seck (2004) *Orientissimo*, CD and cassette, Senegal

Youssou NDour (2004) *Sant*, CD and cassette, Senegal

Films

Danse l'Afrique, Danse ! by Marion Stalens, France, 2012, 52 min.

Djabote: Senegalese Drumming & Song from Master Drummer Doudou N'Diaye Rose, Béatrice Soulé and Eric Millot, France, 1992, 44 min.

Drums, Sand and Shostakovich, by Ken Glazebrook and Alla Kovgan, USA, 2002, 70 min.
Movement (R)evolution Africa, by Joan Frosch & Alla Kovgan, USA, 2007, 65min.
Mudra Afrique by André Waksman, Belgium, 1980, 56 min.

Internet resources
Sabar dancing:
Sabar Dancing in Senegal (2007) by Sophie Schouwenaar.
   http://www.youtube.com/watch?v=RTDC7hJEqT4 [accessed 06.06.2010]
Bakalama:
   http://bakalama-senegal.com/presentation.html
   http://www.myspace.com/bakalama
Danse l'Afrique danse biennale:
   http://www.institutfrancais.com/fr/danse
   2012: http://www.danselafriquedanse.com/
   2010: http://danse-afrique-danse.org/
Compagnie la 5e Dimension:
   http://www.youtube.com/watch?v=0Jg8nJNFaBs [accessed 30.09.2012]

Index